Rover 2000 2300 & 2600 Owners Workshop Manual

by J H Haynes
Member of the Guild of Motoring Writers
and P M Methuen

Models covered
Rover 2000; 1994 cc
Rover 2300 and 2300S; 2350 cc
Rover 2600, 2600S, 2600SE and 2600 Vanden Plas; 2597 cc

Does not cover Diesel engine or V8 models

ISBN 1 85010 444 1

A

Haynes Publishing Group
Sparkford Nr Yeovil
Somerset BA22 7JJ England

Haynes Publications, Inc
861 Lawrence Drive
Newbury Park
California 91320 USA

British Library Cataloguing in Publication Data

Methuen, P. M. (Philip M.)
  Rover 2000, 2300 and 2600 owners workshop manual.
  1. Cars. Maintenance & repair – Amateurs' manuals
  I. Title
  629.28'722
  ISBN 1–85010–444–1

Acknowledgements

Thanks are due to BL Cars UK Limited (Rover Triumph Division) for their help in the provision of technical information and certain illustrations. The supply of technical information and illustrations by the Rover subsidiary of BL Cars UK Limited does not imply that the Rover subsidiary of BL Cars UK Limited has approved the contents of this book or is in any way responsible for the accuracy of any information printed. The copyright in illustrations and other technical material provided by the Rover subsidiary of BL Cars UK Limited remains vested in the Rover subsidiary of BL Cars UK Limited.

The Champion Sparking Plug Company supplied the illustrations showing the various spark plug conditions and Duckhams Oils provided lubrication data.

Special thanks are also due to F J Chalke and Son of Mere, Wiltshire, who were very helpful in providing technical information, and to Vincents of Yeovil Ltd for the loan of a 2000 model used during preparation of the Supplement.

Lastly, thanks are also due to all of those people at Sparkford who helped in the production of this manual.

About this manual

Its aim

The aim of this manual is to help you get the best value from your vehicle. It can do so in several ways. It can help you decide what work must be done (even should you choose to get it done by a garage), provide information on routine maintenance and servicing, and give a logical course of action and diagnosis when random faults occur. However, it is hoped that you will use the manual by tackling the work yourself. On simpler jobs it may even be quicker than booking the car into a garage and going there twice, to leave and collect it. Perhaps most important, a lot of money can be saved by avoiding the costs a garage must charge to cover its labour and overheads.

The manual has drawings and descriptions to show the function of the various components so that their layout can be understood. Then the tasks are described and photographed in a step-by-step sequence so that even a novice can do the work.

Its arrangement

The manual is divided into thirteen Chapters, each covering a logical sub-division of the vehicle. The Chapters are each divided into Sections, numbered with single figures, eg 5; and the Sections into paragraphs (or sub-sections), with decimal numbers following on from the Section they are in, eg 5.1, 5.2, 5.3 etc.

It is freely illustrated, especially in those parts where there is a detailed sequence of operations to be carried out. There are two forms of illustration: figures and photographs. The figures are numbered in sequence with decimal numbers, according to their position in the Chapter – eg Fig. 6.4 is the fourth drawing/illustration in Chapter 6. Photographs carry the same number (either individually or in related groups) as the Section or sub-section to which they relate.

There is an alphabetical index at the back of the manual as well as a contents list at the front. Each Chapter is also preceded by its own individual contents list.

References to the 'left' or 'right' of the vehicle are in the sense of a person in the driver's seat facing forwards.

Unless otherwise stated, nuts and bolts are removed by turning anti-clockwise, and tightened by turning clockwise.

Vehicle manufacturers continually make changes to specifications and recommendations, and these, when notified, are incorporated into our manuals at the earliest opportunity.

Whilst every care is taken to ensure that the information in this manual is correct, no liability can be accepted by the authors or publishers for loss, damage or injury caused by any errors in, or omissions from, the information given.

Introduction to the Rover SD1 models

The Rover 2300 and 2600 SD1 models were introduced in October 1977, using the familiar bodyshell of the Rover 3500 SD1 which was introduced a year earlier. The two newer models replace the ageing Rover 2000 body style, although it had been re-vamped in its later 2200 guise. In the BL Cars range these two new models also replace the Triumph 2000 and 2500.

The six-cylinder engine fitted to the Rover 2300 and 2600 SD1 models is an entirely new design with several interesting features. The engine is basically the same for both models; the 2300 model has however a shorter stroke, thereby giving it a smaller cubic capacity. But apart from the difference in crankshaft and pistons there is little else to separate them.

The bodyshell of the two versions is the same 5-door hatchback design. The fifth door lifts to reveal a very capacious boot area which can be increased still further when the luggage tray is taken out and the rear seat folded down. Its striking shape was evolved from extensive wind tunnel tests and has resulted in an aerodynamically near-perfect shape with very little drag.

The 2600 model shares the same suspension as the Rover 3500, whereas the 2300 has a slightly different type of damper system at the rear. There are other basic simplifications in the 2300 model which include the fitting of a 4-speed gearbox as standard and deletion of

some of the instruments and 'extras', such as warning lights in the rear edge of the front doors. Externally however, apart from the wheel trims and badges, they are identical.

There are many optional extras which can be fitted to both models, although even the smaller engined 2300 model is very well appointed. These include a 5-speed gearbox for the 2300 model or automatic transmission for both models, power steering for the 2300 model, Dunlop Denovo wheels and tyres for both models, sunshine roof etc.

Comfort is of a very high standard and noteworthy is the rear seat arrangement, which has the comfort of any 4 or 5-seater saloon and is contoured although it folds flat to provide estate car type luggage space.

Safety and performance with economy in mind were all prime considerations during the design stage and the application of all these qualities make both the 2600 and 2300 SD1 models very exceptional cars.

The reintroduction of a 2000 model in 1982 coincided with a face-lift for the whole SD1 range. The 2000 model is powered by the well-proven 'O' Series engine found in several other models in the BL range. Details of this model, and of modifications to the other models, will be found in the Supplement at the end of the manual.

Contents

The Rover 2300 SD1

The Rover 2600 SD1

Safety first!

Professional motor mechanics are trained in safe working procedures. However enthusiastic you may be about getting on with the job in hand, do take the time to ensure that your safety is not put at risk. A moment's lack of attention can result in an accident, as can failure to observe certain elementary precautions.

There will always be new ways of having accidents, and the following points do not pretend to be a comprehensive list of all dangers; they are intended rather to make you aware of the risks and to encourage a safety-conscious approach to all work you carry out on your vehicle.

Essential DOs and DON'Ts

DON'T rely on a single jack when working underneath the vehicle. Always use reliable additional means of support, such as axle stands, securely placed under a part of the vehicle that you know will not give way.

DON'T attempt to loosen or tighten high-torque nuts (e.g. wheel hub nuts) while the vehicle is on a jack; it may be pulled off.

DON'T start the engine without first ascertaining that the transmission is in neutral (or 'Park' where applicable) and the parking brake applied.

DON'T suddenly remove the filler cap from a hot cooling system – cover it with a cloth and release the pressure gradually first, or you may get scalded by escaping coolant.

DON'T attempt to drain oil until you are sure it has cooled sufficiently to avoid scalding you.

DON'T grasp any part of the engine, exhaust or catalytic converter without first ascertaining that it is sufficiently cool to avoid burning you.

DON'T allow brake fluid or antifreeze to contact vehicle paintwork.

DON'T syphon toxic liquids such as fuel, brake fluid or antifreeze by mouth, or allow them to remain on your skin.

DON'T inhale dust – it may be injurious to health (see *Asbestos* below).

DON'T allow any spilt oil or grease to remain on the floor – wipe it up straight away, before someone slips on it.

DON'T use ill-fitting spanners or other tools which may slip and cause injury.

DON'T attempt to lift a heavy component which may be beyond your capability – get assistance.

DON'T rush to finish a job, or take unverified short cuts.

DON'T allow children or animals in or around an unattended vehicle.

DO wear eye protection when using power tools such as drill, sander, bench grinder etc, and when working under the vehicle.

DO use a barrier cream on your hands prior to undertaking dirty jobs – it will protect your skin from infection as well as making the dirt easier to remove afterwards; but make sure your hands aren't left slippery. Note that long-term contact with used engine oil can be a health hazard.

DO keep loose clothing (cuffs, tie etc) and long hair well out of the way of moving mechanical parts.

DO remove rings, wristwatch etc, before working on the vehicle – especially the electrical system.

DO ensure that any lifting tackle used has a safe working load rating adequate for the job.

DO keep your work area tidy – it is only too easy to fall over articles left lying around.

DO get someone to check periodically that all is well, when working alone on the vehicle.

DO carry out work in a logical sequence and check that everything is correctly assembled and tightened afterwards.

DO remember that your vehicle's safety affects that of yourself and others. If in doubt on any point, get specialist advice.

IF, in spite of following these precautions, you are unfortunate enough to injure yourself, seek medical attention as soon as possible.

Asbestos

Certain friction, insulating, sealing, and other products – such as brake linings, brake bands, clutch linings, torque converters, gaskets, etc – contain asbestos. *Extreme care must be taken to avoid inhalation of dust from such products since it is hazardous to health.* If in doubt, assume that they *do* contain asbestos.

Fire

Remember at all times that petrol (gasoline) is highly flammable. Never smoke, or have any kind of naked flame around, when working on the vehicle. But the risk does not end there – a spark caused by an electrical short-circuit, by two metal surfaces contacting each other, by careless use of tools, or even by static electricity built up in your body under certain conditions, can ignite petrol vapour, which in a confined space is highly explosive.

Always disconnect the battery earth (ground) terminal before working on any part of the fuel or electrical system, and never risk spilling fuel on to a hot engine or exhaust.

It is recommended that a fire extinguisher of a type suitable for fuel and electrical fires is kept handy in the garage or workplace at all times. Never try to extinguish a fuel or electrical fire with water.

Fumes

Certain fumes are highly toxic and can quickly cause unconsciousness and even death if inhaled to any extent. Petrol (gasoline) vapour comes into this category, as do the vapours from certain solvents such as trichloroethylene. Any draining or pouring of such volatile fluids should be done in a well ventilated area.

When using cleaning fluids and solvents, read the instructions carefully. Never use materials from unmarked containers – they may give off poisonous vapours.

Never run the engine of a motor vehicle in an enclosed space such as a garage. Exhaust fumes contain carbon monoxide which is extremely poisonous; if you need to run the engine, always do so in the open air or at least have the rear of the vehicle outside the workplace.

If you are fortunate enough to have the use of an inspection pit, never drain or pour petrol, and never run the engine, while the vehicle is standing over it; the fumes, being heavier than air, will concentrate in the pit with possibly lethal results.

The battery

Never cause a spark, or allow a naked light, near the vehicle's battery. It will normally be giving off a certain amount of hydrogen gas, which is highly explosive.

Always disconnect the battery earth (ground) terminal before working on the fuel or electrical systems.

If possible, loosen the filler plugs or cover when charging the battery from an external source. Do not charge at an excessive rate or the battery may burst.

Take care when topping up and when carrying the battery. The acid electrolyte, even when diluted, is very corrosive and should not be allowed to contact the eyes or skin.

If you ever need to prepare electrolyte yourself, always add the acid slowly to the water, and never the other way round. Protect against splashes by wearing rubber gloves and goggles.

When jump starting a car using a booster battery, for negative earth (ground) vehicles, connect the jump leads in the following sequence: First connect one jump lead between the positive (+) terminals of the two batteries. Then connect the other jump lead first to the negative (–) terminal of the booster battery, and then to a good earthing (ground) point on the vehicle to be started, at least 18 in (45 cm) from the battery if possible. Ensure that hands and jump leads are clear of any moving parts, and that the two vehicles do not touch. Disconnect the leads in the reverse order.

Mains electricity

When using an electric power tool, inspection light etc, which works from the mains, always ensure that the appliance is correctly connected to its plug and that, where necessary, it is properly earthed (grounded). Do not use such appliances in damp conditions and, again, beware of creating a spark or applying excessive heat in the vicinity of fuel or fuel vapour.

Ignition HT voltage

A severe electric shock can result from touching certain parts of the ignition system, such as the HT leads, when the engine is running or being cranked, particularly if components are damp or the insulation is defective. Where an electronic ignition system is fitted, the HT voltage is much higher and could prove fatal.

General dimensions, weights and capacities

Dimensions

Overall length:
Up to 1981	185.0 in (4.699 m)
Later models	186.5 in (4.737 m)

Overall width:
Up to 1981	69.6 in (1.768 m)
Later models (including mirrors)	78.5 in (1.993 m)

Overall height:
Up to 1981	53.3 in (1.354 m)
Later models	54.5 in (1.385 m)

Wheelbase	110.8 in (2.815 m)

Track (front and rear):
Steel wheels	59.1 in (1.500 m)
Alloy wheels	59.3 in (1.506 m)
Denovo tyres	58.7 in (1.490 m)
Ground clearance	4.3 to 6.1 in (110 to 155 mm) according to model, production date and load

Kerb weights (approx)

2000 model	3049 lb (1383 kg)

2300 model:
Up to 1981	2899 lb (1315 kg)
Later models	3102 lb (1407 kg)

2600 model:
Up to 1981	2954 lb (1340 kg)
Later models	3212 lb (1457 kg)

Capacities

Fuel tank	14.5 gallons (66 litres)

Engine oil, drain and refill:
2000 model (including filter)	7.0 pints (4.0 litres)
2300 and 2600 models (including filter)	10.8 pints (6.1 litres)
Manual gearbox (from dry)	2.8 pints (1.6 litres)

Automatic transmission (from dry):
Borg-Warner	9.3 pints (5.3 litres)
GM 180	12.3 pints (7.0 litres)
Rear axle (from dry)	1.6 pints (0.9 litre)

Cooling system (drain and refill):
2000 model	13.0 pints (7.4 litres)
2300 and 2600 models	18.2 pints (10.3 litres)

Buying spare parts
and vehicle identification numbers

Buying spare parts

Spare parts are available from many sources. BL Cars have many dealers throughout the UK, and other dealers, accessory stores and motor factors will also stock Rover spare parts. Our advice regarding spare part sources is as follows:

Officially appointed vehicle main dealers – This is the best source of parts which are peculiar to your vehicle and are otherwise not generally available (eg complete cylinder heads, internal transmission components, badges, interior trim etc). It is also the only place at which you should buy parts if your vehicle is still under warranty. To be sure of obtaining the correct parts it will always be necessary to give the storeman your vehicle's engine and chassis number, and if possible, to take the 'old' part along for positive identification. Remember that many parts are available on a factory exchange scheme — any parts returned should always be clean! It obviously makes good sense to go straight to the specialists on your vehicle for this type of part, for they are best equipped to supply you.

Other dealers and auto accessory shops – These are often very good places to buy materials and components needed for the maintenance of your vehicle (eg oil filters, spark plugs, bulbs, fan belts, oils and greases, touch-up paint, filler paste etc). They also sell general accessories, usually have convenient opening hours, charge lower prices and can often be found not far from home.

Motor factors – Good factors will stock all of the more important components which wear out relatively quickly (eg clutch components, piston, valves, exhaust systems, brake cylinders/pipes/hoses/seals/shoes and pads etc). Motor factors wil often provide new or reconditioned components on a part exchange basis – this can save a considerable amount of money.

Vehicle identification numbers

Modifications are a continuing and unpublicised process in vehicle manufacture. Spare parts manuals and lists are compiled on a numerical basis, the individual vehicle numbers being essential to identify correctly the component required.

The vehicle identification number is the number used for registration purposes; this is stamped on the right-hand side of the bulkhead panel (photo). On later models, the vehicle identification number will be found on a plate attached to the driver's door post.

The engine number on 2300 and 2600 models is stamped on the right-hand side of the cylinder block, above the alternator rear mounting (photo). On 2000 models the engine number is also on the right-hand side of the block, but it is near the flywheel housing.

The vehicle identification number

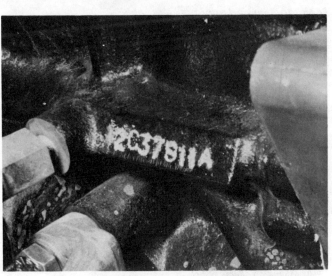

Location of the engine number

Tools and working facilities

Introduction

A selection of good tools is a fundamental requirement for anyone contemplating the maintenance and repair of a motor vehicle. For the owner who does not possess any, their purchase will prove a considerable expense, offsetting some of the savings made by doing-it-yourself. However, provided that the tools purchased are of good quality, they will last for many years and prove an extremely worthwhile investment.

To help the average owner to decide which tools are needed to carry out the various tasks detailed in this manual, we have compiled three lists of tools under the following headings: *Maintenance and minor repair, Repair and overhaul,* and *Special.* The newcomer to practical mechanics should start off with the *Maintenance and minor repair* tool kit and confine himself to the simpler jobs around the vehicle. Then, as his confidence and experience grows, he can undertake more difficult tasks, buying extra tools as, and when, they are needed. In this way, a *Maintenance and minor repair* tool kit can be built-up into a *Repair and overhaul* tool kit over a considerable period of time without any major cash outlays. The experienced do-it-yourselfer will have a tool kit good enough for most repair and overhaul procedures and will add tools from the *Special* category when he feels the expense is justified by the amount of use to which these tools will be put.

It is obviously not possible to cover the subject of tools fully here. For those who wish to learn more about tools and their use there is a book entitled *How to Choose and Use Car Tools* available from the publishers of this manual.

Maintenance and minor repair tool kit

The tools given in this list should be considered as a minimum requirement if routine maintenance, servicing and minor repair operations are to be undertaken. We recommend the purchase of combination spanners (ring one end, open-ended the other); although more expensive than open-ended ones, they do give the advantages of both types of spanner. The fixings used in the Rover 2300/2600 SD1 models are a mixture of metric, UNF and UNC sizes. For this reason, start nuts, bolts and screws with the fingers to ensure thread compatibility.

AF Combination spanners - $\frac{7}{16}$, $\frac{1}{2}$, $\frac{9}{16}$, $\frac{5}{8}$, $\frac{11}{16}$, $\frac{3}{4}$, $\frac{13}{16}$, $\frac{15}{16}$ in
Combination spanners - 10, 13, 17, 19, 22 mm
Adjustable spanner - 9 inch
Engine sump/gearbox/rear axle drain plug key (where applicable)
Spark plug spanner (with rubber insert)
Spark plug gap adjustment tool
Set of feeler gauges
Brake adjuster spanner (where applicable)
Brake bleed nipple spanner
Screwdriver - 4 in long x $\frac{1}{4}$ in dia (flat blade)
Screwdriver - 4 in long x $\frac{1}{4}$ in dia (cross blade)
Combination pliers - 6 inch
Hacksaw, junior

Tyre pump
Tyre pressure gauge
Grease gun (where applicable)
Oil can
Fine emery cloth (1 sheet)
Wire brush (small)
Funnel (medium size)

Repair and overhaul tool kit

These tools are virtually essential for anyone undertaking any major repairs to a motor vehicle, and are additional to those given in the *Maintenance and minor repair* list. Included in this list is a comprehensive set of sockets. Although these are expensive they will be found invaluable as they are so versatile - particularly if various drives are included in the set. We recommend the $\frac{1}{2}$ in square-drive type, as this can be used with most proprietary torque wrenches. If you cannot afford a socket set, even bought piecemeal, then inexpensive tubular box spanners are a useful alternative.

The tools in this list will occasionally need to be supplemented by tools from the *Special* list.

Sockets (or box spanners) to cover range in previous list
Reversible ratchet drive (for use with sockets)
Extension piece, 10 inch (for use with sockets)
Universal joint (for use with sockets)
Torque wrench (for use with sockets)
'Mole' wrench - 8 inch
Ball pein hammer
Soft-faced hammer, plastic or rubber
Screwdriver - 6 in long x $\frac{5}{16}$ in dia (flat blade)
Screwdriver - 2 in long x $\frac{5}{16}$ in square (flat blade)
Screwdriver - 1$\frac{1}{2}$ in long x $\frac{1}{4}$ in dia (cross blade)
Screwdriver - 3 in long x $\frac{1}{8}$ in dia (electricians)
Pliers - electrician's side cutters
Pliers - needle nosed
Pliers - circlip (internal and external)
Cold chisel - $\frac{1}{2}$ inch
Scriber (this can be made by grinding the end of a broken hacksaw blade)
Scraper (this can be made by flattening and sharpening one end of a piece of copper pipe)
Centre punch
Pin punch
Hacksaw
Valve grinding tool
Steel rule/straight edge
Allen keys
Selection of files
Wire brush (large)
Axle-stands
Jack (strong scissor or hydraulic type)

Special tools

The tools in this list are those which are not used regularly, are expensive to buy, or which need to be used in accordance with their manufacturers' instructions. Unless relatively difficult mechanical jobs are undertaken frequently, it will not be economic to buy many of these tools. Where this is the case, you could consider clubbing together with friends (or a motorists' club) to make a joint purchase, or borrowing the tools against a deposit from a local garage or tool hire specialist.

The following list contains only those tools and instruments freely available to the public, and not those special tools produced by the vehicle manufacturer specifically for its dealer network. You will find occasional references to these manufacturers' special tools in the text of this manual. Generally, an alternative method of doing the job without the vehicle manufacturer's special tool is given. However, sometimes, there is no alternative to using them. Where this is the case and the relevant tool cannot be bought or borrowed you will have to entrust the work to a franchised garage.

Valve spring compressor
Piston ring compressor
Balljoint separator
Universal hub/bearing puller
Impact screwdriver
Micrometer and/or vernier gauge
Carburettor flow balancing device (where applicable)
Dial gauge
Stroboscopic timing light
Dwell angle meter/tachometer
Universal electrical multi-meter
Cylinder compression gauge
Lifting tackle
Trolley jack
Light with extension lead

Buying tools

For practically all tools, a tool factor is the best source since he will have a very comprehensive range compared with the average garage or accessory shop. Having said that, accessory shops often offer excellent quality tools at discount prices, so it pays to shop around.

Remember, you don't have to buy the most expensive items on the shelf, but it is always advisable to steer clear of the very cheap tools. There are plenty of good tools around at reasonable prices, so ask the proprietor or manager of the shop for advice before making a purchase.

Care and maintenance of tools

Having purchased a reasonable tool kit, it is necessary to keep the tools in a clean serviceable condition. After use, always wipe off any dirt, grease and metal particles using a clean, dry cloth, before putting the tools away. Never leave them lying around after they have been used. A simple tool rack on the garage or workshop wall, for items such as screwdrivers and pliers is a good idea. Store all normal spanners and sockets in a metal box. Any measuring instruments, gauges, meters, etc, must be carefully stored where they cannot be damaged or become rusty.

Take a little care when tools are used. Hammer heads inevitably become marked and screwdrivers lose the keen edge on their blades from time to time. A little timely attention with emery cloth or a file will soon restore items like this to a good serviceable finish.

Working facilities

Not to be forgotten when discussing tools, is the workshop itself. If anything more than routine maintenance is to be carried out, some form of suitable working area becomes essential.

It is appreciated that many an owner mechanic is forced by circumstances to remove an engine or similar item, without the benefit of a garage or workshop. Having done this, any repairs should always be done under the cover of a roof.

Wherever possible, any dismantling should be done on a clean flat workbench or table at a suitable working height.

Any workbench needs a vice: one with a jaw opening of 4 in (100 mm) is suitable for most jobs. As mentioned previously, some clean dry storage space is also required for tools, as well as the lubricants, cleaning fluids, touch-up paints and so on which become necessary.

Another item which may be required, and which has a much more general usage, is an electric drill with a chuck capacity of at least $\frac{5}{16}$ in (8 mm). This, together with a good range of twist drills, is virtually essential for fitting accessories such as wing mirrors and reversing lights.

Last, but not least, always keep a supply of old newspapers and clean, lint-free rags available, and try to keep any working area as clean as possible.

Spanner jaw gap comparison table

Jaw gap (in)	Spanner size
0.250	$\frac{1}{4}$ in AF
0.276	7 mm
0.313	$\frac{5}{16}$ in AF
0.315	8 mm
0.344	$\frac{11}{32}$ in AF; $\frac{1}{8}$ in Whitworth
0.354	9 mm
0.375	$\frac{3}{8}$ in AF
0.394	10 mm
0.433	11 mm
0.438	$\frac{7}{16}$ in AF
0.445	$\frac{3}{16}$ in Whitworth; $\frac{1}{4}$ in BSF
0.472	12 mm
0.500	$\frac{1}{2}$ in AF
0.512	13 mm
0.525	$\frac{1}{4}$ in Whitworth; $\frac{5}{16}$ in BSF
0.551	14 mm
0.563	$\frac{9}{16}$ in AF
0.591	15 mm
0.600	$\frac{5}{16}$ in Whitworth; $\frac{3}{8}$ in BSF
0.625	$\frac{5}{8}$ in AF
0.630	16 mm
0.669	17 mm
0.686	$\frac{11}{16}$ in AF
0.709	18 mm
0.710	$\frac{3}{8}$ in Whitworth; $\frac{7}{16}$ in BSF
0.748	19 mm
0.750	$\frac{3}{4}$ in AF
0.813	$\frac{13}{16}$ in AF
0.820	$\frac{7}{16}$ in Whitworth; $\frac{1}{2}$ in BSF
0.866	22 mm
0.875	$\frac{7}{8}$ in AF
0.920	$\frac{1}{2}$ in Whitworth; $\frac{9}{16}$ in BSF
0.938	$\frac{15}{16}$ in AF
0.945	24 mm
1.000	1 in AF
1.010	$\frac{9}{16}$ in Whitworth; $\frac{5}{8}$ in BSF
1.024	26 mm
1.063	$1\frac{1}{16}$ in AF; 27 mm
1.100	$\frac{5}{8}$ in Whitworth; $\frac{11}{16}$ in BSF
1.125	$1\frac{1}{8}$ in AF
1.181	30 mm
1.200	$\frac{11}{16}$ in Whitworth; $\frac{3}{4}$ in BSF
1.250	$1\frac{1}{4}$ in AF
1.260	32 mm
1.300	$\frac{3}{4}$ in Whitworth; $\frac{7}{8}$ in BSF
1.313	$1\frac{5}{16}$ in AF
1.390	$\frac{13}{16}$ in Whitworth; $\frac{15}{16}$ in BSF
1.417	36 mm
1.438	$1\frac{7}{16}$ in AF
1.480	$\frac{7}{8}$ in Whitworth; 1 in BSF
1.500	$1\frac{1}{2}$ in AF
1.575	40 mm; $\frac{15}{16}$ in Whitworth
1.614	41 mm
1.625	$1\frac{5}{8}$ in AF
1.670	1 in Whitworth; $1\frac{1}{8}$ in BSF
1.688	$1\frac{11}{16}$ in AF
1.811	46 mm
1.813	$1\frac{13}{16}$ in AF
1.860	$1\frac{1}{8}$ in Whitworth; $1\frac{1}{4}$ in BSF
1.875	$1\frac{7}{8}$ in AF
1.969	50 mm
2.000	2 in AF
2.050	$1\frac{1}{4}$ in Whitworth; $1\frac{3}{8}$ in BSF
2.165	55 mm
2.362	60 mm

Jacking and towing

The jack supplied with the car should be used whenever it is necessary to raise the car for changing a roadwheel. Jacking points are provided at the front and rear of the car at both sides (photo).

When jacking the car up, the chock supplied in the car's tool kit (photo) should be placed in front of or behind the roadwheel diagonally opposite the wheel being raised, in addition to applying the handbrake.

If the car is to be raised for maintenance/repair operations, it is permissible to jack up on the suspension subframe, rear axle or bodyframe sidemembers. Place a suitable wooden packing piece on the jack head to prevent damage to the car metalwork.

Towing eyes are provided at the front and rear of the bodyframe sidemembers, just behind the bumpers. No other points should be used for towing (photo).

If a Rover SD1 model is to be towed, certain precautions must be observed if transmission damage is to be avoided. These are as follows.

Manual transmission models: The propeller shaft must be removed, or disconnected at the rear axle and securely supported.

Automatic transmission models: The vehicle may be towed no further than 30 miles (50 km) at a speed not exceeding 30 mph (50 kph), provided the transmission is undamaged and an extra 3 pints (1.7 litres) of ATF is added before towing commences. Drain off this excess ATF before driving the vehicle under its own power. If the above conditions cannot be met, or if transmission damage is suspected, the propeller shaft must be removed or disconnected.

The vehicle tool kit consisting of the jack, wheel brace, plug spanner, bar and wheel chock

Jacking point with protective bung and front left towing eye

Right rear towing eye

Recommended lubricants and fluids

Component or system	Lubricant type/specification	Duckhams recommendation
1 Engine*	Multigrade engine oil, viscosity range SAE 10W/30 to 15W/50, to API SE or SF	Duckhams QXR, Hypergrade, or 10W/40 Motor Oil
2 Manual gearbox† Early models Later models	 Hypoid gear oil, viscosity SAE 75W ATF to specification M2C 33G	 Duckhams Hypoid 75 Duckhams Q-Matic
3 Automatic transmission Borg-Warner GM 180	 ATF to specification M2C 33G Dexron IID type ATF	 Duckhams Q-Matic Duckhams D-Matic
4 Rear axle	Hypoid gear oil, viscosity SAE 90EP, to BLS 22-OL-03 or MIL-L-2105B	Duckhams Hypoid 90S
5 Power steering	ATF to specification M2C 33G	Duckhams Q-Matic
6 Wheel hubs	Multi-purpose lithium-based grease, to NLGI No 2	Duckhams LB 10
7 Braking system	Hydraulic fluid to FMVSS 116 DOT 3 or SAE J1703	Duckhams Universal Brake and Clutch Fluid
8 Clutch reservoir	Hydraulic fluid to FMVSS 116 DOT 3 or SAE J1703	Duckhams Universal Brake and Clutch Fluid
9 Cooling system	Antifreeze to BS 3151, 3152 or 6580	Duckhams Universal Antifreeze and Summer Coolant
10 Carburettor dashpots*	Multigrade engine oil, viscosity range SAE 10W/30 to 15W/50, to API SE or SF	Duckhams QXR, Hypergrade, or 10W/40 Motor Oil

Austin Rover specify a 10W/40 oil to meet warranty requirements for models produced after August 1983. Duckhams QXR and 10W/40 Motor Oil are available to meet these requirements.

†*The later fluid type can be used in early gearboxes, but only following a total drain and refill with the later type. Be sure not to mix the early and late types of fluid.*

Routine maintenance

Maintenance is essential for ensuring safety and desirable for the purpose of getting the best in terms of preformance and economy from the car. Over the years the need for periodic lubrication – oiling, greasing and so on – has been drastically reduced if not totally eliminated. This has unfortunately tended to lead some owners to think that because no such action is required the items either no longer exist or will last for ever. This is a serious delusion. It follows therefore that the largest initial element of maintenance is visual examination. This may lead to repairs or renewals.

The manufacturer's recommended service intervals for later models have been increased. The DIY mechanic, who does not have to pay garage charges for his or her own labour, is advised to stick to the intervals given below.

Every 250 miles (400 km) or weekly

Check tyre pressures and inflate if necessary.
Check engine oil level and top-up if necessary (photo).
Check battery electrolyte level and top-up if necessary.
Check windscreen washer fluid level and top-up if necessary (photo).
Check coolant level in reservoir and top-up if necessary (photo).
Check brake fluid level and top-up if necessary (photo).
Check clutch fluid level and top-up if necessary (photo).
Check operation of all lights, instruments and controls.

Every 3000 miles (5000 km) or 3 months, whichever occurs first

Check for oil leaks from engine, transmission, steering rack and rear axle.
Check condition of cooling system hoses.
Check condition and tension of all drivebelts.
Check condition of clutch system in hydraulic pipes.
Check power steering reservoir fluid level; top-up if necessary (photo).
Check power steering system for leaks, chafed or corroded pipes.
Check shock absorbers for fluid leaks.
Check condition of steering/suspension joints and gaiters.
Check condition of brake system hydraulic pipes and hoses.
Check condition of brake discs and pads.
Check condition of brake servo hose.
Check headlamp alignment and adjust if necessary.
Check windscreen wiper blades and renew if necessary (photos).
Check condition of pipes and hoses in fuel system.
Check exhaust system for leaks and security.
Check condition of tyre treads and sidewalls.
Check roadwheel nuts for tightness.
Check condition and security of seats, seatbelts and anchorage points.
Check operation of seatbelt warning system.
Check operation of footbrake and handbrake.

Every 6000 miles (10 000 km) or 6 months, whichever occurs first

Renew engine oil filter (photo).
Renew engine oil.
Unscrew the carburettor piston dampers and top-up the oil level.
Lubricate carburettor linkages and pivots with engine oil or light lubricating oil.
Check engine idle speed and mixture settings.
Clean/adjust spark plugs.
Check crankcase breather system for leaks, security and condition of hoses.
Lubricate distributor, as described in Chapter 4, and check points.
Check and adjust ignition timing.
Check gearbox oil level and top-up if necessary (as applicable).
Check automatic transmission oil level and top-up if necessary (as applicable).
Lubricate exposed linkage of automatic transmission selector linkage (as applicable).

Remove dust and mud from slots and screen or underside of torque converter housing (as applicable).
Check rear axle oil level and top-up if necessary.
Check front wheel alignment (toe-in).
Check handbrake operation and adjust if necessary; lubricate linkage and cable guides.
Check condition of brake linings and drums.
Clean battery terminals and smear with petroleum jelly.
Lubricate all locks, hinges and pivots (except steering lock).
Check all water hoses.
Check condition of drivebelts.
Check steering joints and condition of gaiters (photo).
Check steering rack for oil leaks.
Check power steering system for leaks and level in reservoir.
Check shock absorbers for leaks.
Check self-levelling rear units for leaks (2600 model only).
Check all brake pipes for signs of corrosion.
Check operation of brake fluid level warning light switch.
Check operation of brake pad wear warning system.
Lubricate the sliding roof mechanism (as applicable).
Inspect the bodywork and paintwork for damage and corrosion.
Check that any underbody sealant is intact.
Check engagement of the automatic transmission parking pawl (as applicable).
Check the roadwheels for damage.
Check the antifreeze strength and adjust if necessary.
Clean the distributor cap and coil tower.

Every 12 000 miles (20 000 km) or 12 months, whichever occurs first

Renew carburettor air cleaner elements.
Renew fuel filter(s).
Check air intake temperature control system.
Check operation of distributor vacuum unit.
Renew spark plugs.
Check tightness of propeller shaft coupling bolts.
Lubricate clutch pedal pivots (as applicable).
Check security of suspension fixings.
Adjust front hub bearing endfloat.
Lubricate brake pedal pivots.
Lubricate accelerator control linkage and pedal pivot.

Every 18 000 miles (30 000 km) or 18 months, whichever occurs first

Renew brake fluid.

Every 24 000 miles (40 000 km) or 2 years, whichever occurs first

Drain, flush and refill cooling system with new antifreeze solution.
Inspect camshaft drivebelt and renew if necessary.
Renew the automatic transmission fluid and pick-up filter (GM 180 only).
Adjust the automatic transmission brake band(s) (as applicable).

Every 36 000 miles (60 000 km) or 3 years, whichever occurs first

Renew brake servo filter.
Renew all rubber seals and hoses in the braking system.
Renew brake pressure reducing valve.

Every 48 000 miles (80 000 km) or 4 years, whichever occurs first

Renew camshaft drivebelt

Topping-up the engine oil level

Checking windscreen washer reservoir fluid level

Topping-up the coolant level

Topping-up the brake fluid level

Checking the clutch fluid level

Checking the power steering reservoir fluid level

Removing the protective cap fitted over the windscreen wiper arm securing nut

Changing a wiper blade

Manual gearbox filler/level plug (arrowed) is located on left-hand side of rear extension

Oil filter viewed from underneath car

Steering gaiter in good condition

Chapter 1 Engine

For modifications, and information applicable to later models, see Supplement at end of manual

Contents

Specifications

General

	2300	2600
Type	6 cylinder, in-line	6 cylinder, in-line
Bore	3.189 in (81 mm)	3.189 in (81 mm)
Stroke	2.992 in (76 mm)	3.307 in (84 mm)
Cylinder capacity	143.4 cu in (2350 cc)	158.3 cu in (2597 cc)
Compression ratio	9.25:1	9.25:1
BHP (DIN)	123 at 5000 rpm	136 at 5000 rpm
Maximum torque	134 lbf ft at 4000 rpm	152 lbf ft at 3750 rpm
Firing order	1, 5, 3, 6, 2, 4	1, 5, 3, 6, 2, 4
Engine weight	432 lbs (196 kilos)	432 lbs (196 kilos)

Lubrication system

Oil pressure	60 to 65 lbf in² (4.22 to 4.57 kgf cm²) at 2000 rpm
Oil pump type	Holbourne-Eaton eccentric lobe, driven off front end of crankshaft
Oil filter type	Full-flow, disposable element
Oil type/specification*	Multigrade engine oil, viscosity range SAE 10W/30 to 15W/50, to API SE or SF (Duckhams QXR, Hypergrade, or 10W/40 Motor Oil)
Sump and filter capacity	10.8 pints (6.1 litres)
Sump (drain and refill) capacity	9.7 pints (5.5 litres)

Austin Rover specify a 10W/40 oil to meet warranty requirements for models produced after August 1983. Duckhams QXR and 10W/40 Motor Oil are available to meet these requirements

Camshaft

Location	Right-hand side of camshaft carrier
No of bearings	7
Diameter of journals	2.0079 to 2.0084 in (51.0 to 51.013 mm)
Endfloat in carrier	0.002 to 0.006 in (0.050 to 0.144 mm)
Diameter of carrier bore	2.0104 to 2.0114 in (51.063 to 51.090 mm)
Clearance in carrier	0.002 to 0.003 in (0.050 to 0.090 mm)
Cam dwell period	238°

Valve timing
Inlet opens . . . .   12° BTDC
Inlet closes . . . .   52° ABDC
Exhaust opens . . . .   52° BBDC
Exhaust closes . . . .   12° ATDC
Valve clearances:
    Inlet . . . .   0.018 in (0.46 mm)
    Exhaust . . . .   0.018 in (0.46 mm)
Timing marks:
    Camshaft . . . .   Notch in drive pulley and notch in carrier
    Crankshaft . . . .   Mark on crankshaft pulley and timing scale on oil pump cover

Valves
Inlet (single spring):
    Overall length . . . .   4.636 to 4.654 in (117.75 to 118.20 mm)
    Head diameter . . . .   1.653 in (42.00 mm)
    Angle of face . . . .   45°
    Stem diameter . . . .   0.3107 to 0.3113 in (7.892 to 7.907 mm)
    Stem to guide clearance . . . .   0.0019 to 0.0012 in (0.05 to 0.03 mm)
    Guide length . . . .   1.820 in (46.25 mm)
    Spring free length . . . .   1.62 in (41.15 mm)
    Tappet diameter . . . .   1.3767 to 1.3772 in (34.968 to 34.980 mm)
Exhaust (double springs):
    Overall length . . . .   4.649 to 4.665 in (118.09 to 118.54 mm)
    Head diameter . . . .   1.4016 in (35.60 mm)
    Angle of face . . . .   45°
    Stem diameter . . . .   0.3100 to 0.3106 in (7.874 to 7.889 mm)
    Stem to guide clearance . . . .   0.002 to 0.0024 in (0.05 to 0.06 mm)
    Guide length . . . .   2.402 in (61.0 mm)
    Spring free length:
       Inner spring . . . .   1.42 in (36.07 mm)
       Outer spring . . . .   1.62 in (41.15 mm)

Rocker shafts
Shaft diameter . . . .   0.747 to 0.748 in (18.987 to 19.0 mm)
Bore inside diameter . . . .   0.749 to 0.750 in (19.025 to 19.043 mm)

Connecting rods
Length between centres . . . .   5.127 to 5.123 in (130.225 to 130.124 mm)
Small-end bush inside diameter . . . .   0.937 to 0.938 in (23.818 to 23.825 mm)

Big-end bearings
Type . . . .   Vandervell
Diametrical clearance . . . .   0.0027 to 0.001 in (0.068 to 0.025 mm)
Side-play on crankpin . . . .   0.005 to 0.013 in (0.16 to 0.34 mm)
Undersizes . . . .   0.010 and 0.020 in (0.254 and 0.508 mm)

Gudgeon pins
Length . . . .   2.626 to 2.638 in (66.70 to 67.00 mm)
Diameter . . . .   0.937 to 0.9376 in (23.811 to 23.815 mm)
Clearance (push fit):
    Con-rod . . . .   0.0003 to 0.0004 in (0.007 to 0.010 mm)
    Piston . . . .   0.0003 to 0.0004 in (0.0067 to 0.0098 mm)

Pistons
Type:
    2600 . . . .   Aluminium alloy, strutted, by Mahle
    2300 . . . .   Aluminium alloy, W-slotted skirt type, by Hepworth and Grandage
Clearances:
    Top land . . . .   0.018 to 0.024 in (0.450 to 0.613 mm)
    Skirt bottom . . . .   0.0005 to 0.0015 in (0.012 to 0.038 mm)
Oversizes . . . .   0.010 and 0.020 in (0.25 and 0.50 mm)

Piston rings
Number one compression ring type . . . .   Chrome periphery
Number two compression ring type . . . .   Stepped 'L' shape marked 'TOP' on upper face
Compression ring gap in bore:
    Top ring . . . .   0.013 to 0.018 in (0.33 to 0.46 mm)
    No 2 ring . . . .   0.009 to 0.014 in (0.23 to 0.36 mm)
No 1 and No 2 compression ring to piston groove clearance . . . .   0.0019 to 0.0032 in (0.050 to 0.082 mm)
Oil control ring type . . . .   1 ring in 3 parts. A centre expander with an identical chrome rail above and below

Oil control ring gaps:
    Rail . . . .   0.015 to 0.055 in (0.38 to 1.40 mm)
    Expander . . . .   Nil (the ends butt)

Crankshaft

Material	EM 16 steel with induction hardened journals
No of bearings	4
Main journal diameter	2.768 to 2.771 in (70.311 to 70.3833 mm)
Minimum regrind diameter	2.766 to 2.7685 in (70.260 to 70.3198 mm)
Crankpin journal diameter	1.988 to 1.9885 in (50.4952 to 50.5079 mm)
Minimum regrind diameter	1.9855 to 1.986 in (50.4317 to 50.4444 mm)
Endthrust	Taken on thrustwashers on No 3 main bearing
Endfloat	0.003 to 0.011 in (0.076 to 0.279 mm)
Endfloat adjustment:	
Thrustwasher oversizes available	0.002, 0.005, 0.010, 0.015 , 0.020 in (0.05, 0.127, 0.25, 0.379 mm)

Main bearings

Type	Vandervell, with numbered caps
Number	4
Undersizes	0.01 and 0.02 in (0.254 and 0.508 mm)

Torque wrench settings

	lbf ft	Nm
Cylinder head bolts	100 to 105	136 to 142
Camshaft carrier bolts	37	50
Camshaft drive pulley	37	50
Camshaft cover baffle plate	7	10
Main bearing cap bolts	75	102
Big-end bearing cap bolts	44	60
Clutch to flywheel	21	28
Flywheel (Driveplate) to crankshaft bolts . . .	52	70
Crankshaft pulley	147	200
Exhaust manifold bolts	30	40
Inlet manifold bolts	21	28
Oil pump bolts	21	28
Oil suction pipe:		
To sump	21	28
To pump	7	10
Sump bolts	10	14
Sump drain plug	30	40
Rear oil seal housing to block	21	28
Water elbow bolts	21	28
Water pump bolts	21	28
Power steering pump securing and adjusting nuts and bolts	21	28
Power steering pump pulley	21	28
Alternator securing and adjusting nuts and bolts	21	28
Front engine mounting brackets to engine:		
Upper bolts	18	24
Lower bolts	50	67
Front engine mounting bracket to mounting, nuts	40.5	54
Front engine mounting to front crossmember, nuts	40.5	54
Clutch housing:		
To cylinder block and engine plate	21	28
To sump and engine bracing	37	50
Slave cylinder bolts	25	34
Starter motor bolts	35	52

1 General description

The Rover 2300 and 2600 share basically the same robust straight 6-cylinder engine. The only major differences are the crankshaft and the pistons. The engine has a light alloy crossflow head with a cast-iron block. There is a single overhead camshaft (driven by a toothed belt) which directly operates the inlet valves via bucket-type tappets and at the same time operates rockers which in turn operate the exhaust valves. The valves are inclined at an angle of 40°. The rockers and camshaft are housed in a separate carrier bolted to the cylinder head.

The bore in both versions is the same at 81 mm but the strokes are different. In the 2300 model the stroke is 76 mm, producing a cubic capacity of 2350; whereas the 2600 model has a longer stroke of 84 mm, raising the capacity to 2597 cc.

The crankcase, being cast iron, is extremely tough and has convoluted sides rather like a diesel engine. The skirt extends well down below the bearings to give added rigidity. The crankshaft which is

carried by four main bearings is made out of special EM16 steel and the journals are specially hardened.

The combustion chambers are formed both in the cylinder head and in the piston crown.

As with the Rover 3500 (SDI) the fan is connected via a viscous coupling to limit its speed. The water pump is mounted on the front of the block and incorporates the only block drain plug.

The oil pump is mounted on the front end of the crankshaft and driven straight off it.

The carburation is the same in both models. That is, twin SU HS6 carburettors with long induction tracts, which are water heated to ensure efficiency of the crossflow system. The air temperature control system regulates the temperature of the air fed into the carburettors. The exhaust arrangement is unusual in that there is no manifold gasket. It is bolted straight on to the block and secured by two bolts per outlet.

The distributor is mounted horizontally in the side of the camshaft carrier and driven directly off the front end of the camshaft.

Fig. 1.1 Longitudinal view of 6-cylinder engine (Sec 1)

Fig. 1.2 Cross-sectional view of 6-cylinder engine (Sec 1)

2 Major operations possible with the engine fitted in the car

The following major operations can be carried out with the engine still in position in the car:

(1) Removal and refitting of the radiator
(2) Removal and refitting of the water pump and fan assembly
(3) Removal and refitting of the alternator
(4) Removal and refitting of the power steering pump
(5) Removal and refitting of the carburettors and ancillaries
(6) Removal and refitting of the starter motor assembly
(7) Removal and refitting of the distributor
(8) Removal and refitting of the camshaft carrier assembly
(9) Renewal of the camshaft front oil seal
(10) Renewal of the tappets and adjustment of the valve clearances
(11) Renewal of the valves and valve springs
(12) Removal and refitting of the cylinder head
(13) Removal and refitting of the gearbox – manual and automatic
(14) Removal and refitting of the clutch assembly
(15) Removal and refitting of the flywheel/driveplate (automatic transmission)
(16) Removal and refitting of the crankshaft rear oil seal
(17) Removal and refitting of the engine/gearbox mountings
(18) Removal and refitting of the oil pressure relief valve
(19) Removal and refitting of the sump
(20) Removal and refitting of the oil pump
(21) Removal and refitting of the pistons and connecting rods
(22) Renewal of the piston rings
(23) Renewal of the big-end bearings

3 Major operations requiring engine removal

The following operations can only be carried out after the engine has been removed from the car:

(1) Removal and refitting of the main bearings
(2) Removal and refitting of the crankshaft
(3) Reboring of the cylinder block

Note: *Many of the other operations listed in Section 2 are more easily performed with the engine out of the car, although it is feasible to do them in situ. These include:*

(a) Removal and refitting of the sump
(b) Removal and refitting of the oil pump
(c) Removal and refitting of the pistons and connecting rods
(d) Renewal of the piston rings
(e) Renewal of the big-end bearings

If therefore it is likely when starting a job that further stripping will have to be carried out which may require the engine to be taken out of the car, then it is advisable to do so at the outset and make the job easier.

4 Engine – removal with manual gearbox

Note: *Rover recommend that the engine is lifted out complete with the manual gearbox or automatic transmission unit. However, the gearbox can be removed first, followed by the engine if sufficiently heavy lifting tackle is not available or space is limited. The engine unit alone weighs approximately 432 lb (196 kg) and has to be lifted at least three feet to be removed from the car. At no time during the lifting operation should anyone be directly beneath this heavy suspended weight. It is not recommended that this job is tackled by one person alone.*

1   Before commencing work it is advisable to cover the wings with protective sheets or similar. Also ensure that there is sufficient storage space for all the parts you will have to remove from the car.
2   Disconnect the terminals and remove the battery.
3   Mark around the bonnet hinge positions and disconnect the windscreen washer feed pipe at the T-piece.
4   To remove the bonnet itself is a 2 man job. Holding the bonnet open, disconnect the stay rod by removing the split-pin and washer and then fold it down out of the way.
5   Undo the bolts and lift the bonnet away. Store it in a safe place where it will not become damaged. If it has to be stored upright, ensure that rags or some form of similar protection are placed under the corners on which it rests. Screw hinge bolts and plates lightly back into their respective holes for safety.
6   Drain down the cooling system. See Chapter 2.
7   When the system has drained, remove the top hose, bottom hose and expansion hose from the radiator (photo).
8   Undo the bolts that secure the top radiator bracket to the front body panel and lift the radiator straight out. Ensure the hoses and fan blades do not snag the radiator matrix as it is removed. Note that there are no bolts securing the bottom of the radiator. It is located by two pegs which seat in grommets in the front sub-frame.
9   Remove the air temperature control system as a complete assembly (photo). Disconnect the worm drive clips that secure the hoses to the air cleaner and heater box or the manifold, and the two nuts and bolts that secure the control valve to the body mounting bracket. Slide the front cold airfeed hose rearwards through the guide bracket and place the whole assembly in a safe place.
10   Remove the 6 bolts that secure the air cleaner to the twin carburettors.
11   Release the fuel feed pipe from the two plastic clips on the rear of the air cleaner casing and lift out the air cleaner (photo).
12   Disconnect the throttle cable and remove the stop/adjuster from

4.7 Top, bottom and expansion coolant hoses viewed from above

4.9 The complete air temperature control system before removal

4.11 Removing the air cleaner

4.12 The throttle cable and adjuster before removal

4.13 The choke/mixture cable attached to trunnion

4.16 In-line fuel filter (arrowed)

4.18 Disconnecting the wiring harness multi-plug

4.21 Undoing the alternator harness plug

4.27 Disconnecting the heater rail hoses at the bulkhead

4.28 The camshaft cover special retaining bolt

4.30 Undoing the nuts that secure the right-hand engine mounting

4.31 Undoing the nuts and bolts to release the left-hand engine mounting

4.33 The earth strap connected to the lower starter bolt

4.34 Preparing to remove the rear main crossmember bolts

the bracket. Tuck it out of the way (photo).

13 Disconnect the choke cable from the trunnion, remove the hairpin spring clip from beneath the cable stop bracket and withdraw the cable. Tuck it out of the way (photo).

14 Disconnect the servo hose from the manifold and tuck it out of the way.

15 Remove the overflow pipes (green) from the left and right-hand float chambers. Store safely.

16 Release the clip on the outlet end of the fuel filter and separate the fuel feed pipework to the carburettors (photo). Then unclip the fuel feed pipe (with filter attached) from the bulkhead clips and secure out of the way.

17 Remove the fuel feed pipe to both float chambers by releasing the spring clips; store safely.

18 Disconnect the wiring harness multi-plug just below the expansion tank and release the harness strap (photo).

19 Disconnect the HT lead to the coil and the LT leads from it.

20 Undo the positive battery clamp bolt and separate the parts. The wiring can then be tucked away and lifted out with the engine and removed later with greater ease.

21 Undo the alternator harness plug. Slide the red locking clip against the spring and pull out (photo).

22 Slacken off the alternator adjusting bolts and power steering pump adjuster bolts and remove the belts from the pulleys.

23 Withdraw the bolt that secures the adjusting bracket to the alternator and push the bracket up and out of the way.

24 Remove the two bolts and the plate that secure the power steering pump quadrant.

25 Undo the nut and withdraw the common pivot bolt for both the power steering pump and alternator whilst supporting both components. Remove the alternator from the car and place it to one side.

26 Place the power steering pump to one side in the engine bay but do not disconnect the hoses. Make sure it is not going to be in the way when the engine is removed.

27 Disconnect the heater hoses where they pass through the bulkhead at the rear of the engine on the nearside (photo).

28 Remove the special retaining bolt at the centre rear of the camshaft cover or it will snag the bulkhead on removal (photo).

29 Remove the 3 nuts that secure the front exhaust pipe to the lower manifold flange.

30 Remove the 2 self-locking nuts that secure the right-hand front engine mounting rubber to the engine mounting bracket (photo).

31 Remove the 2 nuts from the bolts that secure the left-hand front engine mounting rubber to the subframe (photo).

32 Refer to Chapter 6, Section 2 and follow paragraphs 2 to 15. Paragraph 9 will have already been carried out.

33 Undo the lower starter bolt and nut and remove the earth strap, then refit the nut (photo).

34 Ensure that a jack is placed under the gearbox (preferably a trolley jack if working on hard ground) and remove the four bolts, washers

and the 2 plates that secure the rear main crossmember to the body (photo).

35 Lower the jack to allow clearance between the transmission tunnel and the transmission so as to ease the removal of the assembly.

36 Ensure that both the speedometer drive cable and the reverse light switch cable are tied carefully out of the way.

37 Attach the lifting tackle to the front-left and rear-right lifting eyes.

38 Take the weight of the engine and gearbox assembly on the lifting tackle and remove the two bolts from the left-hand front engine mounting bracket, having previously removed the nuts. Protect the front valance.

39 Carefully lift the engine and gearbox clear, ensuring that all connections are released and that none of the ancillary equipment (cables or leads) snags or gets fouled as the assembly is removed (photo).

40 As the hoist is raised, so the jack under the gearbox must be lowered; also as the engine is raised so the hoist must be pulled forward and away from the car.

41 Once the assembly is removed, the engine and gearbox can be separated. Refer to Section 33 for the correct procedure.

42 The engine oil can be drained off before removal of the engine from the car or it can be done with the engine on the bench, whichever is more convenient (photo).

5 Engine – removal with automatic transmission

1 This operation can be carried out in a similar fashion to the one already described in Section 4. Either the complete assembly can be removed as one, or the automatic transmission unit can first be removed. Refer to Chapter 6 for the correct procedure for this operation.

2 However, there are some special points to note if the assembly is going to be removed as one unit. These are as follows:

3 When removing the radiator of automatic transmission models, two additional hoses will be found. These are the flow and return hoses for the transmission oil cooler. The oil cooler is incorporated as an integral part of the engine cooling radiator. When disconnected, the ends of the hoses and the radiator connections should be plugged to prevent the ingress of dirt and the loss of transmission fluid.

4 Automatic transmission models are fitted with a kickdown (downshift) facility which is connected to the throttle linkage. This must be disconnected. Refer to Chapter 6 if necessary.

5 Disconnect the wires from the inhibitor/reverse lamp switch. Refer to Chapter 6.

6 Move the selector lever to the 'P' position and from underneath the car remove the split-pins, washers and clevis pins that secure the selector rod in position. Remove the rod from the gearbox and control lever. Refer to Chapter 6.

4.39 Carefully lifting the engine and gearbox clear

4.42 The sump drain plug

6 Engine – refitting with manual gearbox

Note: *This section assumes that the engine and gearbox assemblies have been separated and are now awaiting reassembly on the bench.*

1 Lightly grease the gearbox input shaft splines. Engage a gear (temporarily refit the gear lever if necessary) and offer the gearbox to the engine, engaging the input shaft splines with the clutch plate. Do not allow the weight of the gearbox to hang on the input shaft.

2 Push the gearbox fully home, making sure that the dowel on the engine backplate enters the hole in the gearbox bellhousing.

3 Fit three securing bolts, evenly spaced, to secure the gearbox to the engine, but do not tighten them yet. Refer to paragraph 5 to identify the different lengths of bolt.

4 Refit the main dowel bolt through the hole in the left-hand side of the bellhousing (photo). This is a specially long bolt which passes through the crankcase. Fix the nut to the dowel bolt and tighten the bolt, then tighten the three securing bolts previously fitted.

5 Refit the remaining bellhousing to engine bolts. Note that the bolts are of three different lengths. The longest ones bolt directly into the engine block. The medium length bolts locate through the adaptor plate with the nuts on the engine side. The shorter bolts secure the flywheel cover plate in place, also with nuts on the engine side. Note that the top centre hole is blanked off.

6 Ensure that the following brackets etc are correctly located as follows (viewed from the rear):

(a) The water rail rear bracket; secured by a bolt at the top of the bellhousing just right of top centre. This bracket also has a transducer cable clip fitted to it

(b) The transducer cable bracket (next to the transducer itself); located by a bolt at the 11 o'clock position

(c) The diagnostic socket bracket; located on the engine side of the adaptor plate and positioned by two lugs. The bolt and nut above the upper starter motor bolt locate it in position. Do not forget to reconnect the harness plug to the socket assembly (photo).

7 Refit the transducer and secure it with the bolt and washer. Then clip the cable into the two cable clips mentioned in paragraph 6.

8 Note that at this stage all ancillaries such as the manifolds, fan, starter motor, carburettors, distributor, plugs, leads etc should all have been refitted if the engine has been stripped down. If the electrical harness has been removed, this also should have been refitted.

9 Refill the gearbox with the correct grade and quantity of oil before refitting, as it is much easier to do at this stage. Recheck the level when installed and top-up if necessary.

10 Using a suitable hoist, attach chains to the lifting eyes and position the engine in position in front of the car. This is a 2 man operation and should not be attempted by anyone on their own. **Note:** *The smallest lifting hoist that should be used is a ½ ton type, which will support 5 cwt at its longest arm extension (photo).*

6.4 Main dowel bolt securing bellhousing to crankcase (arrowed)

11 Place a protective mat or cover over the front valance and number plate area and then raise the assembly on the hoist.

12 Due to the angle at which the engine/gearbox naturally hangs, it may be found necessary to lift the gearbox end to clear the front valance whilst pushing the assembly in slowly. Keep the assembly in a straight line.

13 As the gearbox nears the bulkhead, lower the hoist and push in further. Ensure that none of the ancillaries or cables become snagged and especially, keep an eye on the engine mounting brackets. They can easily catch the headlamps.

14 Lower further and push in until the rear end of the camshaft carrier is almost touching the bulkhead and the sump is almost resting on the steering rack (photo).

15 Place a jack (a trolley type is preferable, as it will move) under the gearbox mounting bracket and raise the jack until the transmission is as high as it can be without touching the tunnel.

16 Then gently release the hoist and lower the engine to locate the front mountings. Fit the right-hand one first and then the left. Place the nuts on the right-hand mounting and refit the bolts and nuts on the left-hand side. Do not tighten the bolts.

17 Release the tension on the hoist and check the engine position. If satisfactory, tighten up the mounting nuts and bolts.

18 Remove the hoist.

19 Raise the jack and refit the bolts, washers and plate to secure the rear crossmember to the body. Then remove the jack.

20 Feed the reverse light switch cable over the gearbox, locate it in the clips on top of the gearbox and push in the snap connectors (photo).

21 Refit the propshaft, ensuring that the gear lever is in the neutral position. Rotate the shaft/flange and line up the scribe marks made on removal. Insert the four bolts and refit the locknuts (photo). Tighten to the correct torque.

22 Refit the sump stiffening plate bolts and tighten them.

23 Refit the speedometer drive cable and secure the bracket (photo).

24 Refit the exhaust pipe to the manifold, inserting a new gasket. Tighten the three nuts to the correct torque.

25 Refit the front exhaust bracket.

26 Refit the clutch slave cylinder.

27 Refit the earth strap to the lower starter motor bolt.

28 Check the gearbox oil level and top up if necessary.

29 Refit the power steering pump and alternator on the common pivot bolt.

30 Refit the adjustment link on the alternator and refit the two bolts and plate to the adjuster quadrant for the power steering pump.

31 Refit the drive belts, alternator first, and adjust the belt tensions (photo). Tighten up the adjuster and pivot bolts. See Chapter 2 for the correct tension.

32 Refit the alternator harness plug.

33 Reconnect the main harness multi-plug (below the expansion tank) and the harness strap.

34 Reconnect the coil leads and dust cap (photo).

35 Refit the special camshaft cover bolt to the rear centre of the cover.

36 Refit the fuel feed pipework to the carburettors and secure with spring clips.

37 Reconnect the fuel filter and feed pipe with the spring clip and secure the fuel line in the bulkhead clips.

38 Refit both overflow pipes (green) to the float chambers.

39 Reconnect the brake servo hose to the manifold. There is no clip. It simply pushes on (photo).

40 Reconnect the throttle cable to the linkage. Note that the cable has a threaded outer and black plastic stop/adjuster which when located in the linkage bracket can be simply rotated to adjust the cable.

41 Reconnect the choke/mixture cable at the trunnion. Note the hairpin type small spring clip which locates the outer cable in the stop bracket by holding it from underneath the bracket.

42 Refit the heater hoses at the bulkhead.

43 Refit the radiator by locating the pegs in the grommets and secure the top bracket by the 2 bolts through the front panel. Ensure that the drain tap is turned off.

44 Reconnect the top hose, bottom hose and expansion hose.

45 Refit the air temperature control system as a complete assembly. Tighten up the worm drive clips.

46 Refill the engine with the correct grade and quantity of oil.

47 Refill the cooling system with a water/antifreeze mixture. See

6.6 Reconnecting the harness to the diagnostic socket

6.10 Positioning the engine ready for refitting

6.14 Lowering the engine and gearbox into the car

6.20 Refitting the reverse light switch cable at the connectors

6.21 Refitting the propeller shaft to the drive flange

6.23 Speedometer cable and front exhaust bracket refitted

6.31 View of engine showing alternator and power steering pump refitted and the belts in position

6.34 Reconnecting the leads to the ignition coil

6.39 Servo hose, throttle cable, choke cable, fuel feed pipes all reconnected

Chapter 2. Check and top-up only after refitting is completed.
48 Refit the battery and connect the terminals. Remember to rebuild the positive terminal that was stripped out on removal.
49 Refill/check the carburettor dashpot levels.
50 Check the static ignition timing and adjust if necessary. Refer to Chapter 4 for the correct procedure.
51 Refit and line-up the bonnet using the scribe marks. Refit the 2 bolts and plate per hinge. Then refit the bonnet stay, held in place by a washer and split-pin.
52 Reconnect the screen washer feed pipe at the T-piece.
53 Check the line-up of the bonnet and the locking effectiveness. This ensures that the bolts have been refitted correctly.
54 Refit the gear lever with its anti-rattle spring and plunger (See Chapter 6, Section 2 for details) and refit the bias spring and cap.
55 Refit the lower boot, followed by the foam pad and the upper boot and console plate. Then screw on the gear lever knob and sleeve.
56 Start the engine up, check that the warning lights for oil and ignition go out (if not, stop the engine), re-check the timing and adjust if necessary (Chapter 4). Check the balance of the carburettors and the

idling speed and adjust if necessary (Chapter 3); then replace the air cleaner and secure it with the 6 bolts. Ensure also that the air temperature control hose is repositioned and located on the air cleaner and that the fuel feed pipe is located in the plastic clips on the casing of the air cleaner.
57 Check and top-up the cooling system (see Chapter 2).
58 After running the engine for the first test, check to ensure that there are no oil, water or petrol leaks. Remove any tools that may have been left in the engine bay.
59 Check all fluid levels before using the car on the road.

7 Engine – refitting with automatic transmission

1 Fit the automatic transmission to the engine as described in Chapter 6 (Part B).
2 Refitting of the engine/transmission assembly is basically similar to that described in the preceding section for cars with manual gearboxes.

3   As with removal, there are special points to be noted.
4   The speed selector mechanism must be reconnected and checked for correct operation.
5   The inhibitor switch/reverse light plug must be reconnected.
6   The kickdown cable must be refitted and adjusted.
7   The transmission cooler hoses must be reconnected to the radiator. Basically the reverse procedure to removal.
8   The transmission must be filled up with the correct grade and quantity of fluid.
9   If there are any doubts when refitting an automatic transmission, refer to Chapter 6 (Part B) for guidance.

8 Engine mountings – removal and refitting

Front

1   Disconnect the battery negative terminal.
2   Support the weight of the engine, either using a hoist above or

Fig. 1.3 Front engine mountings (Sec 8)

    3 *Mounting rubber to engine bracket nut*
    4 *Mounting rubber to subframe bolt*
    5 *Left-hand mounting rubber*
    6 *Right-hand mounting rubber*

8.4 Left-hand front engine mounting bolts being removed

jack beneath the sump with a bearer in between the sump and the jack.
3   The engine mounting rubber is secured to the engine bracket by 2 nuts and washers. Remove these first.
4   The mounting rubber is also secured to the subframe by 2 bolts and nuts. Remove these next (photo).
5   The mounting rubber can now be withdrawn and renewed.
6   Refitting is the reverse procedure to removal, but note that the bolts which secure the mountings to the subframe have their heads facing to the rear. Tighten all four nuts loosely first and when they are lined-up correctly, tighten them to the specified torque.

Rear

1   Jack the car up and support the body side-members on stands.
2   Support the weight of the gearbox with a jack.
3   Slacken and remove the centre bolt and locknut complete with spacer and washers.
4   Undo the nuts that hold the mounting rubbers to the cross-member.
5   Remove the 2 bolts and plate that hold each side of the rear crossmember in position and remove the crossmember.
6   Unscrew the two mounting rubbers from the gearbox casing.
7   Refitting is the reverse procedure to removal, but note that the centre bolt should be refitted so that there is a gap of 3 mm (0.118 in) between the crossmember and the spacer; when this gap exists the locknut can be tightened.

9 Camshaft cover – removal and refitting

1   Remove the engine breather hose from the camshaft cover.
2   Disconnect and remove the air inlet hose to the air cleaner.
3   Remove the distributor cap and unclip the lead guides from the brackets attached to the camshaft cover. Place them to one side.
4   Remove the nine cover securing screws, taking care not to lose the cable brackets and noting their positions. Also remove the one special bolt at the centre rear of the cover.
5   Carefully ease the cover from under the drivebelt cover bracket and remove it followed by the gasket.
6   Refitting is the reverse procedure to removal, but remember to use a new gasket and to grease both sides first to keep it in position. Also refit the baffle plate with the 2 screws if it has been removed.

10 Camshaft drivebelt cover – removal and refitting

1   Undo the bolt that retains the cover to the bracket attached to the

Fig. 1.4 Rear engine mounting assembly (Sec 8)

    4 *Locknut*   8 *Retaining plate*
    5 *Centre bolt and spacer*   9 *Rear crossmember*
    6 *Mounting rubber securing nut*

Fig. 1.5 Camshaft drivebelt cover (Sec 10)

1 Special manifold stud and nut
2 Top retaining bolt
3 Right-hand bracket to water elbow bolt
4 Common bolt
5 Alternator adjuster link bolt

10.5 Removing the drivebelt cover

camshaft cover. There is a fixed nut on the bracket.
2 Take off the nut and washer that retain the cover to the special stud at the front end of the inlet manifold.
3 Undo the bolt that secures the right-hand upper bracket on the cover to the water elbow.
4 Withdraw the bolt that retains both the cover and alternator adjustment link to the oil pump cover. It is also helpful to slacken the clamp bolt on the adjustment link itself.
5 The drivebelt cover can now be removed (photo).
6 Refitting is the reverse procedure to removal. Remember to tension the alternator drivebelt when the link has been refitted on the common bolt (see Chapter 2).

11 Camshaft drivebelt – removal, refitting and adjusting

1 Disconnect the battery negative terminal.
2 Take off the drivebelt cover as described in the previous Section.
3 Slacken the power steering pump adjuster quadrant bolts, push the pump towards the engine and remove the drivebelt.
4 Remove the alternator/fan drivebelt.

Fig. 1.6 Setting the engine at TDC on the crankshaft pulley (Sec 11)

1 Timing scale

Fig. 1.7 Lining up the timing marks (Sec 11)
1 Grooves in drive wheel and camshaft carrier

5 Rotate the crankshaft so that the notch in the pulley is aligned with the 'O' on the timing scale. The engine is now at TDC. The groove in the camshaft drive wheel should also be lined up with the groove in the camshaft carrier. Do not move the crankshaft from now on.
6 Slacken the belt tensioner pivot and adjustment bolts and pull the tensioner outwards to slacken the belt.
7 Slide the toothed belt from the camshaft drive wheel.
8 Remove the bolts that secure the timing scale to the oil pump housing and then slip the camshaft drivebelt off the pulley and remove it over the fan blades.
9 Refitting is basically the reverse procedure to removal. Ensure that the position of the crankshaft is the same as before (at TDC) and the grooves in the drive wheel and carrier are lined up before slipping the belt onto the camshaft drive wheel (photo). If fitting a used belt, be sure it will run in the same direction as before.
10 Before attempting to tension the drivebelt, ensure that the drive side (right) of the belt is tight and that the teeth are slotted correctly into the grooves in the drive wheel. To achieve this, rotate the crankshaft one complete turn once the belt has been refitted.
11 To adjust the tension of the drivebelt correctly, proceed as follows: Firstly ensure that the tensioner bracket moves freely.
12 Place a $\frac{3}{8}$ in square drive extension into the square hole in the tensioner bracket and, with a torque wrench attached, set to 20 lbf in (2.3 Nm). Rotate the bracket to tension against the belt and when the correct torque is achieved, tighten the adjuster and pivot bolts (photo).
13 Check again that the timing marks are correctly aligned.
14 Take great care with this type of toothed drivebelt. If contaminated with oil it must be discarded as it will slip. Be careful that the belt is not bent or handled in a rough manner as it could easily fracture the reinforcing glass fibre and so shorten its life.
15 Refit and tension the alternator and power steering pump drivebelts (see Chapters 2 and 11).

11.9 Line up the grooves in the camshaft drive wheel and carrier

12 Camshaft drive wheel – removal and refitting

1   Disconnect the battery negative terminal.
2   Refer to Section 10 and remove the camshaft drivebelt cover.
3   Loosen the bolt that secures the drive wheel to the camshaft.
4   Refer to Section 11 and follow paragraphs 5 to 7.
5   Withdraw the drive wheel retaining bolt, washer and spacer, being careful not to turn the camshaft. Remove the drive wheel.
6   Refitting is the reverse procedure to removal, but ensure that the drive wheel locates correctly over the roll pin.
7   Re-tension the belt as described in the previous Section (paragraphs 9 to 13).

13 Camshaft front oil seal – renewal

1   Refer to the previous Section and follow paragraphs 1 to 5.
2   Unless you have the proper extractor, proceed as follows:
3   Drill two small holes in the outer face of the seal on opposite sides of the camshaft nose.
4   Insert a selftapping screw into each hole and screw halfway home, leaving enough to grip with a mole wrench.
5   Grip the screws with a mole wrench and lever out the old seal.
6   Clean out the seal housing.
7   Lubricate the seal inside lip and the outside diameter.
8   Feed the seal over the nose of the camshaft and fit it evenly into the front of the housing (photo).

Fig. 1.8 The camshaft belt tensioner (Sec 11)

6 Pivot and adjustment bolts
7 Drivebelt

Fig. 1.9 The camshaft drive wheel (Sec 12)

6 Retaining bolt
7 Drive wheel
8 Roll pin

11.12 Tensioning the drivebelt

13.8 Fitting a new front oil seal to the camshaft

9 Using a suitable piece of tube with a washer in between, tap the seal carefully into the housing ensuring that it goes in level. Tap it right home.

10 Refit the camshaft drive wheel and follow instructions 6 onwards in the preceding Section.

14 Camshaft carrier – removal and refitting

1 Disconnect the battery negative terminal.

2 Remove the camshaft cover and drivebelt cover. See Sections 9 and 10 respectively.

3 Refer to Section 11 and remove the drivebelt from the drive wheel (paragraphs 5 to 7). Note also that the rotor arm in the distributor points to the No 6 cylinder position when the engine is set at TDC with the camshaft drive wheel and carrier grooves lined up.

4 Disconnect the vacuum advance pipe and low tension lead from the distributor.

5 Undo and remove the seventeen bolts that retain the camshaft carrier to the cylinder head.

6 Lift the carrier carefully and place a wooden bearer, about 1 to $1\frac{1}{4}$ in square (25 to 31.75 mm), under each end of the carrier and let it rest on the cylinder block. Then push the tappets down the tappet guides in the carrier so that they seat over their respective valves. By doing it carefully, the pallet shims on the exhaust valves will not become lost or dislodged (photo).

7 Remove the carrier assembly once you have released the tappets from the guides.

8 To refit the carrier assembly, firstly turn the crankshaft 45° from TDC to prevent any damage occuring to the valves or pistons. Also clean the carrier and cylinder head mating faces.

9 Remove the tappets from their respective inlet valves and insert them into their respective guides in the camshaft carrier, having inverted it first. Grease both tappets and guides well with heavy grease to ensure that they stay in place during the refitting operation (photos).

10 Grease all the pallet shims so that they will not jump out of place and refit them in the top collars of their respective valves (photo).

11 Place the two wooden bearers, used previously, in position at either end of the cylinder block. Turn the camshaft so that the groove in the drive wheel is at the one c'clock position (with reference to the normal fitted position of the carrier).

12 Carefully turn the carrier over (with the tappets inserted) and lower it gently into position over the valves (photo). In order to push the tappets down the guides and onto their respective valves, the carrier will have to be offset slightly to the right of the bolt holes because of the angle of the valves. **Note:** *Do not put sealant on the carrier mating face at this stage. The clearances must be checked first and the procedure then repeated.*

13 Carefully push the tappets down the guides and over the valves but do not push them out of their guides completely or it will not be possible to lower the carrier into position.

14 Remove the blocks one at a time and carefully lower the carrier onto the cylinder head.

15 Insert three retaining bolts, one at each end and one in the middle,

Fig. 1.10 The camshaft carrier assembly (Sec 14)

1 One of the 17 carrier retaining bolts

14.6 Lift the camshaft carrier and support it on blocks

14.9a Removing the tappets from the inlet valves

14.9b Invert the camshaft carrier and insert the tappets in their guides

14.10 Pallet shims refitted on all valves

14.12 Lower the camshaft carrier into position carefully

15.5 The camshaft key location

in the holes nearest the camshaft. Tighten the bolts evenly until the camshaft carrier just contacts the dowels in the cylinder head. Make sure that the carrier remains parallel to the head.

16 Lightly strike the camshaft carrier with a soft-faced hammer to align the dowels with the holes in the carrier, at the same time tightening the three bolts evenly. (Look down the dowel holes to determine in which direction to strike).

17 When the carrier has made contact with the cylinder head, insert the remaining bolts and washers and tighten them evenly to the specified torque.

18 Check the valve clearances and adjust if necessary as described in Section 17.

19 Remove the camshaft carrier again and apply a continuous bead of RTV jointing compound to its cylinder head mating face.

20 Refit the camshaft carrier, this time without the aid of the wooden blocks. Align the dowel holes again if necessary as described in paragraph 16. When the securing bolts have been tightened, recheck the valve clearances to ensure that no shims have dropped out.

21 Lubricate the rockers and cams, then turn the camshaft to line up the grooves in the camshaft drive wheel and the carrier.

22 Turn the crankshaft back to TDC until the notch in the pulley lines up with the 'O' on the timing scale.

23 Ensure that the distributor rotor arm is pointing to the No 6 cylinder firing position.

24 Refit the camshaft drivebelt and adjust the tension (see Section 11).

25 Refit the camshaft cover (see Section 9)..

26 Refit the camshaft drivebelt cover (see Section 10).

27 Reconnect the vacuum advance pipe and the low tension leads to the distributor. Reconnect the negative battery terminal.

15 Camshaft – removal, inspection and refitting

1   Remove the camshaft carrier as described in the previous Section.

2   Undo the bolt and remove the washer, spacer and camshaft drive wheel.

3   Remove the camshaft oil seal as described in Section 13.

4   Mark the rotor arm to body positions and remove the distributor (1 nut) (see Chapter 4).

5   Remove the camshaft key located in the first journal (photo).

6   Hold the rockers out of the way whilst removing the camshaft from the carrier. This can be a difficult operation and can be simplified by sliding a piece of wire the length of the carrier under the rockers to keep them clear of the camshaft. Removal is then made much easier (photo).

7   Thoroughly clean and dry the camshaft before inspection.

8   Examine all the bearing surfaces for wear, score marks or obvious defects. Also carefully inspect the cam lobes.

9   Check the condition of the distributor driving gear.

10 Check the bearing surfaces in the camshaft carrier for wear or score marks and also ensure that the key fits snugly and correctly in the keyway. Also check the condition of the tappets and the tappet bores in the carrier.

11 If in doubt seek professional advice and/or replace with a new component.

12 To refit; clean and lubricate the bearing surfaces in the carrier and the camshaft. Ensure that the camshaft oilways are clear.

13 Follow in reverse the instructions for removal. Check the endfloat after refitting the key. Use of selective keys governs the amount of endfloat on the camshaft. Use a dial gauge to check the endfloat (see Specifications).

15.6 Holding the rockers out of the way

16 Rocker shafts and rockers – removal, inspection and refitting

Note: *The rockers are held in place by two shafts of equal length, one is inserted from the front, the other from the rear and both hold three rockers. There are no springs or washers between the rockers and the rocker shaft guides in the carrier casting.*

1   Refer to Section 14 and remove the camshaft carrier as a complete assembly. Place the assembly on a level working surface.

2   To remove the front rocker shaft, firstly remove the front blanking plug (Fig. 1.11).

3   Take out the front rocker shaft locating screw.

4   Withdraw the shaft. If it is very tight, then screw a slave bolt into the blanking plug hole and gain extra purchase to remove the shaft.

5   When the shaft is out the three rockers can be removed.

6   Similarly, the rear rocker shaft and the rear 3 rockers can be removed. Note that in the rear rocker shaft there is also a blanking plug and locating screw.

7   Check the rocker shafts for wear, pitting or scoring, or any other obvious defects.

Fig. 1.11 Front rocker shaft removal (Sec 16)

4 *Blanking plug*
5 *Locating screw*
6 *Rocker shaft*
9 *O-ring*

8   Check the rocker pads for wear. If there is considerable wear then they must be renewed. This type of cast iron rocker cannot be ground.
9   Check the rocker bores for wear. Again if there is excessive lateral movement on the shaft they must be renewed.
10   Check that the oilways in the rocker shafts are clear.
11   Before refitting the rocker shafts renew the O-rings.
12   Place the rockers 1, 2 and 3 in position as the front rocker shaft is slid into position, lining up the locating screw hole in the shaft with the hole in the carrier before pushing home (photo).
13   Screw in the locating screw and refit the blanking plug, having removed the slave bolt if used.
14   Repeat the above procedure with the rear rocker shaft and rocker Nos 4, 5 and 6.
15   Oil all the bearing surfaces.
16   Refer to Section 14 and refit the camshaft carrier assembly.

17 Valve clearances – checking and adjusting

Note: *If the valves are to be checked or adjusted whilst the cylinder head is in the car, the crankshaft must be turned 45° from TDC to prevent damage occurring to the valves and pistons caused by the valve heads impinging on the piston crowns.*

   If this operation is being carried out with the cylinder head on the

bench, then the cylinder head must be supported clear of the bench, allowing space for the valves to move when the camshaft is turned to check the clearances.

1   Assuming that the engine is in the car, then refer to Sections 9, 10, 11 and remove the camshaft cover, drivebelt cover and slip the drivebelt off the drive wheel, having first ensured the correct settings.
2   Turn the engine 45° from TDC by rotating the crankshaft.
3   Before checking the clearances, ensure that the camshaft carrier is bolted down to the correct torque.
4   Place an open-ended spanner on the hexagon nut on the camshaft to the rear of the keyway and turn the camshaft so that No 1 inlet valve is fully open. Check the clearances (inlet and exhaust are both the same at 0.018 in (0.46mm)) on No 6 inlet valve and No 4 exhaust valve using a feeler gauge. Record the clearances in both cases. **Note:** *To check the inlet valve clearances, insert the feeler gauge between the tappet bucket and cam. To check the exhaust valve clearances, insert the feeler gauge between the cam and the rocker pad* (photos).
5   Then turn the camshaft again so that No 2 inlet valve is fully open. Check the clearances on No 5 inlet and No 6 exhaust. Note down the clearances of both.
6   Do this for all the valves in the following order, recording the clearances each time:

   With No 3 inlet valve open – check No 4 inlet and No 5 exhaust valves
   With No 4 inlet valve open – check No 3 inlet and No 2 exhaust valves
   With No 5 inlet valve open – check No 2 inlet and No 1 exhaust valves
   With No 6 inlet valve open – check No 1 inlet and No 3 exhaust valves

7   Provided the clearances are within ± 0.002 in of the specified gap no further action need be taken. If however the gaps vary widely then they must be adjusted. To do so can be a time consuming operation. Make sure all the clearances are recorded accurately to start with. Clearances are adjusted by altering the sizes of the pallet shims in the tops of the valves.
8   Refer to Section 14. Remove the camshaft carrier and place it to one side.
9   Remove the tappets from the inlet valves and place them in a sectioned box in the correct order. Make sure the pallet shims remain on top of the valves (photo).
10   Check with a micrometer the size of the pallets for all the valves that need their clearances adjusted and note them down alongside the clearances taken earlier.
11   The next step is to calculate the thickness of the new shims required to adjust the gap to reach the correct clearance. The method is really quite simple: If the clearance is too small (less than 0.018 in), subtract the clearance noted from the required clearance and take the difference away from the existing pallet shim size. This will give you the pallet shim size that should be fitted to that valve. If the gap is too large (more than 0.018 in), then subtract the required gap from the clearance noted down and add the difference to the existing pallet shim size to calculate the size of the new shim to be fitted.

16.12 Refitting the front rocker shaft and rockers

17.4a Checking No 4 inlet valve, note spanner on hexagon to turn shaft

17.4b Checking No 5 exhaust valve

17.9 Removing the tappets from the inlet valves

18.8a Compress the valve spring to remove the collets ...

18.8b ... then remove the collar and spring ...

18.8c ...followed by the oil seal (when fitted)...

18.8d ...noting that the exhaust valves have double springs

18.12a Cylinder head with valves removed showing valve guides

18.12b Refitting an inlet valve

18.12c Refitting an exhaust valve

18.12d Refitting the lower collar and seal

18.14 Compressing the spring to insert the collets

18.15 Releasing the spring compressor with the collets in position

Examples are:

Gap too small		Gap too large	
Clearance noted . .	0.006 in		0.025 in
Specified clearance	0.018 in		0.018 in
Difference	0.012 in		0.007 in
Existing pallet shim size	0.142 in		0.137 in
Subtract the difference	0.012 in	Add the difference	0.007 in
Pallet shim size required	0.130 in		0.144 in

Note that pallet shims are available from Rover dealers in a wide variety of thicknesses from 3.200 to 4.550 mm. Alternatively, it is possible to grind them down to the necessary size required but ensure that the ground face is perfectly flat when finished.

12 Using thick grease, fit the new pallet shims to the valves and refit the camshaft carrier as described in Section 14, having fitted the tappets into the inverted camshaft carrier with grease.

13 Once the carrier has been screwed down, recheck the clearances as before. If any clearances are not within ± 0.002 in of the specified gap required then you will have to recalculate the pallet shim sizes again.

14 If there is a valve which has either no clearance or a very large one it could be caused either by a pallet shim jumping out and sticking halfway under a tappet or by one being knocked out of position completely. This can only be checked and rectified by lifting off the camshaft carrier and then checking again on refitting. From experience it has been found that it can be a very difficult job, especially after an engine overhaul, and great care must be exercised when refitting the camshaft carrier assembly as the pallet shim on both sets of valves jump out very easily.

15 It is suggested that after an engine overhaul the use of a nominal size pallet shim of around 0.020 in (0.508 mm) smaller than the original may make the operation easier, as it is likely that all the clearances will be larger than the original due to the valve grinding which has taken place.

18 Valves and valve springs – removal, renewal and refitting

1 Refer to Section 14 and remove the camshaft carrier.
2 The valve springs can be removed and changed with the engine in the car provided that you have the special tools available. Refer to the tool manufacturer's instructions and change the springs. Note that the engine crankshaft must be turned so that each piston comes to TDC in turn. This will prevent the valves falling into the piston chamber should any difficulty arise and the valves be released.
3 The valve springs can also be changed on the bench and if it is the intention to remove the valves then it is easier to carry out the whole operation on the bench.
4 Remove the camshaft carrier and cylinder head together and place the assembly on the bench (see Section 22).
5 Undo the 17 camshaft carrier retaining bolts and separate the carrier from the cylinder head (see Section 14).

6 Identify and remove the tappets and pallet shims from the inlet valves and place them in a sectional box for easy recognition and reassembly.
7 Carry out the same procedure for the exhaust valve pallet shims.
8 Turn the cylinder head on its side and using a G-clamp compress each valve in turn (or the ones that need regrinding or renewing) and remove the collets (photos). Release the clamp and remove the collar, spring(s) and seal for each valve (photo). Note that the exhaust valves have double springs (photo). Seals may not be fitted to the exhaust valves on later models.
9 Keep all the valves and ancillaries in complete sets for identification and reassembly. If possible, use a large sectional box for this purpose. If no box is available then use a sheet of card with 12 holes punched in it and marked accordingly for 1 - 6 inlet and exhaust. Push the valves through the cardboard and slip the ancillaries over the stems.
10 Clean and inspect all parts (see Section 19).
11 Refit the valves to the correct positions as follows:
12 Lubricate the valve stem and insert it into the respective guide. Place in position the lower collar and (when fitted) the seal (photos).
13 Refit the single spring in the case of the inlet valves or double springs in the case of the exhaust valves.
14 Refit the top collar and compress the valve spring using a G-clamp or similar tool (photo).
15 Refit the collets and release the tension on the valve spring compressor ensuring that the collets do not jump out (photo).
16 Repeat the above procedure for each valve that has been removed.
17 Refit the pallet shims on top of the valves and refit the camshaft carrier to the cylinder head as described in Section 14. Check the valve clearances and adjust as necessary, as described in Section 17.

19 Cylinder head – removal with the engine in the vehicle

1 Refer to Section 14 and carry out paragraphs 1 to 4.
2 Drain the cooling system and then disconnect the radiator top hose from the water elbow and the water rail hose from the bottom of the thermostat housing (see Chapter 2 for details).
3 Remove the HT leads from the spark plugs and put the leads and distributor cap safely out of the way.
4 Disconnect the water temperature sensor lead.
5 Refer to Chapter 3 and remove the inlet manifold from the cylinder head. Leave the manifold in the engine bay.
6 Slacken the nut and bolt that secure the front exhaust pipe to the bracket attached to the gearbox.
7 Undo and remove the 12 bolts that hold the exhaust manifold in position and pull it slightly away.
8 Undo and remove the 14 cylinder head retaining bolts. They are removed through the camshaft carrier itself. Reverse the tightening sequence (Fig. 1.12). The order then becomes N, M, L, K, J, I, H, G, F, E, D, C, B, A.
9 Lift off the cylinder head complete with the camshaft carrier and place the assembly flat on a bench with a protected surface.
10 Take off the cylinder head gasket.
11 To further strip the cylinder head and camshaft carrier assembly, refer to Section 14, paragraphs 5 to 7. Also refer to Section 18 if the valves are going to be removed prior to further work being done on the cylinder head such as decarbonisation.

Fig. 1.12 Bolt tightening sequence for cylinder head (Sec 21)

20 Cylinder head – decarbonisation

1   Remove the spark plugs.

2   With the cylinder head off, carefully remove with a wire brush and blunt scraper all traces of carbon deposits from the combustion spaces and the ports. The valve stems and valve guides should also be freed from any carbon deposits. Wash the combustion spaces and ports down with petrol and, using a cup shaped wire brush and an electric drill, remove any carbon deposits from the cylinder head surface. Sometimes hard spots of carbon are not easily removed, except by a blunt scraper. Take care when using a scraper, not to damage the surface in any way.

3   Clean the pistons and top of the cylinder bores. If the pistons are still in the block, then it is essential that great care is taken to ensure that no carbon gets in the cylinder bores as this could scratch the cylinder walls or cause damage to the piston rings. To ensure this does not happen, first turn the crankshaft so that two of the pistons are at the top of their bores. Stuff rag into the other four bores, or seal them off with paper and masking tape. The waterways should also be covered with small pieces of masking tape to prevent particles of carbon entering the cooling system and damaging the water pump.

4   There are two schools of thought as to how much carbon should be removed from the piston crown. One school recommends that a ring of carbon should be left around the edge of the piston and on the cylinder bore wall as an aid to low oil consumption. Although this is probably true for early engines with worn bores, on later engines the thought of the second school can be applied, which is that for effective decarbonisation, all traces of carbon should be removed.

5   If all traces of carbon are to be removed, press a little grease into the gap between the cylinder walls and the two pistons which are to be worked on. With a blunt scraper, carefully scrape away the carbon from the piston crown, taking great care not to scratch the aluminium. Also scrape away the carbon from the surrounding lip of the cylinder wall. When all carbon has been removed, scrape away all the grease which will now be contaminated with carbon particles, taking care not to press any into the bores. To assist prevention of carbon build-up, the piston crown can be polished with a metal polish. Remove the rags or masking tape from the next two cylinders and turn the crankshaft so that the two pistons come to the top of their bores. Place rag or masking tape in the cylinders which have been decarbonised and proceed as just described. Repeat the procedure for the final two pistons.

6   If a ring of carbon is going to be left round the piston, this can be helped by inserting an old piston ring into the top of the bore to rest on the piston and ensure that carbon is not accidentally removed. Check that there are no particles of carbon in the cylinder bores. Decarbonising is now complete.

7   As soon as the spark plugs have been cleaned or renewed they can be refitted (see Section 9, Chapter 4).

21 Cylinder head – refitting

1   Refit the valves if removed (see Section 18).

2   Refit the camshaft carrier to the cylinder (see Section 14).

3   Adjust the valve clearances (see Section 17).

4   Thoroughly clean the cylinder head and block mating surfaces.

5   Fit a new cylinder head gasket, ensuring that the oil and waterways are aligned carefully. The gasket has a tab on one end marked 'TOP REAR' to ensure that it is fitted correctly (photo).

6   Ensure that none of the pistons are at TDC. Turn the crankshaft so that it is 45° from TDC.

7   Carefully lower the cylinder head assembly into position, taking great care not to move the gasket.

8   Lightly oil the heads and threads of the cylinder head bolts, and insert them into their respective holes, ensuring that the gasket has not moved.

9   Tighten the bolts to the correct torque in the sequence shown in Fig. 1.12 (photo).

10   Refit the exhaust manifold and tighten the retaining bolts to the correct torque. Note that there is no gasket (see Chapter 3).

11   Re-tighten the nut and bolt that secure the front exhaust pipes to the gearbox bracket.

12   Refit the inlet manifold and rear lifting eye (see Chapter 3).

13   Reconnect the water temperature sensor lead.

14   Refit the water rail hose to the bottom of the thermostat housing (see Chapter 2).

15   Reconnect the top hose to the water elbow outlet.

16   Reconnect the HT leads to the spark plugs.

17   Refer to Section 14 and follow the instructions 21 to 27 in order to refit the remainder of the components.

18   Refill the cooling system with a water/antifreeze mixture as described in Chapter 2. Then run the engine and recheck the mixture level.

22 Valves and valve springs – servicing

1   Examine the heads of the valves for pitting and burning, especially the heads of the exhaust valves. The valve seating should be examined at the same time. If the pitting on valve and seat is very slight, the marks can be removed by grinding the seats and valves together with coarse, and then fine grinding paste. Where bad pitting has occurred to the valve seats, it will be necessary to recut them and fit new valves. If the valve seats are so worn that they cannot be recut then it will be necessary to fit new valve seat inserts. These latter two jobs should be entrusted to the local Rover agent. In practice, it is seldom that the seats are so badly worn that they require renewal. Normally, it is the exhaust valve that is too badly worn and the owner can easily purchase a new set of valves and match them to the seats by valve grinding.

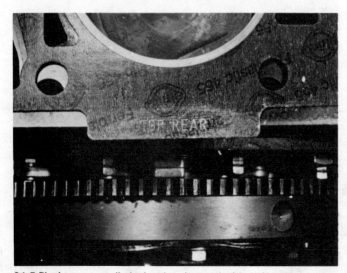

21.5 Placing a new cylinder head gasket on the block. Note the markings

21.9 Tightening the cylinder head bolts to the correct torque (head being refitted on the bench without camshaft carrier)

2 Clean the valves. Remove all the hard carbon deposit from the tops and underside using a blunt knife blade. Care should be taken not to mark or score the valve seating faces. Finish off the valve cleaning with a wire brush.

3 Valve springs should be checked for cracks and distortion. Check also that they compress properly and have not lost their strength. Renew any that are suspect.

23 Valves – grinding

1 Support the head on wooden blocks and start with No 1 valve.

2 Smear a trace of coarse or medium carborundum paste on the seat face and apply a suction grinder tool to the valve head. With a semi-rotary motion, grind the valve head to its seat, lifting the valve occasionally to redistribute the grinding paste. When a dull matt even surface finish is produced on both the valve seat and the valve, then wipe off the paste and repeat the process with fine carborundum paste, lifting and turning the valve to redistribute the paste as before. A light spring placed under the valve head will greatly ease this operation. When a smooth unbroken ring of light grey matt finish is produced, on both valve and valve seat faces, the grinding operation is completed. Scrape away all carbon from the valve head and the valve stem. Carefully clean away every trace of grinding compound, taking great care to leave none in the ports or in the valve guides. Clean the valves and valve seats with a paraffin soaked rag then with a clean rag. If an air line is available, blow the valves, valve guides and valve parts clean.

3 Finally give the cylinder head a rinse in clean paraffin to remove any remaining traces of valve grinding paste. Discard this paraffin and dry the head with a clean non-fluffy rag.

4 Draw a clean rag through each guide bore.

5 Refit the valves into their correct positions, oiling the stems as each valve is refitted in its respective guide.

24 Valve guides – checking for wear

1 With the valves removed from the cylinder head, check the valve guide bores for wear.

2 Insert a new valve into the guide and try to tilt it. If the movement across the valve seat is in excess of 0.020 in (0.508 mm), the guide needs to be renewed (see Fig. 1.13).

3 This is not a job which can be done unless the proper equipment is available. It is much easier to get it done professionally as it is very easy to damage an alloy cylinder head.

25 Lubrication system – general description

The oil is drawn up from the sump through a strainer by an eccentric rotor type of oil pump which is driven directly from the nose of the crankshaft. The pump in turn passes the oil to the canister type oil filter via the oil pressure relief valve. This ensures that the pressure is limited to that which is required to satisfactorily feed the engine with oil at all times. Any excess oil is fed back into the sump (Fig. 1.14).

From the oil filter, the oil feeds into the main oil gallery on the right-hand side of the engine. Drilled passages in the crankcase allow oil to be fed to the 4 main bearings. Further drillings take the oil through the crankshaft to the big-end bearings and up through the con-rods themselves where small outlets allow the oil to spray onto the inside of the pistons. This helps engine cooling.

There is also a feed from the main gallery running up through the cylinder block and head to supply the camshaft, rocker shafts and valve gear. There is a pressure reducing restrictor and non-return valve fitted in this feed passage in the cylinder block face, since the supply to the camshaft carrier does not require the same pressure as the engine. The non-return valve means that there is always a supply of oil ready in the oilways, even when the engine is stopped. Excess oil in the camshaft carrier assembly drains back into the sump via passages at the front and rear of the engine.

Along the main gallery in the outside of the block are tappings to accommodate the oil pressure switch (nearest the front) and oil pressure transmitter (only fitted to the 2600 model). Both are operated by oil pressure. The one common to both models operates a light extinguishing circuit on the panel, which indicates that oil pressure exists

Fig. 1.13 Checking valve guide wear (Sec 24)

0.020 in

in the engine. The oil transmitter sends signals to the oil pressure gauge fitted to the panel in the 2600 version.

26 Oil filter – renewal

1 Disconnect the battery negative terminal, having driven the front wheels onto ramps.

2 Although difficult to reach through the large hole in the right-hand side of the bottom panel, it is possible to remove the filter using a small filter wrench, unless the filter is very tightly fitted.

3 If it cannot be easily undone, although a screwdriver knocked through the canister can help to get the leverage required, then remove the bottom panel for access to the filter (Fig. 1.15).

4 Unscrew the old filter and throw it away, together with the old seal. Remember the filter is full of oil.

5 Clean the oil filter housing.

6 Fit a new seal smeared with grease.

7 Screw in the new filter and tighten only by hand.

8 Check the engine oil level.

9 Connect the battery and start the engine. Ensure there are no oil leaks.

10 Refit the bottom panel if removed and drive the car off the ramps.

27 Sump – removal with the engine in the vehicle

1 Disconnect the negative battery terminal.

2 Jack up the front of the car and support it on axle stands or packing blocks.

3 Remove the bottom panel and drain the sump (Fig. 1.16).

4 Support the weight of the engine using a hoist or crane from above.

5 Remove the front engine mounting nuts and bolts; 2 per side (photo) (see Section 8).

6 Support the subframe with a trolley jack for preference, but an ordinary pillar jack will do.

7 Remove the 4 nuts and bolts that secure the front and rear of the subframe (photo).

8 Scribe a line across the lower steering column coupling and shaft and slacken the pinch-bolt (photo).

9 Gently lower the subframe on the jack and ease the steering coupling from the shaft.

10 Undo the bolts that secure the clutch slave cylinder in position and move the cylinder to one side.

11 Undo the four nuts and bolts that secure the flywheel cover plate in position and remove it.

12 Remove the two sump stiffening plate bolts.

13 Undo the nut fitted to the stud at the centre front of the sump (this holds the bottom water pipe in position).

14 Undo and remove the sump retaining bolts. Scribe the position of the front stud.

15 Whilst tilting the subframe to the rear, remove the sump pan then remove the gasket.

Fig. 1.14 The lubrication system diagram (Sec 25)

1	Strainer	4	Oil filter	7	Rocker shafts	10	Connecting rod journals
2	Oil pump	5	Main oil gallery	8	Camshaft	11	Main bearings
3	Pressure relief valve	6	Restrictor	9	Oil pressure switch	12	Oil spray to pistons

Fig. 1.15 The oil filter with bottom panel removed (Sec 26)

28 Sump – removal with the engine removed from the vehicle

1   With the engine on the bench, remove the following components (Unless already removed), ensuring that all oil has been drained from sump first:

   (a) *The exhaust manifold (see Section 22)*
   (b) *The water rail hose connections at the bottom of the thermostat housing and the rear of the inlet manifold heater pipe*
   (c) *The left-hand front engine mounting bracket (4 bolts)*
   (d) *The bottom water pipe nut attached to the stud situated at the centre bottom of the sump*

2   Turn the engine over on to the left-hand side to gain access to all the sump retaining bolts (photo).
3   Remove the 2 sump stiffening plate bolts (if the gearbox is still attached).
4   Remove the flywheel cover plate, secured in position by 4 nuts and bolts (if the gearbox is still attached).
5   Undo and remove the sump retaining bolts, marking the position of the stud holding the bottom water pipe bracket.
6   Remove the sump and gasket.

Fig. 1.16 Removing the sump with the engine in the vehicle (Sec 27)

6   Front engine mounting bolts
8   Rear subframe bolts and nuts
9   Front subframe bolts and nuts
11   Steering column pinch-bolt
16   Sump stiffening plate bolts
18   Sump bolts

27.5 Front engine mounting left-hand side

27.7 Right-hand side subframe bolts and nuts (arrowed)

27.8 Slacken the steering column pinch-bolt (arrowed)

28.2 The sump retaining bolts

29 Sump – refitting

1   Before refitting, ensure that the sump has been cleaned inside and out and that all traces of sludge have been removed from inside. Use paraffin to wash out the inside.
2   Scrape off the remains of the old sump gasket from the mating surfaces of both the sump and the crankcase.
3   Take a new gasket, apply jointing compound to both sides of the gasket and place it in position. If the engine is out of the car, position the gasket on the crankcase and offer the sump to it. Where the operation is being carried out in situ, place the gasket in position on the sump and tilt the subframe slightly to place the sump and gasket in position.
4   Refit the sump retaining bolts and tighten them evenly and in a diagonal pattern to the correct torque.
5   Refit the sump stiffening plate bolts (if removed).
6   Refit the flywheel cover plate and secure it with the 4 nuts and bolts.
7   When carrying out this operation with the engine in the car, follow in the reverse order paragraphs 1 to 10, Section 27. Ensure that the steering column is correctly aligned by the scribe marks or the steering will be offset.
8   Having reassembled the components, refill the engine with the correct grade and quantity of oil. Start the engine and check that there are no leaks.
9   Check that the sump plug is tightly fitted to the correct torque (see Specifications).

30 Oil pump – removal and refitting

This operation is described as though the engine is in the car. However, this operation can be carried out equally well with the engine on the bench. If the engine has already been removed from the car, certain instructions on both the removal and refitting will not apply. These have been marked *.
1*   Refer to Section 11 and remove the camshaft drivebelt, the alternator/fan belt and the power steering drivebelt.
2   Undo the four nuts and bolts and remove the fan blades (see Chapter 2).
3   Remove the water pump (see Chapter 2 for the procedure) having first drained the cooling system.
4   Remove the sump as described in Sections 27 or 28.
5   Remove the bolt and spacer that retain the crankshaft pulley, taking care not to turn the crankshaft (see Section 41).
6   Pull off the pulley. It should slide off quite easily without the use of a puller. Note that there may be a further spacer behind the pulley if the engine is fitted with an undersize crankshaft.
7   Do not remove the Woodruff key from the crankshaft.

8   Undo the two bolts that hold the oil pick-up pipe to the oil pump. Then remove the bolt that locates the pipe to the crankcase. The oil pick-up pipe and strainer can now be removed (photo).
9*   Withdraw the two adjuster bolts from the quadrant of the power steering pump.
10*   Remove the common pivot bolt for both the alternator and power steering pump and place the units to one side.
11   Remove the other 6 bolts and remove the oil pump assembly complete. Note both the location and length of the bolts.
12   The filter can be removed at this stage if required.
13   Before refitting, clean the mating faces of both the pump and the crankcase. Also grease the oil seal inner lips.
14   Apply a thin bead of RTV sealant to the pump face and slide the assembly over the crankshaft. Locate the driving dog on the Woodruff key in the crankshaft in position (photo). Take care that the inner lips of the front oil seal are not damaged by the driving dog.
15   Refit the six bolts in their respective positions and tighten to the specified torque.
16   Refit the pick-up pipe and strainer. To secure the 2 bolts into the pump casing and the one bolt into the crankcase, use a thread locking compound.
17   Refit the sump (see Section 29).
18   Refit the ancillary components removed if the operation was performed with the engine in the car and then refit the crankshaft pulley and camshaft drivebelt (see Section 11).
19   When refitting the crankshaft pulley, ensure that the spacer is fitted behind the pulley (if one was removed from that position) or the drivebelts will not line up correctly. Also lock the flywheel with a plate or large screwdriver when torquing up the retaining bolt, to prevent the crankshaft turning.
20   Refit the water pump as described in Chapter 2.
21   Refit the fan blades as described in Chapter 2.
22*   Refit and adjust the alternator and power steering pump drivebelts to their correct tension (see Chapter 2 and 11).
23*   Refill the cooling system as described in Chapter 2.
24*   Refill the engine with the correct grade and quantity of oil. See the Specifications.
25*   Reconnect the battery terminal and start the engine. Check for oil and water leaks. Recheck the oil level and top-up the cooling system.

31 Oil pump – overhaul and inspection

1   Remove the oil pump as described in the previous Section.
2   Clean off all excess oil and dirt, after removing the oil filter.
3   Undo the 5 screws amd remove the cover plate.
4   Remove the circlip.
5   Push out the driving dog and inner rotor.
6   Remove the O-ring and then the outer rotor.
7   Remove the oil relief valve split-pin.

30.8 The oil assembly and pick-up pipe with sump removed

30.14 Slide the oil pump assembly over the crankshaft

Fig. 1.17 Exploded view of the oil pump assembly (Sec 31)

2 Circlip	6 O-ring	10 Valve plug	14 Oil seal
3 Driving dog	7 Inner rotor	11 O-ring	
4 Screws	8 Outer rotor	12 Spring	
5 Cover plate	9 Split-pin	13 Plunger	

8 Push the plug in and let it go to remove it.

9 Remove the spring and plunger.

10 Remove the O-ring from the plug.

11 Clean all the components and check the gears, driving dog, casing, oil relief valve and spring for obvious signs of wear or cracks.

12 Reassemble the rotors and driving dog, with the chamfered edge of the outer rotor towards the casing and the arrow head on the inner rotor also towards the casing.

13 Use a feeler gauge to check the clearances between the inner and outer rotor lobes — 0.001 to 0.008 in (0.025 to 0.203 mm) and between the outer rotor and the casing — 0.004 to 0.007 in (0.102 to 0.178 mm).

14 Check also the clearance between the rotors and the cover plate. Place a straight-edge across the casing above the gears and measure the clearance. This should be 0.001 to 0.003 in (0.025 to 0.076 mm).

15 Check the fit of the relief valve components in their housing. Renew any parts that are suspect.

16 If the tolerances on the rotors are too great then they will have to be renewed. It is only possible to purchase them in sets as they are matched together as a pair.

17 Before reassembling the oil pump, smear all the parts with engine oil.

18 Refit the oil pressure relief valve components having fitted a new O-ring to the plug. Use a new split-pin to secure the assembly in the pump housing (photo).

19 If the front oil seal has not been removed then reassembly is quite straightforward but take great care that the inner lips of the oil seal are not damaged when fitting the driving dog. Grease the oil seal inner lip first.

20 Refit the outer rotor to the casing (chamfered edge facing the casing).

21 Fit a new O-ring (photo).

22 Engage the dog and inner rotor and refit the circlip.

23 Refit the cover-plate and screw it down. Note that it can only be fitted one way round (photo).

24 The oil pump is now ready to be refitted to the engine. Check beforehand that the gears rotate freely in the casing.

25 Refer to the previous Section for reassembly instructions.

32 Oil pressure relief valve – removal and refitting

1 This operation can be done with the engine in the car (photo), although it has already been described in Section 31. If there is a problem with the oil pressure and the relief valve is suspect, or if the

Fig. 1.18 Checking the clearance between inner and outer rotor (Sec 31)

Fig. 1.19 Checking the clearance between the rotors and cover plate, using a straight-edge (Sec 31)

valve is leaking oil and the O-ring needs renewing, this can be quite a simple operation.

2 Remove the split-pin (Fig. 1.20).

3 Push the valve plug in and release to remove it.

4 Withdraw the spring and plunger.

5 The O-ring can now be withdrawn and renewed if necessary.

6 Refit the components in the reverse order using a new split-pin to secure them.

31.18 Oil pressure relief valve components ready to refit

Fig. 1.20 The oil pressure relief valve components (Sec 32)

1 Split-pin	5 Plunger
2 Valve plug	6 O-ring
4 Spring	

31.21 Fitting the O-ring

32.1 The oil pressure relief valve (arrowed)

31.23 The oil pump cover plate refitted

33 Gearbox – separation from the engine (removed from vehicle)

Having removed the complete engine and gearbox assembly as described in Section 4, proceed as follows:

1   Remove the starter motor bolts (upper and lower) and remove the starter.

2   Undo the clamp bolt and withdraw the transducer from the bellhousing.

3   Undo the nuts and bolts that retain the flywheel cover-plate and remove it.

4   Withdraw the two sump stiffening plate bolts.

5   Undo and remove the bellhousing retaining bolts and nuts. Note that the bolts differ in length and mark their locations on a diagram if necessary. Also note where the transducer cable brackets and diagnostic socket fit.

6   Carefully ease the transmission assembly rearwards and separate it from the engine assembly.

34 Flywheel – removal and refitting

1   Remove the gearbox. Either refer to the previous Section if the whole engine/gearbox assembly has been removed from the car, or to Chapter 6 if the operation is being performed in the car.
2   Remove the clutch assembly. Refer to Chapter 5.
3   Undo and remove the 6 bolts that secure the flywheel in position. Note the position of the dowel.
4   Remove the flywheel
5   Refitting is the reverse procedure to removal, but ensure that the hollow dowel is in the correct position first.
6   Tighten the six retaining bolts to their correct torque. It is advisable to use a thread locking compound when refitting these bolts. Hold the flywheel when tightening up the bolts by inserting a wide-bladed screwdriver through the starter mounting bracket. **Note:** *The small peg in the outer edge of the flywheel is the timing sensor which is picked up by the transducer mounted in the bellhousing.*

35 Driveplate – removal and refitting

On automatic transmission models, the driveplate replaces the flywheel.
1   Refer to Chapter 6 (Part B) and remove the transmission. This can also be done on the bench when the complete engine/transmission assembly has been removed.
2   Wedge the driveplate to prevent it from turning and remove the six retaining bolts. Note that early engines have 8 bolts retaining the driveplate.
3   Remove the spigot bush. Lever it out taking care not to damage the driveplate.
4   Withdraw the reinforcing spacer followed by the driveplate. Note that there is another spacer behind the driveplate and also a hollow dowel to locate the driveplate to the crankshaft flange.
5   Refitting is the reverse procedure to removal but note that you must use *new* bolts to refit the driveplate. Tighten the bolts to the correct torque.
6   Fit a new spigot bush and tap evenly home, ensuring that it stays square.

36 Connecting rods and pistons – removal

The pistons complete with con-rods are removed through the top of the cylinder bores. This job can be done in situ, but it is necessary to provide a method of supporting the weight of the engine once the cylinder head has been removed but prior to removing the sump. A suggested method is to provide a strong angle bar and rest it, suitably padded to prevent damage to the bodywork, across the front of the engine bay. Make up another plate and through 2 suitably spaced holes, screw it to the front end of the block with 2 cylinder head bolts. Using either a bottle screw tensioner with hooks at either end or a suitable length of chain, attach the plate to the cross-bar and take the weight of the engine (Fig. 1.23). The sump may now be removed. This operation is however much simpler when performed with the engine removed from the vehicle.
Note: *If only the big-end bearings are going to be renewed, then there is no need to remove the complete piston/con-rod assembly. Having removed the upper shell bearing from the con-rod (paragraph 7) push the assembly up as far as will allow the crankshaft to turn without coming into contact with the connecting rod bolts. It is however advisable to place some form of protection, such as short lengths of plastic tubing or tape, over the connecting rod bolts to prevent any scratching or damage, either to the bores or to the crankshaft journals.*
1   Remove the cylinder head as described in Section 21.
2   Arrange the engine support system, as described in the foregoing note to this Section, or using a similar effective method.
3   Remove the sump as described in Section 27 or 28. If working on an automatic model, remove the torque converter cover plate. This gives access to the sump rear fixing and will also enable the engine to be turned over using the drive plate as a crank. If the engine/transmission assembly is out of the car, then refer to Section 33 and separate the two assemblies first.
4   Remove the three bolts that secure the oil pick-up pipe and

Fig. 1.21 Flywheel removal (Sec 34)

1 Retaining bolt

Fig. 1.22 Driveplate removal (Sec 35)

1 Dowel	*4 Reinforcing spacer*
2 Spacer	*5 Retaining bolt*
3 Driveplate	

Fig. 1.23 Supporting the weight of the engine (Sec 36)

Fig. 1.24 The big-end bearings (Sec 36)

4   Retaining nuts   9   Connecting rod and upper shell (note the tags)   10 Bearing cap and lower shell

strainer and remove it.

5   Rotate the crankshaft to gain easy access to the connecting rod bearing caps in turn. Note that each connecting rod and cap is numbered (1 to 6) on the right-hand side (photo). When removing them keep them in sets. Start at No 1 and remove them in order, so that the caps and shells cannot be muddled.

6   Undo the nuts that retain the big-end cap. Remove the cap and lower shell.

7   Push the piston and connecting rod up the bore so that the upper shell bearing can be removed.

8   Then push the piston and con-rod all the way up the bore and withdraw it from the top of the block (photo). Take care that the connecting rod bolts do not scratch either the bore or the crankshaft.

9   Place the complete set of pistons and connecting rods, together with the upper and lower bearing shells and cap and 2 nuts, all together in a sectioned box or similar.

10   Repeat the same process with each piston/con-rod assembly, turning the crankshaft each time to ensure that the bearing cap nuts are in the most convenient position to be undone.

37 Connecting rods and pistons – overhaul

1   The condition of the pistons, rings, big-end bearings and small-end bushes will be governed by many factors, but principally they are:

   (a) The total mileage covered by the car
   (b) The maintenance of oil level and regular oil and oil filter changes
   (c) The way in which the car has been driven and uses to which the car has been subjected

2   Having removed the connecting rod and piston assemblies from the car, overhaul them one set at a time otherwise mixing of parts is liable to occur.

3   Remove one of the gudgeon pin circlips and warm the piston in hot water.

4   The gudgeon pin is a push fit at 68°F (20°C) (photo).

5   Having separated the piston and connecting rod, carefully remove the piston rings and retain them in the correct order.

36.5 Connecting rod and caps are numbered on the right-hand side

36.8 Removing a piston and connecting rod

37.4 Circlip removed and gudgeon pin pushed out

6 If new rings only are being fitted, then the pistons and connecting rods can remain together.

7 Clean all the parts thoroughly and remove the carbon from the piston. Clean out the piston ring grooves.

8 Examine the piston for damage, cracks or scoring. Examine the crown for any dents or marks made by foreign bodies in the combustion chamber; broken rings etc. Rings that have broken during running will have caused damage to the grooves in the piston making the rings sloppy due to excessive clearance in the grooves. Damaged or faulty pistons of this nature will have to be renewed. It is also possible that broken rings will have damaged the cylinder wall. In bad cases this will require a rebore.

9 If the engine has been rebored, then oversize pistons of 0·020 in (0·50 mm) are available.

10 Check the gudgeon pin bush for any sign of wear. When refitting, ensure that the oil hole in the bush and connecting rod are exactly lined up.

11 To refit the piston to the gudgeon pin and connecting rod, hold the connecting rod in the left hand with the cylinder number uppermost. The piston is then refitted with the word 'FRONT' (on the skirt) on the right-hand side.

12 Refit the gudgeon pin retaining clip.

38 Fitting new piston rings

1 When fitting new rings it is advisable to remove the glaze from the cylinder bores. It is strongly advised that the deglazed bore should have a cross hatch finish (diamond pattern) and should be carried out in such a way as not to increase the bore size in any way. This cross hatch finish provides the cylinder walls with good oil retention properties. The careful use of glasspaper will produce a suitable finish.

2 The top compression ring is surfaced with a chrome material and must only be fitted in the top piston ring groove. The second compression ring is of the stepped type and must only be fitted in the groove second from the top of the piston. The second compression ring is marked 'T' or *Top* and it is this side of the ring which must face uppermost.

3 Before fitting the rings however, a word on gapping. Push a compression ring down the cylinder bore using a piston to position it squarely at about 1 in (25 mm) below the top of the block and measure the piston ring gap with a feeler gauge. The gap should be as quoted in the Specifications for each of the 2 compression rings.

4 If required, file the gap using a flat 'fine cut' file. Exercise care and judgement not to overdo it. Refit the ring, square off the piston as before and re-measure. Repeat the process until correct.

5 The special oil control ring needs no gapping, but care must be taken to ensure that the ends of the expander, (fitted first), do not overlap but just abut each other. Fit the rails, one at a time, bottom one first, making sure that they locate snugly within the piston groove.

6 Fit the rings by holding them open, using both hands, thumbs at the gaps with fingers around the outer edges, easing them open enough to slip over the piston top and straight to the groove in which they belong. Use feeler gauges or strips of tin as guides to prevent the rings dropping into the wrong groove. Do not twist the rings whilst doing this or they will snap.

7 Once the rings have been fitted to the piston, then the vertical clearance in the groove should be checked. See Specifications (Fig. 1.28).

8 Fit the oil control rings so that the ring gaps are all at one side, between the gudgeon pin and piston thrust face. Locate the gaps in the rail rings approximately 1 in (25 mm) either side of the expander ring join. The compression rings should be positioned so that the gaps in each ring are on opposite sides of the piston, between the piston thrust face and gudgeon pin. This procedure will ensure good compression (Fig. 1.29).

Fig. 1.25 Piston, gudgeon pin and rings removal (Sec 37)

3 Gudgeon pin circlips
4 Gudgeon pin
5 Piston rings in order (top, scraper and oil control)

Fig. 1.26 Exploded view of pistons rings (Sec 38)

A Oil control expander rail
B Oil control bottom chrome rail
C Oil control top chrome rail
D Scraper or second compression ring
E Top compression ring

Fig. 1.27 Gapping a compression ring in the cylinder bore (Sec 38)

Fig. 1.28 Checking the ring clearance in the groove (Sec 38)

Fig. 1.29 Correct location of piston ring gaps (Sec 38)

A Compression ring gaps on opposite sides of piston
B Oil control ring gaps staggered on same side of piston

39 Connecting rods and pistons – refitting

1   Ensure all parts are thoroughly cleaned and smeared with clean engine oil, including the cylinder bores.
2   Ensure that the correct piston/connecting rod assembly is fitted to the correct bore. Remember that one side of the big-end of each connecting rod is numbered, as is its corresponding cap.
3   Having staggered the fit of the piston rings, fit the ring compressor round the piston.
4   Insert the piston into the bore from the top of the block, ensuring that the words 'FRONT' on both the crown and skirt of the piston face towards the front of the engine. Tap the piston into the bore using a wooden mallet or hammer handle (photo).
5   Ensure that the connecting rod bolts do not come into contact with the cylinder bores or crankshaft while refitting.
6   Pull the connecting rod down and refit the upper shell, noting that the tags are correctly located. Oil the shell and crankpin thoroughly, ensuring that the crankpin is clean.
7   Pull the connecting rod onto the crankpin, making sure that the upper shell is still in its correct place.
8   Oil the bearing cap and lower shell and fit these together ensuring that the tags locate properly (photo).
9   Fit the cap and lower shell to the crankpin ensuring that the tags marry-up and that the cylinder numbers on the cap and the connecting-rod are also side by side. Both should be on the right-hand side of the engine (photos).
10 Refit the bearing cap nuts and tighten to the correct torque (see Specifications).
11 Repeat the same process with the other 5 cylinders.
12 When all connecting rod/ piston assemblies have been refitted, refit the oil strainer, sump and cylinder head assemblies, removing the engine support if the operation has been carried out in the car. See Sections 30, 29 and 21.
13 If the operation has been carried out without removing the engine, then the cooling system will have to be refilled (see Chapter 2) and the engine refilled with the correct grade and quantity of oil.

40 Cylinder bores – examination and renovation

1   The cylinder bores must be examined for taper, scoring and scratches. Start by carefully examining the top of the cylinder bores. If they are at all worn, a very slight ridge will be found on the thrust side. This marks the top of the piston ring travel. The owner will have a good indication of the bore wear prior to dismantling the engine, or removing the cylinder head. Excessive oil consumption, accompanied by blue smoke from the exhaust, is a sure sign of worn cylinder bores and piston rings.
2   Measure the bore diameter just under the ridge with a micrometer, and compare it with the diameter at the bottom of the bore, which is not subject to wear. If the difference between the two measurements is more than 0·006 in (0·1524 mm) then it will be necessary to fit special pistons and rings or to have the cylinders rebored and to fit oversize pistons. If no micrometer is available, remove the rings from a piston and place the piston in each bore in turn about ¾ in (19 mm) below the top of the bore. If an 0·010 in (0·2540 mm) feeler gauge can be slid between the piston and the cylinder wall on the thrust side of the bore, then remedial action must be taken.
3   Pistons are available in an oversize 0·020 in (0·5080 mm). These are accurately machined to just below these measurements to provide correct running clearances in bores bored out to the exact oversize dimensions.
4   If the bores are slightly worn but not so badly worn as to justify reboring them, then special oil control rings and pistons can be fitted which will restore compression and stop the engine burning oil. Several different types are available, and the manufacturer's instructions concerning their fitting must be followed closely.
5   If new pistons are being fitted and the bores have not been reground, it is essential to slightly roughen the hard glaze on the sides of the bores with fine glass paper so the new piston rings will have a chance to bed in properly.

41 Crankshaft pulley – removal and refitting

Section 30 of this Chapter, which deals with the removal of and refitting of the oil pump, covers the steps required to remove and refit the crankshaft pulley. It may however be found easier to leave out the final removal stage of the camshaft drivebelt until the pulley is removed.

42 Crankshaft front oil seal – renewal

If the oil pump is going to be removed then it is easier, unless you happen to posses the special tool, to remove the oil seal by driving it out from inside the oil pump cover. If however the oil seal is leaking and it alone needs renewing, then follow this procedure:
1   Refer to Section 30 and follow the instructions as far as removing the crankshaft pulley.
2   Drill 2 small holes into the outer face of the seal casing and at opposite sides to each other. Screw 2 selftapping screws into the holes. Use a molegrip wrench to lever the old seal out using the selftapping screws as a grip.
3   To fit a new front oil seal, first smear the outside diameter and inside lip with grease.
4   Slide the seal over the crankshaft nose taking care not to damage the inner lip of the seal.
5   Using a tube of larger diameter than the crankshaft and a spacer/washer in between the seal and tube, gently and squarely tap the seal home into its housing.
6   Refer to refit the components removed in the reverse order.

43 Crankshaft rear oil seal – renewal

1   Jack the car up and support it on stands or blocks under the side-members.
2   Disconnect the negative battery lead.
3   Remove the gearbox or automatic transmission. See Chapter 6.
4   Remove the clutch (manual gearbox). See Chapter 5.
5   Remove the flywheel (Section 34) or driveplate (Section 35).

39.4 Refitting a connecting rod and piston into the bore

39.8 Fit the cap and lower shell together

39.9a Refit the cap and lower shell, ensuring that the tangs marry up ...

39.9b ...and the cylinder numbers on cap and con-rod agree

43.7 Undo the 7 bolts to remove the housing (engine out and stripped for clarity)

44.11 Note the main bearing caps are numbered

6   Undo and remove the two bolts at the rear of the sump.

7   Undo and remove the 7 bolts that retain the oil seal housing to the crankcase and then remove the housing itself complete with the seal (photo).

8   Push out the old seal from inside the housing.

9   Clean the housing where the seal fits and also the mating faces of the housing and crankcase.

10 Lubricate the outer edge of the new seal with clean engine oil.

11 Place the seal housing face downwards and position the seal, lip side first, into the housing.

12 Using a block of wood, wide enough to cover the whole seal, tap the seal home ensuring that it is kept square. It should end up flush with the outside face of the housing.

13 Apply a suitable RTV sealant to the mating face of the seal housing and grease the inside lip of the seal itself.

14 Ease the seal and seal housing over the crankshaft flange taking great care not to damage the lip of the seal.

15 Refit the 7 bolts and tighten to the correct torque.

16 Remove any excess sealant that has been squeezed out.

17 Refit the two rear sump bolts, tightening them to the correct torque.

18 Refit the other assemblies removed following the reverse procedure. Refer to the appropriate Sections where necessary.

44 Crankshaft and main bearings – removal

This job has to be carried out on the bench. It is normal to have to renew the main bearings if the engine is making loud knocking noises accompanied by engine vibration and a drop in oil pressure. If there is noise without the vibrations, although the oil pressure may drop, then it is probably the big-end bearings that are badly worn and need renewing.

1   Remove the sump plug and drain the oil into a suitable container.

2   Remove the engine/gearbox assembly as described in Section 4.

3   Separate the two assemblies as described in Section 33.

4   Remove the clutch assembly, see Chapter 5.

5   Remove the flywheel (Section 34) or driveplate (Section 35).

6   Remove the rear oil seal and housing as described in Section 43.

7   Remove the sump as described in Section 28.

8   Remove the oil pump as described in Section 30. Before taking off the crankshaft pulley, turn it 45° from TDC to avoid internal damage.

9   Remove the connecting rod (big-end) bearing caps and lower the shells, noting their numbers and keeping them separate.

10 Push protective lengths of polythene tubing (or similar) over the connecting rod bolts to avoid the bolts damaging the crankpins.

11 Undo the bolts and remove the 4 main bearing caps. Note that they are numbered 1 to 4 front to rear (photo). The position of the numbers is nearest the left-hand side of the engine. If they are refitted the wrong way round the mistake can then be spotted.

12 Remove the thrustwashers from No 3 main bearing. There is one fitted at either side to take up the endfloat in the crankshaft. Note that the oil grooves in the thrustwashers face outwards.

13 Lift out the crankshaft.

14 The inner shells can then be removed noting which positions they belong to (photo).

45 Crankshaft – inspection and renovation

1   Examine the crankpins and main journals for signs of scoring or scratches. Check the ovality of the crankpins at different positions with a micrometer. If more than 0·0025 in (0·0635 mm) out of round, the crankpins will have to be reground. They will also have to be reground if any scores or scratches are present. Also check the journals in the same fashion. See the Specifications for wear allowed. If it is necessary to regrind the crankshaft and fit new bearings, your local Rover dealer or engineering works will be able to decide how much metal to grind off and therefore, the correct undersize shells to fit.

2   Crankshaft bearings (big-end and main) should only be re-used if they are known to have done a very low mileage (less than 15 000 miles). As new bearings are relatively cheap, it is false economy to refit the old ones. Where the condition of the bearings and journals is so bad that the crankshaft has to be reground, new bearings of the correct undersize will be provided by the firm which carried out the regrinding.

44.14 Removing the inner main bearing shells

4 Smear grease on the flat side of the thrust washers and fit one either side of the No 3 bearing location (photo). Remember that the oil grooves in the thrustwashers face outwards.

5 Clean and refit the crankshaft. When in position, check that the inner shells have not moved and are still flush with the housing.

6 Check the crankshaft endfloat using a feeler gauge (or dial gauge if you possess one) (photo). Lever the crankshaft one way and then the other and then check the gap between the crankshaft and thrustwasher. If the gap is more than the specified gap of 0·003 to 0.011 in (0.076 to 0.279 mm), remove the selective thrustwashers and refit slightly thicker ones until the gap is within the tolerance allowed. See the Specifications.

7 Fit the outer bearing shells into the caps making sure that the locating tags slot in correctly.

8 Oil the shells and fit them, noting that the tags in the outer and inner shells must marry-up (photo). Note also that the cap numbers are in the correct sequence (1 to 4 from front to rear) with the numbers on the left of the engine.

9 Tighten the cap bolts alternately to the specified torque (photo).

10 Refit the connecting rods to the crankpins and remove their protective covering.

11 Refit the big-end bearing caps, ensuring the identification numbers marry up and are on the right-hand side of the engine (see Section 39).

12 Tighten the nuts to the specified torque.

13 Check the big-ends for side-play. See Specifications.

14 Refit the remaining components and assemblies in the reverse order to that in which they were removed. Refer to any of the foregoing Sections as necessary.

46 Crankshaft and main bearings – refitting

When refitting the crankshaft and main bearings, lie the engine on its side as for removing the sump.

1 If the main bearing shells are being renewed, note the numbers on the rear of the shell (photo) and determine whether it is undersize or not by consulting with a Rover dealer.

2 Refit the inner shell with the locating tag in its groove.

3 Lubricate the shells and grooves (photo).

47 Crankshaft spigot bearing – renewal

1 The spigot bearing can be renewed with the engine in the car. First remove the gearbox (Chapter 6) and clutch assembly (Chapter 5).

2 If the engine is undergoing complete workshop overhaul and is out of the car the job is much easier and should be considered at this time.

3 Remove the old bearing which is fitted into the crankshaft end

46.1 Note the number on rear of shell to determine size

46.3 Lubricate the shells

46.4 Fitting the thrustwashers to No 3 bearing

46.6 Checking the crankshaft endfloat

46.8 Refit the shells ensuring the locating tags marry-up

46.9 Tighten the bearing cap bolts to the correct torque

Fig. 1.30 Fitting a new spigot bearing (Sec 47)

2 *Bearing washer*
3 *Bearing*
5 *Concave face*

flange. Lever out the spigot bearing washer and remove the spigot bearing.
4　Fit a new spigot bearing to the crankshaft.
5　Insert the bearing washer with the concave face towards the bearing.
6　Use a drift to spread the washer to hold it in place.
7　Refit the flywheel, clutch and gearbox in the reverse order to that in which they were removed.

48 Starter ring gear – removal

Note: *Where automatic transmission is fitted, the starter ring gear is attached to the driveplate and cannot be removed separately. The driveplate must be renewed as an assembly.*
1　On manual transmission models, with the flywheel removed from the engine, drill a hole, approximately 0.375 in (10 mm), through the starter ring gear. Take care not to allow the drill to enter or score the flywheel or flange. The hole should be made at the root of any gear tooth. This will weaken the ring gear and facilitate removal by breaking with a cold chisel (Fig. 1.31).
2　Hold the flywheel in a soft jawed vice.
3　**Warning:** *Beware of flying fragments. A piece of cloth draped over the whole assembly will protect the operator from possible injury.*
4　Split the starter ring gear with a hammer and chisel.

49 Starter ring gear – refitting

1　The new starter ring gear must be heated uniformly. The expansion of the metal permits it to fit over the flywheel and against the flange. Heat to between 338 and 347°F (170 to 175°C). *Do not exceed the specified temperature.*
2　Place the flywheel on a flat surface with the flange side downwards.
3　Offer up the heated ring to the flywheel with the chamfered inner diameter downwards (Fig. 1.32), pressing it firmly against the flange until the ring contracts sufficiently to grip the flywheel. Allow cooling to take place naturally and do not attempt to hasten cooling in any way as this could cause weakening by setting up internal stresses in the ring gear leading to later break up. Where the ring gear is chamfered on both sides it may be fitted either way round.

50 Diagnostic socket and transducer

1　The diagnostic socket and transducer fitted to the new Rover models are a new idea that is designed to make servicing and tuning of these cars quicker and easier when carried out by a Rover dealer (photo).

Fig. 1.31 Removing a damaged starter ring gear from the flywheel (Sec 48)

A *Hole drilled in ring gear to weaken it*
B *Rag to protect operator*
C *Chisel*

Fig. 1.32 Fitting a new starter ring gear to the flywheel (Sec 49)

1 *Chamfered edge*

50.1 Diagnostic socket and transducer (removed from car)

2　The service department of your local dealer has electronic tuning/performance equipment such as 'SUN' or 'CRYPTON' and this is plugged directly into the socket mounted on the right rear of the engine.
3　From the socket there is a lead to the transducer mounted in the bellhousing and this picks up the sensor which is mounted in the outer

diameter of the flywheel, as the engine rotates.

4   There are other leads from the socket to help monitor performance and idling speed.

5   Being able to plug monitoring equipment quickly and directly into the car's sytem will obviously be easier and save time, but it is only intended for the use of Rover dealers who are equipped to use it.

51 Fault diagnosis – engine

Symptom	Reason/s
Engine will not turn over when starter switch is operated	Flat battery Bad battery connnections Bad connections at solenoid switch and/or starter motor Defective starter motor
Engine turns over normally but fails to start	No spark at plugs No fuel reaching engine Too much fuel reaching the engine (flooding)
Engine starts but runs unevenly and misfires	Ignition and/or fuel system faults Sticking or leaking valves Burnt out valves Worn out piston rings
Lack of power	Ignition and/or fuel system faults Burnt out valves Worn out piston rings
Excessive oil consumption	Oil leaks from crankshaft oil seals, timing cover gasket, rocker cover gasket, oil filter gasket, sump gasket, sump plug Worn piston rings or cylinder bores resulting in oil being burnt by engine Worn valve guides and/or defective inlet valve stem seals
Excessive mechanical noise from engine	Worn crankshaft bearings Worn cylinders (piston slap) Slack or worn timing chain and sprockets

Note: *When investigating starting and uneven running faults do not be tempted into snap diagnosis. Start from the beginning of the check procedure and follow it through. It will take less time in the long run. Poor performance from the engine in terms of power and economy is not normally diagnosed quickly. In any event, the ignition and fuel systems must be checked first before assuming any further investigation needs to be made.*

Chapter 2 Cooling system

For modifications, and information applicable to later models, see Supplement at end of manual

Contents

Specifications

Type .... Pressurised system, pump and fan assisted, with separate expansion tank to ensure no loss of coolant

Circulation .... Thermostatically controlled flow with impeller type pump

Fan .... Thirteen bladed, 14.5 in diameter with viscous coupling to limit fan speed

Cap pressure .... 15 lbf/in² (1.05 kgf/cm²)

Thermostat
Type .... Wax
Starts to open .... 82°C (180°F) or as stamped on unit

Coolant
Type/specification .... Antifreeze to BS 3151, 3152 or 6580 (Duckhams Universal Antifreeze and Summer Coolant)
Capacity .... 18.2 pints (10.3 litres), including heater and reservoir

Fan belt adjustment .... Deflection on mid-point of longest run: 0.375 to 0.75 in (10 to 19 mm)

Torque wrench settings

	lbf ft	Nm
Water pump housing bolts	21	28
Thermostat housing bolts	21	28
Fan to viscous coupling nuts	11	15
Water pump drain plug	7	10

1 General description

The engine cooling system is conventional, acting on the thermo-syphon pump assisted principle. The coolant flow is controlled by a thermostat which is fitted at the forward end of the cylinder head casting in the thermostat housing. The purpose of this thermostat is to prevent the full flow of the coolant around the system before the most efficient operating temperature is reached.

The purpose of pressurising the cooling system is to prevent premature boiling in adverse conditions and also to allow the engine to operate at its most efficient running temperature.

The overflow pipe from the radiator is connected to an expansion tank which makes topping-up unnecessary. The coolant expands when hot, and instead of being forced down an overflow pipe and lost, it flows into the expansion tank. As the engine cools, the coolant contracts and, because of the pressure differential, flows back into the top tank of the radiator. Excess pressure is vented to the atmosphere via a pressure relief valve fitted to the expansion tank filler cap.

The cooling system comprises the radiator, water pump, thermostat, interconnecting hoses and waterways in the cylinder block and head. The water pump is driven from the engine crankshaft pulley by a V-belt. The water pump is mounted on the front of the cylinder block and incorporates the only drain plug apart from the radiator one.

The cooling fan is connected to a Holset viscous coupling which limits the fan speed at high engine revolutions. This works in a similar manner to a torque converter, and provides a 'slipping clutch' effect; its aim is to reduce noise and engine loading.

2   Cooling system – draining

With the car on level ground and the system *cold*, proceed as follows:

1   Move the heater control lever to the *HOT* position.
2   Depress and remove slowly the expansion tank filler cap (photo).
3   Unscrew and remove the hexagon radiator filler plug (photo).
4   If antifreeze is used in the cooling system, and has been in use for less than two years, drain the coolant into a container of suitable capacity.
5   To drain the radiator, reach up through the hole provided in the underbelly panel and turn the drain tap in an anti-clockwise direction (photo).
6   The block drain plug is located in the left lower section of the water pump casing. Remove the plug to drain the block (photo).

Note: *There is a fibre washer to prevent leakage and this must be renewed when refitting the plug.*

3   Cooling system – flushing

1   With the passing of time, the cooling system will gradually lose its efficiency as the radiator becomes choked with rust, scale deposits from water and other sediment. To clear the system out, initially drain

the system as described previously, then detach the lower radiator hose.

2   Using a garden hose, allow water to enter the radiator via the radiator filler plug. It will be necessary to refit the cylinder block drain plug during this operation.

3   Allow the water from the hose to run through the radiator for several minutes until it emerges clean, then refit the lower hose.

4   When it is desired to flush the cylinder block, simply remove the radiator filler plug and the cylinder block drain plug. The removal of the cylinder block drain plug will permit speedy clearance of the sediment and scale deposits. The garden hose can be inserted in the radiator filler plug hole as described in paragraph 2. It may be necessary to remove the water pump front cover to clean any really bad blockages in the cylinder block. See Sections 9 and 10. This allows maximum access to the cylinder block waterways.

5   If when flushing the radiator the sediment and scale deposits are very dirty, then it will be found desirable to remove the radiator and reverse flush it. Reverse flushing simply means feeding the clean flushing water into the lower radiator connection and expelling the sediment from the top radiator connection.

6   The alternative to the reverse flushing method, described in paragraph 5, is the use of a proprietary brand of radiator descaler available at most motor accessory shops or garages. The correct usage of the descaler compound is described on the container, but generally necessitates its leaving in the cooling system for a short period to free

2.2 The expansion tank and filler cap

2.3 The radiator hexagon filler plug

2.5 The radiator drain tap (viewed from beneath)

2.6 Removing the block drain plug from the water pump casing

the deposits which can then be flushed out as described in paragraphs 3 and 4.

4 Cooling system – filling

1   The importance of refilling with the correct mixture of antifreeze/inhibitor and water, or inhibitor only with water cannot be over emphasised. Antifreeze solution conforming to British Standard 3151, 3152 or 6580.
2   When mixing water with the antifreeze/inhibitor, or just inhibitor, it is better to use soft tap water or rain water, the mixing being carried out in a plastic bucket. It is not necessary to mix the whole amount required to fill the system, as further topping-up can be done once the initial coolant mix has been poured into the system.
3   Use the following table to ensure adequate protection according to the local climatic conditions:

Amount of antifreeze	Solution	Protection provided down to:
4.6 pts (2.6 litres)	*25%*	*-13°C (9°F)*
6.1 pts (3.5 litres)	*33%*	*-19°C (-2°F)*
9.1 pts (5.2 litres)	*50%*	*-36°C (-33°F)*

4   Make sure that all drain plugs and taps are closed, that all hoses are in good condition and that their clips are secure.
5   Fill the cooling system with the prescribed mixture through the filler plug hole in the top of the radiator, or the filler plug hole in the thermostat housing (as applicable).
6   When the system appears to be full, start the engine and run it at 1500 rpm for five minutes. During this period, continue to top up the cooling system via the radiator filler plug hole.
7   With the engine still running at 1500 rpm, refit the radiator filler plug and tighten it.
8   With the engine still running at 1500 rpm, top up the expansion tank to the bottom of the filler neck. Fit the pressure cap to the expansion tank.
9   Switch off the engine and allow it to cool. Top up the expansion tank further as necessary when cooling has occurred.

5 Radiator – removal and refitting

1   For safety reasons, disconnect the battery negative terminal.
2   Drain the cooling system as described in Section 2.
3   Disconnect the following hoses at the radiator (photo):

   (a)   Top hose
   (b)   Bottom hose
   (c)   Expansion hose

4   On automatic transmission models, two further hoses will be found connected to the radiator. These additional hoses are the flow and return for the automatic transmission oil cooler, which is an integral part of the radiator.
5   Disconnect the oil cooler hoses at the radiator and either plug or clamp them to prevent the loss of fluid and the possible ingression of dirt. Place blanking plugs in the oil cooler inlet and outlet orifices.
6   Remove the 2 bolts that secure the radiator top bracket to the front panel.
7   Lift the radiator out in a vertical plane, ensuring that all the water has drained out beforehand and that the loose hose ends or fan blades do not snag the radiator as it is removed.
8   Note that the radiator has no bottom bolts and is located by 2 pegs which seat in rubber grommets in the front crossmember.
9   If the radiator is to be exchanged or renewed it will then be necessary to remove the securing bracket from the top of the radiator, which is held in place by 4 bolts.
10 Refitting is the reverse procedure to removal, but remember to ensure that the bottom locating pegs on the radiator seat into their grommets correctly.
11 After refitting, refill the system with water/antifreeze mixture as described in Section 4.

6 Fan blades – removal and refitting

1   Disconnect the battery negative terminal.

5.3 The radiator hoses (arrowed)

Fig. 2.1 Fan blades removed (Sec 6)

1 Bolts   2 Nuts and washers

2   Remove the four nuts, bolts and washers that secure the fan blades to the viscous coupling (Fig. 2.1).
3   Pull the blades forward slightly and lift out.
4   Refitting is the reverse procedure to removal, but note that the nuts fit behind the viscous coupling and not in front of the fan.
5   Tighten to the recommended torque (see Specifications).

7 Viscous coupling – removal and refitting

1   Remove the water pump assembly as per Section 9.
2   Support the assembly with the coupling on wooden blocks and space underneath for the pump body.
3   Press the pump driveshaft out of the coupling and remove the tolerance ring.
4   To refit the coupling, first support the pump with the blocks under the pulley, shaft upwards (Fig. 2.2).
5   Place a new tolerance ring on the shaft using grease to keep it in position.
6   Squeeze the ring and press the viscous coupling onto the shaft ensuring that it goes right home.
7   Then refit the water pump as per Section 10.

8 Fan/alternator drivebelt – removal, refitting and adjustment

1   Loosen the alternator mounting and adjuster nuts and bolts.
2   Push the alternator in towards the engine and slip the belt from the pulleys.
3   Loosen the power steering pump adjuster bolts (if fitted) and push

Fig. 2.2 Refitting the viscous coupling (Sec 7)

1 Coupling
2 Tolerance ring
3 Pump driveshaft

8.7 Fan/alternator belt and power steering drivebelt correctly fitted
(fan blades removed for clarity)

Fig. 2.3 Water pump casing bolts (Sec 9)

1 Retaining bolts

in towards the engine. Slip the belt off the pump pulleys. The fan and
alternator drivebelt can now be removed.

4   Refitting is the reverse of removal, but it is important to tension
the belt(s) correctly.

5   Pull the alternator away from the engine until the tension of the
drivebelt is such that deflection on the mid-point of the longest run is
approximately 0.375 to 0.750 in (10 to 19 mm).

6   When the tension is correct, tighten the adjuster block and nuts.

7   Carry out the same procedure having refitting the power steering
pump drivebelt. The deflection in the centre of this belt should be
between 0.25 and 0.375 in (6 to 9 mm) (photo).

8   If a new drivebelt(s) has been fitted, recheck the tension as above
after approximately 250 miles (400 km).

---

9   Water pump – removal

1   Disconnect the battery negative terminal.

2   Drain the cooling system as described in Section 2.

3   Remove the fan blades as described in Section 6. It is not
necessary to do so, but it may be found easier if the radiator is
removed (see Section 5). Access to the water pump is easier and there
is no chance of damaging the radiator whilst removing the water pump
unit.

4   Refer to Chapter 1 and remove the camshaft drivebelt cover.

5   Remove the alternator/fan drivebelt as described in Section 8.

6   Remove the bolt in the water pump housing that secures the alternator adjuster link.

7   Disconnect the inlet and outlet hoses from the water pump.

8   Line-up the camshaft gear timing marks so that No 6 piston is at
TDC (see Chapter 1).

9   Loosen the camshaft belt tensioner and take the belt off the top
drivewheel (see Chapter 1).

10   Undo and remove the 7 bolts that secure the water pump in position (Fig. 2.3).

11   Remove the complete assembly and gasket noting that there may
still be some water in the housing and block.

12   If required, the viscous coupling can be separated from the water
pump as described in Section 7.

13   The pump drive pulley is part of the pump unit and is not remov-
able. If the pulley or the impeller and bearings are badly worn, then a

new unit must be obtained. In most cases it is cheaper and less
frustrating in the long run to renew the unit than to renew just the
impeller and bearings.

---

10   Water pump – refitting

1   If a new unit is being fitted, firstly refit the viscous coupling as
described in Section 7.

2   Clean the cylinder block and water pump mating faces.

3   Take a new gasket and smear it lightly with grease to help keep it
in place on the pump flange whilst offering up the pump to the cylinder
block.

4   Secure the pump in position with the 7 retaining bolts. Tighten to
the specified torque (see Specifications).

5   Ensure that the drain plug and fibre washers are fitted to the
pump.

6   Ensure that the engine is at TDC on No 6 piston and refit the
camshaft drivebelt.

7   Adjust the drivebelt tensioner (see Chapter 1).

8   Reconnect the inlet and outlet hoses to the water pump.

9   Refit the alternator/fan drivebelt and adjuster link pivot bolt.

10   Adjust the tension of the drivebelt (see Section 8).

11   Refit the camshaft drivebelt cover (see Chapter 1).

12   Refit the fan blades (and the radiator if removed).

13   Refill the cooling system as described in Section 4.

14   Reconnect the battery negative terminal.

Fig. 2.4 Thermostat and housing assembly (Sec 11)

    3 *Elbow securing bolt*
    4 *Water elbow*
    5 *Thermostat (correctly lined up in housing)*
    7 *Gasket*
    8 *Jiggle pin (correctly positioned)*

Fig. 2.5 Testing a thermostat (Sec 11)

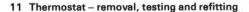

11 Thermostat – removal, testing and refitting

1   If the engine tends to overheat, the cause is most likely to be due to a faulty thermostat that is failing to open at a predetermined temperature setting.

2   Conversely, where the thermostat is stuck permanently open, it will be found that the engine takes a long time to warm-up. In cold weather, this results in having to drive considerable distances using the choke. If in doubt take out the thermostat and test it.

3   There is no need to drain the whole system, but simply drain coolant from the radiator until the level of the coolant is down to the top of the cylinder block. This level will have to be achieved by trial and error. Drain off some coolant and close the radiator drain tap. Carefully remove the engine outlet hose at the elbow. If water is present, refit the hose quickly and drain some more coolant.

4   Once the coolant has reached a suitable low level, then the elbow can be removed and the thermostat exposed.

5   There are two bolts that secure the thermostat housing elbow to the front of the engine. These should be removed, and the housing elbow lifted off (Fig. 2.4).

6   Remember to have a new gasket available for reassembly.

7   Carefully remove the thermostat which should just lift out.

8   With the engine cold, examine it carefully to ascertain whether or not it is stuck open. If so, there is no point in making further tests; it should be renewed.

9   If the thermostat looks normal then proceed as follows:

10 Place the unit in a saucepan of cold water. Do not allow it to touch the bottom. Suspend it with a piece of wire or string (Fig. 2.5).

11 Heat the saucepan and raise the temperature to that at which the thermostat is specified to open. The specified temperature is stamped on either the upper or lower face of the thermostat.

12 Should the thermostat fail to operate correctly, renew it with one of the correct type.

11.15 Fitting the thermostat with the bridge in-line with the crankshaft

13 If it happens that you do not have a spare, the car will run quite well for a day or so without a thermostat until a replacement can be obtained, but the engine will take much longer to reach operating temperature.

14 Refit the elbow and thermostat housing cover using a new gasket.

15 When the thermostat is inserted into the housing, ensure that the word 'TOP' is uppermost. Also check that the bridge on the thermostat lies parallel to the crankshaft (photo). The jiggle-pin (the little loose pin in the centre plate) has to be positioned at the five-to-twelve location when viewed from the front of the engine. This prevents airlocks occuring (photo).

16 Finally reconnect the radiator hose, top-up the cooling system and check for leaks.

See overleaf for 'Fault diagnosis – cooling system'

12 Fault diagnosis – cooling system

Symptom	Reason/s
Overheating	Insufficient water in cooling system
	Fan belt slipping (accompanied by a shrieking noise on rapid engine acceleration)
	Radiator core blocked or radiator grille restricted
	Thermostat not opening properly
	Ignition timing incorrectly set (accompanied by loss of power and perhaps misfiring)
	Carburettors incorrectly adjusted (mixture too weak)
	Exhaust system partially blocked
	Oil level in sump too low
	Blown cylinder head gasket (water/steam being forced down the radiator overflow pipe under pressure)
	Engine not yet run-in
	Brakes binding
Overcooling	Thermostat jammed open
	Incorrect thermostat fitted allowing premature opening of valve
	Thermostat missing
Loss of cooling water	Loose clips on water hoses
	Top, bottom, or bypass water hoses perished and leaking
	Radiator core leaking
	Expansion tank pressure cap spring worn or seal ineffective
	Blown cylinder head gasket
	Cylinder wall or head cracked

Chapter 3 Fuel and exhaust systems

For modifications, and information applicable to later models, see Supplement at end of manual

Contents

Specifications

Fuel pump .... Electric type, immersed in fuel tank

Fuel filter .... In-line, renewable

Carburettors
Type .... Twin sidedraught SU-HS6 Unicon
Needle:
    2300 model .... BEA or BEB
    2600 model .... BEC
Jet size .... 0.10 in (2.54 mm)
Piston spring .... Yellow
Damper oil* .... Multigrade engine oil, viscosity range SAE 10W/30 to 15W/50, to API SE or SF (Duckhams QXR, Hypergrade, or 10W/40 Motor Oil)

Austin Rover specify a 10W/40 oil to meet warranty requirements for models produced after August 1983. Duckhams QXR and 10W/40 Motor Oil are available to meet these requirements

Idling speed .... 750 to 800 rpm

Fast idling speed
Cold .... 1100 to 1300 rpm
Hot .... 1500 rpm

CO emission (at idling speed) .... 0 to 4.5%

Air cleaner type .... Twin disposable paper elements in a single housing

Fuel tank capacity .... 14.5 gallons (65.9 litres)

Torque wrench settings

	lbf ft	Nm
Exhaust manifold bolts	30	40
Hot air manifold bolts	30	40
Inlet manifold bolts	21	28
Air cleaner to carburettors	15	20
Heat chamber to exhaust manifold	21	28
Throttle linkage brackets on inlet manifold	6	8
Fuel tank mountings:		
Front to body	20	27.5
Rear bracket to body	40	54
Rear bracket to tank	20	27.5
Carburettors to manifold	16 to 21	22 to 28

---

1 General description – fuel system

The fuel system comprises a fuel tank at the rear of the car, from which the electrically operated pump delivers fuel to the carburettors.

The electrical fuel pump is not fitted in a conventional way. It is immersed in the fuel tank and not externally mounted as is the usual practice of car manufacturers. At the inlet side of the fuel pump is a filter. Another filter of the in-line type is incorporated in the fuel delivery line just ahead of the carburettors.

2　General description – air cleaner and air intake temperature control system

The air cleaner is a flat oval-shaped metal canister bolted on to the carburettors, into which two renewable paper elements are fitted. They act both as air cleaners and silencers. Air is fed into the air cleaner via the air temperature control system.

The temperature of the incoming air to the air cleaner is maintained to approximately 100°F (38°C) by an air temperature control system. The air temperature control unit consists basically of two inlet connections and a sponge rubber flap valve connected to a bi-metallic strip (photo). One of the inlet connections feeds air to the air temperature control unit from the atmosphere via flexible trunking, whilst the other inlet is connected by a further length of trunking to a heat chamber which is bolted to the exhaust manifold.

The system works basically as follows: When the engine is cold, the flap valve closes the cold air intake and the air supplied to the carburettors is heated, being drawn from the exhaust manifold region. As the engine warms up, the bi-metallic strip expands and in so doing lifts the flap valve away from the cold air intake and a controlled mixture of both heated and cool air is drawn into the carburettors. Further

warming-up of the engine will cause the bi-metallic strip to expand even further until eventually the hot air intake is closed and the incoming air is drawn only from the atmosphere via the cold air intake (photo).

The air temperature control system helps to establish low emission levels and reduces the amount of choke usage, thus bringing about a fuel saving. A general improvement in cold engine performance is also a further benefit of employing such a system.

3　Air cleaner assembly – removal and refitting (including renewal of elements)

1　Remove the air intake hose from the air cleaner.
2　Undo and withdraw the six retaining bolts.
3　Unclip the air cleaner from the fuel pipe. The pipe is attached by two plastic clips on the air cleaner backplate.
4　Lift out the air cleaner and make sure the two gaskets are retained.
5　To renew the paper elements, undo the single bolt in the backplate and split the container in two. Then remove the two elements and discard them (photo).

Fig. 3.1 Air temperature control valve (Sec 2)

A Inlet from exhaust manifold heater
B Inlet from atmosphere
C Outlet to air cleaner

2.0a Air temperature control valve assembly (head-on view)

2.0b Air temperature control system pipework and valve

Fig. 3.2 Exploded view of the air cleaner assembly (Sec 3)

1 Air intake hose
2 Canister securing bolt
3 Fuel pipe and clips
4 Renewable element
5 Air cleaner outer case
6 Air cleaner mounting bolt holes
7 Gasket

3.5 The air cleaner separated, showing renewable elements

4.0 The overrun valve in the butterfly (arrowed)

5.9 Throttle linkage bracket bolts (arrowed)

6   Having cleaned out the container, fit the new elements, and bolt the two sections together again.

7   To refit the air cleaner, follow in reverse the procedure for removal.

4   Carburettors – general description

The SU carburettors fitted to the Rover 2300 and 2600 are of the variable choke type. The fuel, which is drawn into the air passage through a jet orifice, is metered by a tapered needle which moves in and out of the jet, thus varying the effective size of the orifice. This needle is attached to, and moves with, the air valve piston which controls the variable choke opening.

There is a special overrun valve built-in to the throttle butterfly. This is a small spring-loaded valve which operates automatically to reduce the depression built in the carburettor during overrun conditions and thereby reduces the carbon emission by ensuring that the correct amounts of fuel and air are fed in to the engine (photo).

In addition, there is another device fitted to prevent over-rich running. This is a temperature compensator or 'Capstat' which is designed to control the fuel flow automatically as the engine temperature rises, without the needle position altering. In most UK models, the carburettors are fully adjustable. For export, carburettors are also made in a tamper-proof form. This is due to the legislation regarding carburation and emission control in various countries. The only outward adjustment that can be made is via the fast idle speed screw. There is a sleeve round the mixture control nut and also over the slow-running adjuster screw. This makes stripping and overhaul a limited operation.

5   Carburettors – removal and refitting

1   Remove the air cleaner as described in Section 3.

2   Disconnect the throttle cable as described in Section 9.

3   Disconnect the choke/mixture cable from the trunnion next to the right-hand carburettor. See Section 10.

4   Undo the spring clips and remove the fuel feed pipes to both left and right float chambers (Fig. 3.3). Tie up the pipes to ensure the fuel supply is cut off.

5   Remove the overflow pipes from the left and right float chambers.

6   Remove the engine breather hoses from both carburettors.

7   Unhook the throttle return springs (attached to the manifold plate) if fitted.

8   Remove the brake servo hose from the manifold and the vacuum advance hose from the right carburettor.

9   Free the throttle linkage bracket from the manifold under the left carburettor (2 bolts) (photo).

10   Each carburettor is held in place by 4 nuts and washers. Undo them all and remove both carburettors together with the linkage. Note that the top inside nuts of both carburettors cannot be removed until the carburettors are pulled forward slightly.

11   Remove the gaskets.

12   Refitting is the reverse of the removal procedure, but note the following points first:

13   Clean the manifold and carburettor flange faces and fit new gaskets.

14   Fit both carburettors together with the linkage correctly assembled (photo).

15   Tighten the nuts that secure the carburettors to the manifold to the correct torque (see Specifications).

16   After fitting, it will be necessary to tune and adjust the carburettors as described in Section 7.

6   Carburettors – needle and jet renewal

Needle renewal

1   Remove the air cleaner as per Section 3.

2   Give both carburettors a preliminary clean and wipe dry with a clean rag.

3   Unscrew the damper and give it a sharp tug to release the retaining clip (photo). Withdraw the damper and sealing washer (Fig. 3.4).

4   Mark the relationship of the suction chamber (dashpot) and carburettor body. Undo the three fixing screws. Lift the chamber away without tipping it (photo).

Fig. 3.3 Removal of the twin carburettors (Sec 5)

4	Fuel feed pipe clips	
7	Throttle return spring (where fitted)	
10	Throttle linkage bracket and bolts	
11	Carburettor securing nuts	
12	Gasket	

5.14 Carburettors refitted with linkage correctly assembled

6.3 Withdrawing the damper and retaining clip

5   Remove the piston return spring. Note that some carburettors may have smaller diameter springs than others.

6   Carefully withdraw the piston assembly and empty the oil from the piston rod.

7   To remove the jet needle, remove the needle locking screw and withdraw the needle complete with the spring and guide (Fig. 3.6) (photo). Note that the needle is fully floating.

8   Check the needle carefully for damage and wear and renew it (if necessary) with the correct type of needle for the car model (see Specifications).

9   Clean all parts before reassembly.

10   Refit the spring and guide to the needle and fit the assembly into the base of the piston; before tightening the locking screw ensure that the shoulders of the needle are flush with the piston base (photo).

11   Ensure that the piston key is securely located in the body (see Fig. 3.5.).

Fig. 3.4 Removing the suction chamber (Sec 6)

1 *Fixing screws*   3 *Damper*
2 *Dashpot*   4 *Sealing washer*

Fig. 3.5 Removing the piston assembly complete (Sec 6)

10 *Piston key*   12 *Return spring*
11 *Piston and needle*

6.4 Lifting the dashpot and piston out

6.7 Removing the needle, spring and guide

6.10 Checking that the needle is fitted
correctly using a straight-edge

Fig. 3.6 The jet needle assembly (Sec 6)

6 *Needle locking screw*
7 *Location of needle in base of piston*
9 *Needle spring and guide*

Fig. 3.7 The damper retainer (arrowed) (Sec 6)

6.15 Refilling the damper chamber with oil

12 Carefully refit piston assembly into the carburettor body.
13 Refit the piston return spring, refit the dashpot (lining up the marks) and screw it down.
14 Insert the damper into the piston whilst holding the piston up. Check to ensure that the retainer is firmly seated in position (Fig. 3.7).
15 Fill the damper chamber with engine oil, until the oil is just visible at the bottom of the retainer (photo). Move the damper up and down a few times to make sure the oil has gone right down. Then screw the damper down finger-tight.
Note: *Because of the nature of the tamperproof carburettors (where fitted) it is not recommended that they are stripped for overhauling any further than described above. In some countries, if you break the seals and alter the mixture and running settings, it can lead to prosecution for violating emission control laws. If it is essential to alter the pre-set adjustment, break the seals and adjust using an exhaust gas analyser and tachometer. Fit new seals to the adjustment screws on completion (refer to Section 7).*

Jet renewal

16 This procedure should only be attempted on cars which are produced for the UK market, which up to late 1979 did not have tamperproof carburettors fitted as standard. See the note following paragraph 15 of this Section.
17 Follow paragraphs 1 to 6 of this Section before attempting to remove the jet assembly.
18 Remove the linkage clip to the jet assembly (photo).
19 Undo the float chamber feed pipe union.
20 Carefully withdraw the complete jet assembly (photo). Note the colour coding rings on the fuel feed pipe from the float chamber. This is to identify the jet size. Ensure that the new jet is exactly the same (see Specifications).
21 The jet assembly is renewed as one unit. It cannot be stripped any further as the capstat (see Section 4) is incorporated in the base of the assembly.
22 Reassembly is the reverse of the removal procedure.

6.18 Unclip the linkage to the jet assembly

7   Carburettors – adjustments and tuning

Note: *Before trying to adjust or tune the carburettors you must ensure that the following points have been checked and clearances etc reset if necessary (see Specifications):*

    (a)   Ignition timing (see Chapter 4)
    (b)   Valve clearances (see Chapter 1)
    (c)   Spark plugs (see Chapter 4)
    (d)   Distributor contact points (see Chapter 4)

Also for this next Section you will need 3 special items of equipment:

    (a)   An exhaust gas analyser
    (b)   An airflow or balancing meter
    (c)   An accurate external tachometer

1   Take off the air cleaner. See Section 3.
2   Check to ensure that the throttle operation is smooth and does not stick.
3   Remove the tamperproof covers from the mixture control and idling speed adjuster screw (if fitted).

6.20 Draw the complete jet assembly downwards to remove

4   Unscrew the fast idle adjuster screws so that they are not touching the cams (photo).

5   Disconnect the choke cable at the carburettor linkage end.

6   Turn the idle adjuster screws (B) until they are just clear of the throttle levers (with the throttle closed). Now turn them 1½ turns in a clockwise direction (see Fig. 3.8).

7   Check to see that each piston can operate freely. Lift it up and see that it falls cleanly onto the bridge. If either piston sticks, remove and clean both piston and dashpot (see Section 6).

8   Lift the piston of each carburettor in turn and wedge it in the raised position so you can see the jet.

9   Turn the jet adjuster nuts so that the jets are raised flush with the carburettor bridge (Fig. 3.9).

10 Also ensure that the shoulders of the needles are flush with the bases of the pistons.

11 Unscrew the jet adjusters 2 complete turns (photo).

12 Fill the damper chamber with oil; see Section 6, paragraph 15. Ensure that the retainer stays in position.

13 Start up the engine and run it at fast idle speed (1200 rpm) until it reaches normal operating temperature, then continue for a further 5 minutes at 1500rpm.

14 Before starting adjustments or attempting to take readings, run the engine for 30 seconds at 2500 rpm to clear it. This procedure should be carried out every three minutes when adjusting the carburettors to ensure that you do not obtain false readings.

15 Using the exhaust gas analyser, insert the probe into the exhaust pipe following the manufacturers instructions.

16 Fit the accurate external tachometer to the engine.

17 Slacken both nuts and bolts on the throttle spindle and jet control connecting rods (photo).

18 Using an airflow meter (balancing meter), check the carburettors for balance. Various types of meter are available on the market, but all

7.4 The fast idle adjuster screw (arrowed), left-hand carburettor

Fig. 3.8 Carburettor adjusting screws (Sec 7)

A Mixture control nut/jet adjuster
B Idle adjuster screw
C Fast idle adjuster screw

Fig. 3.9 View of carburettor (from above) with dashpot and piston assembly removed (Sec 7)

1 Carburettor bridge (insert with jet flush to bridge)

7.11 Unscrew the jet adjuster nuts (right-hand side shown)

7.17 Slacken both nuts and bolts on both interconnecting rods

Fig. 3.10 Airflow/balancing meter (Sec 7)

operate on the same principle. Firstly you need to zero the gauge by means of the adjusting screw. Then fit the gauge, ensuring that there are no air leaks.

19 With the engine running, note the reading on the gauge. If the pointer remains or settles in the zero area of the scale, then no adjustment is necessary. If the needle moves to the right, reduce the airflow entering the left-hand carburettor by *unscrewing* the idle adjustment screw. Alternatively, increase the airflow through the right-hand carburettor by *screwing up* the idle adjuster on that carburettor. If conversely, the needle moves to the left, then reverse the procedure.

20 If the idling speed rises too high or drops during these checks, adjust to the correct idle speed, maintaining the gauge needle in the zero area.

21 The difference in engine speeds set with and/or without the balancer in position will be negligible, being in the region of plus or minus 25 rpm.

22 A wide variation in speeds would indicate a basic carburettor fault that may only be remedied by an overhaul, or replacement units. It should be borne in mind that with the SU HS6, only limited overhaul is possible (see Section 6 of this Chapter).

23 To weaken or enrich the mixture, turn the jet adjuster nuts up or down (up to weaken, down to enrich) by the same amount until the tachometer registers its highest speed.

24 Then turn each nut up one flat at a time until the rpm just begins to fall.

25 Now turn the nuts down by the smallest amount possible to regain the highest speed.

26 Check the idle speed and adjust if needed by turning the idle adjuster screws the same amount.

27 Check that the CO reading on the exhaust gas analyser is within the accepted limits of the 2% to 4%. If the reading is outside this, then reset both jet adjusting nuts by the smallest variation possible to bring the CO level within tolerance.

Note: *If the adjustment exceeds 3 flats ($\frac{1}{2}$ turn) to rectify the setting,*

then the carburettors need to be renewed. Check the throttle control linkage setting as follows:

28 Slacken the locking nut on the progression lever adjusting screw.

29 Turn the screw against the lever until the top edge of the lever is just in contact with the link rod at point 'A' and at the top, the slot at point 'B'. See Fig. 3.12. then tighten the locknut.

30 Turn the driving lever on the throttle connecting shaft on both carburettors so that you have a clearance of 0.01 in (0.25 mm) between the driving lever tongue and the upper arm of the fork.

31 Tighten the driving lever clamp bolts and nuts.

32 If necessary, adjust the throttle cable to take up any slack you may have created.

33 Check the accelerator pedal stop to ensure it opens fully. Adjust if necessary.

34 Recheck the balance of the carburettors using the airflow meter with the engine running at 1500 rpm.

35 With the fast idle cams against their stops, tighten up the jet control connecting clamps so that both start to move together. Check the choke (mixture) control cable movement as follows:

36 Reconnect the choke control cable to the trunnion. Check that you have $\frac{1}{16}$ in (1.6 mm) free play before the cams move.

37 Pull up the choke lever until the jet is about to move.

38 Using the airflow meter to ensure equal adjustment, turn the fast idle screws to give the correct fast idle speed on the tachometer. Then tighten the locknuts.

39 Refit the seals to the idle speed adjuster screws and the mixture control nuts.

40 Refit the air cleaner and make a last check of the CO reading at the correct idle speed. Then remove the probe.

41 If you adjust the throttle linkage on automatic models then it must follow that an additional check and possible re-adjustment may have to be carried out on the downshift cable, so ensuring that the downshift cable has not suffered any movement or change in relation to the new linkage adjustment. Refer to Chapter 6.

Fig. 3.11 Carburettor linkage control connecting rods (Sec 7)

1 Throttle spindle clamp nuts and bolts   2 Jet control connecting rod clamp nuts and bolts

Fig. 3.12 Throttle and choke linkage settings (Sec 7)

1 Driving lever clamp   4 Locknut
2 Throttle cable   A and B Progression lever
3 Driving lever tongue   contact points

4   Take off the cover and gasket.
5   Remove the float pivot pin, float, needle and seat (photo).
6   Having cleaned and inspected the moving parts and cleaned out the chamber itself (taking care to remove all sediment), the unit is now ready to be reassembled.
7   Reassembly is the reverse of the dismantling procedure but remember to fit a new gasket.

Fig. 3.13 Float chamber components – right-hand unit (Sec 8)

3 Securing screw   7 Float
4 Cover   8 Needle
5 Gasket   9 Needle seat
6 Pivot pin

---

8   Float chamber – dismantling and reassembly

1   Disconnect the fuel supply line to the float chamber.
2   Remove the float chamber cover securing screws and identity tag (Fig. 3.13).
3   Mark the cover to body relationship for easy reassembly.

---

9   Throttle cable – removal and refitting

1   Take off the air cleaner (see Section 3).
2   Undo the throttle cable adjuster and release the cable from the bracket.
3   Remove the split-pin, washer and clevis pin which attach the throttle cable to the carburettor linkage (Fig. 3.14).
4   From inside the car, having removed the driver's side glovebox (see Chapter 12), release the throttle cable from the pedal.

8.5 The float chamber parts – cover, needle, float and pivot pin

5   Then pull the whole cable (inner and outer) through the bulkhead, complete with grommet.

6   Refitting is the reversal of removal. Do not overtighten the pedal end securing clamp or the cable may be distorted . Also remember that you may have to adjust the cable to take up any slack and (if applicable) reset the automatic transmission downshift cable (Chapter 6). Do this before refitting the air cleaner.

10 Choke cable – removal and refitting

1   Undo the trunnion pinch-bolt and pull the front end of the cable (inner and outer) away from the right carburettor (Fig. 3.15) (photo).

2   Remove the driver's side glovebox (see Chapter 12).

3   Lift up the console rear panel and remove the screw that locates the choke lever assembly.

4   Unclip the securing clip that holds the inner cable rod end (Fig. 3.16) (photo) and disconnect the electrical connections.

5   Lift the console away.

6   Remove the complete cable from inside. When withdrawing the cable through the bulkhead, it may be found easier if you lightly lubricate the outer cable.

7   Refitting is the reverse procedure to removal. Remember to feed the cable underneath the heater unit. Also ensure that the outer cable is firmly located in the plastic clip on the underside of the choke lever assembly (Fig. 3.17).

Fig. 3.14 Throttle cable attachment (Sec 9)

2 Cable adjuster
3 Cable to linkage clevis pin

10.1 The choke cable prior to removal

Fig. 3.15 Choke cable attachment – front end (Sec 10)

1 Trunnion pinch-bolt

Fig. 3.16 Choke lever assembly showing inner cable rod clip (Sec 10)

10.4 Choke lever raised showing rod and clip (arrowed)

Fig. 3.17 Choke lever assembly showing outer cable securing clip
(Sec 10)

11 In-line fuel filter – removal and refitting

1   Rover recommend that the in-line fuel filter be renewed at 12000 mile (20000 km) intervals or annually, whichever occurs first.
2   Disconnect the fuel inlet pipe from the filter by undoing the union nut. Tie the inlet pipe up on the bulkhead to avoid fuel spillage (Fig. 3.18).
3   Pull off the outlet pipe.
4   Remove the filter and replace it with a new one.
5   Fitting the new filter is the reverse procedure to removal, but note that it is important that the end of the filter marked IN be connected to the fuel inlet pipe.
6   After fitting the new filter, start the engine and check that there are no leaks.

3   Fold down the rear seat squab and pull the luggage compartment covering back to reveal a large rubber grommet.
4   Pull out the grommet and disconnect the wiring plug from the socket (photo).
5   Disconnect the fuel feed pipe from the pump/tank outlet.
6   Chock the front wheels, raise the rear of the car and support it on axle-stands or strong packing blocks.
7   Remove the left-hand rear roadwheel to gain access to the fuel filter pipe connecting hose (Fig. 3.19).
8   Clean away the road dirt in the area around the fuel filler connecting hose then loosen the clips sufficiently to enable the hose to be slid up clear of the tank filler neck.

Fig. 3.18 In-line fuel filter (Sec 11)

1 Inlet pipe and nut
2 Outlet pipe and clip
3 Fuel filter

12.4 Access to the fuel pump/tank gauge unit is through a hole in the rear floor area

12 Fuel tank – removal and refitting

Warning: *Due to the high fire risk do not use a naked light. It is preferable to work on the car out in the open taking advantage of the natural light and breeze to dispel any petrol vapours.*
1   For safety reasons, immobilise all electrical circuits by disconnecting the battery negative terminal connection.
2   Should the fuel tank be over a quarter full, then for ease of handling, syphon out the fuel into a suitable clean container using a length of hose.

9   Pull off the fuel tank vent hose.
10 Place a trolley jack directly underneath the fuel tank to support it. Insert a suitable piece of flat wood between the tank and the jack lifting pad to prevent damage to the tank.
11 Release the fuel feed pipe from the right-hand side of the fuel tank. Access to these is from beneath the car.
12 Ensure that the jack is supporting the fuel tank centrally, then remove the remaining two bolts (front end) and the two nuts (rear end) that secure the tank (Fig. 3.20) (photos).
13 Lower the jack slowly and draw the fuel tank out from beneath the car.

12.12a Nuts securing fuel tank at forward end

12.12b Nuts securing fuel tank at rear end

Fig. 3.19 Location of the filler pipe connecting hose (Sec 12)

Fig. 3.20 Location of the nuts and bolts that retain the fuel tank (Sec 12)

14 If the tank is to be renewed, then it will be necessary to remove the vent hose and the fuel feed line clips in order to extract the fuel pump and tank unit assembly. In addition, any surplus fuel left in the old tank will have to be drained out.

15 Non-professional home repairs on the fuel tank, if split or leaking, are not recommended. The only remedy for such faults is to fit a new tank or a professionally reconditioned unit. Generally it will be found that a radiator repair specialist will also undertake fuel tank repairs.

16 Refitting of the fuel tank is the reverse of the removal procedure. **Note:** *When fitting the fuel pump and tank gauge unit, use a new gasket.* Details of the fuel pump/tank gauge assembly is covered in Section 13.

---

13 Fuel pump and tank gauge unit – removal and refitting

1   Disconnect the negative battery terminal.
2   Fold the rear seat squab forward and then roll the luggage compartment floor covering back towards the rear of the car.
3   Roll back the extreme left-hand felt strip and remove the large rubber grommet from the luggage compartment floor panel.
4   Disconnect the wiring plug from the socket fitted into the upper exposed section of the fuel tank.
5   Undo the fuel outlet union connection situated next to the wiring socket.
6   Remove the six retaining screws that secure the fuel pump/tank gauge unit to the fuel tank.
7   Withdraw the assembly up through the top of the fuel tank and remove the gasket (Fig. 3.21).

8   The pump can be separated from the assembly after releasing the spring clip, elbow hose, terminal cover and two electrical leads.
9   Refitting the pump to the tank gauge unit is the reverse of removal. When connecting the pump cables, the black cable is fitted to the (-) terminal and the red cable to the (+) terminal.

Fig. 3.21 The fuel pump and tank gauge unit (Sec 13)

10 Gasket   13 Elbow hose
11 Pump and retaining clip   14 Terminal cover
12 Spring clip

10 When fitting the assembly, use a new gasket and reverse the removal procedure.

Note: *The electric feed supply to the fuel pump is taken from the starter motor solenoid and the engine oil pressure switch; consequently, the fuel pump is only operative when the engine is being turned by the starter motor or is running with sufficient oil pressure.*

14 Emission control systems – general description

With the new 6-cylinder engines, a great deal of thought has gone into making this engine as efficient as possible with as low a fuel consumption rate as can be achieved whilst still having regard for reducing pollution in the form of emission controls.

The emission control system comprises basically the following two systems, although it must be emphasised that many other components play a contributory part in maintaining the low emission levels.

Air intake temperature control system: A description of this system is given in Section 2.

Crankcase emission control system: In this system the crankcase fumes and blow-by gases are recirculated through the induction manifold and burned in the normal combustion process.

The breathing cycle is initiated by the inlet manifold which creates a depression, thus drawing fumes from the crankcase up through the rear oil drain passage in the cylinder block and head. There is an area in the camshaft cover into which the fumes are then drawn and this is covered by a baffle plate. Finally the fumes are fed to the depression side of the carburettors by rubber hoses. Then they are fed into the engine and burned.

15 Emission control systems – maintenance

Air intake temperature control system

1   This system is basically maintenance free, apart from a periodic inspection of the hot and cold air flexible hoses.
2   A function test can be carried out quite simply to check the operation of the flap valve and bi-metallic strip.
3   With the engine cold, disconnect the cold air intake flexible hose and check that the flap valve is covering the cold air inlet port. Reconnect the hose and run the engine until normal operating temperature is reached, then disconnect the hot air intake flexible hose. The flap valve should in this condition be covering the hot air intake port. Reconnect the hot air intake hose (Fig. 3.1).
4   If the function of the air intake temperature control system does not follow that described in paragraph 3, the only remedy is to renew the assembly.

Crankcase emission control system

5   Periodically disconnect the interconnecting hoses between the carburettors and the camshaft cover. Inspect the hoses carefully for deterioration and interior fouling up.
6   Clean the hoses by passing a short length of cloth through them.
7   Refit the hoses ensuring that the spring clips are correctly positioned.

16 Exhaust system – general

1   The exhaust system is of a three-section conventional design with the first two sections being mainly twin-pipe and the rear section single-pipe (photos) (Fig. 3.22). This enables easy renewal of corroded or damaged parts.

Fig. 3.22 Layout and detail of the exhaust system (Sec 16)

2   When removing any section, apply penetrating oil liberally to the nuts and bolts and obtain new gaskets, where necessary, before reassembly.

3   Examine the rubber support rings and mounting brackets and renew them if weak or worn (photo).

4   When assembling the exhaust system, do not tighten the coupling nuts and bolts any more than finger-tight before the whole system is in place.

5   Start securing from the mainfold flange rearwards but take care that undue strain is not placed on any joint due to misalignment. A badly fitted system will have a much shorter life due to any additional strain it may be forced to bear.

6   After fitting any new part of the exhaust system, start the engine and check for any leakage from the joints.

7   Allow the system to cool down, then recheck the security of the entire system as some settling is bound to have occurred due to expansion and contraction.

17 Exhaust manifold – removal and refitting

1   Remove the hot air intake pipe from the heat chamber.

2   Remove the three nuts and washers that secure the front exhaust pipe to the manifold flange.

3   Remove the 12 bolts that secure the manifold to the cylinder head (photo).

4   Lift the manifold vertically so that the studs disengage from the front exhaust pipe flange, then remove it. If necessary, the remaining bolt that secures the heat chamber can be removed and the heat chamber can then be taken off.

5   Remove the manifold to front pipe flange gasket. Note that there is no manifold to cylinder head gasket.

6   Before refitting, clean the mating faces of both the mainfold and

cylinder head, and also the manifold and front exhaust pipe.

7   Fit a new gasket over the studs on the bottom manifold joint and refit the heat chamber if removed.

8   Lower the manifold into position, ensuring that the studs engage in the front exhaust pipe flange.

9   Screw in all the manifold retaining bolts, finger-tight first, then progressively tighten to the specified torque.

10 Secure the front exhaust pipe to the manifold with the three nuts and washers.

11 Refit the hot air intake pipe.

12 Start the engine and run till hot; check for exhaust gas leaks.

13 Stop the engine and allow the system to cool down. Then check again the tightness of the manifold bolts and front exhaust flange nuts.

18 Inlet manifold – removal and refitting of gasket

1   Drain the cooling system. See Chapter 2.

2   Take off the air cleaner. See Section 3.

3   Remove the cover for the camshaft drivebelt. See Chapter 1.

4   Remove the breather hose from the camshaft cover.

5   Disconnect the hose to the water pump at the manifold end.

6   Remove the 9 bolts that secure the manifold to the cylinder head. Remove the rear lifting eye and spacers.

7   Lift the manifold away from the cylinder head. Then remove the gasket.

8   Clean the mating faces thoroughly.

9   Refit a new gasket.

10 Refitting of the manifold is the reverse procedure to removal, remembering to tighten the manifold bolts to the correct torque (see Specifications).

16.1a Front exhaust pipe bracket to gearbox

16.1b U-bolt clamps secure first to second sections

16.1c Flange connection secures middle to tail section

16.3 Support rings for rear silencer

17.3 Manifold bolts pictured with engine out of the car

19 Fault diagnosis – fuel system

Symptom	Reason/s
Carburation and ignition faults	Air cleaner choked and dirty giving rich mixture Fuel leaking from carburettor/s or fuel lines Float chamber flooding Generally worn carburettor/s Balance weights or vacuum advance mechanism in distributor faulty
Poor performance	Carburettor/s incorrectly adjusted, mixture too rich or too weak Idling speed too high Distributor points gap incorrect Carburettors require balancing Incorrectly set spark plugs Tyres under-inflated Wrong spark plugs fitted Brakes dragging Petrol tank air vent restricted Partially clogged fuel pump or in-line filter Dirt lodged in float chamber needle housing Incorrectly seating valves in fuel pump Too little fuel in fuel tank (prevalent when climbing steep hills)
Air leaks	Union joints on pipe connections loose Inlet manifold to block joint, or inlet manifold to carburettor/s gasket leaking
Fuel pump faults	Disconnected cables at pump Wires disconnected at oil pressure switch; this switch affects the fuel pump operation Fuel pump filter clogged Suction pipe or fuel pump disconnected

Chapter 4 Ignition system

For modifications, and information applicable to later models, see Supplement at end of manual

Contents

Specifications

Distributor

Type	Lucas 54 D6 fitted to both models. Part Nos vary – check No stamped on body of distributor before ordering spare parts
Rotation	Anti-clockwise
Contact breaker gap	0.014 to 0.016 in (0.35 to 0.40 mm)
Dwell angle	$37° \pm 5°$
Condenser capacity	0.18 to 0.23 mfd

Spark plugs

Type	Champion BN-12Y
Electrode gap	0.025 in (0.64 mm)

Ignition coil

Type	Lucas 16 C6 with ballast resistor
Primary resistance	1.3 to 1.45 ohms

Engine firing order

1, 5, 3, 6, 2, 4

Ignition timing

Static or at idle	10° BTDC
Dynamic (distributor vacuum pipe disconnected):	
2300	24° BTDC at 2500 rpm
2600	20° BTDC at 2500 rpm
Location of timing marks	Scale on oil pump cover and notch in crankshaft pulley.

Torque wrench settings

	lbf ft	Nm
Spark plugs	6 to 8	8 to 11
Distributor to camshaft carrier nut	15	20

1 General description

In order that the engine may run correctly, it is necessary for an electrical spark to ignite the fuel/air charge in the combustion chamber at exactly the right moment in relation to engine speed and load. The ignition system is based on supplying low tension voltage from the battery to the ignition coil where it is converted to high tension voltage by virtue of contact breaker operation. The high tension voltage is powerful enough to jump the spark plug gap in the cylinder many times a second under high compression pressure, providing that the ignition system is in good working order and that all adjustments are correct.

The ignition system comprises two individual circuits known as the low tension circuit and the high tension circuit.

The low tension (or primary) circuit comprises the lead from the positive terminal of the 12 volt battery, the ignition/starter switch, a ballast resistor wire, the primary winding of the 6 volt ignition coil, the contact breaker points of the distributor (which are bridged by the condenser) and an earth connection. Since the negative terminal of the battery is also earthed, current will flow in the low tension circuit when the distributor contacts are closed and a magnetic field will be set up in the primary winding of the coil.

The high tension (or secondary) circuit comprises the secondary winding of the ignition coil (one end of which is connected internally to the output terminal of the primary winding), the heavily insulated ignition lead from the centre of the coil to the centre of the distributor cap, the rotor arm, the spark plug leads and the spark plugs.

When the contacts open, the magnetic field in the primary coil winding collapses rapidly and induces a voltage in the secondary winding. At this instant, the distributor rotor is bridging the coil output terminal and one of the spark plug connections in the distributor cap, and a spark therefore jumps the electrode gap. The condenser across the contacts serves the dual purpose of assisting the rapid collapse of the magnetic field in the primary winding and acts as a spark suppressor for the contacts.

The whole cycle is repeated when the contacts open again which will be when the distributor has turned through 45°, but this time the next spark plug in the ignition sequence will fire.

During the starting sequence, the ballast resistor or resistor wire in series with the coil primary winding is bypassed so that the full battery voltage (which will be low anyway due to the high current drawn by the starter motor) is passed to the 6 volt coil. In this way a bigger secondary voltage will be induced and therefore a bigger spark will result.

Whilst the above sequence is apparently satisfactory, in that the distributor can be physically set to provide a spark when it is needed, some variation of ignition timing is required to obtain optimum efficiency under varying conditions of engine load and speed. A centrifugal advance mechanism is used inside the distributor body which will give an increasing amount of spark advancement (ie, firing earlier in the cycle) as the engine speed increases. Additionally, a vacuum device is fitted, which is operated by the depression in the inlet manifold and will give additional spark advancement at low and moderate throttle openings, eg when the car is cruising. At wide throttle openings, eg, when hill climbing there is less suction in the inlet manifold and hence there will be little or no additional advancement. The combination of the two devices will provide a wide range of ignition advancement or retardation according to the engine requirements at any particular time.

2 Condenser – removal, testing and refitting

1 The purpose of the condenser (sometimes known as the capacitor) is to ensure that when the contact breaker points open, there is no sparking across them which would waste voltage and cause wear. It also boosts the HT voltage.
2 The condenser is fitted in parallel with the points. If it develops a short circuit, ignition failure will result as the points will be prevented from interrupting the low tension circuit.
3 If the engine becomes very difficult to start or begins to 'miss' after several miles running and the points show sign of excessive wear/burning, then the condition of the condenser must be suspect.
4 Without special equipment the only way to check whether the condenser is faulty is to fit a new one and observe the results.
5 To remove the condenser from the distributor, take off the distributor cap and rotor arm. Now remove the condenser locating screw and lead connection.
6 Fitting of the condenser is the reverse of the removal procedure, but take care that the lead cannot contact the moving parts or become trapped when the cap is refitted.

3 Contact breaker points – adjustment

1 Remove the HT lead from the distributor cap.
2 Undo the two clips, remove the distributor cap and put it to one side.
3 Remove the rotor arm.
4 Turn the crankshaft to position the heel of the contact on one of the cam peaks.
5 Prise the contact points apart and examine the condition of their faces. If in any doubt, refer to the next Section of this Chapter for removal, cleaning and refitting.
6 Provided the condition of the points is satisfactory, check the gap between them using a feeler gauge. The 0·015 in (0·38 mm) feeler

should just slide between them (photo).
7 To adjust the gap, first slacken the lockscrew (photo).
8 Then move the contact plate to adjust the gap. There is a slot in the end into which a screwdriver can be inserted to make it easier (photo).
9 Having set the gap correctly, tighten the lockscrew, recheck the gap and then refit the rotor.
10 Before refitting the distributor cap, check the condition of the rotor contact and the electrodes in the cap itself. The rotor arm contact can be cleaned with fine emery cloth and the electrodes scraped clean with a small screwdriver or penknife.

4 Contact breaker points – removal, cleaning and refitting

1 Carry out the procedure as described in paras 1 to 3 of Section 3.
2 Undo and remove the lockscrew and washers.
3 Lift out the contact breaker assembly.
4 Separate the contact spring from the insulator pad.
5 Remove the terminal clip from the contact spring.
6 If the points are to be cleaned and re-used, then rub the faces of the contacts on fine emery cloth or fine carborundum paper (400 grade wet and dry). It is important that the faces are kept flat and parallel otherwise they will not meet properly when refitted and ignition problems may easily recur.
7 Refitting of the now cleaned set of points or the fitting of a new set, is simply the reverse procedure to removal. Remember to clean any preservative off a new set of points before fitting them.
8 Before fitting the rotor, adjust the gap correctly. See Section 3.

Fig. 4.1 End-on view of the distributor (Secs 2, 3 and 4)

1 Distributor cap securing clip
2 Condenser (capacitor)
3 Cam peak
4 Contact breaker assembly lockscrew
5 Contact breaker assembly
6 Insulation pad
7 Terminal clip
8 Adjustment slot

3.6 Checking the contact points gap

3.7 Releasing the contact points lockscrew

3.8 Adjusting the contact points gap

5   Distributor – removal and refitting

1   Remove the HT lead from the distributor cap.
2   Undo the 2 clips that hold the cap in place and remove the cap. Place safely out of the way.
3   Turn the engine over until you obtain TDC with No 6 cylinder firing. The rotor arm should be pointing at No 6 cylinder position. The notch on the crankshaft pulley must be aligned with the 0° on the scale (photo).
4   Disconnect the spade connector on the distributor low tension lead.
5   Pull off the vacuum advance pipe rubber connector.
6   Undo the nut and washer that hold the distributor to the camshaft carrier.
7   Carefully withdraw the distributor.
8   To refit, ensure that the distributor is held against its recess with its mounting flange positioned at the top. Set the rotor arm about 30° past the No 6 cap contact so that as the distributor is pushed into position and the drivegears mesh, the rotor will turn anti-clockwise to align with No 6 cap contact.

Fig. 4.2 Distributor with cap off showing location (Sec 5)

1 Rotor arm before installation of distributor
3 Rotor arm after installation (pointing to No 6 cylinder position)
4 Low tension lead and connector
5 Vacuum advance pipe
6 Distributor securing nut

5.3 The timing scale bracket and crankshaft pulley

9   Fit the nut and washer but do not tighten.
10   Check and adjust the timing (static) if necessary. See Section 8.
11   Tighten the securing nut.
12   Connect the low tension lead and refit the cap. Push in the HT lead.
13   Check the ignition timing (dynamic) when the engine is running. See Section 8.
14   Refit the vacuum advance pipe.

6   Distributor – dismantling, overhaul and reassembly

1   Remove the distributor from the engine as described in Section 5 and take off the rotor arm.
2   Remove the felt pad and contact breaker set (see Fig. 4.4).
3   Undo the condenser screw and manipulate the low tension lead (complete with grommet) so that it can be removed through the body of the distributor from the inside together with the condenser.
4   Undo the 2 screws that secure the vacuum advance unit and remove it.
5   Undo and remove the 2 screws that hold the moving plate, withdraw the earth lead and then the plate assembly itself.
6   Take off the drivegear by tapping out the pin with a small pin punch. Remove it with the thrustwasher.
7   Pull the shaft out carefully and check to see that it is not burred. Remove the collar.
8   Disconnect and carefully remove the control springs.
9   No further dismantling should be attempted.
10   Clean the mechanical parts carefully in petrol, then examine them for wear as described in the following paragraphs:
11   Check the fit of the balance weights on the distributor shaft. If the pivots are loose or the holes excessively worn, the relevant parts must be renewed. The springs are best renewed anyway.
12   Examine the driving gear teeth for wear and renew if necessary.
13   Check the fit of the driveshaft in the housing. If excessive wear is present, the parts must be renewed.
14   Check that the vacuum unit is working correctly by sucking through the tube and checking that the linkage moves.
15   Check the metal contact on the distributor rotor for security of fixing and burning. Small burning marks can be removed with a smooth file or very fine emery paper, but if anything else is wrong the rotor should be renewed. Look also for cracks in the plastic moulding.
16   Check the distributor cap in a similar manner, renewing it if necessary.
17   Reassembly is essentially the reverse of the dismantling procedure, but the following points should be noted:

   (a) Lubricate the weight assembly with a dry lubricant
   (b) Lubricate the shaft with a dry lubricant
   (c) Lubricate the moving plate pin with a dry lubricant
   (d) Lubricate the distributor as described in Section 7

Fig. 4.3 Distributor drivegear (cut-away to show camshaft) (Sec 5)
1 Distributor drivegears
2 Locating bracket

7 Distributor – lubrication

1 During routine maintenance and where otherwise stated in this Chapter, the distributor should be lubricated as follows:

2 Remove the distributor cap and rotor arm.

3 Apply a few drops of engine oil to the felt pad to lubricate the cam spindle bearing.

4 Squirt a few drops of engine oil through the lubrication holes to oil the centrifugal timing control.

5 Lubricate the contact plate bearing by putting one drop of engine oil in each of the oil holes in the plate.

6 Grease the cam with a light smear of general purpose grease.

7 The contact post may be lubricated in the same manner.

Fig. 4.4 Exploded view of Lucas distributor (Sec 6)

1	Felt pad	6	Moving plate assembly	11	Contact post
2	Contact breaker set	7	Driving gear and pin	12	Moving plate pin
3	Condenser screw	8	Collar	13	Cam
4	Vacuum advance control	9	Control springs	14	Distributor cap
5	Earth lead retaining screw	10	Cam assembly	15	Rotor arm

16 Distributor body
17 Low tension lead

8 Ignition timing – checking and adjustment

1   In this Section, procedures are given for static and dynamic checking. The static setting is satisfactory for most practical purposes.

Static setting

2   Initially check the contact breaker gap and adjust or clean the contacts as necessary. Disconnect the low tension lead from the distributor at the snap connector.

3   Using a 12 volt bulb of up to 5 watts rating (eg sidelamp or instrument panel lamp), connect it between the end of the distributor/coil (–ve) lead and the battery positive terminal (Fig. 4.5).

4   Rotate the crankshaft in the normal direction of rotation and check that as the notch in the crankshaft pulley is moving towards the 0-marking on the scaleplate, ie top-dead-centre (TDC), the lamp is on until 10° before TDC is reached, and then goes off (see photo 5.3).

5   If the requirement described in paragraph 4 is not satisfied, slacken the distributor mounting nut then initially turn the distributor anti-clockwise past the point at which the lamp illuminates, whilst maintaining the notch on the crankshaft pulley at 10° before TDC.

6   Now turn the distributor slowly and carefully clockwise until the lamp just goes off; then tighten the clamp nut on the distributor without allowing the distributor to move.

7   The setting can now be rechecked using the procedure previously described.

8   Finally, remove the test lamp and reconnect the lead to the ignition coil. Note: *If it is not possible to use the recommended octane fuel, audible detonation or pinking can be expected to occur with lower grades of fuel. In cases like this, the ignition timing should be retarded just enough to prevent pinking from occurring, then should be reset correctly, as soon as the correct grade of fuel can be used.*

Dynamic setting

9   Before commencing, check the contact breaker gap.

10   If possible, use an external tachometer attached to the engine. You will have to do this in 2300 models since there is no tachometer fitted as standard equipment; however in the 2600 model, the dashboard gauge can be used if no external one is available.

11   Disconnect the vacuum advance pipe from the distributor and plug the open end of the pipe.

12   Using a proprietary stroboscopic timing light connected in accordance with the manufacturers instructions, run the engine at the speed indicated in the Specifications and check the timing. The engine is timed on No 6 cylinder which is at the rear of the engine. If the timing is correct, the crankshaft pulley notch will appear to be in alignment with the specified (BTDC) scale mark.

13   Should the timing not be as quoted, then slacken the distributor clamp nut and turn the body slightly in a clockwise direction to advance the timing, or anti-clockwise direction in order to retard it. Note: *This must be done with the engine stopped.* Restart the engine and check the alignment of the timing marks.

14   Tighten the clamp nut and repeat paragraph 13 onwards.

15   Should the ignition timing be satisfactory at the lower engine speeds, but fail to remain accurate as the engine speed is increased, then it is reasonable to assume that the mechanical advance weights are sticking. One possible cause of sticking advance weights is the use of a non-specified lubricant.

16   On completion, remove the stroboscopic timing light and reconnect the No 6 spark plug HT lead.

9 Spark plugs – removal and refitting

1   Remove the plug cap by pulling on the cap itself, not the HT lead. Blow or brush away any dirt from around the plug seat.

2   Unscrew the plug using a proper spark plug spanner or socket. Having started the plug with the spanner, it should be possible to unscrew and remove it by hand (photo).

3   Before refitting note that these plugs have a tapered seat and no gasket. The cylinder head threading and the plug seats are made from soft aluminium alloy. They only require half the amount of torque to do them up, as compared with the more usual torque specified. See the Specifications.

4   Screw the plug in finger-tight having ensured that it is positioned

Fig. 4.5 Checking the ignition timing (static) (Sec 8)

1 *Distributor*   4 *Test lamp, 5 watts maximum*
2 *Coil*   5 *Battery*
3 *Negative coil lead*

9.2 Unscrew and remove the spark plug

correctly. It is extremely easy to cross-thread the soft alloy plugs and holes and make a costly job out of a simple operation.

5   Tighten the plug to the specified torque. There is now available a special plug spanner for this operation, pre-set to the correct torque.

10 Spark plugs and HT leads

1   The correct functioning of the spark plugs is vital for the correct running and efficiency of the engine.

2   At intervals of 6000 miles (10 000 km) the plugs should be removed, examined, cleaned and if the electrodes are worn, renewed. The spark plugs should be renewed in any event every 12 000 miles (20 000 km).

3   The condition of the spark plugs will also tell much about the overall condition of the engine.

4   If the insulator nose of the spark plug is clean and white, with no

Measuring plug gap. A feeler gauge of the correct size (see ignition system specifications) should have a slight 'drag' when slid between the electrodes. Adjust gap if necessary

Adjusting plug gap. The plug gap is adjusted by bending the earth electrode inwards, or outwards, as necessary until the correct clearance is obtained. Note the use of the correct tool

Normal. Grey-brown deposits, lightly-coated core nose. Gap increasing by around 0.001 in (0.025 mm) per 1000 miles (1600 km). Plugs ideally suited to engine, and engine in good condition

Carbon fouling. Dry, black, sooty deposits. Will cause weak spark and eventually misfire. Fault: over-rich fuel mixture. Check: carburettor mixture settings, float level and jet sizes; choke operation and cleanliness of air filter. Plugs can be re-used after cleaning

Oil fouling. Wet, oily deposits. Will cause weak spark and eventually misfire. Fault: worn bores/piston rings or valve guides; sometimes occurs (temporarily) during running-in period. Plugs can be re-used after thorough cleaning

Overheating. Electrodes have glazed appearance, core nose very white – few deposits. Fault: plug overheating. Check: plug value, ignition timing, fuel octane rating (too low) and fuel mixture (too weak). Discard plugs and cure fault immediately

Electrode damage. Electrodes burned away; core nose has burned, glazed appearance. Fault: pre-ignition. Check: as for 'Overheating' but may be more severe. Discard plugs and remedy fault before piston or valve damage occurs

Split core nose (may appear initially as a crack). Damage is self-evident, but cracks will only show after cleaning. Fault: pre-ignition or wrong gap-setting technique. Check: ignition timing, cooling system, fuel octane rating (too low) and fuel mixture (too weak). Discard plugs, rectify fault immediately deposits, this is indicative of a weak mixture, or too hot a plug (a hot plug transfers heat away from the electrode slowly, a cold plug transfers heat away quickly).

5   If the top and insulator nose is covered with hard black deposits, then this is indicative that the mixture is too rich. Should the plug be black and oily, then it is likely that the engine is fairly worn, as well as the mixture being too rich.

6   If the insulator nose is covered with light tan to greyish brown deposits, then the mixture is correct and it is likely that the engine is in good condition.

7   If there are any traces of long brown tapering stains on the outside of the white portion of the plug, then the plug will have to be renewed. This shows that there is a faulty joint between the plug body and the insulator allowing compression to leak away.

8   Plugs should be cleaned by a sand blasting machine, which will free them from carbon more thoroughly than cleaning by hand with a wire brush. The machine will also test the condition of the plugs under compression. Any plug that fails to spark at the recommended pressure should be renewed.

9   The spark plug gap is of considerable importance, as, if it is too large or too small, the size of the spark and its efficiency will be seriously impaired. The spark plug gap should be set to the specified gap.

10 To set it, measure the gap with a feeler gauge, and then bend open, or close, the outer plug electrode until the correct gap is achieved. The centre electrode should never be bent as this may crack the insulation and cause plug failure, if nothing worse.

11 Refit the distributor HT leads in the correct firing order. This is 1, 5, 3, 6, 2, 4.

12 The plug leads require no routine maintenance other than being kept clean and wiped over regularly.

---

11 Fault diagnosis – ignition system

Engine fails to start

1   If the engine fails to start and the car was running normally when it was last used, first check there is fuel in the fuel tank. If the engine turns over normally on the starter motor and the battery is evidently well charged, then the fault may be in either the high or low tension circuits. **Note**: *If the battery is known to be fully charged, the ignition light comes on and the starter motor fails to turn the engine, check the tightness of the leads on the battery terminal and also the secureness of the earth lead to its connection to the body. It is quite common for the leads to have worked loose, even if they look and feel secure. If one of the battery terminal posts gets very hot when trying to work the starter motor this is a sure indication of a faulty connection to that terminal.*

2   One of the commonest reasons for bad starting is wet or damp spark plug leads and distributor. Remove the distributor cap; if condensation is visible internally, dry the cap with a rag and also wipe the leads. Refit the cap.

3   If the engine still fails to start, check that current is reaching the plugs by disconnecting each plug lead in turn at the spark plug end and hold the end of the cable about $\frac{1}{8}$ in (3 mm) away from the cylinder block. Spin the engine on the starter motor.

4   Sparking between the end of the cable and the block should be fairly strong with a regular blue spark. Hold the lead with a dry cloth or rubber glove to avoid electric shocks. If current is reaching the plugs, remove, clean and regap them. The engine should now start.

5   If there is no spark at the plug leads, take off the HT lead from the centre of the distributor cap and hold it to the block as before. Spin the engine on the starter once more. A rapid succession of blue sparks between the end of the lead and block indicates that the coil is in order and that the distributor cap is cracked, the rotor arm faulty, or the carbon brush in the top of the distributor cap is not making good contact with the spring on the rotor arm.

6   If there are no sparks from the end of the lead from the coil, check the connections at the coil end of the lead. If it is in order, start checking the low tension circuit.

7   Use a 12 volt voltmeter, or a 12 volt bulb and two lengths of wire. With the ignition switched on and the points open, test between the low tension wire to the coil connection (+ve) and earth. No reading indicates a break in the supply from the ignition switch. Check the connections at the switch to see if any are loose. Refit these and the

Fig. 4.6 HT lead connection diagram (No 1 spark plug at front of engine) (Sec 10)

engine should run. A reading shows a faulty coil or condenser, or broken lead between coil and distributor.

8   Take the condenser wire off the points assembly and with the points open, test between the moving points and earth. If there now is a reading, the fault is in the condenser. Fit a new one and the fault should be cleared.

9   With no reading from the moving point to earth, take a reading between the earth and the negative (–ve) terminal of the coil. A reading here shows a broken wire (which will need to be renewed) between the coil and distributor. No reading confirms that the coil has failed and must be renewed. Remember to refit the condenser wire to the points assembly. For these tests it is sufficient to separate the points with a piece of dry paper whilst testing with the points open.

Engine misfires

10 If the engine misfires regularly, run it at a fast idling speed. Pull off each of the plug caps in turn and listen to the note of the engine. Hold the plug cap in a dry cloth or with a rubber glove as additional protection against a shock from the HT supply.

11 No difference in engine running will be noticed when the lead from the defective circuit is removed. Removing the lead from one of the good cylinders will accentuate the misfire.

12 Remove the plug lead from the end of the defective plug and hold it about $\frac{1}{8}$ in (3 mm)) away from the block. Restart the engine. If the sparking is fairly strong and regular, the fault must lie in the spark plug.

13 The plug may be loose, the insulation may be cracked, or the electrodes may have burnt away, giving too wide a gap for the spark to jump. Worse still, one of the electrodes may have broken off. Either renew the plug or clean it; reset the gap, and then test it.

14 If there is no spark at the end of the plug lead, or if it weak and intermittent, check the ignition lead from the distributor to the plug. If the insulation is cracked or perished, renew the lead. Check the connections at the distributor cap.

15 If there is still no spark, examine the distributor cap carefully for tracking. This can be recognised by a very thin black line running between two or more electrodes or between an electrode and some other part of the distributor. These lines are paths which conduct electricity across the cap thus letting it run to earth. The only remedy is a new distributor cap.

16 Apart from the ignition timing being incorrect, other causes of misfiring have already been dealt with under the section dealing with the failure of the engine to start. To recap – these are that:

   (a) *the coil may be faulty giving an intermittent misfire*
   (b) *there may be a damaged wire or loose connection in the low tension circuit*
   (c) *there may be a mechanical fault in the distributor*

17 If the ignition timing is too far retarded, it should be noted that the engine will tend to overheat and there will be a quite noticeable drop in power. If the engine is overheating and the power is down and the ignition timing is correct, then the carburettor should be checked, as it is likely that this is where the fault lies.

Chapter 5 Clutch

For modifications, and information applicable to later models, see Supplement at end of manual

Contents

Specifications

Type . . . . Single dry plate diaphragm type, hydraulic actuation

Clutch driven plate diameter . . . . 9 in (228.6 mm)

Fluid
Type/specification . . . . Hydraulic fluid to FMVSS 116 DOT 3 or SAE J1703 (Duckhams Universal Brake and Clutch Fluid)

Torque wrench settings

	lbf ft	Nm
Clutch assembly to flywheel bolts	21	28
Slave cylinder bolts	25	34
Clutch housing to engine and sump bracer bolts	37	50
Clutch housing to cylinder block and engine plate bolts	21	28
Release arm pivot post	37	50
Flywheel cover plate bolts	15	20

1 General description

The clutch fitted to manual transmission models is of the single dry plate diaphragm spring type and is hydraulically operated.

The unit comprises a steel cover which is dowelled and bolted to the rear face of the flywheel and contains the pressure plate, diaphragm spring and fulcrum rings.

The clutch disc is free to slide along the splined first motion shaft and is held in position between the flywheel and the pressure plate by the pressure of the pressure plate spring. Friction lining material is riveted to the clutch disc and it has a spring cushioned hub to absorb transmission shocks and to help ensure a smooth take off.

The circular diaphragm spring is mounted on shoulder pins and held in place in the cover by two fulcrum rings. The spring is also held to the pressure plate by three spring steel clips which are riveted in position.

The clutch release mechanism consists of a hydraulic master cylinder and slave cylinder and the interconnecting pipework, a release arm and a sealed ball type release bearing (the latter being in permanent contact with the fingers of the pressure plate assembly).

As the friction linings on the clutch driven plate wear, the pressure plate automatically moves closer to the driven plate to compensate. This makes the centre of the diaphragm spring move nearer to the release bearing, so decreasing the release bearing clearance. Depressing the clutch pedal actuates the clutch release arm by means of hydraulic pressure. The release arm pushes the release bearing forwards to bear against the release fingers, so moving the centre of the diaphragm spring inwards. The spring is sandwiched between two annular rings which act as fulcrum points. As the centre of the spring is pushed in, the outside of the spring is pushed out, so moving the pressure plate backwards and disengaging the pressure plate from the clutch disc.

When the clutch pedal is released, the diaphragm spring forces the pressure plate into contact with the high fulcrum linings on the clutch disc and at the same time pushes the clutch disc a fraction of an inch forwards on its splines so engaging the clutch disc with the flywheel. The clutch disc is now firmly sandwiched between the pressure plate and the flywheel so the drive is taken up.

2 Maintenance

1   This consists of occasionally checking the security of the bolts which retain the master and slave cylinders and applying a little engine oil to the operating rod clevis joints.
2   Periodically check the hydraulic pipes and unions for leaks, corrosion or deterioration.
3   At weekly intervals, remove the clutch master cylinder cap and check the fluid level (photo). Before unscrewing the cap wipe it clean to prevent the ingress of dirt. Use only the recommended type of clutch fluid. If topping-up becomes a common occurrence then carry out a visual inspection of the clutch hydraulic system. Any leakage of fluid would then be evident.

3 Master cylinder – removal and refitting

1   From within the car, remove the split-pin, washer and clevis pin that secure the clutch master cylinder pushrod to the clutch pedal.
2   From the engine compartment, disconnect the metal hydraulic pipe at the master cylinder union. Plug the end of the pipe and the hole in the master cylinder to prevent the escape of the fluid. Remember that the fluid is corrosive and will have a detrimental effect on paintwork. If any fluid should be spilt, wipe it up immediately.
3   Remove the two nuts, spring washers and plain washers that

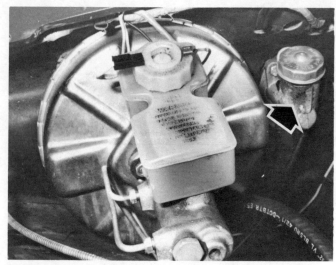

2.3 The clutch master cylinder reservoir (arrowed)

secure the master cylinder to the scuttle/pedal assembly.
4   The master cylinder can now be withdrawn.
5   Refitting is the reverse of the removal procedure, but the following points should be noted:
6   Fit a new split-pin to the clevis pin and remember to separate the ends of the split-pin to prevent it from falling out.
7   Bleed the clutch hydraulic system as detailed in Section 8.

4   Master cylinder – overhaul

1   Remove the master cylinder as described in the previous Section.

2   Unscrew the reservoir cap and drain out the fluid.
3   Refer to Fig. 5.1 and slide the rubber boot off the master cylinder and ease it over the pushrod end yoke.
4   From the pushrod end of the master cylinder extract the circlip that retains the pushrod.
5   Withdraw the pushrod dished washer.
6   Invert the master cylinder and bump the pushrod end into the palm of your hand to dislodge the piston assembly or alternatively, apply air supplied from a tyre foot pump to the outlet port.
7   Withdraw the piston, spring and seal assembly from the master cylinder bore.
8   Prise up the locking prong that retains the spring and separate it from the piston.
9   Remove the piston seal and discard it.
10 Compress the spring so that the valve stem is in-line with the larger hole in the spring retainer. Remove the spring and retainer.
11 Remove the valve spacer and spring washer from the valve stem.
12 Remove the valve seal and discard it.
13 Examine all the components for scores or 'bright' wear areas and if evident, renew the complete master cylinder. Wash all components in methylated spirit or clean hydraulic fluid.
14 If the master cylinder is serviceable, obtain a repair kit which includes new seals and other components.
15 *Reassembly:* Use Castrol Girling rubber grease to coat the new seals. The remaining parts should be smeared with Castrol Girling Brake and Clutch fluid.
16 The new valve seal should be fitted (flat side on first) to the end of the valve stem.
17 The spring washer fits over the small end of the stem, domed side first.
18 Now fit the spacer, again over the small end, legs first.
19 Place the spring in position on the valve stem and insert the retainer into the spring. Compress the spring that holds the retainer and engage the valve stem into the keyhole slot in the retainer.
20 Fit the new piston seal to the piston, making sure that the larger diameter goes on last.
21 Bring the piston and the spring retainer together fitting the piston into the retainer until the locking prong engages.

Fig. 5.1 Sectioned and exploded view of the clutch master cylinder (Sec 4)

1   Pushrod
2   Rubber boot
3   Circlip
4   Dished washer
5   Piston
6   Piston seal
7   Thimble
8   Spring
9   Valve seal spacer
10 Seal
11 Valve stem
12 Dished washer

22 Apply Castrol Girling rubber grease to the piston and seal, and insert the whole assembly, valve end first, into the cylinder.
23 Refit the pushrod and secure with its retaining washer and circlip.
24 Having rechecked that all the operations have been correctly carried out and there are no components left on the workbench, the unit can now be refitted to the car.

5 Slave cylinder – removal and refitting

1 Tape over the vent hole in the master cylinder reservoir cap. This measure prevents the fluid syphoning out when the slave cylinder is removed.
2 Raise the car and support it securely.
3 Clean the external surface of the slave cylinder, especially in the region of the fluid pipe and union nut.
4 Undo the union nut, pull aside the fluid pipe and plug the end.
5 Remove the two bolts and spring washers that secure the slave cylinder to the bellhousing (photo).
6 Withdraw the slave cylinder gently, avoid jerking it in a forward direction as the pushrod can easily dislodge the release arm. If the release arm is dislodged then it will be necessary to remove the gearbox in order to refit it.
7 Refitting of the slave cylinder is the reverse of removal, but make sure that the bleed nipple is located above the fluid pipe union nut as it is possible to fit the slave cylinder in an upside-down position.
8 After refitting it will be necessary to bleed the clutch hydraulic system as described in Section 8.

6 Slave cylinder – overhaul

1 Remove the slave cylinder as detailed in Section 5.
2 Clean the exterior of the unit, prior to dismantling, using clean brake fluid or methylated spirit.
3 Obtain the necessary servicing kit of spares which will include the required seal and dust cover. In the case of a high mileage car, the piston return spring should also be renewed.
4 Dismantle the unit by first removing the dust cover after which the piston can usually be dislodged by bumping the open end down onto the palm of your hand. Alternatively, apply compressed air generated by a tyre foot pump to the fluid inlet port (Fig. 5.2).
5 Extract the piston assembly followed by the conical spring.
6 Unscrew the bleed nipple and clean all the components in clean hydraulic fluid or methylated spirit.
7 Discard the rubber piston seal and the dust cover.
8 Examine the piston surface and cylinder bore for scoring or 'bright' wear areas. If these are evident, renew the complete slave cylinder.
9 Treat the new piston seal with a smear of Castrol Girling rubber grease, and to the remainder of the internal parts apply a film of clean hydraulic fluid.
10 Fit the seal (smaller diameter first) to the piston.
11 Locate the spring, again with the smaller diameter towards the piston.
12 Apply a smear of Castrol Girling rubber grease to the piston assembly and insert (spring first) into the slave cylinder body.
13 Smear the inside of the new rubber boot with Castrol Girling rubber grease and fit it over the end of the slave cylinder.
14 Screw in the bleed nipple and fit the slave cylinder as described in Section 5.

7 Clutch pedal assembly – removal and refitting

This procedure is covered in Chapter 9, Section 13.

8 Bleeding the hydraulic system

Whenever the clutch hydraulic system has been overhauled, a part is renewed, or the level in the reservoir is too low, air will have entered the system necessitating its bleeding. During this operation the level of hydraulic fluid in the reservoir should not be allowed to fall below half full, otherwise air will be drawn in again.
1 Obtain a clean, dry, glass jar, a length of plastic or rubber tubing which will fit the bleed nipple of the clutch slave cylinder and which is

5.5 The clutch slave cylinder

Fig. 5.2 Slave cylinder components (Sec 6)

1 Bleed nipple 4 Piston seal
2 Cylinder body 5 Piston
3 Spring 6 Boot

about 12 in (300 mm) long, a supply of the correct type of fluid and the services of an assistant.
2 Check that the master cylinder reservoir is full and, if not, fill it to within $\frac{1}{4}$ in (6·5 mm) of the top. Also add about one inch of fluid to the jar.
3 Remove the rubber dust cap from the slave cylinder bleed nipple, wipe the nipple clean then attach the bleed tube.
4 With the other end of the tube immersed in the fluid in the jar (which can be supported on the subframe if required), and the assistant ready inside the car, unscrew the bleed nipple one full turn.
5 The assistant should now pump the clutch pedal up and down until the air bubbles cease to emerge from the end of the tubing. Check the reservoir frequently to ensure that the hydraulic fluid does not drop too far, so letting air into the system.
6 When no more air bubbles appear, tighten the bleed nipple at the bottom of a downstroke.
7 Fit the rubber dust cap over the bleed nipple.
Note: *Never re-use the fluid bled from the hydraulic system but discard it or retain for bleed jar purposes only.*

9 Clutch – removal, inspection and refitting

1 Remove the gearbox as described in Chapter 6.
2 The clutch cover is secured to the flywheel by a peripheral ring of bolts. Mark the position of the clutch cover in relation to the flywheel.
3 Unscrew the securing bolts evenly, a turn at a time in diametrically

Fig. 5.3 Major clutch components (Sec 9)

A Clutch cover and bolt   C Recessed bolts (not to be
B Driven plate   unscrewed)

9.3 Undoing the clutch cover bolts

9.11 Driven plate fitted and centralised

opposite sequence, to avoid distortion. The three bolts located in the deep recesses of the cover should not be disturbed (photo).

4   When the bolts are finally removed, withdraw the pressure plate assembly from the flywheel and catch the driven plate as it is released from the face of the flywheel.

5   The pressure plate assembly should not be dismantled but if worn, cracked or distorted, it should be renewed on an exchange basis.

6   Examine the driven plate for wear. If the linings are worn almost down to the rivets then a factory reconditioned unit should be obtained on an exchange basis. Do not waste your time trying to reline the plate, it seldom proves satisfactory.

7   If there is evidence of oil staining, find the cause which will probably be a faulty gearbox input shaft oil seal or a crankshaft rear oil seal.

8   Check the machine surfaces of the flywheel and pressure plate; if grooved or scored, then the flywheel should be machined (within the specified limits – see Chapter 1), and the pressure plate assembly renewed.

9   Check the release bearing for smooth operation. There should be no harshness or slackness in it and it should spin reasonably freely bearing in mind that it is grease sealed. (Refer to next Section).

10   It is important that no oil or grease gets on the clutch plate friction linings or the pressure plate and flywheel faces. It is advisable to refit the clutch with clean hands and to wipe down the pressure plate and flywheel faces with a clean rag before assembly begins.

11   Place the clutch plate against the flywheel, ensuring that it is the correct way round. The flywheel side of the driven plate has the shorter hub boss. If the plate is fitted the wrong way round, it will be quite impossible to operate the clutch (photo).

12   Fit the clutch cover assembly loosely on the dowels. Refit the six bolts and spring washers and tighten them finger tight so that the clutch plate is gripped but can still be moved. The clutch disc must now be centralised so that when the engine and gearbox are mated, the gearbox first motion shaft splines will pass through the splines in the centre of the driven plate.

13   Centralisation can be carried out quite easily by inserting a round bar or long screwdriver through the hole in the centre of the clutch, so that the end of the bar rests in the small hole in the end of the crankshaft containing the spigot bush. Ideally an old first motion shaft should be used.

14   Using the first motion shaft spigot bush as a fulcrum, moving the bar sideways or up and down will move the clutch disc in whichever direction is necessary to achieve centralisation.

15   Centralisation is easily judged by removing the bar and viewing the driven plate hub in relation to the hole in the centre of the clutch cover plate diaphragm spring. When the hub appears exactly in the centre of the hole, all is correct. Alternatively, the first motion shaft will fit the bush and centre of the clutch hub exactly, obviating the need for visual alignment.

16   Tighten the clutch bolts firmly in a diagonal sequence to ensure that the cover plate is pulled down evenly and without distortion of the flange. Finally tighten the bolts down to the recommended torque setting.

10 Clutch withdrawal mechanism – removal, inspection, overhaul and refitting

1   Remove the gearbox as described in Chapter 6.

2   Using the service tool ST 1136 or a suitably cranked spanner, unscrew the release arm pivot post. This will then enable you to withdraw the release bearing. However, it has been found that the release lever can be removed without undoing the pivot post. If you pull the lever away from the release bearing, at the same time unhooking the spring legs behind the lever from the pivot ball, you can then pull the lever and pushrod out of the casing.

3   Slide the release bearing off the input shaft.

4   If the whole assembly was removed together, then slide the release bearing away from the release lever slipper pads (photo).

5   Clean all the components, excluding the release bearing, in either paraffin or a suitable cleaning solution.

6   Examine the various components for wear and renew as found necessary.

7   The release bearing is sealed for life and as such cannot be cleaned or repacked with grease. (Fig. 5.5).

8   Spin the bearing by hand whilst holding the sleeve. If the bearing

Fig. 5.4 Clutch release lever and bearing (Sec 10)

1 Release lever
2 Release bearing assembly
3 Slipper pads
4 Pivot post
5 Pushrod
6 Pushrod retainer

Fig. 5.5 Sectional view of the release bearing and sleeve (Sec 10)

10.4 The release bearing in position

10.10 Release arm, bearing and pushrod ready for refitting

10.13 Release arm and bearing correctly located in the bellhousing

is unserviceable it can be pressed or driven off the sleeve and a new one fitted. When pressing on the new bearing, the pressure must only be applied to the inner race. Ensure the release face is outermost.

9   Before reassembly, apply a light smear of general purpose grease to the slipper pads, the ball part of the pivot post and the inner bore of the release bearing sleeve.

10 Fit the release arm assembly by following the reverse of the removal procedure. If the pivot post was not removed, then reassembly is basically the same although a little more difficult (photo). Position the release bearing on the input shaft.

11 Hook the spring legs on the rear of the release lever, partly over the pivot head.

12 Line up the slipper pads on the release lever with the channels in the release bearing sleeve.

13 Push the lever inwards and at the same time towards the release bearing. This will cause the slipper pads to locate in the channels in the sleeve and the spring to slide over the pivot head and secure itself (photo).

11.1 Clutch hydraulic damper

11 Clutch hydraulic damper – description

1   Some models may be found equipped with a clutch hydraulic damper (photo). The function of this damper is to limit the rate at which pressure in the slave cylinder is reduced if the clutch pedal is suddenly released. Snatch and judder are thereby avoided.

2   No repair is possible to the damper. If it leaks or is suspected of malfunction it must be renewed.

3   It may be found that the damper presents problems when bleeding the hydraulic system. The use of a proprietary pressure bleeding kit should reduce such problems to a minimum.

12 Fault diagnosis – clutch

Symptom	Reason/s
Judder when taking up drive	Loose engine mountings Worn or oil contaminated driven plate friction linings Worn splines or driven plate hubs or first input shaft Worn crankshaft spigot bush (pilot bearing)
Clutch slip	Damaged or distorted pressure plate assembly Driven plate linings worn or oil contaminated
Noise on depressing clutch pedal	Dry, worn or damaged clutch release bearing Excessive play in input shaft splines
Noise as clutch pedal is released	Distorted driven plate Broken or weak driven plate hub cushion coil springs Distorted or worn input shaft Release bearing loose
Difficulty in disengaging clutch for gearchange	Fault in master cylinder or slave cylinder Air in hydraulic system Driven plate hub splines rusted on shaft

Chapter 6
Manual gearbox and automatic transmission

For modifications, and information applicable to later models, see Supplement at end of manual

Contents

Specifications

Manual gearbox

Type

Rover 2600	5-speed, synchromesh on all forward gears
Rover 2300:	
Standard	4-speed, synchromesh on all forward gears
Optional	5-speed, synchromesh on all forward gears

Gearbox ratios

5th	0.833:1
4th	1.000:1
3rd	1.396:1
2nd	2.087:1
1st	3.321:1
Reverse	3.428:1

Gearbox lubricant

Type/specification:*	
Early models	Hypoid gear oil, viscosity SAE 75W (Duckhams Hypoid 75)
Late models	ATF to specification M2C 33G (Duckhams Q-Matic)
Capacity:	
4 and 5-speed	2.8 pints (1.6 litres)

The later fluid type can be used in early gearboxes, but only following a total drain and refill with the later type. Be sure not to mix the early and late types of fluid

Torque wrench settings

	lbf ft	Nm
Bellhousing to sump bracing bolts	37	50
Bellhousing to engine bracing bolts	37	50
Bellhousing to gearbox casing bolts	59	80
Bellhousing to cylinder block bolts	21	28
Flywheel cover plate to bellhousing bolts	15	20
Driving flange to mainshaft locknut	150	200
Rear cover, centreplate and front cover bolts	21	28
Mounting bracket bolts	21	28
Magnetic drain plug	26	35
Propeller shaft to gearbox nuts	37	50
Remote control assembly to rear cover bolts	15	20

Automatic transmission

Type .... Borg Warner model 65

Transmission conversion range
3rd .... 1.00 to 1.98
2nd .... 1.45 to 2.87
1st .... 2.39 to 5.80
Reverse .... 2.09 to 4.14

Final drive ratios
2300 model 3.45:1
2600 model 3.08:1

Shift speeds *

Throttle position	Selection	Shift	Speed mph (km/h) 2300	2600
Closed	1	2 to 1	19 to 34 (31 to 55)	21 to 38 (34 to 61)
Light throttle	2	1 to 2	7 to 24 (11 to 39)	8 to 27 (18 to 43)
Light throttle	D	2 to 3	9 to 27 (15 to 43)	10 to 30 (16 to 48)
Part throttle	D	3 to 2	47 (76) max	53 (85) max
Kickdown	D	1 to 2	37 to 39 (60 to 79)	42 to 55 (68 to 89)
	D	2 to 3	64 to 73 (103 to 118)	72 to 82 (116 to 132)
	D	3 to 2	58 to 70 (93 to 113)	65 to 78 (105 to 126)
	D	3 to 1	26 to 41 (49 to 66)	29 to 46 (47 to 74)
	2	1 to 2	37 to 49 (60 to 79)	42 to 55 (68 to 89)
	2	2 to 1	26 to 41 (42 to 66)	29 to 46 (47 to 74)

All shift speeds given are applicable to models fitted with 175 HR 14 tyres

Automatic transmission lubricant
Type/specification .... ATF to specification M2C 33G (Duckhams Q-Matic)
Capacity (with oil cooler) .... 9.3 pints (5.3 litres)

Torque wrench settings

	lbf ft	Nm
Torque converter housing to gearcase bolts:		
10 mm	20	27
12 mm	40	54
Oil pan bolts	7	10
Inhibitor switch bolt	24	33
Driveplate to torque converter bolts	30	41
Torque converter housing to engine bolts	25	34
Rear extension housing bolts	50	68
Output flange bolt (use thread locking compound)	40	54

PART A : MANUAL TRANSMISSION

1   General description

This gearbox was designed specifically for the Rover 3500 (SD1) and was fitted to the Triumph TR7 as an option. Because of its modular construction it is very easy to make it either a 4 or 5 speed box. The 5th speed gearing is located in the rear casing, which in the 4-speed box is left empty. Therefore the 2600 and 2300 models share what is basically a common gearbox. The 2300 model can of course be fitted with the 5-speed box as an optional extra. The most unusual feature of this gearbox is the use of taper roller bearings for the mainshaft/input shaft and layshaft, which provide for a less bulky gearbox using standard bearings, and also simplifies assembly.

The gearbox is built up on a centre plate, a rigid iron casting between the tailpiece and the main housing. Since taper rollers come apart easily, the shafts and gears can be simply placed in position and jiggled around until the gears mesh; all that is needed is for the shaft and play to be adjusted, which is a relatively straightforward operation.

A single shaft selector mechanism is used for the gear selection. Gears 1 to 4 are arranged in the usual H-pattern, but reverse and 5th (where fitted) are left-forward and right-forward respectively. The single shaft has two operating dowels, the rear one engaging reverse and the front one engaging the forward gears, via bosses on the selector forks. An interlock arrangement prevents engagement of more than one gear at the same time.

The selector mechanisms are mounted on the centre plate. A simple externally mounted hairpin-type spring gives the gear lever a natural bias to the $\frac{3}{4}$ plane. This bias has to be overcome in progressive steps to obtain the $\frac{1}{2}$ plane, 5th gear and reverse gear in order, the latter having a separate biassing arrangement.

With the exception of 5th, which overhangs the centre plate to the rear, the gear layout and mode of operation is conventional.

2 Gearbox – removal and refitting

Note: *As described here, the gearbox can be removed separately from the engine. However, the complete assembly of engine and gearbox can be removed together when required (see Chapter 1).*

1   Detach the battery negative lead.
2   With neutral selected, unscrew and remove the gear lever knob and pull out the gear lever shroud and top panel assembly.
3   Withdraw the sponge rubber insert, followed by the draught excluder and flange assembly.
4   Remove the countersunk screw and slacken off the bolt that holds the bias spring rear clamp. Swing the clamp to one side and remove the insert.
5   The spring legs can now be carefully prised clear of the gear lever pins and pushed down to rest on the bolts beneath (photo).
Warning: *It is possible to force the spring legs over the gear lever pins without undoing the clamp first, but if you do this you will seriously risk damaging the bias action of the spring.*
6   Remove the bolt and washer that hold the gear lever ball cap (photo).
7   Carefully lift out the gear lever, ensuring that the anti-rattle spring and nylon plunger are not lost (photo).
8   Raise the car and support it on blocks beneath the bodyframe side-members for access to the gearbox area.
9   Disconnect the front exhaust pipes from the manifold flange.

Fig. 6.1 Sectional view of 4-speed gearbox (Sec 1)

1 Selector shaft	3 Input shaft	5 Layshaft	7 Main driving flange
2 Remote control shaft	4 Mainshaft	6 Oil pump driveshaft	8 Gearbox

Fig. 6.2 Sectional view of rear section of 5-speed gearbox showing 5th gear mechanism (Sec 1)

1 Bias spring right leg
2 Countersunk screw
3 Retaining bolt holding spring clamp rear
4 Gearlever ball cap

Fig. 6.3 Remote control assembly showing bias spring arrangement (Sec 2)

2.5 Prising the bias spring legs clear of the gear lever pins

2.6 Remove the gear lever ball cap retaining bolt (arrowed)

2.7 Carefully lift out the gear lever

2.12 Disconnect the speedometer cable by undoing the single bolt (arrowed)

2.13 Reverse lamp switch and cable clip

10 Undo the front exhaust securing bracket attached to the bracket on the rear of the gearbox and push the exhaust system to one side.

11 Scribe the front propshaft to driveflange location and remove the four locknuts and bolts that secure it. Push the propshaft to one side.

12 Disconnect the speedometer cable from the gearbox by undoing the single bolt and lifting away the U-shaped clamp plate. Pull away the speedometer cable and tie it back out of the way (photo).

13 Pull off the electrical leads of the reverse light switch and disconnect the cable from the retainer clip fitted to the upper face of the gearbox casing (photo).

14 Undo the two bolts that secure the clutch slave cylinder and carefully withdraw it. Tie the slave cylinder to one side, taking care not to strain the flexible hydraulic hose.

15 Remove the two bolts and washers from the sump stiffening plate.

16 Remove the 3 bolts, nuts and washers that secure the flywheel cover-plate to the bellhousing.

17 Remove the lower bolt and nut that secure the starter motor and take off the earth strap, then remove the upper retaining bolt and nut. Remove the starter from its housing and place it safely out of the way.

18 Undo the nut and bolt that secure the engine diagnostic unit to the clutch housing, also undo the screw that holds the transducer in place in the bellhousing. Remove the complete assembly.

19 Place a jack underneath the sump with a wooden protective block inserted between the two. Raise the jack to just take the weight of the engine.

20 Remove the special retaining bolt on the rear of the camshaft cover, otherwise it will foul the bulkhead when the assembly is lowered to undo the upper bellhousing bolts (see Chapter 1, Section 4).

21 Remove the 4 bolts, spring washers and the 2 plates that secure the rear mounting plate (crossmember) to the body.

22 Carefully lower the jack under the sump so that you can gain access to the bolts that secure the bellhousing.

23 Now remove the dowel bolt and locknut and the other bolts and nuts that secure the bellhousing noting their length and positions. To remove the dowel bolt, undo the locknut on the engine side of the casing and tap it out.

24 Before removing the last two bolts, place a jack, preferably a trolley one, under the gearbox to support it. This will ensure that you

can remove the gearbox rearwards easily and not strain the input shaft. Make sure that the water rail is not fouled.

25 With the aid of an assistant, remove the gearbox. Note that the gearbox weighs around 110 lb (50 kg).

26 Refitting the gearbox is basically the reverse of the removal procedure. Refer to Chapter 1, Section 6, paragraphs 1 to 7, for further details.

27 It is recommended that, when reconnecting the propeller shaft to the gearbox, new locknuts are fitted.

28 Refitting the gear lever anti-rattle spring and plunger is rather awkward. The method is to fit the gear lever, minus spring and plunger, and select 2nd or 4th gear. Withdraw the gear lever and refit it together with the spring and plunger. A large screwdriver can be used to slightly compress the plunger and spring to assist the entry of the assembly.

29 Check if the gearbox has been drained of lubricant then refill it after refitting.

3 Manual gearbox – dismantling (4 and 5-speed)

1 Before commencing to dismantle the gearbox, clean the exterior with a water-soluble solvent. This will make the gearbox easier to handle, and possibly prevent dirt from contaminating the internal parts. Drain the gearbox oil, then refit the magnetic plug (photo).

2 Remove the clutch release bearing and lever arm as described in Chapter 5.

3 Remove the bolts and washers, and withdraw the bellhousing. Note that the bottom-right and top-left bolts are longer and have locating dowels.

4 Make up a suitable bracket which can be bolted to the mainshaft flange and which will wedge against the remote control extension, then unscrew the flange nut and washer (photo).

5 Pull off the mainshaft driveflange.

6 Remove the nut and pin which are used to connect the remote control shaft to the selector shaft (photo).

7 Remove the four bolts, spring washers and plain washers that

3.1 The gearbox drain plug

3.4 Remove the output flange nut

3.6 Selector shaft nut (arrowed)

3.8 Removing the speedometer driven gear

3.9 Removing the rear (5th gear) spool locating boss

3.10 Withdrawing the rear cover

3.12 Removing the 5th gear selector fork and bracket

3.13 Removing the selector shaft circlip

secure the remote control housing to the gearbox rear cover. Note the positions of the plastic bushes and tubular spacers when the housing is removed.

8 Remove the speedometer driven gear and housing (photo).

9 Remove the two bolts and spring washers and withdraw the locating boss for the 5th gear (rear) selector spool (5-speed gearboxes only) (photo).

10 Remove the ten bolts, spring washers and flat washers and withdraw the rear cover and gasket. Note the positions of the tubular dowels (photo).

11 Remove the oil pump driveshaft from the end of the layshaft or oil pump so that the shaft is not lost. Note: *Paragraphs 12 to 15 concern the removal of the 5th gear only. Procedure for the 4-speed boxes continues from paragraph 16 onwards.*

12 Remove the two bolts and spring washers, and take off the 5th gear selector fork and bracket (photo).

13 Remove the circlip from the selector shaft and withdraw the 5th gear selector spool. Note that the longer cam is pointing downwards (photo).

14 Remove the circlip and withdraw the 5th gear synchro assembly, 5th gear and spacer from the mainshaft (Fig. 6.4).

15 Remove the circlip that retains the layshaft 5th gear, then use a 2 or 3-legged puller to remove the gear (photo). The gear is actually held in place by a retaining collar. Note that the outer face of the centre section of the layshaft 5th gear has a groove running round it. This easily identifies which way it goes back on rebuild.

16 In 4-speed boxes, since there is no actual gearing mechanism in the rear section of the box, the space on the selector shaft which normally carries the 5th gear selector spool is taken up with a spacer tube held in position by a circlip. Remove the spacer tube and circlip.

17 Withdraw the spring-clip from the mainshaft.

18 Remove the six bolts and spring washers, then remove the gearbox front cover and gasket.

19 Remove the selective washers and bearing tracks from the input shaft and layshaft (photo).

20 Remove the two bolts and spring washers, and withdraw the locating boss for the front selector spool.

21 Remove the selctor plug, spring and ball from the drilling in the

Fig. 6.4 5th gear synchro and associated parts (Sec 3)

3.15 Removing the layshaft 5th gear

Fig. 6.5 Gearbox front cover, spacers and bearing tracks (Sec 3)

3.19 Removing the selective washers from the front cover

3.21 Selector plug, spring and ball

3.26 Reverse selector lever pivot pin (arrowed)

3.31 The layshaft showing the bearings

3.32 Removing the oil pump cover and pick-up pipe

3.33 The oil pump gears

centre plate (photo).
22 Support the gearbox on the centre plate and pull off the main casing.
23 Remove the synchro cone and the input shaft.
24 Withdraw the layshaft gear cluster from the centre plate.
25 Using a vice with protective jaw covers, support the centre plate.
26 Remove the retaining circlip and take out the reverse lever pivot pin. The reverse lever and slipper pad can now be taken out (photo).
27 Slide the reverse shaft rearwards so that the reverse gear spacer, mainshaft, selector shaft, selector shaft fork and spool can be drawn forwards and away from the centre plate.
28 Withdraw the selector fork and spool. Note that the shorter cam is pointing towards the bottom of the gearbox.
29 Remove the nut and spring washers, if necessary, and remove the reverse gear pivot shaft.
30 If subsequent inspection shows the input shaft bearing to be defective, the outer race can be driven out of the casing using a soft drift. The inner race and bearing can then be pulled or levered off.
31 If the subsequent inspection shows the layshaft bearings to be faulty, the outer races can be driven out of the casing and centre plate. Then the inner race and bearings can be pulled or levered off (photo).
32 Remove the bolts and spring washers and take off the oil pump cover and intake pipe (photo).
33 Remove the oil pump gears (photo).
34 Remove the rear cover oil seal, bearing, speedometer, gear, circlip and sleeve, and oil sleeve.
35 If subsequent inspection shows the mainshaft bearing to be defective, the outer race can be driven out of the centre plate. Removal of the inner race and bearing is dealt with in Section 5.

4 Manual gearbox – examination

1 The gearbox has been stripped probably, because of wear or malfunction, possibly excessive noise, ineffective synchromesh or failure to stay in a selected gear. The cause of most gearbox ailments is the failure of the taper bearings on the input or mainshaft and wear on the synchro-rings, both the cup surfaces and the dogs. The nose of the mainshaft, which runs in the needle roller bearing in the input shaft, is also subject to wear. This can prove very expensive as the mainshaft would need to be renewed and this could represent about 20% of the total cost of a replacement gearbox.
2 Examine the teeth of all gears for signs of uneven or excessive wear and, of course, chipping. If a gear on the mainshaft requires renewal, check that the corresponding lay gear is not equally damaged. If it is, the whole lay gear may need renewing also.
3 All gears should be a good running fit on the shaft with no signs of rocking. The hubs should not be a sloppy fit on the splines.
4 Selector forks should be examined for signs of wear or ridging on the faces which are in contact with the operating sleeve.
5 Check for wear on the selector rod and interlock spools.
6 The taper bearings may not be obviously worn, but if one has gone to the trouble of dismantling the gearbox it would be advantageous to renew them. The same applies to the synchronizer rings, although for these, the mainshaft has to be completely dismantled for the new ones to be fitted.

7 Examine for wear the bush in the reverse idler gear. If any is found, press out the old bush and then press in a new one, so that it is flush with the boss opposite the collar of the operating lever. It may be found necessary to ream the bush after fitting.
8 Examine the oil pump gears for wear and damaged teeth, renewing parts as necessary.
9 Examine the oil pump driveshaft; if worn or damaged then renew it.
10 It is recommended that new oil seals are fitted. These should be fitted with the lip towards the gearbox.
11 Before finally deciding to dismantle the mainshaft and renew parts, it is advisable to make enquiries regarding the availability of parts and their cost. It may still be worth considering an exchange gearbox even at this stage. Your old gearbox will have to be reassembled for exchange.

5 Manual gearbox mainshaft – dismantling and reassembly

1 From the front end of the mainshaft, remove the pilot bearing and spacer.
2 Remove the mainshaft bearing circlip, then use a lead hammer or similar item to drive the mainshaft out of the 1st gear. In this way the gear, bush and bearing can be removed together (photo).
3 From the front end of the mainshaft, pull off the 3rd gear and the 3rd/4th synchronizer hub and sleeve (photo).
4 Now take off the 1st/2nd gear hub, sleeve, synchro cones and 2nd gear (this assembly incorporates the reverse gear).
5 Clean all parts in petrol or paraffin, and dry them in a lint-free cloth.
6 On the assembled synchro assemblies, check that a load of 18 to 22 lbf (8·2 to 10 kgf) is required to push the synchro hub through the

5.2 Driving 1st gear off the mainshaft

Fig. 6.6 Exploded view of the mainshaft gears (Sec 5)

a 3rd/4th synchro hub and sleeve, and 3rd gear   b 1st/2nd gear assembly, including reverse gear   c 5th gear assembly

5.3 Pulling 3rd gear off the mainshaft

Fig. 6.7 Spacer dimensions for checking 1st gear bush endfloat (Sec 5)

14 Using an old circlip and the feeler gauges, check the endfloat. This should be 0·0002 to 0·002 in (0·005 to 0·055 mm).

15 If necessary, select a new rear spacer to provide this clearance.

16 Remove the circlip, spacer and 5th gear assembly from the mainshaft.

17 Ensure that the 1st/2nd synchro is assembled with the short splines on the inner member towards 2nd gear.

18 Fit the 3rd gear, baulk ring, and the synchro sleeve and hub, so that the longer boss of the hub is towards the front of the gearbox. Also fit the bearing (photos).

19 Fit the 2nd gear, baulk ring, synchro hub and sleeve (selector fork annulus towards the rear of the gearbox), baulk ring, 1st gear and selective bush, bearing and a new circlip. **Note:** *During fitment, the circlip internal diameter must not be opened out beyond 1.272 in (32.3 mm)* (photos).

6   Manual gearbox – reassembly

1   Commence reassembly by fitting new bearings if the old ones were removed. Also fit new bearing tracks to the centre plate and front cover if necessary.

2   It has been found through practical experience that it is easier to rebuild the gearbox in a vertical plane in the early stages. Take two

outer sleeve in either direction.

7   Manufacture a spacer to the dimensions shown in Fig. 6.7, so that the 1st gear bush endfloat can be checked as described in paragraphs 8 to 11 below.

8   Fit 2nd gear, 1st/2nd synchro hub and 1st gear to the mainshaft; then fit the spacer.

9   Using an old circlip and a set of feeler gauges, check the clearance between the spacer and circlip. This should be 0·0002 to 0·002 in (0·005 to 0·055 mm).

10   If necessary, select a new bush with a collar thickness which will give this dimension.

11   Remove the circlip, spacer, bush, synchro hub, and 2nd gear from the mainshaft.

12   Check the 5th gear endfloat as described in paragraphs 13 to 16 below.

13   Fit the 5th gear assembly to the mainshaft (this comprises the front spacer, 5th gear, synchro hub, rear plate and spacer).

5.18a Fitting the baulk ring ...

5.18b ...the 3rd/4th synchro sleeve and hub ...

5.18c ...and the input shaft/mainshaft pilot bearing

5.19a Fitting 2nd gear and baulk ring ...

5.19b ...1st/2nd synchro hub and sleeve (including reverse gear) and baulk ring ...

5.19c ...1st gear and selective bush ...

5.19d ...followed by the bearing ...

5.19e ...and new circlip to the mainshaft

similar sized boxes or blocks, stand them slightly less than the width of the centre plate apart and lay the centre plate flat on top. Ensure there is sufficient room beneath the centre plate for the mainshaft to hang down without touching the bench.

3 Fit the rebuilt mainshaft and selector shaft together to the centre plate, having slotted the selector forks into their respective synchro sleeves first (photo).

4 Ensure the selector spool is set up correctly with the shorter cam facing down.

5 Fit the circlip to the lower side of the centre plate to retain the mainshaft.

6 Refit the layshaft, engage the gears and line-up with the mainshaft (photo).

7 Refit the selector shaft ball, spring and plug to the centre plate drilling.

8 If removed, refit the reverse gear shaft.

9 Fit the gear with the slipper pad lip to the front.

10 Refit the reverse lever, slipper pad, pivot pin and circlip (photo).

11 Position the centre plate front gasket, having greased it on both sides.

12 Place the input shaft in position on the top of the mainshaft (photo) and then gently lower the main gearcase into position. Do not force it and ensure the dowels are in position first. Also ensure that the internal bearing tracks are in good condition or have been changed before refitting the main gearcase. Secure the casing to the centre plate using the 4 slave washers and bolts.

13 Fit the bearing tracks to the input and layshafts (photo).

14 Fit the spacers to the front cover and use a smear of grease to hold them in position. Use a layshaft spacer of 0.040 in (1.02 mm).

15 Fit a new gasket to the front (top) of the main gearcase; grease it on both sides first.

16 Carefully slide down the front cover into position and tighten the bolts (photo).

17 Check the layshaft endfloat using a dial gauge.

18 The layshaft preload required is 0.001 to 0.002 in (0.025 to 0.051 mm). Add the temporary spacer thickness, the measured endfloat and

H.5931

Fig. 6.8 Drive flange and associated parts (Sec 6)

6.3 Fit the selector and mainshaft together to the centre plate

6.6 Refit the layshaft

6.10 Reverse gear mechanism refitted

6.12 Place the input shaft on the front (top) end of the mainshaft

6.13 Fit bearing tracks and spacer to layshaft

6.16 Slide the front cover into position

the preload figure together to obtain the required spacer thickness.

19 Remove the front cover and insert the correct size spacer for the layshaft.

20 Refit the front cover using the selected spacer and recheck the specified endfloat.

21 Place a small steel ball on the machined centre of the end of the input shaft so that the stylus of a dial gauge can be rested on it.

22 Check and record the combined endfloat of the input shaft and mainshaft. If it is found that side movement of the input shaft prevents an accurate reading from being obtained, it is permissible to remove the front cover and wrap about 6 turns of masking tape around the input shaft below the splines; this will stop any side movement.

23 Having determined the endfloat, select a spacer for the front cover which will give a final endfloat of 0.0002 to 0.002 in (0.005 to 0.055 mm).

24 Remove the front cover (and tape, if used). If the front cover oil seal has not yet been renewed, this should be done first. Fit it with the lips facing the gearbox, then lubricate the lips with gearbox oil.

25 Carefully fit the front cover so that the seal lips are not marked by the shaft splines. Tighten the 6 bolts to the correct torque.

26 Remove the slave bolts from the centre plate.

27 Place the gearbox in a horizontal plane.

28 Refit the nut and washer on the reverse gear pivot shaft.

29 In 4-speed boxes, it is now necessary to refit the spacer tube on the selector shaft and secure it with the circlip.

30 With 5-speed boxes, it is now necessary to rebuild the 5th gear assembly. Start by refitting the layshaft 5th gear with its retaining collar and circlip. Continue to paragraph 36.

31 Then refit the spacer, 5th gear, baulk ring, synchro-hub and sleeve, spacer and circlip to the mainshaft, in that order.

32 Refit the selector fork and bracket and secure with the 2 bolts and washers (photo).

6.32 Refitting the selector fork and bracket

6.33 Refit the 5th gear selector spool

6.40 Refitting the speedometer driving gear

6.42 Refit the spacer, bearing and seal to the rear end of the mainshaft

33 Refit the 5th gear selector spool, ensuring it is fitted the correct way, and push home the circlip (photo).
34 Rebuild the oil pump in the rear casing and fit the driveshaft into the pump; ensure the oil pump gears are in good condition as they are made of tough plastic but can be damaged quite easily by swarf.
35 Place the rear cover gasket on the centre plate, having greased it first. Also grease the bushes in the end of the rear cover.
36 Offer up the rear cover to the centre plate. Feed the mainshaft and selector shaft through the bushes in the rear of the cover.
37 Ensure that the oil pump driveshaft is in the right attitude to engage in the end of the layshaft.
38 Push the rear cover home and secure with the bolts. Ensure different length bolts go in the correct holes. The longer bolts fit in the dowel holes.
39 Refit the rear selector spool locating boss.
40 Fit the speedometer driving gear to the mainshaft. Note that the face with the small notches in it faces to the rear (photo). The gear has to locate on the mainshaft flats. Tap the gear home using a tube.
41 Refit the speedometer driven gear.
42 Refit the spacer, bearing and seal to the rear end of the mainshaft (photo). Grease the inside of the seal before sliding it over the shaft.
43 Replacement seals have been found by experience to look very different from the original ones.
44 Grease the seal contact area on the driving flange and fit it.

45 Refit the washers and nut. Use a bracket to stop the mainshaft turning whilst it is tightened to the correct torque.
46 Refit the pin to the end of the selector shaft, nut uppermost.
47 Refit the remote control housing, ensuring the selector pin engages in the bush in the remote control shaft.
48 Secure the housing in position with the 2 bolts and washers at the forward end and the 2 bolts and bushes at the sides.
49 Insert the gearlever into the housing (minus the plunger and spring) and check the reassembly of the gearbox. Ensure that all gears engage correctly and in the right order, working relative shaft speeds to the lever positions. Turn the box on the input shaft.
50 Refit the bellhousing if it was removed to start with.
51 Refit the clutch release bearing and lever (see Chapter 5).
52 Refill the gearbox with the correct grade and quantity of oil.

7 Manual gearbox gearchange remote control assembly – dismantling and reassembly

1 With the assembly removed from the transmission as described in Section 3, remove the two bolts and countersunk head screws that secure the bias spring bridge plates.
2 Remove the bridge plates, bridge plate liners and hairpin-type bias spring.

3   Remove the bias spring adjustment bolts and locknuts.
4   Remove the two bolts and washers that secure the reverse baulk plate assembly; withdraw the reverse baulk plate, springs and spacers.
5   Remove the four bolts and washers, and take off the bottom cover plate.
6   Remove the reverse light switch and locknut, referring to Chapter 10 if necessary.
7   Remove the square-headed pinchbolt and take off the selector shaft elbow. Now withdraw the selector shaft.
8   Press out the selector shaft bushes from the casing.
9   Remove the circlips. Press out the pivot balls and bushes from the selector shaft elbows.
10 Reassembly is the reverse of the dismantling procedure. Use a thread locking compound on the square-headed pinchbolt. On completion, with the assembly attached to the gearbox, the reverse baulk plate, 1st/2nd stop gate and gear lever hairpin bias spring should each be adjusted by following the procedure given in Section 8.

8   Manual gearbox gearchange remote control assembly – adjustment of reverse baulk plate and bias spring

1   To adjust the reverse baulk plate, proceed as follows:
2   Remove the remote control assembly bottom cover plate.
3   With the gear lever vertical and neutral selected, loosen the baulk plate adjusting bolts until the plate contacts the backing plate.
4   Tighten the adjusting bolts equally until they just start to move the baulk plate away from the backing plate.
5   Using a piece of cord and a spring balance, check that the force required at the gear lever knob to overcome the resistance of the reverse baulk plate is between 30 and 35 lbf (13.6 and 15.9 kgf). Adjust if necessary by means of the baulk plate adjusting bolts.
6   When the above condition has been met, check that the clearance between the upper face of the baulk plate and the lower edge of the gear lever bush ('B' in Fig. 6.9) is at least 0.01 in (0.25 mm).
7   The 1st/2nd gate stop must now be adjusted as follows. Begin by engaging 1st gear. Check that the clearance between the side of the gear lever and the edge of the baulk plate is between 0.01 and 0.05 in (0.25 and 1.25 mm). Adjust if necessary by adding or removing shims ('C' in Fig. 6.9).
8   Repeat the check in paragraph 7, this time with 2nd gear engaged.

Fig. 6.9 Remote control assembly adjustment (Sec 8)

B Gearlever bush/baulk plate clearance
C 1st/2nd gate stop shims

Refit the bottom cover plate when adjustment is correct.
9   To adjust the gear lever bias spring, first engage 3rd gear. Position the hairpin spring bias screws so that there is a clearance of 0.02 in (0.5 mm) between the spring legs and the crosspin on each side. Do not tighten the locknuts.
10 Apply a light load to move the gear lever to the right to take up the free play, then adjust the right-hand screw downwards until the spring leg just makes contact with the crosspin.
11 Repeat paragraph 10, moving the gear lever to the left, then adjust the left-hand screw downwards to just contact the crosspin.
12 Move the gear lever to neutral, rock it across the gate and check that it comes to rest in the 3rd/4th plane.
13 Tighten the locknuts.
14 Adjust the reverse light switch as described in Chapter 10.

---

9   Fault diagnosis – manual gearbox

Symptom	Reason/s
Weak or ineffective synchromesh	Synchronising cones worn, split or damaged Synchromesh dogs worn or damaged
Jumps out of gear	Gearbox coupling dogs badly worn Selector forks or slipper pads badly worn
Excessive noise	Incorrect grade of oil in gearbox or oil level too low Bushes or bearings worn or damaged Gear teeth excessively worn or damaged

PART B : AUTOMATIC TRANSMISSION

10   General description

The Borg-Warner 65 automatic transmission is available as an optional extra for certain versions of the Rover 2300 and 2600. It is a light-weight version of the earlier Borg-Warner 35 and due to the resighting of the hydraulic control unit to within the sump, the unsightly bulge in the transmission tunnel which was associated with former versions is no longer necessary. The system comprises two main components: the first being a three element hydrokinetic torque converter coupling capable of torque multiplication at an infinitely variable ratio between 2.08 : 1 and 1: 1. The second being a torque/speed responsive hydraulic epicyclic gearbox comprising a planetary gear set providing three forward ratios and one reverse ratio. Selection of the required ratio is by means of a console-mounted lever, with the selector positions, P, R, N, D, 2, 1 marked.

It is not possible to start the engine unless the selector is in the P or N positions. This prevents inadvertent movement of the vehicle, and is controlled by an inhibitor switch mounted on the transmission unit.
The six selector positions are stepped to control the selector lever movement. The positions normally used in a particular sequence are grouped together. To prevent accidental engagement of R or P, the selector lever is spring loaded and so biassed away from the operating plane of these selector positions

Note: *It is essential that a transmission oil cooler be installed where automatic transmission is fitted.*

Owing to the complexity of the automatic transmission unit, it is not recommended that stripping the unit is attempted. Where the unit is known to be faulty, and the fault cannot be rectified by following the procedures given in the following Sections of this Chapter, the repair should be entrusted to a Rover dealer or an automatic transmission specialist.

11 Automatic transmission – removal and refitting

1   Initially drive the car onto ramps, or have available adequate jacks and axle stands to permit access to the underside of the car.
2   Select N and chock the roadwheels remaining on the ground.
3   Open the bonnet and disconnect the battery negative terminal.
4   Remove the air cleaner assembly as described in Chapter 3.
5   Disconnect the downshift.
6   Release the transmission dipstick/filler tube from its cylinder head fixing and likewise release the transmission breather pipe from the clip at the rear of the cylinder head.
7   Unscrew the union at the base of the filler pipe and drain the fluid into a container of at least 9.5 pints (5.4 litres) capacity.
8   Disconnect the exhaust system from the manifold flanges to the intermediate pipe. Remove the bolts and nuts that secure the exhaust pipes to the transmission bracket and lift away this forward section.
9   Remove the propeller shaft as described in Chapter 7.
10   Remove the selector rod by withdrawing the split-pins and clevis pins at either end. Do not alter the adjustment of this rod during the removal procedure and remember to remove the nylon bushes from the levers.
11   Remove the rear, right-hand engine sump bolt and then undo the bolts that secure the torque converter access plate in position. Lift the access plate away.
12   Through the access hole, remove the four bolts and thick washers that secure the torque converter to the engine driveplate (photo).
13   Support the transmission unit using an ordinary jack or ideally a trolley jack. A flat piece of timber placed between the jack lifting pad and the transmission sump pan will spread the load and prevent damaging the sump.
14   Remove the two bolts, spring washers and plain washers that secure the sump reinforcement plate to the torque converter bellhousing.
15   Remove the four bolts, spring washers and plates that retain the transmission rear mounting platform.
16   Lower the transmission support jack sufficiently to gain access to the torque converter bellhousing bolts and oil cooler pipe unions.
17   With the engine/transmission assembly so inclined disconnect the following units:

(a) oil cooler pipes
(b) speedometer cable
(c) starter/inhibitor reverse lamp switch leads

18   Place a support under the engine sump in a similar manner to that employed under the transmission sump.
19   Undo and remove the bolts and spring washers that secure the transmission unit to the engine. Note the positions of any wiring harness clips.
20   Draw the transmission unit away from the engine but do not lower

it until the torque converter is clear of the crankshaft spigot. Some fluid is certain to flow out during this operation so conveniently placed newspapers or rags will be useful.
21   When refitting the automatic transmission unit, first align the slots in the pump driving gear with the driving fingers of the converter hub.
22   Whilst employing an assistant to turn the crankshaft pulley as necessary, raise the transmission unit and insert the input shaft into the torque converter. As the input shaft splines align, the unit can be pushed fully home.
23   The remainder of the refitting procedure is the reverse of that used during removal.
24   On completion, top up the transmission to the *Cold-High* mark on the transmission dipstick.
25   After warming up the engine, recheck the fluid level as described in Section 25.

12 Downshift cable – checking and adjustment

Note: *The downshift cable has been preset at the Rover factory during manufacture and should not normally require adjustment. However, if the carburettors have been adjusted or a previous owner has interfered with the cable adjustment, the following checks can be carried out:*
1   Select P, start the engine and run it until the normal operating temperature has been reached (ie five minutes after the opening of the thermostat).
2   Refer to Chapter 3 and tune the carburettors. Check that the throttle linkage is set correctly.
3   Remove the air cleaner assembly to gain access to the downshift cable and throttle linkage.
4   Check the clearance between the downshift cable ferrule and adjusting nut. If the clearance is not 0.020 to 0.025 in (0.51 to 0.63 mm) loosen the locknut and adjust the clearance.
Note: *Incorrect setting of the downshift cable will result in the wrong oil pressure, which in turn will give rise to possible transmission clutch failure.*

13 Downshift cable – pressure test

1   Run the engine until the normal operating temperature is reached.
2   Refer to Chapter 3 and tune the carburettors.

11.12 Removing the torque converter to engine driveplate bolts

Fig. 6.10 Checking the downshift cable adjustment (Sec 12)

3   *Locknut*
4   *Clearance between ferrule and cable adjusting nut*

0.022ins
(0.55mm)

3   Stop the engine and raise the car to provide access to the transmission. If jacks are used, adequately chock the wheels. Remove the plug situated in the cut-away on the lower edge of the transmission rear extension flange and fit a pressure gauge suitable for reading up to 100lbf/in² (7 kgf/cm²).

4   Lower the car to the ground and apply the footbrake and handbrake as well as having the wheels chocked.

5   Start the engine and select D. Check that the gauge pressure is between 55 and 70lbf/in² (3.8 and 4.9 kgf/cm²) at idle speed.

6   Increase the speed to 1250 rpm and check that the pressure increases by 15 to 20 lbf/in² (1.0 to 1.4 kgf/cm²).

7   Stop the engine.

8   If the downshift cable has been set correctly as described in Section 12 but the operating pressures are incorrect, then the gearbox can be suspected of having an internal fault. **Note:** *an incorrect pressure reading will result if the fluid level is incorrect.*

9   It is not a satisfactory practice to adjust the downshift cable merely as an attempt to correct the pressure readings. In such instances it is advisable to seek the expertise of your Rover dealer or automatic transmission specialist.

14 Front brake band – adjustment

1   Raise the car for access to the transmission and select N.

2   Slacken the locknut on the adjustment screw then tighten the adjuster screw (using a torque wrench) to a torque setting of 5 lbf ft (0.7 kgf m), then back it off ¾ of a turn.

3   Hold the adjuster screw stationary in this position and tighten the locknut.

4   Lower the car to the ground.

15 Rear brake band – adjustment

1   Select N and raise the car for access to the transmission unit.

2   Slacken the locknut and then tighten the adjuster screw to a torque setting of 5 lbf ft (0.7 kgf m). Remember to use a torque wrench for this operation as 'guess work' is not at all satisfactory. If a torque wrench is not available, attach a spring balance to the ends of a wrench 1ft in length.

3   Having tightened the adjuster screw to this setting back it off by ¾ of a turn.

4   Hold the adjuster screw stationary in this position and tighten the locknut.

5   Lower the car to the ground.

16 Front servo – removal, overhaul and refitting

1   With the handbrake on and N selected, raise the vehicle to gain access to the transmission unit. If you are using a jack remember to use some supplementary method of support as mentioned previously.

2   Disconnect and remove the forward section of the exhaust system between the manifolds and the intermediate pipe.

3   Remove the propeller shafts as described in Chapter 7.

4   Disconnect the selector arm and rod from the transmission unit.

5   Support the transmission unit with a suitable jack placed beneath the sump. Use a block of timber to spread the load.

6   Undo the four bolts that secure the transmission crossmember to

Fig. 6.11 Checking the downshift cable (pressure test) (Sec 13)

1 Blanking plug
2 Pressure gauge (scale up to 100lbf/in² – 7 kgf/cm²)

Fig. 6.12 Front brake band adjustment point (Sec 14)

1 Adjuster   2 Locknut

Fig. 6.13 Rear brake band adjustment point (Sec 15)

1 Adjuster
2 Locknut

Fig. 6.14 Component parts of front servo (Sec 16)

1 Joint washer (gasket)   5 Piston
2 O-ring   6 Cover O-ring
3 Spring   7 Cover
4 Piston O-rings   8 Screw

the chassis frame.

7   Lower the support jack just enough to gain access to the front servo unit. Do not lower the jack too far as the air cleaner body will foul the bulkhead.

8   Take out the four cover bolts and withdraw the servo assembly, spring and joint washer.

9   Remove the spring and withdraw the piston.

10   Take off all the O-rings from the piston and body, and discard them.

11   Clean all parts in petrol and wipe them dry with a lint-free cloth.

12   Inspect the piston for scoring, corrosion or other damage and renew if necessary.

13   Inspect the cover for damage and check that the passages are unobstructed.

14   It is preferable to renew the spring, unless it is known to be fairly new.

15   Assemble the unit in reverse order to dismantling, using new O-rings and a new gasket.

16   Raise the support jack, relocate and tighten the crossmember bolts.

17   Refit the selector arm and lever, propeller shaft and exhaust system section by reversing the removal procedures.

17   Rear servo – removal, overhaul and refitting

1   With the handbrake on and N selected, raise the vehicle and support it to gain access to the transmission unit.

2   Remove the forward section of the exhaust system between the manifolds and the intermediate pipe.

3   Refer to Chapter 7 and remove the propeller shaft.

4   Disconnect the selector arm and rod from the transmission unit.

5   Locate a support jack under the transmission sump pan. Place a flat block of wood on the jack lifting pad to prevent damaging the sump pan.

6   Having supported the transmission in this manner, remove the four bolts that secure the transmission crossmember to the chassis frame.

7   Lower the support jack just enough to gain access to the rear servo unit. If the jack is lowered too far, the air cleaner body will foul the bulkhead and possibly cause damage to other components.

8   Take out the six bolts that secure the rear servo cover.

9   Withdraw the servo assembly, joint washer, spring and pushrod.

10   Remove the pushrod and spring, then withdraw the piston.

11   Take off all the O-rings from the piston and body, then discard them.

12   Clean all the parts in petrol and wipe them dry with a lint-free cloth.

13   Inspect the piston for scoring, corrosion or other damage and renew if necessary.

14   Inspect the cover for damage and check that the passages are unobstructed.

15   It is preferable to renew the spring, unless it is known to be fairly new.

16   Assemble the unit in the reverse order to dismantling using new O-rings and a new gasket.

17   Raise the support jack, relocate and tighten the four crossmember bolts.

18   The selector arm and lever, propeller shaft and front exhaust section can all be refitted by reversing the removal procedures.

18   Rear extension – removal and refitting

1   Drive the car onto a ramp or have jacks and axle stands available, chock the wheels and select N.

2   Disconnect the transmission fluid filler tube from the cylinder head and sump pan. Have ready a container of at least 9.5 pints (5.5 litres) as the fluid will drain from the transmission when the union at the base of the filler tube is unscrewed.

3   Disconnect and remove the forward section of the exhaust system between the manifolds and the intermediate pipe.

4   Remove the four bolts that secure the front end of the propeller shaft. Move the propeller shaft to one side and support it.

5   In order to prevent the output flange from turning when undoing the flange retaining bolt, it will be necessary to construct a simple tool. A flat steel bar is ideal and can be drilled and then bolted to the flange. Hold the bar and undo the flange bolt, then pull off the flange.

6   Support the transmission unit under its sump, using a suitable jack. Place a flat wooden block on top of the jack lifting pad to spread the load.

7   Unscrew and remove the four bolts, spring washers and the two plates that secure the transmission crossmember to the chassis frame.

8   Undo the two nuts and separate the crossmember bracket from the extension housing.

9   Unscrew the two bolts and remove the exhaust system support bracket.

10   Lower the transmission support jack sufficiently to gain access to the extension housing retaining bolts.

11   Disconnect the speedometer cable by undoing the single bolt, removing the U-shaped clamp and pulling the cable away.

12   Undo the extension housing retaining bolts and withdraw the rear extension housing.

13   Refitting is a straightforward reversal of the removal procedure, but make sure that a new flange gasket is used.

Fig. 6.15 Component parts of rear servo (Sec 17)

1 Screw
2 Cover
3 Piston O-rings
4 Piston
5 Spring
6 Pushrod
7 Joint washer (gasket)
8 O-rings

19 Extension rear oil seal – renewal

1   Drive the car on to a ramp or have jacks and axle stands available. Chock the wheels and select N.

2   Mark the relationship of the propeller shaft and transmission drive flanges for re-alignment purposes.

3   Remove the four bolts that secure the front end of the propeller shaft. Move the propeller shaft to one side and support it.

4   In order to undo the transmission flange bolt it will be found necessary to construct a simple tool to hold the drive flange still. A flat steel bar is ideal for this purpose and can be drilled and then bolted to the flange.

5   Hold the end of the tool firmly with one hand and undo the flange retaining bolt.

6   Pull off the drive flange.

7   Prise out the old oil seal.

8   Using a suitable drift, carefully drive in a new oil seal. Lightly lubricate the lip of the seal.

9   Refit the parts in the reverse order to removal. Use thread locking compound on the threads of the transmission flange bolt, and tighten it to the specified torque.

Fig. 6.16 Rear extension oil seal (Sec 19)

1 Oil seal	4 Washer
2 Rear extension	5 Bolt
3 Drive flange	

20 Governor – removal, overhaul and refitting

1   Remove the rear extension as described in Section 18.

2   Withdraw the speedometer drive gear.

3   Unscrew the counterweight from the base of the governor, taking note of the spring washer.

4   Withdraw the governor from the shaft.

5   Prise off the retaining circlip and remove the weight.

6   Withdraw the stem, spring and valve.

7   Wash all the parts in petrol and dry with a lint-free cloth.

8   Check the parts for burrs and scoring, and for any signs of thread damage.

9   It is best to renew the spring, even if apparently satisfactory.

10 When reassembling, first insert the valve into the body.

11 Next, fit the spring to the stem, then fit both parts into the body.

12 Refit the weight and a new circlip.

13 Refit the governor, the counterweight and the spring washer.

14 Refit the speedometer drive gear, followed by the rear extension. Remember to use a new gasket.

21 Selector rod – removal, refitting and adjustment

1   Drive the vehicle onto a ramp or raise it up using jacks and axle stands.

2   Select P and apply the handbrake.

3   Slacken the locknut on the selector rod. Remove the split-pins and clevis pins, then lift the rod away. Note the locations of the spacer washers.

4   Check that the hand selector lever and the transmission selector lever are both in the P position.

5   Fit the selector rod to the gearbox selector lever.

6   Lift the front of the rod up and adjust the clevis fork until the clevis pin holes in the fork and cross-shaft lever are aligned.

7   Fit the clevis pin, washers and split pins.

8   Tighten the locknut.

22 Transmission sump – draining and refilling

1   Drive the vehicle on to a ramp or have adequate jacks to provide access to the underside of the car.

Fig. 6.17 Removing the governor (Sec 20)

1 Circlip	5 Counterweight
2 Weight	6 Valve
3 Governor body	7 Stem
4 Spring washer	8 Spring

Fig. 6.18 Adjusting the selector rod (Sec 21)

1 Selector rod	4 Clevis pin
2 Locknut	5 Spacer washers
3 Clevis fork	6 Split pin

2   Select P and apply the handbrake.
3   Raise the ramp, or jacks.
4   Wipe around the area of the filler tube union at the transmission and then unscrew the union, drain the contents into a suitable container. **Note:** *It is not possible to drain the torque converter completely.*
5   Tighten the union nut; then add fresh fluid via the filler tube until the level is no higher than the *Cold-High* mark on the dipstick.
6   Give the car a warming-up run and re-check the fluid level when hot, by following the procedure given in Section 25.

Fig. 6.19 The transmission sump (Sec 23)

1   *Sump pan*
2   *Gasket*
3   *Bolt and spring washer*

Fig. 6.20 Starter inhibitor/reverse lamp switch (Sec 24)

1   *Electrical leads*   3   *Bolt*
2   *Thread protector*   4   *Switch*

23 Transmission sump – removal and refitting

1   Drive the vehicle on to a ramp or raise it up using jacks to gain access to the underside of the transmission. Select P and apply the handbrake.
2   Unscrew the filler tube union at the transmission and drain the contents into a suitable container.
3   Unscrew the twelve sump pan bolts and remove the sump with its gasket.
4   When refitting the sump, make sure that the mating surfaces are clean. Use a new gasket and tighten the bolts evenly to the recommended torque setting.
5   Refit the filler tube and then refill with new fluid as described in Section 22.

24 Starter inhibitor/reverse lamp switch – removal and refitting

1   Drive the car on to a ramp or have adequate jacks to permit access to the transmission. Select P and apply the handbrake.
2   Disconnect the battery negative terminal connection.
3   Take off the thread protector from the switch cover (where fitted).
4   Disconnect the switch leads. Note their colour coding and their relative positions for correct refitting later.
5   Take out the retaining bolt and remove the switch.
6   Refitting is a reversal of the removal procedure.

25 Fluid level – checking

The automatic transmission fluid level check can be carried out with the system either *Cold* or *Hot* as follows:

Cold check
1   Park the vehicle on a level surface, apply the footbrake and handbrake. Start the engine.
2   With the engine running, move the selector through the complete range of shift positions. Continue this operation for a period of two minutes to ensure that the system is fully primed.
3   After this period select P, still allowing the engine to idle.
4   Open the bonnet, withdraw the transmission dipstick, wipe it clean.
5   Insert the dipstick fully and withdraw it immediately.
6   The fluid level should be on the *cold* side of the dipstick blade.
7   Top-up as required to the *High-Cold* mark, but do not overfill.
8   Repeat paragraphs 1 to 7 as necessary.

Hot check
9   The transmission should be at normal operating temperature when carrying out this check, ie after a run of approximately 20 miles (30 km).

Fig. 6.21 the Transmission fluid dipstick – location and detail (Sec 25)

1   *Dipstick – showing 'Cold' side markings*
2   *Combined dipstick/filler tube*

10 Park the vehicle on a level surface, apply the footbrake and handbrake.

11 While holding the brakes on in this manner, allow the engine to idle and move the selector lever through the complete range of shift positions.

12 Continue to move the shift lever through the shift range for a period of two to three minutes in order to fully prime the transmission.

13 Having primed the system, move the selector lever to P and allow the engine to remain at idling speed.

14 Open the bonnet, withdraw the transmission dipstick and wipe it clean.

15 Insert the dipstick to its full depth and withdraw it immediately.

16 The fluid level should be on the *hot* side of the dipstick blade.

17 Top-up as necessary to the *High-Hot* mark, but do not overfill.

18 Repeat paragraphs 9 to 17 as necessary.

26 Stall test

This test can only be satisfactorily carried out with an engine which is in good condition and capable of developing full power. **Note**: *during the test it is important that the temperature of the transmission fluid does not exceed 110°C (230°F) at any time.*

1 Run the engine until normal operating temperature has been reached and then check the fluid level as described in Section 25 (hot check).

2 Chock the rear wheels. Also apply the foot and handbrakes for the duration of the test.

3 If possible, connect an auxiliary type of tachometer which can be observed from the driver's seat.

4 Start the engine and with the brakes applied, select D and allow the engine to idle for approximately one minute to ensure full circulation of the transmission fluid.

5 After this period, depress the accelerator pedal to the full throttle position *(not Kick-down)* and take a note of the tachometer reading which should be in the region between 1900 and 2100 rpm. *Under no circumstances hold the throttle pedal in this position for longer than ten seconds as the transmission will overheat.*

6 If the tachometer reading obtained during the test is between 1300 and 1900 rpm, then the engine is probably not developing full power. Readings less than 1300 rpm indicate suspected stator slip in the torque converter. Where readings in excess of 2300 rpm are obtained, this is usually an indication of defective brake bands or clutches within the transmission unit.

7 If the test is to be repeated, allow 10 to 15 minutes for the heat in the transmission fluid to dissipate.

27 Road tests

The following tests will give an indication of the condition of the automatic transmission. Check that the unit functions properly in all the tests mentioned.

Owing to the complicated construction and the finely adjusted settings within the unit, it is recommended that any repairs or adjustments, other than those we explain, should be entrusted to an appointed Rover workshop or an automatic transmission specialist.

Note: *The term 'full throttle' refers to approximately seven-eighths of the available pedal travel and 'kick-down' is equivalent to full pedal travel.*

Procedure

1 Check that the starter motor operates only with the selector lever at P or N and that the reverse lights operate only at R.

2 Apply the handbrake. With the engine idling, select N-D, N-2, N-R. Engagement should be positive (a cushioned 'thump' under fast idling conditions is to be expected).

3 With the transmission at normal running temperature, select D. Release the brakes and accelerate with minimum throttle. Check the 1-2 and 2-3 shift speeds and the smoothness of the change.

4 Stop the vehicle, select D then re-start using full throttle. Check the 1-2 and 2-3 shift speeds and the smoothness of the change.

5 At a maximum speed of 50 mph (80 km/h), kick-down fully. The transmission should immediately change down into second gear.

6 Stop the vehicle, select D, then re-start using kick-down, check the 1-2 and 2-3 gearchange speeds.

7 At 65mph (107 km/h), select 2 and simultaneously release the throttle, check the 3-2 changedown.

8 At 35 mph (56 km/h), select 1 and simultaneously release the throttle; check the 2-1 changedown.

9 With 1 still engaged, stop the car and using kick-down accelerate to over 40 mph (65 km/h). Check for 'slip', 'squawk' and loss of upward gearchanges.

10 Park the vehicle on a gradient. Apply the handbrake and select P then release the handbrake and check that the parking pawl holds. Check that the selector lever is firmly locked in P.

Converter diagnosis

Inability to start on steep hills, combined with poor acceleration from rest and low stall speeds (1300 rpm), indicates that the converter stator unidirectional clutch is slipping. This permits the stator to rotate in an opposite direction to the impeller and turbine, preventing torque multiplication. Poor acceleration in third gear above 30 mph (50 km/h) and reduced maximum speed, indicates that the unidirectional clutch has seized. The stator will not rotate with the turbine and impeller and the 'fluid flywheel' effect cannot occur. This condition will also be indicated by excessive overheating of the transmission although the stall speed will be satisfactory.

28 Fault diagnosis – automatic transmission

Due to the complexity of the transmission unit, fault diagnosis should be limited to the information given in Section 26 and 27. Most problems encountered are likely to be linked to the following:

1 *Low fluid level*
2 *Incorrectly adjusted downshift cable*
3 *Incorrectly adjusted selector mechanism*

Chapter 7 Propeller shaft

Contents

Specifications

Type	Single piece, tubular with constant velocity joints at either end

Torque wrench settings

	lbf ft	Nm
Gearbox and rear axle flange nuts	37	50

1 General description

Drive is transmitted from the gearbox unit to the rear axle by a finely balanced tubular propeller shaft. At either end of the shaft are constant velocity joints which allow for vertical movement of the rear axle. The design of the constant velocity joint also permits a small amount of longitudinal movement to allow for the fore-and-aft movement of the rear axle.

Flanges are used at each end for attachment to the gearbox mainshaft flange and rear axle driveflange.

No provision is made for lubrication during service life.

2 Propeller shaft – removal and refitting

1   Jack up the rear of the car and position on firmly based axle-stands located at the body jacking points. Alternatively, position the rear of the car over an inspection pit or on a ramp.
2   If the rear of the car is jacked up, always supplement the jack with supporting axle-stands or blocks so that danger is minimised should the jack fail.
3   When the rear wheels are off the ground, place the car in gear or apply the handbrake. This is to ensure that the propeller shaft does not turn when an attempt is made to loosen the nuts that secure the propeller shaft universal joint flanges to the rear of the gearbox and to the final drive extension shaft flange (photo).

2.3 Propeller shaft constant velocity joint at gearbox end

Fig. 7.1 The propeller shaft (Sec 1)

Fig. 7.2 Sectional view of the propeller shaft, showing the constant velocity joints (Sec 3)

4   The propeller shaft is carefully balanced to fine limits and it is important that it is refitted in exactly the same position it was in prior to its removal. Index mark the edges of the propeller shaft flanges and the corresponding edges of the front and rear driving flanges.

5   Undo and remove the four nuts and bolts that hold the rear flange of the propeller shaft to the flange on the final drive extension shaft.

6   Push the propeller shaft forwards, lower the rear end of the propeller shaft and support it.

7   Undo and remove the four nuts and bolts that hold the forward flange of the propeller shaft to the flange at the rear of the gearbox unit.

8   Remove the propeller shaft from the car.

9   Refitting is the reverse of the removal procedure, but ensure that the index marks are aligned. **Note:** *Owing to the fact that the spacing of the propeller shaft front and rear flange holes are not the same, it will be found that the propeller shaft can be fitted in one position only.*

3   Constant velocity joints – checking for wear

1   Wear in the propeller shaft constant velocity joints can be indicated by vibration or 'clunks' in the transmission, particularly when the drive is being taken up or when going to over-run. (Backlash in the rear axle has the same effect, so check both assemblies, if symptoms occur).

2   It is easy to check the constant velocity joints whilst the propeller shaft is still in position. Try to turn the shaft with one hand and grip the other side of the joint with the other hand. There should be no movement across the joint. Check also by trying to lift the shaft and noting any movement in the joints.

3   If any wear is detected when carrying out the checks mentioned above, then a replacement propeller shaft will have to be obtained as the constant velocity joints are non-repairable items.

4   Fault diagnosis – propeller shaft

Symptom	Reason/s
Vibration	Misalignment Wear in constant velocity joints Loose flange nuts
Noisy operation	Wear in constant velocity joints Loose flange nuts

Chapter 8 Rear axle

For modifications, and information applicable to later models, see Supplement at end of manual

Contents

Specifications

Type . . . .   Semi-floating live axle with hypoid bevel gears and two pinion
differential

Lubricant
Type/specification . . . .   Hypoid gear oil, viscosity SAE 90EP, to BLS 22-OL-03 or
MIL-L-2105B (Duckhams Hypoid 90S)

Capacity   . . . .   1.6 pints (0.91 litres)

Final drive ratio
2300 and 2600 Manual 3.45:1
2600 Automatic 3.08:1

Torque wrench settings

	lbf ft	Nm
Halfshaft bearing retainer plate set-screws	37	50
Extension housing to axle casing (nuts and bolts)	37	50
Extension housing to mounting bracket bolts	37	50
Oil filler level plug	26	35
Oil seal housing to hypoid housing set-screws	37	50
Brake pipe bracket set-screws	21	28
Shock absorber locknut	33	45
Shock absorber nut	45	61
Radius rod nuts	41	54
Watts linkage pivot nut	41	54

1 General description

The semi-floating 'live' rear axle consists of a conventional hypoid final drive and differential units.

The axle casing is located at its forward end by semi-trailing arms and a torque tube (pinion housing extension). Shock absorber struts and coil springs also assist. Sideways location of the rear axle is provided by a Watts type pivoting linkage arrangement, which is transversely mounted at the rear of the axle casing.

Drive from the propeller shaft is taken to the bevel pinion via the extension shaft. From the bevel pinion, the drive is transmitted to the crownwheel and differential unit which together form the differential assembly.

The differential assembly (including the crownwheel but excluding the bevel pinion) is free to revolve within the axle casing, being mounted at either side on taper roller bearings and retained to the casing by two semi-circular bearing housing caps. This arrangement enables the differential assembly to be removed from the rear axle casing without the necessity to remove the rear axle.

The procedures given in this Chapter enable the owner to carry out certain operations but owing to the need for specialised tools and the necessary expertise, it is not recommended that the owner should attempt to either remove, dismantle or make adjustments to the differential or bevel pinion assemblies. It is far better to entrust work of this complex nature to your local Rover dealer who will have the necessary equipment and trained personnel at hand.

2 Halfshaft – removal and refitting

1   The halfshafts may be withdrawn without disturbing the differential gear.

2   Chock the front roadwheels and raise the appropriate rear roadwheel clear of the ground. Support the car with either an axle stand or strong wooden packing blocks.

3   Remove the rear roadwheel and release the handbrake.

4   Undo the single countersunk screw and withdraw the brake drum. Should it be found difficult to remove refer to Chapter 9 for further details.

5   Through the large hole in the halfshaft flange, undo the four bolts and nuts that secure the halfshaft assembly and brake backplate to the axle tube flange.

6   Rover recommend that a slide hammer tool be used to withdraw the halfshaft, but if such a tool is not at hand, the brake drum and a heavy soft-faced hammer will suffice.

7   Temporarily fit the brake drum so that the inside of the drum is facing towards you. Retain the drum to the halfshaft by using the wheelnuts secured on the wrong way round (taper edge outwards).

8   Using a heavy soft-faced hammer, or an ordinary hammer and a hardwood block, tap the drum from behind whilst rotating it to draw out the halfshaft complete with the bearing.

9   Refitting is basically the reverse of the removal procedure, but the following points should be noted:

Fig. 8.1 Halfshaft location (Sec 2)

1   Retaining nuts (4 off)
2   Access hole in halfshaft flange

(a) *The interior of the axle tube/halfshaft bearing area should be smeared with a lithium-based grease*
(b) *Likewise smear a little lithium-based grease on the bearing and the oil seal*
(c) *Slide the halfshaft carefully in through the axle tube and turn it slowly until its splined end engages with the differential splines*
(d) *Push the halfshaft inwards and check that the bearing and oil seal enter the axle tube squarely*
(e) *Fit the securing bolts and nuts, taking care to tighten them evenly*
(f) *Wipe away any surplus lubricant and grease, to prevent the possibility of brake lining contamination*

3   Halfshaft bearing and oil seals – removal and refitting

1   Because of the special tools required to draw off the spacer ring and halfshaft bearing retainer oil seal, this job should be entrusted to a Rover dealer. However, the halfshaft can be removed as described in the previous Section to minimise labour costs.
2   To remove the oil seal from the axle tube, first remove the halfshaft as described in Section 2.
3   Prise out the seal from the axle tube.
4   Smear the replacement seal with axle oil, ensure that the bore of the axle tube is clean, then fit the seal with the lip towards the differential.
5   Fit the halfshaft as described in Section 2.

4   Pinion extension housing – removal and refitting

1   Chock the front roadwheels, raise the rear of the car and support it on strong wooden packing blocks or axle-stands.
2   Release the handbrake.
3   Disconnect the propeller shaft at the extension housing drive flange (photo).
4   Remove the clip that retains the handbrake cable to the extension housing.
5   Undo the two bolts that secure the flexible brake hose bracket to the extension housing.
6   Place a support jack under the differential pinion ensuring that it is clear of the extension housing flange.
7   Remove the two bolts, together with their spring washers, that secure the mounting bracket to the extension housing.
8   Release the mounting bracket from the extension housing.
9   Lower the support jack until the extension housing is clear of the

Fig. 8.2 Sectional view of the rear hub assembly (Sec 2)

Fig. 8.3 Halfshaft and bearing/seal arrangement (Sec 3)

1 Halfshaft	*4 Oil seal*
2 Wheel stud	*5 Bearing*
3 Retainer plate	*6 Lockring*

car body.
10   Remove the three bolts and spring washers, and one bolt, nut bracket and locknut that secure the extension housing rear flange to the axle casing.
11   The extension housing can now be withdrawn.
12   Refitting is the reverse of the removal procedure.

5   Pinion extension housing bearing – removal and refitting

1   Remove the pinion extension housing as described in Section 4.
2   Scribe a line on the extension housing to coincide with the amount of overlap of the mudshield. This facilitates accurate refitment later.
3   Using a wedge-shaped drift, tap the mudshield forwards towards the drive flange. Great care must be taken when doing this as the

Fig. 8.4 Axle tube and oil seal (Sec 3)

4.3 Rear axle extension housing bracket and drive flange connection

1 Extension shaft
2 Extension housing
3 Mudshield
4 Circlip
5 Bearing
6 Circlip

Fig. 8.5 Sectional and exploded view of the pinion extension housing assembly (Sec 4)

mudshield will distort if tapped unevenly or too hard.

4   Using a suitable pair of circlip pliers, extract the end circlip which retains the bearing and shaft.

5   Pull the shaft and bearing out of the extension housing.

6   Remove a further circlip directly behind the bearing.

7   The bearing can now be either pressed or driven off the shaft.

8   Fit the new bearing and locate it with the circlip.

9   Fit the bearing and shaft into the housing and fit the circlip to the housing.

10   Slide the mudshield back along the shaft into its original position. When correctly fitted, there should be a gap of $\frac{5}{32}$ in (4 mm) between the edge of the mudshield and the machined lip of the extension housing.

11   Refit the extension housing by reversing the removal procedure.

Fig. 8.6 Fitting the pinion oil seal (Sec 6)

6.9 Rear axle oil filler/level plug

6 Differential pinion oil seal – renewal

Note: *Rover recommend that certain special service tools are used to carry out this operation. However, this task can be carried out without them if some care is exercised. The main problem will be pulling out the seal housing – Rover use a universal puller on a U-shaped plate slotted behind the lip on the housing.*

1   Remove the pinion extension housing as described in Section 4.
2   Carefully remove the pinion seal housing.
3   Extract the pinion seal from the housing.
4   Fit a new pinion oil seal to the housing, taking great care to prevent damaging the seal lip. The lip of the seal must face away from the arrow-marked housing face.
5   Wrap a narrow strip of masking tape over the pinion shaft. This measure will protect the seal during fitment of the seal housing. Position the masking tape in such a way that it can be easily removed after

fitting the seal housing.
6   Lubricate the lip of the seal and the masking tape.
7   Fit the seal and housing and insert them evenly into the axle casing. Note that the arrow-marked face must be fitted outermost and the arrow must point downwards. Tap the seal housing evenly and gently into position.
8   Fit the extension housing by reversing the removal procedure.
9   Finally check and if necessary, top-up the rear axle oil level (photo).

7 Rear axle – removal and refitting

1   Raise the rear of the car and support it using suitable stands or blocks beneath the bodyframe side-members. Chock the front wheels for safety.
2   Remove the rear roadwheels and release the handbrake.

Fig. 8.7 Removing the rear axle (illustrations indicating some of the components which must be either removed or disconnected) (Sec 7)

1   *Watts linkage pivot*
2   *Handbrake cable fork ends*
3   *Handbrake cable guide*
4   *Handbrake compensator unit*
5   *Shock absorber lower mounting*
6   *Radius rod end nut*

3 Place a supporting jack, ideally a trolley jack, under the differential unit.
4 Disconnect the rear end of the propeller shaft from the final drive flange. Move the propeller shaft to one side and support it.
5 Disconnect the flexible brake hose from the bracket attached to the pinion extension housing. Cap the open ends of the hose and pipe in order to prevent loss of hydraulic fluid.
6 Undo the two bolts that secure the bracket to the pinion extension housing. Ease the bracket off the locating dowels.
7 Loosen the clip on the extension housing and separate the handbrake cable support clip from it.
8 Disconnect the handbrake cable fork ends from the backplate levers by withdrawing the split-pins and clevis pins.
9 Release the handbrake cable from the guide fitted to the rear of the axle casing.
10 Disconnect the handbrake cable compensator by removing the nut and bolt that clamp the compensator and releasing the handbrake cable trunnion.
11 Tie the handbrake cables back out of the way.
12 Disconnect the radius arms from the axle brackets by undoing the

nuts and withdrawing the large plain washers and rubber bushes. See Chapter 11.
13 Undo the nut and remove the plain washer that secure the Watt's linkage to the differential housing. Pull the Watt's linkage central pivot arm back clear of the central pivot post.
14 Disconnect the shock absorbers from the axle simply by removing the locknut, nut and washer.
15 Lower the support jack slowly and at the same time draw the axle clear of the radius rods.
16 The axle can now be pulled out from under the car with the road springs attached. These can easily be removed by removing the spring bracket. They can then be lifted off as a complete assembly with the spring upper seats and bump stops.
17 Refitting is basically the reverse of the removal procedure, but the following points should be noted:
18 When locating the axle, tighten each of the various nuts and bolts only finger-tight at first. After everything is reconnected is this manner, progressively tighten the nuts and bolts to the recommended torque setting.
19 One of the final tasks will be to bleed the brakes. This operation is described in Chapter 9.

8 Fault diagnosis – rear axle

Symptom	Reason/s
Vibration	Worn halfshaft bearings Loose drive flange bolts Propeller shaft out-of-balance Wheels require balancing
Noise	Insufficient lubricant Worn differential gears
'Clunk' on acceleration or deceleration	Incorrect crownwheel and pinion mesh Excessive backlash due to wear in differential gears Worn halfshaft or differential side gear splines Loose drive flange bolts Worn drive pinion flange splines
Oil leakage	Faulty pinion or halfshaft seals Blocked axle housing breather

Chapter 9 Braking system

For modifications, and information applicable to later models, see Supplement at end of manual

Contents

Specifications

System type . . . . Dual hydraulic, front disc and rear drums, with vacuum servo and rear wheel pressure reducing valve. Cable operated handbrake to rear wheels. Warning lamp on facia operated by a pressure differential switch.

Front brakes
Type . . . . Disc and caliper
Disc diameter (nominal) . . . . 10.15 in (258 mm)
Disc thickness:
    New . . . . 0.55 in (14 mm)
    Refinishing limit . . . . 0.51 in (13 mm)
Pad lining minimum thickness . . . . 0.12 in (3.0 mm)

Rear brakes
Type . . . . Drum, single leading shoe, self-adjusting
Drum internal diameter (nominal) . . . . 9 in (228 mm)
Drum width (internal) . . . . 2.25 in (57 mm)
Shoe lining minimum thickness . . . . 0.12 in (3.0 mm)

Vacuum servo unit
Type . . . . Direct acting
Boost ratio 3.08:1

Handbrake
Type . . . . Cable operated to rear wheels from floor mounted lever

Brake fluid specification . . . . Hydraulic fluid to FMVSS DOT 3 or SAE J1703 (Duckhams Universal Brake and Clutch Fluid)

Torque wrench settings

	lbf ft	Nm
Pedal bracket to dash bracket screw	20	27.5
Pressure reducing valve to body nut	20	27.5
Front caliper to suspension bolt	55	75
Disc to hub bolt	41	54.5
Disc shield set-screw	8	11
Handbrake lever to body bolt	20	27.5
Handbrake fulcrum to rear axle nyloc nut (M10)	12.5	17
Brake compensator lever to handbrake nut (M6)	8	11
Servo and pedal bracket to dash nut	20	27.5
Brake pipe unions to:		
Calipers	8	11
Drums	6	9
Servo	8	11
Hoses	10	13.5
Pressure valve	6	9

Fig. 9.1 Layout of the brake
system (Sec 1)

1   General description

The brakes fitted to the front two wheels are of the rotating disc and static caliper type, with one caliper per disc, each caliper containing two piston operated friction pads, which on application of the footbrake, pinch the disc rotating between them.

Application of the footbrake creates hydraulic pressure in the master cylinder and fluid from the cylinder travels via steel and flexible pipes to the cylinders in each half of the calipers, the fluid so pushing the pistons, to move the friction pads, into contact with each side of each disc.

Two rubber seals are fitted to the operating cylinders. The outer seal prevents moisture and dirt from entering the cylinder. The inner seal, which is retained in a groove inside the cylinder, prevents fluid leakage and provides a running clearance for the pad irrespective of how worn it is, by moving it back a fraction when the brake pedal is released.

As the friction pad wears so the pistons move further out of the cylinders and the level of the fluid in the hydraulic reservoir drops; disc pad wear is thus taken up automatically and eliminates the need for periodic adjustments by the owner.

The rear brakes are of the self-adjusting, leading and trailing shoe type, with one brake cylinder per wheel for both shoes. A lever assembly is fitted between the two shoes of each brake unit and attached to this is a system of cables which in turn is connected to the handbrake lever. It is unusual to have to adjust the handbrake system as the efficiency of this system is largely dependent on the condition of the brake linings and the adjustment of the brake shoes. The handbrake can however, be adjusted independently from the footbrake-operated hydraulic system if cable stretch requires it.

Connected to the brake pedal is a servo unit onto which is mounted the master cylinder. It increases the hydraulic line pressure whilst decreasing the driver's pedal effort. The master cylinder is a dual-type which means that the front and rear brakes operate independently of each other through a common pedal pushrod. Should one half of the system fail to operate, the brakes on the other half will still operate, although the system efficiency is reduced. A brake pressure regulator is fitted and is designed to prevent the rear wheels from locking. A separate description of this is given in the text (Section 10).

2   Brake hydraulic system – bleeding

1   Removal of all the air from the hydraulic system is essential to the correct working of the braking system, but before undertaking this, examine the fluid reservoir cap to ensure that the vent hole is clear; check the level of fluid and replenish if required.
2   Check all brake line unions and connections for possible seepage, also check the condition of the rubber hoses. These may be perished.
3   If the condition of the wheel cylinders is in doubt, check for signs of possible fluid leakage.
4   If there is any possibility of incorrect fluid having been put into the system, drain all the fluid out and flush through with isopropyl-alcohol or methylated spirit. Renew all piston seals and cups since they will be affected and could possibly fail when under pressure.
5   Gather together a clean jam jar, a 9 in (230 mm) length of tubing which fits tightly over the bleed nipple, and a supply of the correct type of fluid. You will also require the services of an assistant.
6   Disconnect the wires from the brake pressure failure switch, and unscrew the switch from the underside of the master cylinder.
7   To bleed the system, make sure that the car is on a level surface and release the handbrake. To gain better access to the bleed nipples it may be preferable to lift one roadwheel at a time. If this is the case, chock the roadwheels which remain on the ground.

Fig. 9.2 Bleeding a front brake caliper

2.8 Front brake caliper bleed nipple (arrowed)

8   Commence at the front wheel caliper furthest from the master cylinder, remove the rubber cap and wipe carefully around the bleed nipple (photo).
9   Fit one end of the rubber tube over the nipple and place the other end of the tube in a clean glass jar containing sufficient fluid to keep the end of the tube submerged during the operation.
10   Open the bleed valve with a spanner and quickly press down the brake pedal. After slowly releasing the pedal, pause for a moment to allow the fluid to recoup in the master cylinder and then depress again. This will force air from the system. Continue until no more air bubbles can be seen coming from the tube, then, with the pedal depressed, close the bleed nipple. At frequent intervals during the operation, make certain that the reservoir is kept topped-up, otherwise air will enter the system again. Always discard any fluid which is bled off since it probably contains air, dirt and moisture.
11   Now repeat the operation on the other front caliper in the same way. Do not forget to refit the rubber protective cap on the bleed nipple afterwards. This completes the bleeding of the front brakes.
12   The rear brakes should now be bled. There is only one bleed nipple; this is on the right-hand backplate.
13   When the system has been fully bled the pedal action should be firm, and free from any 'sponginess'. If this still appears to be present, there is a likelihood that one of the seals in the master cylinder has failed.
14   On completion, refit the brake pressure failure switch. Note that the tightening torque is only 15 lbf in (0·17 kgf m).

3   Brake disc and disc shield – removal and refitting

1   Remove the front hub, as described in Chapter 11.

Brake disc
2   Remove the five disc-to-hub retaining bolts, and withdraw the disc.
3   Refitting is the reverse of the removal procedure. Tighten the retaining bolts evenly to the specified torque.

Disc shield
4   Remove the three bolts and spring washers. Detach the disc shield from the vertical link.
5   Refitting is the reverse of the removal procedure.

4   Front brake pads – removal and refitting

1   Apply the handbrake, then jack-up the front of the car and remove the roadwheel.
2   Straighten the ends of the split-pins, slightly depress the pad retaining springs and withdraw the split-pins (photo).
3   Lift the retaining springs away and withdraw the pads and shims taking note of their positions (photo). If the lining material on one or more pads has worn down to the specified minimum, all four pads must be renewed.
4   Carefully press the caliper pistons back into their bores. **Note:** *This will cause the reservoir fluid level to rise. Prevent it from overflowing by previously syphoning some fluid from the reservoir with an old clean hydrometer or similar.*
5   Refitting is now the reverse of the removal procedure, but the following points should be noted:

(a) *Ensure that the pad location area in the caliper is free from dust and dirt*
(b) *If the shims are corroded, obtain new ones; they should be inserted with the larger, or only, cut-out at the bottom*
(c) *Use new pad retaining springs and split pins. Fold back one leg of each split-pin*
(d) *Depress the brake pedal several times on completion to correctly locate the pads*
(e) *Check the reservoir fluid level on completion*

5   Front brake caliper – removal, overhaul and refitting

1   Apply the handbrake, then jack-up the front of the car and remove the roadwheel.
2   Disconnect the brake union from the caliper. Seal the fluid connections to prevent the ingress of dirt.
3   Straighten the ends of the tab washers and undo the two bolts that retain the caliper to the damper unit and stub axle assembly.
4   The caliper can now be withdrawn.
5   Remove the brake pads and shims (refer to Section 4, if necessary).
6   Using a small G-clamp and a thin flat strip of wood, clamp one of the pistons in position. Apply a low pressure air line or alternatively a tyre foot pump to the fluid port and eject the piston.
7   Having removed one of the pistons, remove the G-clamp and place the flat piece of wood over the hole vacated by the piston that has just been removed. Carefully clamp the piece of wood in position.
8   Apply the low pressure air source to the fluid port and eject the other piston.
9   Note the exact positions of the two pistons. Under no

4.2 Withdrawing the disc pad retaining pins

4.3 Withdrawing the disc pads and shims

Fig. 9.3 Front brake caliper (Sec 5)

1   Caliper
2   Tab washers
3   Retaining bolts

Fig. 9.4 Rear brake drum (Sec 6)

1	Backplate	11	Steady pin spring
2	Wheel cylinder	12	Steady pin cup
3	Bleed screw	13	Handbrake lever
4	Spring clip	14	Handbrake lever boot
5	Shoes	15	Plug
6	Adjuster components	16	Bolt
7	Cross-lever tension spring	17	Nut
8	Pull-off spring	18	Drum
9	Pull-off spring	19	Screw
10	Steady pin	20	Seal kit

circumstances swop their caliper positions. Should one of the pistons be seized in the caliper, the whole caliper must be renewed.

10 Using a blunt screwdriver, carefully prise out the wiper seal retainers. Do not scratch any metal parts.

11 Extract the wiper dust seals and fluid seals from the bores.

12 Thoroughly clean the metal parts using clean brake fluid, methylated spirit or isopropyl-alcohol. Inspect the caliper bores and pistons for wear, scoring and corrosion, renew parts as necessary. *Do not attempt to separate the two halves of the caliper.*

13 Position new fluid seals in the caliper bores, ensuring that they are properly located. They will stand proud of the bore at the edge furthest away from the mouth of the bore.

14 Lubricate the bores with new brake fluid and squarely insert the pistons in their original positions. Leave about $\frac{5}{16}$ in (8 mm) of each piston projecting.

15 Fit a new wiper seal into each seal retainer, and slide an assembly into each bore.

16 Press the seals and pistons fully home.

17 Refitting of the caliper is now the reverse of the removal procedure. Fit the retaining bolts only finger-tight at first and reconnect the

fluid pipe.

18 Tighten the retaining bolts to the recommended torque setting and bend back the ends of the tab washers. The fluid hose coupling can now be fully tightened.

19 On completion of refitting the brakes will have to be bled as described in Section 2. Fitting of the brake pads is covered in Section 4.

---

6 Rear brake shoes – removal and refitting

1   Jack-up the rear of the car and support it on stands or blocks beneath the rear axle. Chock the front wheels for safety.

2   Remove the roadwheel and release the handbrake.

3   Remove the single countersunk screw and pull off the brake drum (photo). **Note:** *If the drum is difficult to remove, remove the rubber plug on the rear of the backplate and insert a small screwdriver to engage in the small adjusting lever. Press downwards to contract the brake shoes.*

4   Note the fitted positions of the shoes and springs. Remove the steady pin cups and springs by depressing the cups and turning the pins through 90 degrees. The pins can now be withdrawn from the rear of the backplate.

5   Lever the ends of the brake shoes out from the slots in the wheel cylinder piston heads (photo).

6   Remove the clevis pin that secures the yoke end of the handbrake cable to the backplate operating lever.

7   Detach the pull-off springs and the cross-lever tension spring to remove the brake shoes. Retain the piston in the cylinders using a wire

Fig. 9.5 Layout of the right-hand rear brake (Sec 6)

1	Steady pin and cup	5	Wheel cylinder
2	Leading shoe	6	Front pull-off spring
3	Trailing shoe	7	Rear pull-off spring
4	Abutment plate	8	Cross-lever tension spring

6.3 A rear brake assembly with drum removed

clip or strong rubber band.

8   Blow or brush out any dust etc from the brake drum and back-plate. **Warning:** *Take care that the dust is not inhaled since it can be very harmful to the lungs.* If there are signs of fluid leakage from the hydraulic wheel cylinder or oil leakage from the halfshaft or bearing, these points should be investigated and if necessary, remedied at this stage. See Section 7 and Chapter 8. Renew the brake shoes where the linings have worn down to the specified minimum or are likely to wear down to this point during the next few thousand miles of motoring.

9   When fitting the shoes, insert the tension spring hook in the cross-lever and engage the other end in the web of the leading shoe. **Note:** *The springs are in sets for left and right-hand brakes.*

10 Ease the shoe and cross-lever towards the backplate; engage the toe in the piston slot and heel in the abutment slot.

11 Hold the crossmember and shoe against the backplate and fit the steady pin, spring and cup.

12 Hook the pull-off springs into the holes in the shoe webs. Note that they run on the backplate side of the shoes.

13 Pull the trailing shoe into position with the heel in the piston slot and the toe in the abutment slot. Ensure that the cross-lever cut-out engages in the adjuster plate slot.

14 Fit the second steady pin, spring and cup.

15 Refit the handbrake cable and clevis pin to the backplate operating lever using a new split-pin.

16 Provided that care is exercised to prevent the pistons from being forced out, the automatic adjuster action can be checked by gently pressing the brake pedal. As the shoes expand, the ratchet will operate; this can be cancelled by raising the ratchet plate to separate the ratchet teeth and allowing the shoes to retract under spring action. With new shoes, allow them to retract fully.

17 Fit the brake drum and roadwheel, then depress the brake pedal several times to centralize and adjust the brakes.

18 If the brake action is unsatisfactory, test run the car and apply moderately high pedal effort during several test runs at a speed around 20 mph (33 kph). This will help to bed in the linings quickly.

7   Rear wheel cylinder – removal, overhaul and refitting

1   Remove the brake shoes as described in the previous Section.

2   Disconnect the handbrake cable from the lever behind the back-plate by removing the split-pin and clevis pin.

3   Disconnect the pipe union and remove the bleed screw or the feed and transfer pipe unions from the rear of the wheel cylinder, as applicable.

4   Remove the spring clip and take off the wheel cylinder.

5   Remove the rubber boots and take out the pistons; also remove the spring from the bore.

6   Remove the seal from each piston.

6.5 A rear wheel cylinder showing the location of the brake shoe webs and the leading and trailing ends of the linings

Fig. 9.6 Left-hand rear wheel cylinder fixing at backplate (Sec 7)

1	Spring clip	3	Handbrake cable fork clevis
2	Feed/transfer pipe		pin

Fig. 9.7 Exploded view of the rear wheel cylinder unit (Sec 7)

1	*Rubber boot*	3	*Seal*
2	*Piston*	4	*Spring*

7   Thoroughly clean the metal parts using clean brake fluid, methylated spirit or isopropyl alcohol. Inspect the pistons and cylinder bores for wear, scoring and corrosion; renew parts as necessary.
8   Smear the cylinder bore with new brake fluid, then fit a new seal to the large groove of each piston, so that the lip of the seal faces away from the slot.
9   Locate the rubber boots into the smaller groves of the piston, then insert the pistons into the bore with the spring between them.
10 Refitting is the reverse of the removal procedure, but bleed the brakes before test running the car.

8   Rear brake backplate – removal and refitting

1   Remove the halfshaft assembly as described in Chapter 8. Insert a piece of lint-free cloth in the end of the open axle tube to prevent the oil from running. Providing the axle is not overfilled and the car has been raised high enough, no oil should run out.
2   Refer to the procedure given in paragraphs 2 and 3 of the previous Section.
3   Remove the four nuts, spring washers and bolts that secure the backplate. Withdraw the backplate.
4   Refitting is the reverse of the removal procedures, but bleed the brakes on completion (see Section 2).

9   Brake pipes and hoses – inspection, removal and refitting

1   Inspection of the braking system hydraulic pipes and flexible hoses is part of the maintenance schedule. Carefully check the rigid pipes along the rear axle, underbody and in the engine compartment, not forgetting the short runs to the front wheel calipers. Any pipes showing signs of corrosion or damage should be renewed, following which it will be necessary to bleed the system as described previously.
2   Carefully inspect the flexible hoses. There is one flexible pipe to the rear axle and one on each suspension arm. Look for any signs of swellings, cracking and/or chafing. If any of these faults are evident, renew the hoses straight away. Remember that your life could depend on it.
3   Where flexible hoses are to be renewed, unscrew the metal pipe union nut from its connection to the hose, and then holding the hexagon on the hose with a spanner, unscrew the attachment nut and washer.
4   The body end of the flexible hose can now be withdrawn from the chassis mounting bracket and will be quite free.
5   Refitting is the reverse of the removal procedure, following which it will be necessary to bleed the system, as described in Section 2.

10   Brake pressure reducing valve – description of operation

The reducing valve is fitted in the brake circuit between the master cylinder, and the front and rear brakes. Its purpose is to limit the pressure applied to the rear brakes relative to the front brake pressure, thus minimising the possibility of rear wheel locking. In the event of a failure in the front circuit the cut-off pressure is increased and the pressure reduction ratio is altered (Fig. 9.8).

Fig. 9.8 Sectional view of the brake pressure reducing valve (Sec 10)

Fluid from the master cylinder primary chamber is fed into the pressure reducing valve at port A and out to the front brakes via ports C and D. The master cylinder secondary chamber feeds into port B, through the internal passages in the valve plunger, past the metering valve and then to the rear brakes via port E. The large spring S biases the valve plunger to the left. Hydraulic pressure therefore acts on the annular area $(a1 - a2)$ forcing the plunger to the left whilst the force acting on the area $a1$ and annular area $(a4 - a3)$ tries to move the plunger to the right where it is opposed by the spring. When the net force acting to the right overcomes the pre-load provided by the spring, the plunger assembly shifts to the right and closes the metering valve F. Thus pressure at the rear outlet port E falls relative to the input pressure.   As pressure is increased at ports A and B, the plunger is forced to the left, opening the metering valve F and allowing a metered quantity of fluid to be fed to the rear brakes. The resultant increase in pressure acting on area $a1$ causes the plunger to again shift to the right, thus closing the metering valve. This procedure continues until there is no further increase in applied pressure from the master cylinder.

The resultant pressure at outlet E is reduced after cut-off, in proportion to the area $a2$ and the difference between the two annular areas $(a1 - a2)$ and $(a4 - a3)$. This cut-off pressure is equal to the pre-load in the spring S divided by the combined areas $a2$ and $(a4 - a3)$. Should the front brake circuit fail, there will be no pressure acting on the annular area $(a4 - a3)$ so that the net force tending to move the plunger to the right will equal the product of the input pressure and area $a2$. Thus, as the value of the pre-load spring is unchanged, the cut-off pressure will increase considerably.

As the annular area $(a4 - a3)$ is now redundant, the reduction ratio after cut-off changes the area $a2$. Should the rear brake circuit fail, the pressure reducing valve is completely inoperative.

11   Brake pressure reducing valve – removal and refitting

Note: *The pressure reducing valve cannot be dismantled for repair.*
1   Loosen the brake pipe union at the master cylinder and remove the two inlet pipes from the top of the reducing valve (photo).
2   Disconnect the remaining pipes at the pressure reducing valve.
3   Undo the nut, plain washer, spring washer and bolt. Lift the pressure reducing valve from the wheel arch. Wrap it in a lint-free cloth before lifting it clear to avoid the spillage of brake fluid.
4   Refitting is the reverse of the removal procedure, but bleed the brakes on completion.

12   Master cylinder – removal, overhaul and refitting

1   Noting their fitted position, detach the fluid lines from the master cylinder. Plug the pipes and ports to prevent the loss of brake fluid and the ingress of dust, dirt, etc (photo).
2   Detach the leads from the brake pressure failure and low fluid level switches, then remove the master cylinder retaining nuts and washers. Withdraw the master cylinder from the servo.
3   Clean all dirt from the external surfaces of the master cylinder.
4   Unscrew and remove the brake pressure failure switch.
5   Secure the master cylinder in a vice fitted with jaw protectors and remove the two crosshead screws that secure the fluid reservoir. Withdraw the reservoir from the master cylinder body.
6   Extract the two reservoir sealing rings after noting their exact positions.
7   Extract the circlip from the end of the cylinder bore.

11.1 The brake pressure reducing valve (engine removed from car)

12.1 The brake master cylinder and servo unit (arrowed)

1   End plug
2   Distance piece
3   Copper washer
4   Spring retainer
5   Spring
6   Washer
7   Pressure differential piston
8   O-ring seals
9   Stop pin
10 Seals
11 Pressure differential switch
12 Secondary piston return spring and clip
13 Piston seals
14 Secondary piston
15 Secondary piston seal
16 Primary piston return spring and cup
17 Piston seals
18 Primary piston
19 Primary piston seal
20 Circlip

Fig. 9.9 Exploded view of the master cylinder (Sec 12)

8   Withdraw the primary piston and return spring.
9   Using a copper or brass rod, insert it into the cylinder and depress the secondary piston so that the stop pin (situated next to the secondary piston fluid feed port) can be extracted.
10   Withdraw the secondary piston, spring retainer and the return spring.
11   Take a note of the sizes and pistons of the various rubber seals, piston washers and spring retainers.
12   Unscrew and remove the end plug and washer but do not prise off the distance piece from the end plug spigot.
13   Extract the pressure differential assembly, either by shaking it from the body or by applying air pressure to the secondary outlet port.
14   Wash all components in methylated spirit, isopropyl alcohol or clean hydraulic fluid, and examine the surfaces of the pistons and cylinder bore for scoring or 'bright' wear areas. Where these are evident, renew the complete master cylinder.
15   If the components are in good condition, discard all seals and obtain the appropriate repair kit.
16   Fit new O-ring seals to the pressure warning piston.
17   Fit a shim washer to the primary and secondary pistons.
18   Using the fingers only, manipulate the two identical piston seals into place on the primary and secondary piston (lips facing away from the washers).
19   Of the two remaining seals contained in the repair kit, fit the thinner one to the primary piston (lip towards primary spring seat) and the thicker one to the primary piston (lip towards piston seal).
20   Fit the shorter return spring and cup to the secondary piston, dip the assembly into clean hydraulic fluid and insert it into the master cylinder body. Take care not to turn back the lip of the seal.
21   Depress the secondary piston and insert the stop pin after the head of the piston has been seen to pass the feed port.
22   Fit the return spring and cup to the primary piston, dip the assembly into clean hydraulic fluid and insert it into the master cylinder body. Take care not to turn back the seal lips. Refit the retaining circlip.

23   Insert the pressure differential piston into its bore and then fit a new copper sealing washer to the end plug and screw it in, tightening it to the specified torque.
24   Fit new reservoir seals into the cylinder body recesses.
25   Fit the reservoir and tighten the retaining screws to the recommended torque setting.
26   Fit the brake pressure failure switch.
27   Refitting the master cylinder is the reverse of the removal procedure, but on completion bleed the hydraulic system, as described in Section 2.

13   Brake (and clutch) pedal box – removal, overhaul and refitting

1   Remove the driver's side glovebox and hinge.
2   Pull off the side window demister hose.
3   Pull off the wiring block connector to the stop lamp switch.
4   Disconnect the flasher unit from the brackets mounted to the pedal box.
5   Remove the split-pin, clevis pin and washer from the clutch and brake pedals (Fig. 9.11).
6   Undo the top bolt that secures the steady bracket to the pedal box.
7   Loosen the cover bolt that retains the steady bracket to the accelerator pedal and push the assembly to one side.
8   Undo the two nuts and bolts that secure the bulkhead and facia. Lift the pedal box assembly away.
9   Remove the bolts and lift away the pedal stop bracket.
10   Remove the end clips and spacers.
11   Release the clutch pedal return spring and slide the clutch pedal off the pedal shaft.
12   Slide the pedal shaft through the brake pedal, remove the circlip and lift away the brake pedal.
13   Where necessary, renew the pedal pivot bushes, and the pedal rubbers, then reassemble, using other new parts as necessary.
14   Refitting of the pedal box is the reverse of the removal procedure.

1   Pedal box
2   Steering column to pedal box bolts and nuts
3   Nuts retaining pedal box to facia and bulkhead
4   Steering column to pedal box nuts and bolts
5   Steady bracket to pedal box bolt
6   Steady bracket
7   Steady bracket to accelerator pedal bolt
8   Pedal height adjustment bolt and locknut

Fig. 9.10 The brake pedal box assembly (Sec 13)

Fig. 9.11 Exploded view of the pedal box, brake and clutch pedal components (Sec 13)

1	Pedal box	8	Return spring (brake pedal)
2	Clutch pedal	9	Thrustwasher
3	Brake pedal	10	Felt seal
4	Pedal shaft	11	Spacer
5	Retaining clip	12	Spacer
6	Locking washer	13	Circlip
7	Return spring (clutch	14	Felt seal
	pedal)	15	Spacer

Fig. 9.12 Handbrake lever assembly (Sec 14)

1	Handbrake lever	4	Switch
2	Retaining bolts and washers	5	Earth wire connection
3	Clevis pin		

14 Handbrake lever assembly – removal and refitting

1   Chock the roadwheels and release the handbrake lever.
2   Refer to Chapter 12 and remove the centre console.
3   Undo and remove the two handbrake lever mounting bolts and pull the earth wire to one side.
4   Separate the single wiring connector to the handbrake warning light switch.
5   Lift the handbrake lever slightly to gain access to the split-pin and clevis pin that secure the handbrake cable end to the operating lever.
6   Remove the split-pin and clevis pin and lift the handbrake lever away.
7   Reverse the removal procedure for refitting, and then check the handbrake cable adjustment as described in Section 15.

15 Handbrake cable assembly – removal, refitting and adjustment

1   Raise the rear of the vehicle to gain access to the underside. Remember to provide additional support such as axle-stands or packing blocks.
2   Release the handbrake lever.
3   Pull the rubber protective boot away from the underside of the handbrake lever and remove the split-pin and clevis pin that secure the yoke end of the handbrake inner cable to the lever end.
4   Loosen the adjuster locknuts at the abutment bracket and slide the cable away from the bracket via the slotted hole.
5   Pull the protective rubber boot off the cable.
6   Remove the split-pin, washer and clevis pin at each rear brake operating lever on the backplate.
7   Release the cable from the guide piece on the axle tube.
8   Loosen the small nut and bolt at the compensator in order to release the trunnion (photo).
9   Pull the cable assembly out from the rear, taking care to guide the forward section through the two support clips attached to the axle casing.
10 Refitting is the reverse of removal, but the handbrake cable will require adjustment as described in the text below:
11 Ensure that the handbrake lever is fully off.
12 Slacken the handbrake cables by loosening the adjuster locknuts at the abutment bracket (photo) and at the left-hand lever end. Disconnect the cable fork ends from the operating levers at the brake backplate.
13 Start the engine and press the brake pedal hard three or four times. This will bring the brake shoes into the correct position. Stop the engine.
14 Reconnect the left-hand fork end and use its adjuster to take up slack until the compensator lever is 30° to the left of vertical, with the operating lever still in the off position (Fig. 9.14). Tighten the left-hand fork adjuster locknut (photo).
15 Reconnect the right-hand fork end. At the abutment bracket, pull the outer cable to the rear to take up slack until the right-hand operating lever just starts to move. Secure the cable in this position by means of the adjuster nut at the abutment bracket. Give the adjuster nut one whole turn further (in the direction of taking up slack) and secure with the locknut.
16 Apply the handbrake control by one notch and check that the rear wheels will rotate without binding. (A slight drag is permissible). Apply the control a further two notches and check that the rear wheels are locked. Readjust if necessary to achieve this.

16 Brake servo – removal and refitting

1   Remove the driver's glovebox.
2   Remove the split-pin, washer and clevis pin that secure the pushrod end to the brake pedal.
3   Remove the brake master cylinder as described in Section 12.
4   Disconnect the vacuum hose from the servo non-return valve.
5   Remove the four retaining nuts and spring washers. Withdraw the servo.

Fig. 9.13 Layout of the handbrake cable assembly (Sec 15)

15.8 The handbrake cables and compensator

15.12 The handbrake cable adjuster at the abutment bracket

Fig. 9.14 Adjusting the handbrake cable – compensator lever (4) should be at an angle of 30° as shown (Sec 15)

15.14 The left-hand handbrake fork adjuster

Fig. 9.15 Servo fixing points to bulkhead (Sec 16)

Fig. 9.16 Withdrawing the servo non-return valve (Sec 17)

2 Clevis pin (pushrod fork to brake pedal)
5 Servo retaining nuts

6   Refitting is the reverse of the removal procedure, but bleed the brakes on completion (see Section 2).

17 Brake servo non-return valve and filter – removal and refitting

Non-return valve
1   With the engine stopped, depress the brake pedal several times to release the servo vacuum.
2   Pull the vacuum hose off at the non-return valve elbow on the servo.
3   Withdraw the non-return valve.
4   Refitting is the reverse of the removal procedure; where necessary, renew the sealing rubber.

Filter
5   Remove the driver's glovebox.
6   Remove the split-pin, washer and clevis pin that secure the servo pushrod end to the brake pedal.
7   Pull the pushrod from the master cylinder and pull off the rubber boot.
8   Remove the steel ring from the pushrod housing and withdraw the felt and filter.
9   Refitting is the reverse of the removal procedure.

Fig. 9.17 Cross section through the servo/filter assembly (Sec 17)

3 Rubber boot   4 Steel ring   5 Felt and filter

18 Fault diagnosis – braking system

Symptom	Reason/s
Pedal travels almost to floorboards before brakes operate	Brake fluid too low Caliper leaking Master cylinder leaking (bubbles in master cylinder fluid) Brake flexible hose leaking Brake line fractured Brake system unions loose Rear automatic adjusters seized
Brake pedal feels springy	New linings not yet bedded-in Brake discs or drums badly worn or cracked Master cylinder securing nuts loose
Brake pedal feels spongy and soggy	Caliper or wheel cylinder leaking Master cylinder leaking (bubbles in master cylinder reservoir) Brake pipe line or flexible hose leaking Unions in brake system loose Air in hydraulic system
Excessive effort required to brake car	Pad or shoe linings badly worn New pads or shoes recently fitted – not yet bedded-in Harder linings fitted than standard causing increase in pedal pressure Linings and brake drums contaminated with oil, grease or hydraulic fluid Servo unit inoperative or faulty One half of dual brake system inoperative
Brakes uneven and pulling to one side	Linings and discs or drums contaminated with oil, grease or hydraulic fluid Tyre pressures unequal Radial ply tyres fitted at one end of the car only Brake caliper loose Brake pads or shoes fitted incorrectly Different type of linings fitted at each wheel Anchorages for front suspension or rear suspension loose Brake discs or drums badly worn, cracked or distorted
Brakes tend to bind, drag or lock-on	Air in hydraulic system Wheel cylinders seized Handbrake cables too tight

Chapter 10 Electrical system

For modifications, and information applicable to later models, see Supplement at end of manual

Contents

Specifications

System type .... 12 volt, negative earth

Battery
UK models	50 amp hr at 20 hr discharge rate
Export models	66 amp hr at 20 hr discharge rate

Alternator
Type:

All UK and export models	Lucas 23 ACR
Some early 2300 models	Lucas 18 ACR

23 ACR specifications:

Brush length, new	0·5 in (12·70 mm)
Brush length, minimum	0·2 in (5·0 mm) protrusion
Brush spring pressure	9 to 13 ozf (255 to 370 gf)
Stator windings	Three phase – delta connected
Field winding resistance at 20°C (68°F)	3·201 ohms
Regulator type	14 TR

Nominal output, hot:

Alternator speed	6000 rpm
Engine speed	2250 rpm
Control voltage	14 volts
Current	55 amp
Drivebelt tension	0·375 to 0·75 in (10 to 19 mm) at mid-point on longest section

Starter motor
Type	Lucas 2 M 100 PE

Brush length:

New	0·71 in (18·03 mm)
Minimum	0·375 in (9·53 mm)
Brush spring pressure	36 ozf (1 kgf)
Shaft endfloat, maximum	0·01 in (0·25 mm)

Solenoid winding resistance:
Pull-in . . . . 0·25 to 0·27 ohms
Hold-in . . . . 0·76 to 0·80 ohms

Windscreen wiper motor
Type . . . . Lucas
Armature endfloat . . . . 0·002 to 0·008 in (0·05 to 0·20 mm)
Brush length, new . . . . 0·380 in (9·7 mm)
Brush length, minimum . . . . 0·180 in (4·8 mm) or when narrow section is worn away on high
speed brush
Brush spring pressure . . . . 5 to 7 ozf (140 to 200 gf)

Bulbs

	Wattage
Headlamps (dip/main beam):	
2600 model (halogen bulbs)	60/55
*2300 model (tungsten bulbs)	40/45
Front indicator lamp	21
Front parking lamp	5
Tail lamp	4
Reverse lamp	21
Stop lamp	21
Number plate lamp	6
Rear fog lamp	21
Instrument panel illumination	1·2
Hazard warning light	1·5
Boot light	5
Brake failure warning light	5
Handbrake warning light	1·2
Cigar lighter illumination	2·2
Clock illumination	2·2
Interior lamp	6
Fibre optic light source	5 (use a 4W replacement)
Front fog lamp (optional extra)	55
2600 models only:	
Door open guard lamp	5
Map light	6
Glovebox light	6

*Note: *The 2300 model may have halogen bulbs fitted as an optional extra. It is therefore advisable to check the type of bulb fitted before obtaining a replacement.*

Fuses (main fuse box)

	Circuits protected
No 1 – 2	Spare fuse
No 3 – 4 (25 amp)	Heater
No 5 – 6 (25 amp)	Battery control
No 7 – 8 (25 amp)	Hazard flashers
No 9 – 10 (25 amp)	Ignition
No 11 – 12 (35 amp)	Screen washers and wipers
No 13 – 14 (25 amp)	RH main beam
No 15 – 16 (25 amp)	LH main beam
No 17 – 18 (15 amp)	RH dipped beam
No 19 – 20 (15 amp)	LH dipped beam
No 21 – 22 (15 amp)	Side/tail, rear fog and panel lights
No 23 – 24 (25 amp)	Front fog lamps

In-line fuses
50 amp (near fuse box)	Heated rear screen
3 amp (behind radio)	Radio supply

Torque wrench settings

	lbf ft	Nm
Alternator mounting bolts	21	28
Alternator pulley nut	30	40
Starter motor securing bolts	30 to 35	40 to 47

1 General description

The electrical system is of the 12 volt type. The major components comprise a 12 volt battery, of which the negative terminal is earthed; a Lucas alternator is fitted to the front right-hand side of the engine and is driven from the engine crankshaft pulley and a pre-engaged Lucas starter motor is mounted on the rear right-hand side of the engine.

The battery supplies current for the ignition, lighting and other electrical circuits, and provides a reserve of electricity when the current consumed by the electrical equipment exceeds that being replaced by the alternator. Normally the alternator is able to meet any demand placed upon it.

The 2600 model has several extra electrical features over the 2300 model. These are notably the tachometer, halogen (as opposed to tungsten) headlamps, interior illumination for the front underdash lockers and map reading light, additional warning light for bulb failure, oil pressure gauge and intermittent windscreen wipers. Also the 2600 models can have electric window lifts as an optional extra, and on both models front fog lamps are optional. Further details of these features are given in the text.

When fitting electrical accessories to cars with a negative earth system, it is important, if they contain silicone diodes or transistors, that they are connected correctly, otherwise damage may result to the components concerned. Before purchasing any electrical accessory, check that it has or can be adjusted to the correct polarity to suit the car.

It is important that the battery leads are always disconnected if the battery is to be boost charged, or if any body or mechanical repairs are to be carried out using electric arc welding equipment, otherwise, serious damage can be caused to the more delicate instruments, especially those containing semi-conductors.

2 Battery – removal and refitting

On models with a central door locking system, refer also to Chapter 13, Section 12.

1 Detach the negative battery lead followed by the positive battery lead from the battery terminal lugs. Disconnecting the leads in this order prevents the possibility of 'shorting' the battery.
2 Loosen the nuts and swing the battery retainer downwards.
3 Lift out the battery.
4 Before refitting, ensure that the retainer is in the downward position and that the hooks are engaged in the body aperture. Check that the leads and loom wires are not trapped.
5 Fit the battery, then connect the terminal leads, positive first. Do not hammer them on. They may jam or at the worst the battery will crack.
6 Finally, smear the battery terminals and lead ends with a little petroleum jelly or a proprietary brand of battery corrosion inhibitor. Do not use regular lubricating grease as a substitute.

3 Battery – maintenance and inspection

1 Normal weekly battery maintenance consists of checking the electrolyte level of each cell to ensure that the separators are covered by $\frac{1}{4}$ in (6 mm) of electrolyte. If the level has fallen, top-up the battery using distilled water only. Do not overfill. If a battery is overfilled or any electrolyte spilled, immediately wipe away the excess as electrolyte attacks and corrodes very rapidly any metal it comes into contact with.
2 If the battery has the 'Auto-fill' device fitted, a special topping-up sequence is required. The white balls in the 'Auto-fill' battery are part of the automatic topping-up device which ensures correct electrolyte level. The vent chamber should remain in position at all times except when topping-up or taking specific gravity readings. If the electrolyte level in any of the cells is below the bottom of the filling tube, top-up as follows:

(a) *Lift off the vent chamber cover*
(b) *With the battery level, pour distilled water into the trough until all the filling tubes and trough are full*
(c) *Immediately refit the cover to allow the water in the trough and tubes to flow into the cells. Each cell will automatically receive the correct amount of water*

3 As well as keeping the terminals clean and covered with petroleum jelly, the top of the battery, and especially the top of the cells, should be kept clean and dry. This helps prevent corrosion and ensures that the battery does not become partially discharged by leakage through dampness and dirt.
4 Once every three months, remove the battery and inspect the battery securing bolts, the battery clamp plate, tray and battery leads for corrosion (white fluffy deposits, on the metal, which are brittle to the touch). If any corrosion is found, clean off the deposits with ammonia or a solution of bicarbonate of soda and warm water, and paint over the clean metal with anti-rust and anti-acid paint.
5 Cracks are frequently caused to the top of the battery case by pouring in distilled water in the middle of winter *after* instead of *before* a run. This gives the water no chance to mix with the electrolyte and so the former freezes and splits the battery case.
6 If topping-up the battery becomes too frequent and the case has been inspected for cracks that could cause leakage but none are found, the battery is being overcharged and the alternator will have to be checked. Generally, this indicates that the regulator (housed within the alternator end cover) is at fault thus allowing the alternator to operate uncontrolled, delivering full output even when the battery is fully charged. A fairly basic check can be carried out (see Section 7), but as

Fig. 10.1 The battery and retainer (Sec 2)

a general principle this sort of job is best left to a competent auto-electrician or your Rover dealer.
7 With the battery on the bench at the three monthly interval check, measure the specific gravity with a hydrometer to determine the state of charge and condition of the electrolyte. There should be very little variation between the different cells, and, if a variation in excess of 0.025 is present, it will be due to either:

(a) *Loss of electrolyte from the battery at some time caused by spillage or a leak, resulting in a drop in the specific gravity of the electrolyte when the deficiency was replaced with distilled water instead of fresh electrolyte*
(b) *An internal short circuit caused by buckling of the plates or a similar fault, pointing to the likelihood of total battery failure in the near future*

8 The specific gravity of the electrolyte for fully charged conditions at the temperatures indicated, is listed in Table A. The specific gravity of a fully discharged battery at different temperatures of the electrolyte is given in Table B.

Table A

Specific gravity – battery fully charged
1.268 at 100°F or 38°C electrolyte temperature
1.272 at 90°F or 32°C electrolyte temperature
1.276 at 80°F or 27°C electrolyte temperature
1.280 at 70°F or 21°C electrolyte temperature
1.284 at 60°F or 16°C electrolyte temperature
1.288 at 50°F or 10°C electrolyte temperature
1.292 at 40°F or 4°C electrolyte temperature
1.296 at 30°F or -1.5°C electrolyte temperature

Table B

Specific gravity – battery fully discharged
1.098 at 100°F or 38°C electrolyte temperature
1.102 at 90°F or 32°C electrolyte temperature
1.106 at 80°F or 27°C electrolyte temperature
1.110 at 70°F or 21°C electrolyte temperature
1.114 at 60°F or 16°C electrolyte temperature
1.118 at 50°F or 10°C electrolyte temperature
1.122 at 40°F or 4°C electrolyte temperature
1.126 at 30°F or -1.5°C electrolyte temperature

4 Battery electrolyte – replenishment

1 With the battery fully charged, check the specific gravity of the electrolyte in each of the cells. If one or more of the cells reads 0.025, or more, below the others, it is likely that some electrolyte has been lost. Check each cell for short circuits with a voltage meter. A four to seven second test should give a steady reading of between 1.2 and 1.8 volts.
2 Top the cell up with a solution of 1 part sulphuric acid to 2.5 parts of water, bought ready mixed from your garage. If the cell is already

fully topped up, draw some electrolyte out of it with a hydrometer. Continue to top up the cell with the freshly made electrolyte and then recharge the battery and check the hydrometer readings.

5 Battery – charging

Note: *Before charging the battery disconnect the terminal leads, check the electrolyte level and if possible, remove the battery from the car.*

1 In winter time when heavy demand is placed upon the battery, such as when starting from cold and much electrical equipment being continually in use, it is a good idea to occasionally have the battery fully charged from an external source at the rate of 3.5 to 4 amps.
2 Continue to charge the battery at this rate until no further rise in specific gravity is noted over a four-hour period.
3 Alternatively, a trickle charger charging at the rate of 1.5 amps, can be safely used overnight.
4 Specially rapid 'boost' charges which are claimed to restore the power of the battery in 1 to 2 hours are most dangerous, as they can cause serious damage to the battery plates through overheating.
5 Whilst charging the battery, note that the temperature of the electrolyte should never exceed 100°F.
6 Always disconnect both battery cables before the external charger is connected otherwise serious damage to the alternator may occur.

6 Alternator – general description, maintenance and precautions

1 Briefly, the alternator comprises a rotor and stator. Voltage is induced in the coils of the stator as soon as the rotor revolves. This is a 3-phase alternating voltage which is then rectified by diodes to provide the necessary current for the electrical system. The level of the voltage required to maintain the battery charge is controlled by a regulator unit.

2 Maintenance consists of occasionally wiping away any oil or dirt which may have accumulated on the outside of the unit.
3 No lubrication is required as the bearings are sealed for life.
4 Check the drivebelt tension at the intervals given in Routine Maintenance. Refer to Section 8, for the procedure.
5 Due to the need for special testing equipment and the possibility of damage being caused to the alternator diodes if incorrect testing methods are adopted, it is recommended that overhaul or major repair is entrusted to a Lucas or Rover dealer. Alternatively, a service exchange unit should be obtained.
6 Alternator brush renewal is dealt with in Section 9.
7 Take extreme care when connecting the battery to ensure that the polarity is correct, and never run the engine with a battery charger connected. Do not stop the engine by removing a battery lead as the alternator will almost certainly be damaged. When boost starting from another battery, ensure that it is connected positive to positive and negative to negative (photo).

7 Alternator – testing in position in the car

If the alternator is suspected of being faulty, a test can be carried out which can help in isolating any such fault. A dc voltmeter (range 0 to 15V) and a dc ammeter (suitable for the nominal output current – see Specifications) will be required.
1 Check the alternator drivebelt tension and adjust if necessary. See Section 8.
2 Disconnect the brown cable from the starter motor solenoid. Connect the ammeter between this cable and the starter motor solenoid terminal.
3 Connect the voltmeter across the battery terminals.
4 Run the engine at 2250 rpm (6000 rpm of the alternator); the ammeter reading should stabilize.
5 If the ammeter reads zero, an internal fault in the alternator is indicated.
6 If less than 10 amps is indicated, and the voltmeter shows 13.6 to

Fig. 10.2 Exploded view of the Lucas 23ACR alternator (Sec 6)

6.7 The alternator identification plate

14.4 volts, where it is known that the battery is in a low state of charge, the alternator is suspect and should be checked by an auto-electrician. The nominal output is given in the Specifications.
7 If the ammeter reads less than 10 amps and the voltmeter reads less than 13.6 volts, a fault in the alternator internal regulator is indicated. A fault in the regulator is also indicated when the voltage exceeds 14.4 volts.

8 Alternator – removal, refitting and drivebelt adjustment

1 Detach the battery earth lead.
2 Slide the harness plug lock outboard and down to unlock it, then remove the plug.
3 Remove the locknut on the alternator adjustment bolt (4) and slacken off the main pivot bolt (2). See Fig. 10.3.
4 Slacken the adjustment link to engine bolt (3) and the alternator adjustment bolt (4) (photo).
5 Push the alternator in towards the engine and the drivebelt can be removed.
6 Remove the adjustment bolt with its washer and push the link up and out of the way.
7 Remove the main pivot bolt washer and nut whilst supporting the weight of the alternator. Then lift the alternator clear.
8 Take care when withdrawing the main pivot bolt not to lose the

Fig. 10.3 The alternator showing the mounting and adjustment link nuts and bolts (Sec 8)

2 Main pivot bolt and nut
3 Adjustment link to engine bolt
4 Alternator adjustment bolt

8.4 The alternator drivebelt adjustment link

9.1 Remove the two bolts and lift off the alternator cover

9.2a Remove the alternator brush-holder bolts

9.2b Inspecting the condition of the alternator brushes

9.3 Withdrawing the alternator brush and backplate

washers or spacers, which should be as follows:

> Vehicles with power-assisted steering – 4 washers
> Vehicles with manual steering – 2 spacers and 4 washers.

9   Refitting is basically the reverse of the removal sequence. However, before tightening up the mounting bolts, ensure that the belt tension has been checked as described below:

10 Where necessary, slacken the adjustment bolts (4) and (3) and the main pivot bolt (2).

11 Pull the alternator away from the engine and tighten the adjustment bolt (4). Check the belt tension by depressing the belt at the middle of its longest run. Movement should be approximately 0·375 to 0·75 in (10 to 19 mm). Re-adjust if necessary. **Note:** *It is permissible to apply leverage at the drive end bracket if necessary, to obtain the correct tension, but only a softwood lever, or similar item may be used.*

12 Tighten the mounting bolts on completion.

13 If a new belt has been fitted, the belt tension should be rechecked after about 250 miles (400 km) of travelling.

9   Alternator – brush renewal

1   Remove the alternator from the car (see Section 8). Remove the 2 small bolts and take off the cover (photo).

2   Undo the 2 bolts (arrowed) that retain the brush holder (photo) and gently ease the brush holder upwards and invert it to inspect the condition of the brushes. There is no need to remove the wires to do this (photo).

3   To remove the outer brushes, remove the 2 small $\frac{3}{16}$ AF bolts and leads, noting the position of each, and withdraw the brush attached to the backplate (photo).

4   To remove the inner brushes, remove the 2 small $\frac{3}{16}$ bolts and single wire. Withdraw the brush and backplate.

5   Refit the new brushes in the reverse order to removal, connecting up the wires correctly.

6   Ensure all bolts are tight.

7   Refit the cover.

8   Refit the alternator to the car (see Section 8)

10 Starter motor – general description

When the ignition switch is turned, current flows through the solenoid pull-in winding and starter motor, moving the solenoid plunger. At the same time a much smaller current flows through the solenoid hold-in winding directly to earth.

The movement of the solenoid plunger causes the drive pinion to move and engage with the starter ring gear on the flywheel. At the same time the main contacts close and energise the motor circuit. The pull-in winding now becomes ineffective and it remains in the operated condition by the action of the hold-in winding only.

A special one-way clutch is fitted to the starter drive pinion, so that when the engine commences to fire there is no possibility of it driving the starter motor.

When the ignition key is released, the solenoid is de-energised and returns to its original position. This breaks the supply to the motor and returns the drive pinion to the disengaged position.

11 Starter motor – removal and refitting

1   Detach the battery earth lead and raise the front of the car to a suitable working height for access to the starter motor (photo).

2   Remove the nut and spring washer, then disconnect the heavy battery feed cable to the starter motor solenoid.

3   Disconnect the white/yellow and white/brown wires at the solenoid by removing the two cross-head screws. Note the locations of the wires.

4   Using a socket, extension and ratchet spanner, remove the starter motor mounting flange bolts.

5   Lift the starter motor out and downwards from the engine (photo).

6   Refitting is the reverse of removal, but check that the solenoid wires are connected correctly.

7   See the Specifications for mounting bolt torque figures.

12 Starter motor – overhaul

1   Slacken the nut which secures the connecting link to the solenoid terminal 'STA'.

2   Remove the two screws that secure the solenoid to the drive end bracket.

3   Lift the solenoid plunger upwards and separate it from the engagement lever. Extract the return spring seat and dust excluder from the plunger body.

4   Withdraw the block from between the drive end bracket and the starter motor yoke.

5   Remove the armature end cap from the commutator end bracket.

6   Chisel off some of the claws from the armature shaft spire nut so

11.1 The starter motor in position (engine removed)

Fig. 10.4 Exploded view of the starter motor (Sec 10)

11.5 Removing the starter motor

Fig. 10.5 LH headlamp unit with halogen bulb (Sec 14)

that the nut can be withdrawn from the shaft.

7   Remove the two tie-bolts and then withdraw the commutator and cover and starter motor yoke from the drive end bracket.

8   Separate the commutator end cover from the starter motor yoke, at the same time disengaging the field coil brushes from the brush box to facilitate separation.

9   Withdraw the thrustwasher from the armature shaft.

10   Remove the spire nut from the engagement lever pivot pin and then extract the pin from the drive end bracket.

11   Withdraw the armature and roller clutch drive assembly from the drive end bracket.

12   Using a piece of tubing, drive back the thrust collar to expose the jump ring on the armature shaft. Remove the jump ring and withdraw the thrust collar and roller clutch.

13   Remove the spring ring and release the engagement lever, thrustwashers and spring from the roller-clutch drive.

14   Remove the dust excluding seal from the bore of the drive end bracket.

15   Inspect all components for wear. If the armature shaft bushes require renewal, press them out or screw in a $\frac{1}{2}$ in tap. Before inserting the new bushes, soak them in engine oil for 24 hours.

16   If the brushes have worn below the minimum specified length, renew them by cutting the end bracket brush leads from the terminal post. File a groove in the head of the terminal post and solder the new brush leads in to the groove. Cut the field winding brush leads about $\frac{1}{4}$ in (6 mm) from the joint of the field winding. Solder the new brush leads to the ends of the old ones. Localise the heat to prevent damage to the field windings.

17   Check the field windings for continuity using a torch battery and test bulb. If the windings are faulty, removal of the pole shoe screws should be left to a service station having a pressure screwdriver, as they are very tight.

18   Check the insulation of the armature by connecting a test bulb and torch battery. Use probes placed on the armature shaft and each commutator section in turn. If the test bulb lights at any position then the insulation has broken down and the armature must be renewed. Discolouration of the commutator should be removed by polishing it with a piece of glass paper (not emery cloth). Do not undercut the insulation.

19   Reassembly is a reversal of dismantling, but apply grease to the moving parts of the engagement lever, the outer surface of the roller clutch housing and to the lips of the drive end bracket dust seal. Fit a new spire nut to the armature shaft, positioning it to give the specified shaft endfloat. Measure this endfloat by inserting feeler blades between the face of the spire nut and the flange of the commutator end bush.

13   Headlamp unit – removal and refitting

1   Open the bonnet.

14.3 The outer left headlamp wiring plug and rubber cover

2   If the left-hand unit is to be removed, carry out the following operations:

(a)   Remove the screen washer reservoir
(b)   Undo the four bolts that secure the radiator in position

3   If the right-hand unit is to be removed, then it will be necessary to remove the battery (Section 2) for better access.

4   From the rear of the light units, pull off the harness plugs for the dipped/main beam and the main beam lamp.

5   Loosen one of the bolts that secure the headlamp sealing panel. Push the panel inwards slightly to provide clearance.

6   Remove the screws that secure the headlamp assembly by manoeuvering it upwards and forwards from the vehicle body.

7   Refitting is the reverse of the removal procedure.

14   Headlamp – bulb renewal

1   Open the bonnet.

Main/dip beam bulb (outer) – Halogen

2   Pull off the wiring harness plug from the rear of the light unit (photo).

3   Remove the protective rubber cover (photo).

4   Squeeze the ends of the spring retainer clip together and tip the retainer clip outwards to release the bulb holder.

5   Withdraw the bulb, but do not handle the glass part (photo).

14.5 Withdraw the bulb

14.14 Slide the headlamp main beam unit rubber cover back along the wires

Fig. 10.6 LH headlamp unit with tungsten bulb (Sec 14)

6   Insert the new bulb without touching the glass part. It will locate in one position only, this being indicated by the positioning of the pegs and cut-outs. If the glass is accidentally touched, clean it with methylated spirit, using a clean lint-free cloth.
7   Secure the bulb by relocating the spring retainer clip.
8   Refit the rubber cover and wiring harness plug.

Main/dip beam bulb (outer) – Tungsten
9   Pull off the harness plug.
10   Remove the rubber cover.
11   Squeeze and release the ends of the wire clip and swing it back.
12   Remove the bulb.
13   Fit the new bulb ensuring that the lugs fit correctly; the bulb can only fit one way. Refit the wire clip and cover and plug in.

Main beam bulb (inner) – Halogen
14   Disconnect the rubber cover by tilting it and then pull it back along the two wires (photo).
15   Disconnect the two wiring spade connectors.
16   Disengage the wire retainer clip and lift out the bulb. Do not handle the bulb by its glass portion.
17   Fit the bulb so that it is positioned correctly, then refit the spring retainer and wiring connections. If the glass is accidentally touched, clean it with methylated spirit, using a clean lint-free cloth.
18   Slide the rubber cover up the wires and relocate it.

Main beam bulb (inner) – Tungsten
19   Pull off the harness plug and remove the rubber cover. See Fig. 10.6.
20   Unhook the securing ends of the wire clip and swing it back.
21   Remove the bulb.

15.2 The vertical beam adjuster knob

22   Fitting the new bulb is the reverse procedure to removal, but ensure that the bulb is fitted into the holder correctly.

15   Headlamp beam – alignment

1   It is recommended that adjustment of the headlamp beams should only be carried out by a dealer or garage having beam setting equipment. This should always be carried out if a headlamp shell or bulb has been fitted.
2   Where the headlamp beam is known to be greatly out of alignment, it is permissible to make adjustments using the three large plastic knobs located at the rear of the headlamp unit (photo). However, this must only be regarded as a temporary adjustment, and when in doubt, the beams should be set to aim perhaps more towards the ground, in order to obviate glare. This adjustment must be checked at the earliest opportunity by a suitably equipped dealer.

16   Front parking/flasher lamps

Bulb renewal
1   Remove the three screws and withdraw the lens, then remove the

desired bayonet-fitting bulb. Refitting of the bulb is the reverse of this procedure.

Removal and refitting

2   Open the bonnet and disconnect the wiring harness plug.
3   Remove the single retaining nut, spring washer and plain washer.
4   Push out the stud and withdraw the two front spigots from the grommets in the vehicle body.
5   Lift the lamp assembly away and extract the rubber gasket.
6   Refitting is the reverse of the removal procedure.

17 Fog lamp (front)

Bulb renewal

1   Prise the rim of the fog lamp out of its housing.
2   Support the weight of the lamp and pull off the two wiring connectors at its rear.
3   Disengage the ends of the wire retainer clip and withdraw the bulb. Do not touch the glass part of the bulb.
4   Refitting of the bulb rim assembly to the housing is the reverse of the removal procedure. Reconnection of the lamp wires is as follows. The grey wire is the bulb feed and the black wire connects to the lamp body earth terminal.

Removal and refitting

5   Open the bonnet and disconnect the fog lamp wiring harness located next to the rear of the headlamp unit.
6   Attach a short length of cord to the fog lamp harness and tie the other end of the cord to a suitable anchorage. This precaution will prevent the wiring harness from being pulled completely through during the removal operation.
7   Disconnect the two snap connectors.
8   Unscrew the fog lamp adjustment screw, counting the number of turns in order to obtain a satisfactory setting on refitting.
9   Through a hole in the underbelly panel, insert a probe and depress the inner spring retainer. With the spring retainer so depressed, lower the lamp and withdraw the harness.
10   Refitting is the reverse of the removal operation. When reconnecting the snap connectors the blue/yellow cable must be connected into the grey cable and the two remaining black cables connected together.
11   Turn the adjustment screw to its original position and make the final adjustment at night on a suitable stretch of road.

18 Rear lamp assembly

Bulb renewal

1   Open the fifth door.
2   Undo the thumb screws and lift away the cover panel from the rear of the lamp assembly.
3   All the bulb holders except the tail lamp can be removed by twisting them in an anti-clockwise direction (photo). The tail lamp holder is a push fit in the lamp body.
4   Withdraw the bayonet-fitting bulb. Refitting is the reverse of the removal procedure.

Removal and refitting

5   Remove the bulb holders as described in paragraph 3.
6   Disconnect the single connector and terminal end from the tail lamp bulb holder.
7   Undo the six nuts and extract the special anti-vibration washers.
8   Where the left-hand lamp is being removed, the bulb failure indicator unit will have to be removed from the mounting bracket inner studs.
9   Remove the harness earth tag(s) and the single star washer from the upper inboard stud.
10   Remove the harness strap from the upper centre stud and withdraw the lamp assembly, together with the rubber gasket, from the vehicle.
11   Refitting is the reverse of removal. Where any wiring connections have been disconnected they should be refitted as shown in Fig. 10.7.

18.3 Removing the rear fog lamp bulb and holder

Fig. 10.7 LH rear lamp wiring connections (Sec 18)

B	Black	RG	Red/green
GR	Green/red	GN	Green/brown
NP	Brown/purple	R	Red

Note: On RH assemblies the indicator wire is GW. (Green/White)

19 Number plate lamp

Bulb renewal

1   Remove the two screws and withdraw the lens, then remove the festoon-type bulb. Refitting is the reverse of this procedure (photo).

Removal and refitting

2   Remove the two retaining screws and withdraw the lamp from the body, forward edge first.
3   Remove the festoon-type bulb and pull off the two wiring connectors.
4   Refitting is the reverse of removal.

20 Courtesy lamp (centre pillar)

Bulb renewal

1   Disconnect the battery earth terminal connection, for safety reasons.
2   Gently pull the lens out from its centre pillar mounting (photo).
3   Prise out the festoon-type bulb. Refitting is the reverse of removal.

19.1 Removing the number plate lamp bulb

20.2 Centre pillar courtesy light removed

21.2 Removing the luggage compartment courtesy lamp

23.1 Removing the door 'open guard' lamp lens

Removal and refitting
4   Pull the lens out from the centre pillar and remove the festoon-type bulb as described in paragraphs 1 to 3 above.
5   Pull out the single spade connector.
6   Note the positions of the other two terminal wires, then pull them out of their respective location points.
7   Refitting is the reverse of removal.

21 Courtesy lamp (luggage compartment)

Bulb renewal
1   Disconnect the battery negative lead.
2   Carefully prise out the lamp assembly and remove the bayonet type bulb (photo). Refitting is the reversal of removal.

Removal and refitting
3   Extract the lamp assembly from the rear panel as described in paragraphs 1 to 2 above.
4   Note the positions of the two leads and pull them off. Withdraw the lamp.
5   Refitting is the reverse of removal.

22 Map reading lamp

Bulb renewal
1   Pull the lens away from the dashboard sufficiently to deflect the two plastic clips.
2   Withdraw the festoon-type bulb. Refitting is the reverse of removal.

Removal and refitting
3   Remove the lamp as described in paragraph 1. Open the glove box, then disconnect the two wiring connections.
4   Refitting is the reverse of removal. The purple wire is connected to the bulb contact and the black wire to the switch contact.

23 Door 'open guard' lamp

Bulb renewal
1   Open the door and carefully draw the lens out from the plastic rim (photo).
2   Remove the bayonet-type bulb. Refitting is the reverse of removal.

Removal and refitting

3   Disconnect the battery earth lead.
4   Open the door and draw the lens out from the plastic rim.
5   Carefully prise the plastic moulding out from the door frame.
6   Owing to the length and awkward run of the wiring harness, it is advisable to cut the two lamp wires at a distance of approximately 3 in (75 mm) from the lamp to facilitate removal.
7   Refitting of the lamp necessitates joining the wires up. The method recommended is to solder or crimp bullet connectors to the cable ends and then rejoin the cables using single snap connectors. The remainder of the refitting procedure is the reverse of removal.

24 Cigar lighter

Bulb renewal

1   Carefully prise the cigar lighter and plate clear of the console, unclip the bulb and remove the bayonet-type bulb.
2   Refitting is the reverse of removal.

Removal and refitting

3   Disconnect the battery negative lead.
4   Withdraw the heating unit and prise up the centre console panel in order to release the three plastic spigots.
5   Disconnect the two spade connectors and the single snap connector. Note the positions of the leads.
6   Squeeze the sides of the bulb cowl and withdraw it.
7   Using a pair of long-nosed pliers on the inner well cross-piece, unscrew the inner well from the outer well, and then remove the bezel.
8   Refitting is the reverse of the removal procedure; position the bulb cowl as necessary. When connecting the wires, the purple wire should be connected to the centre terminal and the black wire to the unit body.

25 Fibre optic lamp

This type of lamp is fitted to all 2600 models but only to the automatic version of the 2300. It illuminates the gearchange (automatic) and heater controls.

Bulb renewal

1   Remove the glovebox and locate the fibre optic lamp, fitted to the hinge assembly next to the heater (photo).
2   Pull the bulb holder out and remove the bayonet-type bulb. Refitting is the reverse of removal.

Removal and refitting

3   Refer to paragraphs 1 and 2 above and pull out the bulb holder.
4   Pull out the fibre element terminal ends as follows:

    2600 automatic version – 5
    2600 manual version – 4
    2300 automatic version – 1

5   Undo the two screws that secure the lamp to the hinge bracket and lift the lamp away.
6   Refitting is the reverse of removal.

26 Fibre optic system components – removal and refitting

Refer to Fig. 10.8 for details of the system layout. This system is not fitted to the 2300 manual model. In 2300 models only, the automatic gearchange selector panel is illuminated by this method. In 2600 automatic models, the automatic gearchange selector panel and the heater control panel are both illuminated by this method. However, in the 2600 manual model, this system is used to illuminate the heater control panel only. See also Section 25 of this Chapter.

Selector panel illumination

1   Remove the two screws at either end of the panel.
2   Lift the panel sufficiently to expose the fibre optic illumination system.
3   Pull off the single wiring spade connector and withdraw the fibre element terminal end.
4   Lift the panel away.

25.1 The fibre optic lamp (arrowed)

5   Refitting is the reverse of removal, but take care to prevent the fibre element being trapped by the panel.

Heater control illumination

6   Pull off the heater control knobs and remove the two panel retaining screws.
7   Tip the top of the panel away from the housing and pull off the four wiring spade connectors. Withdraw the four fibre element terminal ends.
8   Lift the panel away.
9   Refitting is the reverse of removal.

27 Bulb failure indicator

1   If the bulb failure indicator should fail to illuminate when the ignition switch is in the start position, then move the master light switch to the side light position and check that the side lamps are illuminated. Should the side lights fail to illuminate, then it is reasonable to assume that the bulb failure indicator has become defective.
2   The bulb failure indicator is mounted adjacent to the left-hand rear light cluster.
3   The bulb failure indicator unit can be temporarily by-passed by withdrawing the wiring block connector, breaking off the central locating lug and refitting the block connector after rotating it through 180°.
Note: *This procedure is only intended as a 'get you home' repair, and a new unit should be fitted as soon as possible (photo).*

28 Instrument illumination and panel warning lights

1   Disconnect the battery negative terminal lead.
2   Turn the knob at the left-hand end of the instrument panel through 90°, and withdraw the instrument panel fuse box end cover.
3   Lift the top cover of the instrument panel off and disconnect the two snap connectors which are located in the radio speaker supply cables.
4   If a panel warning light bulb is to be renewed, then lift one spring clip and pull the small panel housing at the front of the instrument panel away to gain access to the bulbs.
5   To renew the instrument illumination bulbs in either the speedometer or tachometer housing, depress the two plastic clips on top of the panel and remove the face panel. In the Rover 2300 models, the same method is used to remove the small instrument housing which takes the place of the tachometer.
6   The centre block can be pulled out on its harness.
7   The bulbs can then be taken out of their holders and renewed.
8   Refitting is the reverse of removal.

Fig. 10.8 The fibre optic system (2600 automatic transmission model shown) (Sec 26)

27.3 The bulb failure indicator unit

Clock illumination

9   Open the glovebox and push the clock out of the facia from the rear.
10 Remove the bulb holder and unscrew the bulb.
11 Renew the bulb and reassemble in the reverse order.

29 Glovebox lamp

Bulb renewal

1   Open the glovebox and carefully prise open the two connector clips to remove the festoon-type bulb. Refitting is the reverse of removal.

Removal and refitting

2   Carry out the removal instructions detailed in paragraph 1 for bulb removal.
3   Disconnect the two wiring connectors and lift away the lamp.
4   Refitting is the reverse of removal.

30 Relays and flasher units – removal and refitting

Hazard flasher unit

1   The hazard flasher unit is located together with the turn signal

flasher unit and attached to the brake pedal mounting bracket (photo).
2   Identify the hazard flasher unit by the wire colour codes blue/brown and light green/purple.
3   Pull the flasher unit away from its retainer clip and pull off the two wiring connections mentioned in paragraph 2. Refitting is the reverse of removal.

Turn signal flasher unit
4   Refer to paragraph 1 for the location of the unit.
5   Identify the turn signal flasher unit by the colour coding of the supply cables attached to it, which are both of the same colour, light green/brown.
6   Removal and refitting is as described in paragraph 3.

Heated rear window relay
7   Disconnect the battery earth lead and remove the passenger glovebox.
8   Loosen the two bolts that locate the relay mounting bracket (photo).
9   Push the relay bracket forwards to disengage its slots from the bolts and allow the bracket to hang down.
10   Identify the heated rear window relay by the brown/yellow, brown/red, white/slate and black wires attached to it.
11   Remove a single nut, spring washer and bolt and disconnect the harness plug.
12   Refitting is the reverse of removal.

Heater motor supply line relay
13   This relay is mounted together with the heated rear window relay and is identified by the brown, brown/blue, white and black wires attached to it.
14   Removal and refitting are identical to the procedures described in paragraphs 7 to 12.

Lighting supply line relay
15   The location, removal and refitting of this relay is identical to that described in paragraphs 7 to 12. The lighting supply line relay can be identified by the brown, red/blue, red/green and black wires attached to it.

Starter motor relay
16   The starter motor relay is located in the engine bay next to the radiator overflow (expansion) tank (photo).
17   Pull the wiring connector block off the relay and undo the single retaining screw.
18   Refitting is the reverse of removal.

Window lift supply line relays
19   These relays, where applicable, are mounted together with the heated rear window, heater motor supply line and lighting supply line relays.
20   Removal and refitting is as described in paragraphs 7 to 12.
21   The rear window lift supply line relay can be identified by the brown/green, light green, brown/purple and black wires attached to it. The front window lift supply line relay has brown/green, green, brown/purple and black wires attached to it.

31 Fuses

1   A list of fuse ratings and the circuits protected by these fuses are given in the Specifications Section. Further details can be obtained by reference to the appropriate wiring diagram or the end of the fuse box end cover.
2   The bulk of the fuses are located in the end of the instrument panel housing. Access to these fuses is achieved by turning the end cover knob through 90° (photo). Additional in-line fuses for the heated rear screen and radio supply are located beneath the instrument panel top cover, well forward behind the speedometer (photo). To remove the instrument panel top cover, remove the screw and clip located at the top of the main fuse box and pull the cover left to release the three cover securing lugs. Lift off the cover (photo). Refitting the cover is the reverse of the removal procedure. The in-line fuse for the central door locking system (if fitted) is located in the right-hand footwell, adjacent

30.1 Flasher unit relays on pedal bracket (arrowed)

30.8 The relay mounting bracket

30.16 The starter motor relay beside the expansion tank

31.2a The main fuse box located in the end of the instrument housing with a list of fuses and protected circuits

31.2b The heated rear screen and radio supply in-line fuses

31.2c Instrument panel top cover fuse information label

to the accelerator pedal.

3   If any item of electrical equipment fails to operate, first check the appropriate fuse. If the fuse has blown the first thing to do is to find the cause, otherwise it will merely blow again (fuses can blow through age fatigue, but this is the exception rather than the rule). Having found the faulty fuse, switch off the electrical equipment and then fit a new fuse. From the Specifications, note which circuits are served by the blown fuse and then start to switch each one on separately in turn. It may be necessary to have the ignition circuit switched on at the same time. The fuse should blow again when the faulty item is switched on. If the fuse does not blow immediately, start again, but this time leave the circuits switched on and build up the cumulative total lead on the fuse. If and when it blows, you will have an indication of which circuits may be causing the problem. If a new fuse does not blow until the car is moving, then look for a loose, chafed or pinched wire.

4   When fitting a new fuse, always use a fuse of the correct rating. Do not, under any circumstances, fit a fuse of a higher rating or use a piece of tin foil as a substitute. It should be clearly understood that fuses are the weakest link in a circuit. Any fault causing shorting or an overload of a particular circuit will cause the fuse wire to melt and thus break the circuit. A higher rated fuse or a piece of tin foil will not break the circuit and in such cases overheating and the risk of fire at the fault source, could easily occur.

5   If a fault occurs in one accessory or component and its rectification defies all efforts, always remember than it could be a relay at fault. Relays cannot be repaired or adjusted and, if faulty, should be renewed as a unit (details given in other Sections of this Chapter).

32   Ignition/starter switch – removal and refitting

1   Disconnect the battery earth lead.
2   Slacken the steering column clamp knob and lower the steering column to its lowest position.
3   Remove the steering column nacelle halves (one screw each).
4   In order to obtain better access, remove the door glass demist hose from the heater outlet.
5   Note the run of the switch harness and remove the three retaining straps (two securing it to the steering column and the third securing it to the mounting bracket).
6   Pull the harness away from the steering column to expose the ignition/starter switch harness plug.
7   Disconnect the harness plug and remove the two screws that secure the switch.
8   Remove the switch together with the wiring harness.
9   Refitting is the reverse of removal.

33   Multi-function stalk switch assembly – removal and refitting

1   Disconnect the battery earth lead.
2   Slacken the steering column clamp knob and lower the steering column to its lowest position.
3   Remove the steering column nacelle halves (one screw each).
4   Refer to Chapter 11 and remove the steering wheel.
5   In order to gain better access, remove the door glass demist hose from the heater outlet.
6   Note the run of the switch harness and remove the three retaining straps (two securing the harness to the steering column, the third retaining it to the mounting bracket).
7   Pull the harness away from the steering column to expose the four harness plugs.
8   Disconnect the three harness plugs associated with the steering column multi-function switch and the master light switch assembly.
9   Loosen the switch assembly clamp screw and remove the assembly complete with its harness.
10   If one of the switches is faulty, then it can be renewed individually by removing the single spire clip and undoing the two outer hexagon screws. Do not loosen or remove the two similar hexagon screws, located at the centre of the switch assembly. Where necessary the master light switch can be removed as described in Section 34.
11   Refitting is the reverse of removal, but where possible, renew the spire clip. Before refitting the switch assembly, ensure that the turn signal cancelling collar is correctly aligned by checking that the arrow on the collar is pointing towards the centre of the trafficator stock. Refer to Chapter 11 for the correct refitting of the steering wheel.

34   Switches – removal and refitting

Master light switch

1   Disconnect the battery negative lead.
2   Slacken the steering column clamp knob and lower the steering column to its lowest position.
3   Remove the steering column nacelle halves (one screw each).
4   Press the two spring clips on the side of the switch body inwards and withdraw the switch from the mounting (Fig. 10.10).
5   Note the positions and cable colour codes and pull off the three single pin connectors.
6   Refitting is the reverse of removal. When reconnecting the switch cables ensure that the brown cable is connected to terminal 3, the red/green cable to terminal 2 and the blue cable to terminal 1.

Fig. 10.9 Multi-function switch assembly detail (Sec 33)

1   Do not slacken or remove these hexagon screws
2   Outer hexagon screws, remove these to split unit
3   Spire clip

Fig. 10.10 The master light switch and wiring connections (Sec 34)

Fig. 10.11 The instrument housing and panel rheostat switch (Sec 34)

Heated rear screen, hazard flasher, front·fog lamp, rear fog lamp and rear window lift isolate switches

7   Disconnect the battery earth lead.

8   Remove the instrument housing end panel by turning the locking knob through 90°.

9   Lift off the lid of the instrument housing and push the appropriate switch out from its housing.

10 Disconnect the appropriate harness plug and withdraw the switch and its attached harness.

11 Refitting is the reverse of the removal procedure.

Panel rheostat switch

12 Disconnect the battery negative lead.

13 Remove the instrument housing end panel by turning the locking knob through 90°.

14 Lift off the lid of the instrument housing and disconnect the two wiring connectors for the radio speaker.

15 Under the facia locate and remove the three bolts, spring washers and plain washers that secure the instrument housing.

16 Release the two plastic clips on the fuse box and swing the fuse box into the instrument housing in order to gain access to a further retaining bolt.

17 Remove this retaining bolt and carefully raise the rheostat switch end of the instrument housing to gain access to the end cover screws.

18 Remove the rheostat end cover screws. Withdraw the end cover, and disconnect the rheostat multi-plug connector.

19 Pull the control knob off the rheostat switch, undo the switch retaining nut and remove the switch from the end panel. Note the position of the spring washer.

20 Refitting is the reverse of removal.

Door switch (courtesy lights)

21 With the door open, remove the single screw, withdraw the switch and detach the wiring connector.

22 Refitting is the reverse of the removal procedure.

Glovebox lamp switch

23 Open the glovebox, remove the single retaining screw and pull off the wiring connector.
24 Refitting is the reverse of the removal procedure.

Seat belt (belt switch)

25 Undo the single bolt to release the switch assembly and separate the harness plug after releasing the harness from the clip fixed to the seat frame.
26 Refitting is the reverse of the removal procedure.

Passengers seat belt (seat) switch

27 Remove the passenger seat as described in Chapter 12.
28 Remove the four screws and prise out the four studs to release the seat side trim mouldings.
29 Release the clip which retains the harness plug to the appropriate seat side trim moulding.
30 Remove the four bolts and any distance washers in order to separate the squab from the cushion.
31 Remove the four wire retainer clips that secure the cushion cover to the seat frame just behind the harness plug.
32 Remove the four clips to release the cushion cover cord from the seat frame.
33 Remove the five clips that secure the rear flap of the seat cushion cover to the seat frame.
34 Fold the cushion cover forward to reveal the switch which is glued to the cushion.
35 Break the adhesive to free the switch and then trace the loom into the cushion and disconnect the two single pin harness plugs.
36 Refitting is the reverse of the removal procedure.

Handbrake switch

37 Disconnect the battery negative lead.
38 On manual gearbox vehicles, pull up the gear lever boot and undo the four retainers. On automatic vehicles, firstly lift out the mat forward of the gear selector then prise out the two screw head covers.
39 Using a wide blade screwdriver, carefully prise up the rear panel of the centre console in order to release the four plastic spigots. Prise up the centre console panel between the handbrake and choke to release a further four plastic spigots.
40 Remove the six screws, two at the centre console side panel and the four that secure the centre console to the body. Raise the rear of the console to gain access to the handbrake switch.
41 Disconnect the switch feed wire connector, undo the single retainer screw and lift the switch away.
42 Refitting is the reverse of the removal procedure.

Choke switch

43 Disconnect the battery negative lead and carefully prise up the rear panel, held by 4 spigots, in the centre of the console.
44 Remove the screw that retains the choke control lever assembly.
45 Lift the rear of the choke control assembly to an angle of approximately 45° and pull it back slightly to release the forward hook.
46 Lift the bonnet and slide the choke cable through the bulkhead grommet by approximately 2.36 in (60 mm).
47 Pull the choke control assembly rearwards by approximately 2.36 in (60 mm) to obtain access to the choke switch.
48 Pull off the two wiring connectors at the switch. Disconnect the choke control rod from the control lever by removing the retaining clip.
49 Remove a single screw and lift away the choke switch.
50 Refitting is the reverse of the removal procedure.

Luggage compartment lamp switch

51 Open the tailgate and pull off the two spade connectors at the switch.
52 Remove the single retaining screw and lift away the switch.

Engine compartment lamp switch

53 Open the bonnet and disconnect the single feed wire at the switch.
54 Remove the single retaining screw and lift away the switch.
55 Refitting is the reverse of removal.

Stop light switch

56 Remove the driver's side glovebox and pull off the two spade connectors at the stop light switch. Undo the special nut and withdraw the

Fig. 10.12 The passenger's seat belt switch (Sec 34)

1·50 to 1·75mm.
0·060 to 0·070 in.

Fig. 10.13 Stop light switch adjustment (Sec 34)

    3   Special nut
    5   Thin nut
   14   Brake pedal bolt and nuts

stop light switch from the support bracket.
57 Where a new stop light switch is being fitted, transfer the thin nut to the new switch.
58 Refitting is basically the reverse of removal, but initially screw the thin nut on to the bottom of the thread.
59 Place the special nut in position between the brake pedal and bracket. Insert the switch through the bracket so that the locating flat is at the bottom.
60 Screw the special nut onto the switch until the nut recess contacts the switch body. Screw the thin nut up to the bracket and tighten it.
61 Measure the gap between the brake pedal bolt and the outer edge of the special nut with the brake pedal in the fully released position. If this clearance gap is between 0.060 and 0.070 in (1.50 to 1.75 mm) then the adjustment is satisfactory and the next paragraph can be ignored.
62 Where found necessary the clearance gap can be adjusted by loosening the brake pedal bolt nuts and altering the effective length of the bolt. After tightening the nuts recheck the clearance gap.
63 Reconnect the switch wires and refit the driver's glovebox.

Reverse lamp switch (manual transmission)

64 Unscrew the gear lever knob and prise out the upper panel housing.
65 Withdraw the rubber draught excluder and the foam rubber insert. Separate the switch wires at the single snap-connectors, slacken the locknut and unscrew the switch (photo). When fitting the switch, select reverse gear and screw in the switch until it just makes contact (this can be checked with a continuity tester or a test lamp and

Fig. 10.14 Reverse lamp switch (Manual gearbox) (Sec 34)

34.65 The reverse lamp switch wiring connector (arrowed)

Fig. 10.15 Reverse lamp switch (automatic transmission) (Sec 34)

2	Thread protector	4	Switch unit
3	Securing bolt	5	Switch leads

Fig. 10.16 Oil pressure switch wiring connections (Sec 34)

WN	White/brown
WP	White/purple
W	White

battery), then screw it in a further 3 flats (180°). Hold the switch in this position and tighten the locknut.
66 The remainder of the refitting procedure is the reverse of that used for removal.

Reverse lamp switch (automatic transmission)

67 Disconnect the negative and positive battery leads and jack up the car. This is a combined switch for the reversing lamp and starter inhibitor and is bolted onto the left-hand side of the gearbox casing. See Fig. 10.15.
68 Remove the thread protector (where fitted) and undo the securing bolt.
69 Remove the spade connectors, noting their locations, and take away the switch.
70 Refitting is the reverse of the removal procedure. Note that the switch retaining bolt torque is 5 lbf ft (7 Nm).

Brake line failure switch

71 Release the harness plug claws and disconnect the plug from the switch on the lower side of the master cylinder.
72 Unscrew the switch.
73 Refitting is the reverse of the removal procedure. Note that the switch tightening torque is only 15 lbf in (0.17 kg fm).

Oil pressure switch

74 Detach the leads from the switch on the right-hand side of the

engine adjacent to the alternator. Some later models have a single plug type connector and not separate leads.
75 Unscrew the adaptor unit from the oil pump and then unscrew the switch from the adaptor.
76 Refitting of the assembly is the reverse of removal, but note that the threads of the adaptor unit are tapered so avoid overtightening it.

35 Instrument housing – removal and refitting

1 Disconnect the battery earth lead.
2 Rotate the recessed control on the end cover through 90° until it releases, then unscrew the metal clip holding the top cover.
3 Pull off the top cover and disconnect the wiring connectors that join the radio speaker leads.
4 Open the driver's glovebox and undo the two straps so that it can be dropped right down.
5 Remove the speedometer face panel by depressing the two plastic clips on top. Be careful not to damage the trip reset button.
6 Remove the five panel housing bolts, spring washers and washers from beneath the facia (see Fig. 10.18). Note that the nut in the bottom of the speedometer housing is loose and can easily be lost.
7 Disconnect the speedometer cable by depressing the locking prong.
8 Pull off the corrugated hose from the air duct at the rear of the instrument housing.
9 Pull the instrument housing forward and disconnect the wiring harness multi-plugs.
10 Pull out the bulb and the white/green lead from the triangular plate at the rear of the gauge housing.
11 Disconnect the leads from the bulb holders fitted to the

Fig. 10.17 The instrument housing end and top cover panels (Sec 35)

2 Recessed control	7 Retaining pins
3 Small metal clip	8 Locking prong and retainer
4 Top cover	slot

Fig. 10.18 Instrument housing fixings (Sec 35)

3 Speedometer cable	7 Air duct hose
6 Retaining bolts (access from	10 White/green lead connection
underneath dash)	point

speedometer, tachometer and turn signal warning lights.

12 Depress the rear retaining lugs on the fuse holder housing and release it from the instrument housing.

13 The instrument housing can now be removed.

14 Refitting is the reverse of removal, but note the following points:

(a) *The pin arrangement pattern of the multi-plugs is designed to avoid incorrect assembly.*

(b) *Red/white and black leads are connected to the bulb holders of the speedometer and tachometer.*

(c) *Green/white and black leads are connected to the right-hand turn signal warning light.*

(d) *Green/red and black leads are connected to the left-hand turn signal warning light.*

(e) *A white/green lead is connected to the terminal at the rear of the gauge housing.*

Note: *The instrument housing on the Rover 2300 differs from that fitted to the 2600 model, but the removal procedure is the same. Disregard any mention of the tachometer when dealing with the 2300 model.*

36 Panel instruments and sender units – removal and refitting

Battery condition indicator, oil gauge, temperature gauge and fuel gauge

1   Disconnect the battery negative lead.

2   Remove the instrument housing end cover by turning the recessed knob through 90°.

3   Lift off the top panel of the instrument housing and disconnect the leads to the radio speaker at the wiring connectors.

4   Press the top retaining lugs down on the front cover of the gauge housing and pull away the cover from the housing.

5   Remove the two gauge housing retaining screws and draw the gauge housing forward.

6   Press down the locking prong at the rear of the housing and withdraw the multi-plug.

7   Pull out the bulb holder from the triangular plate and disconnect the white/green lead from the back of the gauge housing.

8   Withdraw the gauge housing, remove the two screws and lift away the front lens holder.

9   In order to remove any individual gauge, simply undo the retaining nuts and remove the wave washers. The gauge can now be withdrawn see Figs. 10.19 and 10.20

10 Refitting is the reverse of removal.

Clock

Note: *The clock is non-adjustable apart from moving the 'hands' to correct small discrepancies.*

11 Disconnect the battery earth lead.

12 Open the passenger's glovebox, reach in and push the back of the clock from behind, to remove it from the facia.

13 Disconnect the electrical leads from the clock and withdraw the bulb holder.

14 Refitting is the reverse of the removal procedure.

Speedometer

15 Disconnect the battery negative lead.

3 Front cover retaining lugs	4 Screw retaining gauge housing
	5 Gauge housing
	6 Multi-plug
	7 Bulb holder
	8 White/green lead

Fig. 10.19 Fixing details of the panel instruments (front) (Sec 36)

Fig. 10.20 Fixing details of the panel instruments (rear) (Sec 36)

11 *Nuts retaining battery condition indicator*
12 *Nuts retaining oil pressure gauge*
13 *Nuts retaining temperature gauge*
14 *Nuts retaining fuel gauge*
17 *Connection point for white/green lead*

16   Remove the instrument housing end and top panels as described in paragraphs 2 and 3.
17   Depress the locking prong and pull out the speedometer cable from the rear of the speedometer head.
18   Depress the upper retaining lugs on the speedometer front cover and lift the cover away from the instrument housing.
19   Undo the two retaining screws and draw the speedometer forward sufficiently to remove the bulb holders.
20   Refitting is the reverse of removal.

Tachometer

21   Disconnect the battery negative lead.
22   Remove the instrument housing end and top panels as described in paragraphs 2 and 3.
23   Pull out the wiring plug connector from the rear of the tachometer.
24   Depress the upper retaining lugs on the tachometer front cover and lift the cover away.
25   Undo the two tachometer retaining screws. Draw the tachometer forwards and pull out the bulb holders.
26   Refitting is the reverse of the removal procedure.

Temperature gauge transmitter

27   The temperature gauge transmitter is located on the front end of the inlet manifold flange (photo).
28   Drain part of the engine coolant (see Chapter 2).
29   Remove the spade connector.
30   Unscrew the unit from the manifold and remove the washer.
31   Refitting is the reverse procedure to removal, but remember to fit a new sealing washer if possible.

Oil pressure transmitter

32   Disconnect the battery earth lead.
33   Pull off the wiring connector at the transmitter. This is located on the right-hand side of the engine block just in front of the dipstick housing. Nearer the front of the block is the oil pressure switch; this extinguishes the warning light on the dash and indicates the presence of oil in the system (photos).
34   Unscrew the transmitter and withdraw the sealing washer.
35   If the transmitter is suspect, then it can be checked by substitution or by temporarily fitting a pressure gauge in its place.
36   Fitting of the transmitter is the reverse of the removal procedure, but remember to fit a new sealing washer.

36.27 The water temperature gauge transmitter (arrowed)

Fuel gauge tank unit

37   The fuel gauge tank unit is an integral part of the fuel pump assembly. Removal and refitting details for this assembly are given in Chapter 3.

---

37   Central door locking system components – removal and refitting

---

The central door locking system is fitted to 2300 and 2600 models as an optional extra.

Door lock control assembly

1   The door lock control assembly is located behind the carpet covering the right-hand side panel of the luggage compartment.
2   Disconnect the battery negative lead and pull the carpet aside to gain access to the assembly.
3   Remove the four screws and single star washer then carefully manoeuvre the control assembly out from the aperture in the side panel.
4   Disconnect the wires from the six terminals shown in Fig. 10.21.
5   Refitting is the reverse of removal.

Door lock (locking and unlocking) resistors

6   Remove the door lock control assembly as described in paragraphs 1 to 3.
7   In order to gain better access to the resistors, pull back the rubber covers at the inner terminal studs of the relay units. Undo the retaining nuts at these studs and lift away the four harness tags.
8   Identify the required resistor by tracing the appropriate brown/red wire from its relay. Identify the relay by the wires attached to it as shown below:

Locking relay
Brown
Brown/red
Green/black
Green/slate

Unlocking relay
Brown
Brown/red
Blue/black
Blue/orange

9   Note the location of the wires on the terminal block and loosen the two screws in order to remove the appropriate resistor.
10   Refitting is the reverse of removal.

Door lock (locking and unlocking) relays

11   Remove the door lock control assembly as described in paragraphs 1 to 3.

36.33a The oil pressure gauge transmitter

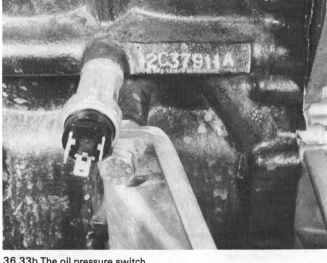

36.33b The oil pressure switch

Fig. 10.21 Door lock control wiring cable colour codes (Sec 37)

GS	Green/slate
GB	Green/black
UB	Blue/black
UO	Blue/orange
N	Brown

37.18 Disconnecting the harness plug from the interior central door lock switch

12 Identify the required relays as described in paragraph 8.
13 Pull off the two spade connectors.
14 Pull back the two rubber covers at the relay terminal studs. Undo the two nuts and lift off the four harness tags.
15 Remove the two nuts, spring washers, plain washers and bolts to release the relay.
16 Refitting is the reverse of the removal procedure.

Door lock interior switch

17 Remove the door trim pad as described in Chapter 12.
18 Release the two fixing claws and separate the harness plug (photo).
19 Push the single plastic clip on the switch inwards and withdraw the switch upwards from the door pull.
20 Refitting of the switch is the reverse of removal, but make sure that the 'door lock open' symbol is facing towards the rear of the car.

Door lock key switch assembly

21 Refer to Chapter 12.

Door lock solenoids

22 Refer to Chapter 12.

38 Windscreen washers

Reservoir – removal and refitting

1 Pull off the washer reservoir pipe from the washer pump, then lift the reservoir from its retaining bracket.
2 Refitting is the reverse of the removal procedure.

Washer jet – removal and refitting

3 Pull off the pipe, then remove the nut and anti-vibration washer, taking care that they are not dropped (Fig. 10.22).
4 Remove the jet and sealing washer.
5 Refitting is the reverse of this procedure. If necessary, rotate the jet using a screwdriver to direct the jet satisfactorily.

Washer pump – removal and refitting

6 Remove the washer reservoir, as previously described.
7 Pull off the two electrical leads from the pump.
8 Undo the two nuts and bolts that secure the washer pump to its mounting bracket (photo).
9 Lift the pump and pull off the inlet and outlet pipes.
10 Refitting is the reverse of removal, but make sure that the inlet and outlet pipes are connected correctly. The direction of water flow is usually denoted by an arrow at the pump inlet and outlet connections.

Fig. 10.22 Screenwasher jet fixing detail (Sec 38)

2   *Delivery pipe*   4   *Jet and sealing*
3   *Nut and anti-vibration washer*   *washer*

38.8 The screen washer pump mounted on a bracket behind the reservoir

The lime green and black power wire should be connected to the (+) terminal of the washer pump.

39 Windscreen wiper arms and blades – removal and refitting

Wiper arm

1   Open the bonnet and carefully prise off the plastic cap from the pivot end of the wiper arm (see routine maintenance).
2   Undo the nut that retains the arm to the spindle.
3   Tilt the arm and blade assembly away from the windscreen and withdraw the wiper arm from the spindle.
4   Refitting is the reverse of the removal procedure. Position the arm on the splines to obtain the most suitable 'Park' position.

Wiper blade

5   Lift the arm and blade away from the windscreen, then simultaneously depress the clip and withdraw the blade pin from the pivot block (see routine maintenance).
6   Refitting is the reverse of the removal procedure.

40 Windscreen wiper motor and drive assembly – removal and refitting

1   Open the bonnet and disconnect the battery earth lead (photo).
2   Remove the four bolts, plate and screw that secure the bonnet lock to the body and move the lock to one side. The location of these bolts is shown in Fig. 10.23.
3   Remove the wiper arms (see Section 39).
4   Undo the two wheel box retaining nuts and extract the spacing washers and rubber seals.
5   Disconnect the wiper motor earthing strap at the wiper motor mounting plate.
6   Remove the nut, bolt and washers that secure the wiper motor mounting plate to the body.
7   Pull off the electrical multi-plug connector from the wiper motor.
8   Tip the assembly to allow the wheel box spindles to fall clear of their location holes and withdraw the assembly from the body aperture.
9   Refitting is the reverse of the removal procedure. Before refitting the wiper arms switch the wipers on and off in order to obtain the 'Park' position.

41 Windscreen wiper motor – removal, overhaul and refitting

1   Remove the wiper motor and drive assembly from the car as described in Section 40.

40.1 View of windscreen wiper motor and bonnet lock

2   Remove the special, serrated face nut from the wiper motor shaft.
3   Undo the three bolts that secure the wiper motor to its mounting plate.
4   Withdraw the wiper motor from its linkage and note the positions of the shim washer and rubber seal fitted to the wiper motor shaft.
5   Undo the three screws that retain the gearbox cover and lift it off.
6   Make sure that the end of the wiper motor shaft is free from burrs, then withdraw it and extract the dished washer.
7   Remove the thrust screw, or thrust screw and locknut from the side of the wiper body.
8   Remove the through-bolts and slowly withdraw the cover and armature. The brushes will drop clear of the commutator, but do not allow them to become contaminated with grease from the worm gear.
9   Pull the armature out of the cover.
10 Undo the three screws that retain the brush assembly.
11 Lift and slide the limit switch sideways, to release it from the spring clip.
12 The brush assembly and limit switch can now be lifted away together.
13 Examine the various components for wear and renew as necessary.
14 Commence the reassembly procedure by sliding the limit switch in position and securing it with the clip.
15 Refit the brush assembly and secure it with the three screws.

Fig. 10.23 Wiper motor and drive assembly fixing detail (Sec 40)

1   Bonnet lock fixing screw
2   Retainer plate
3   Bonnet lock fixing bolts
4   Wiper arm, nut and plastic cap
5   Wheel box fixing nuts, spacing washers and seals
7   Wiper motor mounting plate to body fixing

Fig. 10.24 Wiper motor to linkage fixing detail (Sec 41)

2   Special serrated nut
3   Wiper motor to mounting plate
4   Wiper motor
5   Shim washer and rubber seal

Fig. 10.25 Exploded view of the wiper motor assembly (Sec 41)

1   Rubber seal
2   Gearbox cover plate
3   Wiper motor shaft
4   Thrust screw
5   Through bolts
7   Armature
8   Brush assembly
9   Limit switch

16 Lubricate the cover bearing and soak the cover bearing felt washer with Shell Turbo 41 oil.

17 Refit the armature to the cover, lubricate the self-aligning bearing with Shell Turbo 41 oil, then insert the armature shaft through the bearing whilst restraining the three brushes. Take care when inserting the armature shaft to prevent the brushes from becoming contaminated with grease.

18 Position the cover against the gearbox casing so that the datum lines are correctly aligned.

19 Insert the cover through-bolts and tighten them.

20 Refit the thrust screw, or the thrust screw and locknut and then check the armature endfloat.

21 On types with an adjustable thrust screw, loosen the locknut and screw the adjustment screw inwards until resistance is felt. Turn the screw back by a quarter of a turn and tighten the locknut.

22 On types with a non-adjustable thrust screw, push the armature towards the cover and place a feeler gauge between the armature shaft and the thrust screw. The endfloat at this point should be 0.002 to 0.008 in (0.05 to 0.20 mm). Where the endfloat is insufficient, the only solution is to place a packing washer under the head of the thrust screw. If the endfloat is excessive, then have metal machined from under the head of the thrust screw.

23 Lubricate the final gear bushes with Shell Turbo 41 oil and apply Ragosine Listate grease to the final gear cam.

24 Fit the dished washer with its concave surface facing the final drive gear then insert the shaft.

25 Pack the area around the worm and final gear with Ragosine Listate grease.

26 Reposition the gearbox cover and fit the rubber seal.

27 The wiper motor can now be refitted to the mounting plate by reversing the removal procedure.

42 Wiper motor delay unit – removal and refitting

1 The wiper motor delay unit is retained by a clip and mounted alongside similar units on the body panel behind the driver's glove compartment.

2 Before removing the unit, disconnect the battery negative lead.

3 Open the driver's glove compartment and identify the unit by the colour coding of the wires jointed to it.

Terminal 1   *White with green tracer*
Terminal 2   *Brown with light green tracer*
Terminal 3   *Yellow with light green tracer*
Terminal 4   *Brown with green tracer*

4 Pull off the wiring connections and pull the wiper motor delay unit from its retaining clip.

5 Refitting is the reverse of the removal procedure.

43 Radio – removal, refitting and trimming

1 Disconnect the battery earth lead.

2 Pull off the upper knob, felt washer, lower knob and nut cover from the left-hand control.

3 Pull off the upper knob, lower knob and nut cover from the right-hand control.

4 Undo the two thin nuts and lift away the face panel and support plate.

5 Hold the radio by the two control spindles. Push it downwards and

Fig. 10.26 Cover to gearbox casing alignment marks (Sec 41)

Fig. 10.27 Wiper motor delay unit (Sec 42)

Fig. 10.28 Radio fixing details (Sec 43)

tilt it slightly to release the catch on the lower retaining bracket.

6   Withdraw the radio from the aperture far enough to disconnect the following:

  (a) *Earthing wire at the radio terminal connection*
  (b) *Supply wire, by releasing the bayonet type fitting at the in-line choke*
  (c) *Speaker wires, at the harness plug*
  (d) *The aerial lead, at the plug connector*

7   Refitting is the reverse of removal, but do not fit the right-hand control knob components until the radio has been trimmed.

8   Switch on the radio and tune it to a weak position eg 250 metres (1.2 MHz). Insert a thin screwdriver through the small aperture adjacent to the right-hand control spindle and adjust the trim screw to obtain the maximum volume.

9   Switch off the radio and refit the right-hand control knob components.

44 Electric window lift motors – removal and refitting

1   Disconnect the battery earth lead.
2   Remove the door trim panel, referring to Chapter 12, Section 14, if necessary.
3   Remove the door-mounted speaker, where applicable, then disconnect the motor wires at the multi-plug.
4   If suspected motor failure is being investigated, apply battery voltage at the motor multi-plug. If the motor now operates where it did not before, the fault is in the wiring or control circuitry.
5   If the motor does not operate, it must be renewed. Remove the anti-vibration bracket, the interior door catch and plastic moulding, and the insulating sheet.

6   Disconnect the door catch operating rod. Unhook the lower lifting stud (front doors only) and remove the abutment plate.
7   Remove the motor mounting bolts, then raise the motor and glass so that the window is fully closed. Wedge the glass in this position.
8   On front doors, remove the front channel securing bolt.
9   Slide the linkage backwards and forwards to release the lifting studs from their channels and withdraw the assembly from the door. If difficulty is experienced on rear doors, drill out the rivet securing the secondary link to the quadrant.
10   Commence refitting by applying battery voltage to the motor multi-plug to position the linkage in the fully closed position.
11   Apply grease to the lifting studs and pivots.
12   Fit the assembly to the door, engaging the upper lifting studs in the glass horizontal support channel.

Front doors
13   Screw in one of the motor mounting bolts.
14   Connect the multi-plug and operate the motor until the other mounting holes are aligned, then fit and tighten the bolts.
15   Refit the front channel securing bolt. Position the lower lifting stud in the abutment plate and refit the abutment plate to the door.

Rear doors
16   Engage the lower lifting stud in its support plate.
17   Connect the multi-plug and operate the motor until the mounting holes are aligned, then fit and tighten the bolts.

All doors
18   Remove the wedge, temporarily reconnect the battery and check the window for correct operation.
19   The remainder of the refitting procedure is a reversal of removal.

45 Fault diagnosis – electrical system

Symptom	Reason/s
Starter fails to turn engine	Battery discharged Battery defective internally Battery terminal leads loose or earth lead not securely attached to body Loose or broken connections in starter motor circuit Starter motor switch or solenoid faulty Starter brushes badly worn, sticking, or brush wires loose Starter motor armature faulty Field coils earthed
Starter turns engine very slowly	Battery in discharged condition Starter brushes badly worn, sticking, or brush wires loose Loose wires in starter motor circuit
Starter spins but does not turn engine	Pinion or flywheel gear teeth broken or worn Battery discharged
Starter motor noisy or excessively rough engagement	Pinion or flywheel gear teeth broken or worn Starter motor retaining bolts loose
Battery will not hold charge for more than a few days	Battery defective internally Electrolyte level too low or electrolyte too weak due to leakage Plate separators no longer fully effective Battery plates severely sulphated Fan belt slipping Battery terminal connections loose or corroded Alternator not charging Short in lighting circuit causing continual battery drain Regulator unit not working correctly
Ignition light fails to go out, battery runs flat in a few days	Fan belt loose and slipping or broken Alternator brushes worn, sticking, broken or dirty Alternator brush springs weak or broken Internal fault in alternator
Horn operates all the time	Horn push either earthed or stuck down Cable to horn push earthed

Symptom	Reason/s
Horn fails to operate	Blown fuse Cable or cable connection loose, broken or disconnected Horn has an internal fault
Horn emits intermittent or unsatisfactory noise	Cable connections loose Horn incorrectly adjusted
Lights do not come on	If engine not running, battery discharged Wire connections loose, disconnected or broken Light switch shorting or otherwise faulty
Lights come on but fade out	If engine not running, battery discharged Light bulb filament burnt out or sealed beam units broken Wire connections loose, disconnected or broken Light switch shorting or otherwise faulty
Lights give very poor illumination	Lamp glasses dirty Lamps badly out of alignment
Lights work erratically – flashing on and off, especially over bumps	Battery terminals or earth connection loose Lights not earthing properly Contacts in light switch faulty
Wiper motor fails to work	Blown fuse Wire connections loose, disconnected or broken Brushes badly worn Armature worn or faulty Field coils faulty
Wiper motor works very slowly and takes excessive current	Commutator dirty, greasy or burnt Armature bearings dirty or unaligned Armature badly worn or faulty Brushes badly worn Commutator dirty, greasy or burnt Armature badly worn or faulty
Wiper motor works but wiper blades remain static	Wiper motor gearbox parts badly worn

Fig. 10.29 Supplementary wiring diagram – electrically-operated windows (pre-1982 models)

BAT	Battery supply		8	Front LH console switch
IGN	Ignition switch supply		9	Front LH motor
1	Thermal cut-out		10	Front RH console switch
2	Front supply relay		11	Front RH motor
3	Connection to harness crimp joint – three green wires		12	Rear LH console switch
4	Rear supply relay		13	Rear LH door switch
5	Rear isolate switch		14	Rear LH motor
6	Connection to harness crimp joint – four light green wires		15	Rear RH console switch
			16	Rear RH door switch
7	Connection to harness crimp joint – three light green wires		17	Rear RH motor

Fig. 10.30 Wiring diagram for left and right-hand drive Rover 2600 models

1 Alternator
2 Radio suppressor
3 Battery
4 Starter solenoid
5 Bulkhead terminal stud
6 Ignition/starter switch
7 Fuse
8 Choke
9 Radio
10 Speaker
11 Master light switch
12 Main/dip/flash switch
13 Main beam warning light
14 RH main beam
15 LH main beam
16 RH dip beam
17 LH dip beam
18 Front fog lamp switch
19 Front fog lamp
20 Rear fog lamp switch
21 Rear fog lamp
22 Rear fog lamp warning light
23 Fibre optic lamp
24 Clock illumination
25 Cigarette lighter illumination
26 Plate illumination lamp
27 Tail lamp
28 Stop lamp
29 Front parking lamp
30 RH flasher warning light
31 RH front flasher lamp
32 RH rear flasher lamp
33 LH rear flasher lamp
34 LH front flasher lamp
35 LH flasher warning light
36 Turn signal flasher unit
37 Turn signal switch

38 Hazard flasher unit
39 Hazard switch
40 Headlamp wiper supply
41 Choke warning light
42 Choke switch
43 Brake warning light
44 Brake fluid level switch
45 Brake line failure switch
46 Hand brake warning light
47 Hand brake switch
48 Panel rheostat
49 Tachometer illumination
50 Instrument illumination
51 Speedometer illumination
52 Horn switch
53 Horn
54 Stop lamp switch
55 Passenger's seat switch
56 Passenger's belt switch
57 Seat belt warning light
58 Driver's belt switch
59 Bulb failure warning light
60 Starter inhibitor switch (automatic transmission only)
61 Starter relay
62 Oil pressure switch
63 Fuel pump
64 Oil pressure warning light
65 Ignition warning light
66 Heater motor supply line relay
67 Ignition coil
68 Ignition distributor
69 Engine diagnosis socket
70 Engine diagnosis timing transducer
71 Tachometer
72 Lighting supply line relay
73 Fuse

74 Heated rear window relay
75 Heated rear window
76 Heated rear window switch
77 Heated rear window warning light
78 Fuse box
79 Windscreen wiper switch
80 Windscreen wiper delay unit
81 Windscreen wiper motor
82 Windscreen washer switch
83 Windscreen washer pump
84 Fuel warning light stabilizer
85 Fuel warning light
86 Fuel indicator
87 Fuel tank unit
88 Water temperature indicator
89 Water temperature transmitter
90 Oil pressure indicator
91 Oil pressure transmitter
92 Battery condition indicator
93 Reverse lamp switch
94 Reverse lamp
95 Heater motor
96 Heater resistor
97 Heater switch
98 Luggage bay lamp
99 Luggage bay lamp switch
100 'B' post lamp
101 Front door guard lamp
102 Door switch
103 Map lamp
104 LH glove box lamp
105 LH glove box lamp switch
106 Clock
107 RH glove box lamp
108 RH glove box lamp switch
109 Cigarette lighter

COLOUR CODE

B	Black		P	Purple
G	Green		R	Red
K	Pink		S	Slate
LG	Light Green		U	Blue
N	Brown		W	White
O	Orange		Y	Yellow

Fig. 10.31 Wiring diagram for left and right-hand drive Rover 2300 models

1 Alternator
2 Radio suppressor
3 Battery
4 Starter solenoid
5 Bulkhead terminal stud
6 Ignition/starter switch
7 Radio fuse
8 Radio
9 Speaker
10 Master light switch
11 Main/dip/flash switch
12 Main beam warning light
13 RH main beam
14 LH main beam
15 RH dip beam
16 LH dip beam
17 Front fog lamp switch
18 Front fog lamp
19 Rear fog lamp switch
20 Rear fog lamp
21 Rear fog lamp warning light
22 Fibre optic lamp
23 Clock illumination
24 Cigarette lighter illumination
25 Plate illumination lamp
26 Tail lamp
27 Stop lamp
28 Front parking lamp
29 RH flasher warning light
30 RH front flasher lamp
31 RH rear flasher lamp
32 LH rear flasher lamp
33 LH front flasher lamp

34 LH flasher warning light
35 Turn signal flasher unit
36 Turn signal switch
37 Hazard flasher unit
38 Hazard switch
39 Headlamp wiper supply
40 Choke warning light
41 Choke switch
42 Brake warning light
43 Brake fluid level switch
44 Brake line failure switch
45 Hand brake warning light
46 Hand brake switch
47 Panel rheostat
48 Instrument illumination
49 Speedometer illumination
50 Horn switch
51 Horn
52 Stop lamp switch
53 Passenger's seat switch
54 Passenger's belt switch
55 Seat belt warning light
56 Driver's belt switch
57 Starter inhibitor switch (automatic transmission only)
58 Starter relay
59 Oil pressure switch
60 Fuel pump
61 Oil pressure warning light
62 Ignition warning light
63 Heater motor supply line relay
64 Ignition coil
65 Radio suppressor

66 Ignition distributor
67 Engine diagnosis socket
68 Engine diagnosis timing transducer
69 Lighting supply line relay
70 Fuse
71 Heated rear window relay
72 Heated rear window
73 Heated rear window switch
74 Heated rear window warning light
75 Fuse box
76 Windscreen wiper switch
77 Windscreen wiper motor
78 Windscreen washer switch
79 Windscreen washer pump
80 Fuel warning light stabilizer
81 Fuel warning light
82 Fuel indicator
83 Fuel tank unit
84 Water temperature indicator
85 Water temperature transmitter
86 Battery condition indicator
87 Reverse lamp switch
88 Reverse lamp
89 Heater motor
90 Heater resistor
91 Heater switch
92 Luggage bay lamp
93 Luggage bay lamp switch
94 'B' post lamp
95 Door switch
96 Map lamp
97 Clock
98 Cigarette lighter

COLOUR CODE

B	Black	P	Purple
G	Green	R	Red
K	Pink	S	Slate
LG	Light Green	U	Blue
N	Brown	W	White
O	Orange	Y	Yellow

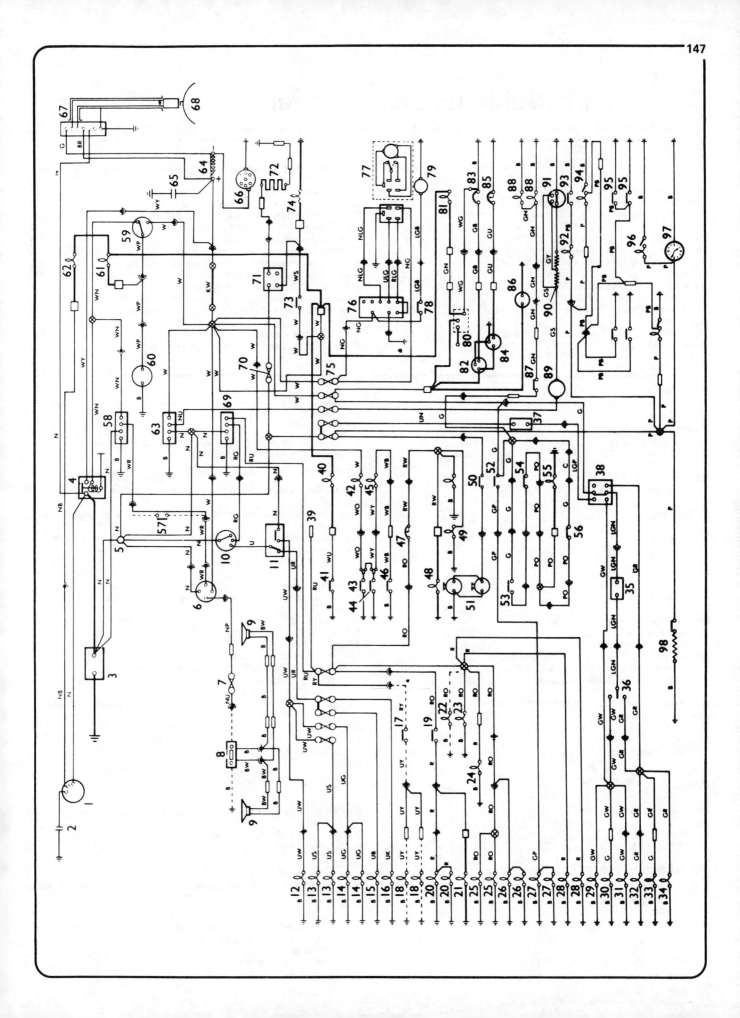

Chapter 11 Suspension and steering

For modifications, and information applicable to later models, see Supplement at end of manual

Contents

Specifications

Front suspension
2300 and 2600 models .... MacPherson strut with integral shock absorbers, eccentrically mounted coil springs and anti-roll bar

Rear suspension
2300 and 2600 models .... Axle located by semi-trailing arms, torque tube and transverse Watts linkage

2300 models .... Suspension provided by telescopic shock absorbers and variable rate coil springs

2600 models .... Suspension provided by Boge-Nivomat self-energising, self-levelling telescopic shock absorbers and constant-rate coil springs

Steering
Type .... Rack-and-pinion, with steering wheel adjustable for reach and height
Power assistance .... Standard on 2600 models from October 1978. Optional on 2300 models

Steering wheel turns, lock-to-lock:
    Power assistance .... 2·70
    Manual rack-and-pinion .... 4·50
Manual steering rack lubricant type/specification .... Multi-purpose lithium-based grease, to NLGI No 2 (Duckhams LB 10)
Power steering reservoir fluid type/specification .... ATF to specification M2C 33G (Duckhams Q-Matic)
Power steering fluid reservoir capacity .... 1·25 pints (0·70 litre)

Steering/front suspension geometry

	Unladen	Laden (Four-up plus full tank)
Castor angle	2° 00'	2° 00'
Camber angle	0°	+ 0° 55'
Kingpin inclination	13° 30'	10° 15'
Front wheel alignment	0 to 0·125 in (0 to 3·0 mm) toe-in	

Wheels
Standard:
    2300 and 2600 models .... Pressed steel disc type, 14 in x 5½J with flat ledge safety rims
Optional:
    2300 models .... Dunlop Denovo wheels and tyres
    2600 models .... Dunlop Denovo wheels and tyres or Cast alloy wheels (6J)

Wheel hub lubricant

Type/specification .... Multi-purpose lithium-based grease, to NLGI No 2 (Duckhams LB 10)

Tyre sizes
Standard .... 175/HR-14 steel braced radial ply tyres now fitted to both models, although earlier 2300 models had ordinary fabric radial tyres and not steel braced
Optional .... 195/70 HR 14 or 195/65 HR 375*
Denovo type manufactured by Dunlop

Tyre pressures

	Front	Rear
175 HR 14:		
Normal	28 lbf/in² (2·0 kgf/cm²)	30 lbf/in² (2·1 kgf/cm²)
Fully laden	30 lbf/in² (2·1 kgf/cm²)	32 lbf/in² (2·2 kgf/cm²)
195/70 HR 14:		
Normal	26 lbf/in² (1·8 kgf/cm²)	26 lbf/in² (1·8 kgf/cm²)
Fully laden	26 lbf/in² (1·8 kgf/cm²)	28 lbf/in² (2·0 kgf/cm²)
195/65 HR 375:		
Normal	23 lbf/in² (1·6 kgf/cm²)	23 lbf/in² (1·6 kgf/cm²)
Fully laden	26 lbf/in² (1·8 kgf/cm²)	28 lbf/in² (2·0 kgf/cm²)

Torque wrench settings

	lbf ft	Nm
Front suspension		
Anti-roll bar crossmember	32	43
Anti-roll bar to lower link	71	95
Subframe attachments	30	40
Lower link to crossmember	59	80
Lower link to strut assembly	36	48
Strut mounting to body	21	28
Steering arm to strut	55	75
Anti-roll bar clamp	41	54
Road spring to strut	30	40
Wheels to hubs (all types)	66	88
Rear suspension		
Trailing link to fork end	41	54
Trailing link fork end to body	41	54
Trailing link to rear axle	41	54
Watts linkage to rear axle	41	54
Rear crossmember body to outer mounting	34	46
Shock absorber to axle and body (nut)	15	20
Shock absorber to axle and body (locknut)	22	32
Bump stop to upper spring cup	20	27·5
Rear crossmember to axle extension	41	54
Wheels to hubs (all types)	66	80
Steering		
Rack to crossmember	32	43
Balljoint to steering arm	36	48
Steering wheel	20	27
Coupling set-screw	20	27·5
Column mounting bracket to dash	20	27·5
Power steering pump valve cap	35	47
Balljoint to tie-rod	47	64
High pressure feed pipe to steering rack	14	19
High pressure feed pipe to steering pump	22	30
Low pressure return pipe (steering pump)	22	30

1 General description

The front suspension is of the MacPherson strut type with integral shock absorbers, offset coil springs and an anti-roll bar. The single lower links are pivoted at their inner ends in rubber bushes set in the subframe assembly. This subframe also carries the anti-roll bar and steering rack assembly. At the upper ends, the springs and dampers are retained in housings in the front wing valances.

The live rear axle is located by semi-trailing arms and the long nose of the final drive housing (acting as a torque tube) at its forward end. Sideways location is provided by a transverse Watts linkage system mounted at the rear of the axle.

For Rover 2300 models the rear suspension is provided by variable-rate coil springs and separately mounted normal telescopic shock absorbers. The rear suspension in the 2600 models is provided by constant-rate coil springs and separately mounted Boge-Nivomat self-energising and self-levelling oil-filled shock absorber units.

In the Rover 2600 models from October 1978 onward, the steering is of the power-assisted rack-and-pinion type with twin tie-rods connecting to the steering arms through balljoints. The power steering pump is belt driven from the engine crankshaft. Earlier 2600 models only had power-assisted steering as an option and as standard equipment they were fitted with a manual form of rack-and-pinion with which the 2300 models are still equipped.

The steering wheel connects through a steering shaft, a universal

Fig. 11.1 Rear suspension layout (left-hand side) (Sec 1)

1	Torque tube	4	Semi-trailing arm
2	Watts linkage	5	Shock absorber unit
3	Rear coil spring		(depicted here is the Boge unit)

joint, an intermediate shaft and a second universal coupling to the steering gear pinion.

The steering and suspension is relatively maintenance-free apart from periodically checking the tension of the steering pump drivebelt, the power steering fluid level and renewing the power steering fluid reservoir filter. It is advisable to periodically inspect the entire steering and suspension systems.

2 Anti-roll bar – removal and refitting

1   Apply the handbrake, then raise the front of the car and support it on blocks or axle-stands beneath the subframe or body frame members. For convenience, also remove the roadwheels.
2   Remove the two bolts and nyloc nuts on each side that secure the anti-roll bar saddle brackets to the subframe.
3   Remove the spring pin, nyloc nut, flat and dished washer, and bush at each end of the anti-roll bar.
4   Remove the bolt and nyloc nut that secure one of the bottom links to the subframe.
5   Pull the bottom link from the subframe bracket, withdraw the anti-roll bar from the car, then take off the inner bush and dished washer from each end.
6   If the rubbers have deteriorated, they should be cut away with a sharp knife. When fitting new items, ensure that the anti-roll bar is clean, then smear it with a proprietary rubber grease or glycerine and slide on the bushes.
7   Refitting is basically the reverse of the removal procedure. Attach the bottom link first and secure it with the bolt and nyloc nut.
8   Offer up the anti-roll bar and align the ends with the mounting

Fig. 11.2 Anti-roll bar mounting bracket (Sec 2)

2 Saddle bracket nuts

Fig. 11.3 Anti-roll bar end mountings (Sec 2)

3 Spring pin, nut, washer and bush assembly

holes in each of the bottom links. The saddle brackets can now be refitted.

3 Front spring and strut – removal and refitting

1   Apply the handbrake, then raise the front of the car at the appropriate side. Support it beneath the subframe or bodywork member.
2   Remove the roadwheel.
3   Fit a brake hose clamp and disconnect the brake caliper pipe union from the brake hose. The use of the brake hose clamp is to prevent the loss of brake fluid due to the syphoning action. The alternative to this method is to tape over the vent hole in the master cylinder filler cap. When the brake union is disconnected, the end can be plugged to prevent any fluid loss.
4   Remove the nyloc nut and plain washer from the track-rod end and separate the track-rod end from the steering arm using either a balljoint separator or split wedges.
5   Remove the nyloc nut and washer that secures the suspension balljoint to the base of the strut. Separate the balljoint taper pin from the strut using the method described in paragraph 4.
6   Remove the three nyloc nuts at the top damper mounting, then pull the strut clear of the car (photo).
7   Using proprietary spring compressors, compress the spring evenly.
8   Prise out the plastic dust cover from the top bearing assembly and undo the nyloc nut from the top of the damper piston rod.
9   Remove the washer, lift off the upper swivel assembly complete with the upper spring pan and shim(s).
10 Withdraw the spring, gaiter retaining plate, gaiter and two rubber bump stops.
11 Reassembly and refitting of the strut is the reverse of the removal and dismantling procedures. After refitting, bleed the brakes as described in Chapter 9.

4 Front subframe – removal and refitting

1   Jack-up the car and support it on the bodyframe side-members so that the weight of the body is just taken off the front suspension.
2   Undo the four nuts and bolts that secure the anti-roll bar and

Fig. 11.4 Front spring and strut assembly (Sec 3)

1	*Plastic dust cover*	*6*	*Spring*
2	*Nyloc nut and washer*	*7*	*Bump stops*
3	*Upper swivel assembly*	*8*	*Gaiter*
4	*Upper spring pan and shim(s)*	*9*	*Spring insulation ring*
5	*Gaiter retaining plate*	*10*	*Strut/shock absorber*

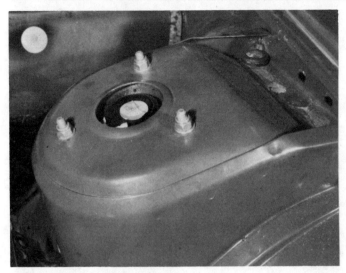
3.6 Top left-hand strut mounting nuts

4.3 Steering rack to subframe nuts and bolts

Fig. 11.5 Front subframe fixing details (Sec 4)

1 Support jacks	4 Nuts and bolts securing	7 Subframe retaining bolts
2 Anti-roll bar fixing to	lower links to subframe	(long)
subframe	6 Engine mounting and	9 Subframe retaining bolts
3 Steering rack to subframe fixing	stabiliser bar	(short)

engine stabiliser to the subframe.

3   Undo the four nuts and washers that secure the steering rack to the subframe (photo).

4   Undo the two nuts and washers that secure the bottom links to the subframe. Withdraw the bolts and release the links. If the bolts cannot be withdrawn, adjust the support jacks to relieve the load on the bolts.

5   Support the engine with a jack placed beneath the sump coupling plate.

6   Disconnect the engine mounting from the subframe and stabiliser by removing the four nuts, bolts and washer.

7   Support the subframe. Remove the two long bolts, nuts and washers at the front end, and the two short bolts, nuts and washers at the rear.

8   Lower the supports and withdraw the subframe.

9   Refitting is the reverse of the removal procedure, but remember to tighten the nuts to the recommended torque setting. Ensure that the steering rack is correctly located.

5   Front hub – removal, dismantling, reassembly, refitting and adjustment

1   Apply the handbrake, then raise the front of the car at the appropriate side. Support it beneath the subframe or bodyframe member.

2   Remove the roadwheel, clamp the flexible brake hose or alternatively, tape over the vent hole in the master cylinder reservoir cap. This measure will prevent the excessive loss of brake fluid when the union is disconnected.

Fig. 11.6 Exploded view of the front hub and disc assembly (Sec 5)

Fig. 11.7 Cross-section through the front hub (Sec 5)

7   Grease cap   8   Split-pin and nut retaining cap

5.3 Disconnect the metal brake pipe at the union with the flexible pipe

5.6 Prise off the grease cap

3   Disconnect the caliper metal pipe at its union with the flexible hose (photo).
4   Bend the tab washer ends back from the caliper retaining bolt heads and remove the two bolts.
5   Lift the brake caliper away.
6   Prise off the grease cap and wipe away the surplus grease from the end of the stub axle (photo).
7   Remove the split-pin, retaining cap, nut and washer.
8   Withdraw the hub and disc, complete with bearings and oil seal.
9   Remove the outer bearing; remove the inner seal and inner bearing.
10   Drive out the bearing inner races from the hub.
11   Clean all the parts carefully in petrol or paraffin and check for obvious wear, scoring, signs of overheating (a bluish colour), etc. Brown grease stains are of no significance. Ensure that the bearings run smoothly when assembled in their outer tracks. Renew bearings, where necessary, as complete assemblies. On no account mix up parts of bearings from one side of the car to the other.
12   Press in the bearing outer tracks, then lubricate the bearing races with a general purpose grease, working it well in with the fingers.
13   Partially pack the hub with grease, then fit the bearing races.
14   Fit a new oil seal with the lips facing the inner bearing then push

on the hub. Take care that the outer bearing is not dislodged.
15   Fit the washer to the stub axle and screw on the nut finger-tight only.
16   Fit the caliper and reconnect the brakepipe. Fit a new caliper lock tab and tighten to the recommended torque setting (Chapter 9).

17 Adjust the hub by tightening the nut to a torque setting of 5 lbf ft (0.69 kgf m) and back it off one flat.
18 Fit the retaining cap and retain it with a new split-pin. Refit the hub grease cap (there is no need to fill it with grease).
19 Before refitting the roadwheel, bleed the brakes as described in Chapter 9.

6 Front suspension lower link and balljoint assembly – removal and refitting

1 Apply the handbrake, then raise the front of the car at the

Fig. 11.8 Front suspension lower link and track-rod end assembly (Sec 6)

6   *Track-rod end locking nut*
7   *Stub axle balljoint securing nut*

appropriate side. Support it beneath the subframe or the bodyframe member.
2 Remove the roadwheel, then detach the end of the anti-roll bar from the lower link (refer to Section 2, if necessary).
3 Remove the nyloc nut and plain washer that secures the lower link balljoint to the base of the strut/stub axle assembly.
4 Pull back the rubber boot from the balljoint, then use a proprietary balljoint separator or split wedges to separate the balljoint taper pin from the strut/stub axle assembly.
5 Remove the bolt and nyloc nut that secures the lower link to the subframe.
6 Withdraw the lower link and balljoint assembly.
7 Refitting is the reverse of the removal procedure.

7 Rear spring and bump stop – removal and refitting

1 Jack-up the rear of the car and support it on blocks or an axle-stand beneath the bodyframe member. Chock the front wheels for safety.
2 Place a jack under the axle to support its weight, but ensure that the car's body weight is still taken by the support placed beneath the bodyframe member.
3 Remove the two 'power lock' bolts that secure the forked end of the trailing link assembly to the inner sill.
4 Undo and remove the bolt, nyloc nut and washer that secure the spring retainer clip to the axle (photo).
5 Disconnect the two nuts that secure the self-levelling damper unit to the axle bracket.
6 Carefully lower the axle support jack, then withdraw the spring and insulating ring.
7 If the bump stop is to be removed, then undo the nut that secures the bump stop to the spring top mounting.
8 Refitting is the reverse of the removal procedure.

8 Rear suspension trailing link – removal and refitting

1 Chock the front roadwheels, raise the rear of the car and support it on axle-stands or packing blocks placed under the bodyframe side-member.

Fig. 11.9 Rear spring and bump stop detail (Secs 7 and 9)

4   *Spring retaining clip assembly*   5   *Shock absorber retaining nuts (lower)*

7.4 Rear spring and retaining clip (arrowed) left-hand side

Fig. 11.10 Component parts at rear end connection of rear suspension trailing link (Sec 8)

| 1 | Bushes | 3 | Washer |
| 2 | Spacer sleeve | 4 | Nyloc nut |

Fig. 11.11 Front fixing view of rear suspension trailing link (Sec 8)

3   Power lock bolts

2   Disconnect the trailing link from the axle locating bracket by removing the nyloc nut, plain washer, rubber bush and distance tube (photo).
3   Undo the two 'power lock' bolts that retain the forked bracket to the inner body sill panel.
4   Pull the trailing link away from the axle and extract the rubber bush from the rear end.
5   If necessary, remove the nut and bolt that secure the eyed end of the trailing link to the fork bracket.
6   Renew the bushes as necessary and refit by reversing the removal procedure.

9   Rear shock absorber – removal and refitting

1   Raise the rear of the car and support it with packing blocks or stands placed under the bodyframe side-member. Remember to chock the front roadwheels.
2   Fold down the rear seat and pull away the carpet from the region of the wheel arch to expose the top mounting of the shock absorber (photo).
3   Place a support jack under the axle to support its weight.
4   Undo the locknut, nut and dished washer that secure the shock absorber to the body.
5   Lower the axle support jack. Undo the locknut and nut that secure the lower end of the shock absorber unit to the axle bracket. Note that a dished washer is positioned above these retaining nuts (photo).
6   Withdraw the shock absorber unit. Remove the metal spacing sleeves from the body and axle bracket rubber bushes.
7   Remove the rubber bushes from the body and axle mounting holes.
8   Refitting is the reverse of the removal procedure. When fitting the rubber bushes it may be found beneficial to lubricate them with a proprietary brand of rubber grease.

10 Watts linkage assembly – removal and refitting

1   Chock the front roadwheels, raise the rear of the car and support it on axle-stands or strong packing blocks.
2   Remove the bolts and nyloc nuts that secure the side links to the side brackets.
3   Undo the central pivot nut, remove the plain washer and slide the complete assembly off (photo).

8.2 Rear suspension trailing link (arrowed) right-hand side

9.2 Top rear shock absorber mounting behind rear seat

9.5 Locknut, nut and dished washer securing bottom end of damper

Fig. 11.12 Layout of Watts transverse linkage system (Sec 10)

1   Side link bolt and nut (right-hand)   *2   Side link bolt and nut (left-hand)*   *6   Bush, washer and nyloc nut (centre pivot)*

10.3 Watts linkage, central mounting

11.9 Power steering flexible hoses

4   With the assembly removed from the car, check the condition of the pressed-in rubber bushes. Renew the bushes as necessary.
5   Refitting of the assembly is the reverse of the removal procedure.

11   Steering rack (power assisted) – removal and refitting

Note: *When dismantling or disconnecting any part of the power steering system, it is very important to ensure that complete cleanliness is observed. Exposed ends of pipes, hoses or parts should be sealed in some way to prevent the ingress of foreign matter. Do not at any time start the engine until the fluid reservoir has been filled, otherwise the hydraulic pipe will be seriously damaged.*

1   Lift the bonnet and remove the air cleaner assembly as described in Chapter 3.
2   Apply the handbrake, then raise the front of the car and support it on blocks or axle-stands placed beneath the bodyframe members. For convenience also remove the roadwheels.
3   With the wheels in the straight-ahead position, index mark the pinion shaft and the lower steering coupling to assist with alignment when refitting. (This is not necessary if the steering rack is to be renewed).
4   Remove the nuts from the tie-rod balljoints on the steering arms.

5   Pull back the rubber boot on each balljoint, then use a proprietary balljoint separator, or split wedges, to separate the balljoint from the steering arm.
6   Remove the nut and bolt that secure the lower steering universal joint coupling to the rack pinion.
7   Loosen the bolt and nut that secure the universal joint coupling to the intermediate shaft.
8   Remove the bolt that retains the flexible pipe clip to the rack body.
9   Place a suitable receptacle under the steering rack valve housing. Disconnect the feed and return flexible hoses from the valve housing and allow the fluid to drain (photo). **Note**: *Do not re-use the fluid drained from the system.*
10   Position a jack under the engine sump. Place a flat block of wood on the lifting pad to spread the load and to prevent damaging the sump.
11   With the engine so supported, remove the engine mounting bolts and nyloc nuts.
12   Remove the two bolts that secure the right-hand engine tie-rod to the subframe and lift the tie-rod away.
13   Raise the engine support jack to lift the engine clear of the rack.
14   Turn the right-hand front wheel to the full right-hand lock position.
15   Remove the four bolts, washers and nuts that secure the steering rack to the subframe.

16 Separate the lower coupling from the rack pinion shaft and manoeuvre the rack out of the right-hand wheel arch.

17 If the steering rack is worn or faulty then it is advisable to entrust the repairs to your local Rover dealer or obtain a new or reconditioned unit.

18 Refitting is the reverse of the removal procedure. If a different rack is being fitted then it will be necessary to centralise it. To centralise the rack, remove the centre plug from the thrust pad. Locate the dimple in the rack shaft by passing stiff wire through the plug aperture. Move the pinion shaft as necessary to get the dimple in the centre of the aperture. Fit a bolt in place of the centre plug and lightly tighten it to hold the rack in the centred position.

19 After fitting, refit the damper plug, fill and bleed the hydraulic system as described in Section 18. The front wheel alignment will need checking and possibly adjusting. Refer to Section 14 for details.

12 Steering rack (manual) – removal and refitting

1   Apply the handbrake and raise the front of the car. Support it on blocks or axle-stands placed beneath the bodyframe members.
2   Set the roadwheels so that they point straight-ahead.
3   Scribe the pinion shaft and the lower steering coupling to assist with alignment on refitting (this need only be done if the original equipment is going to be refitted without having been dismantled).
4   Disconnect the rack tie-rod outer balljoints from the steering arms.
5   Remove the nut and bolt that secure the steering lower coupling to the rack pinion.
6   Remove the four nuts, bolts and brackets that hold the rack to the subframe.
7   Remove the pinion shaft from the lower coupling.
8   Remove the rack.
9   If the steering rack is worn or faulty then it is advisable to entrust the repairs to your local Rover dealer or obtain a new or reconditioned unit.
10   Refitting is the reverse of the removal procedure. If a different rack is being fitted, see Section 11 for the correct procedure.
11   After fitting, refit the centre plug having removed the bolt used to hold the pinion shaft in place. Check that the rack contains multipurpose grease (see Specifications).
12   The front wheel alignment will need checking and possible adjusting. Refer to Section 14 for details.

13 Steering tie-rod balljoints and rack gaiters – removal and refitting

1   Carefully mark the position of the tie-rod outer balljoint locknut so that it can be refitted in the same position and thus prevent upsetting the front wheel alignment. If new balljoints are to be fitted, note the distance from the beginning of the tie-rod screw thread to the centre of the outer balljoint cap. This is because a new item may differ slightly in dimension when compared with the original one (photo).
2   Slacken the outer balljoint locknut.
3   Detach the outer balljoint as described in paragraphs 4 and 5 of Section 11.
4   Unscrew the balljoint and locknut from the tie-rod.
5   Remove the gaiter retaining clips and slide the gaiter off the tie-rod.
6   When fitting, lubricate the inner balljoint with a general purpose grease and slide on the gaiter.
7   With the rack centralised, fit the inboard clip on the gaiter.
8   Fit the outboard clip on the gaiter whilst checking that the steering can be moved from lock-to-lock without the gaiter being strained.
9   Fit the balljoint on the tie-rod. If the original position is not known, screw it on until the distance between centres of the balljoints is approximately 13.33 in (338 mm)
10   The remainder of the fitting procedure is the reverse of that used when removing.
11   On completion, if there is any doubt about the balljoint(s) not being fitted in their original positions, the front wheel alignment must be checked – see Section 14.

13.1 Tie-rod balljoint

14 Front wheel alignment – checking

1   In order to minimize tyre wear and retain the correct steering and roadholding characteristics, it is essential that the front wheels are correctly aligned. Ideally, the alignment should be checked using special gauges. It is therefore recommended that the job is done by a Rover dealer. However, it is possible to do the check with a reasonable amount of accuracy if care is taken.
2   The front wheels are correctly aligned when they are turning inwards at the front by the specified amount; this is the toe-in. This measurement is made with the wheels in the straight-ahead position, with the steering rack in the mid-position of its travel, the ball centres of the tie-rod equal and the steering wheel centre spot horizontal.
3   It is important that the measurement is taken on a centre-line drawn horizontally and parallel to the ground through the centre-line of the hub. The exact point should be in the centre of the sidewall of the tyre and not on the wheel rim which could be distorted and so give inaccurate readings.
4   The adjustment is effected by loosening the locknut on each tie-rod outer balljoint and also slackening the rubber gaiter clip holding it to the tie-rod, both tie-rods being turned equally until the adjustment is correct.
5   Castor and camber angles are set during production; there is no provision for adjustment. The angles should be checked however after a front-end collision.

15 Power steering pump – removal and refitting

1   Open the bonnet and remove the filler cap of the power steering reservoir situated on top of the pump (photo)
2   Place a suitable receptacle underneath the power steering pump; detach the inlet hose from the pump and drain the fluid.
3   After draining the fluid, seal the end of the hose to prevent the ingress of dirt and refit the reservoir cap.
4   Disconnect the outlet hose from the pump and seal its end to prevent the ingress of dirt.
5   Slacken the adjustment nuts and bolts.
6   Remove the drivebelt, undo the nut and washer and remove the pulley.
7   Undo the pump body clamp bolt and slide the pump out of the clamp to the rear (photo).
8   Refitting the pump is the reverse procedure to removal.

16 Power steering pump – servicing

The pump is a Hoburn-Eaton sealed unit and it is not possible to service it. If it malfunctions then a replacement exchange unit will have to be purchased.

15.1 Removing the power steering reservoir filler cap

15.7 Pump mounting clamp (surrounding components removed for clarity)

19.2 Steering wheel retaining nut

17 Power steering pump drivebelt. – removal, refitting and adjustment

1   Loosen off the power steering pump pivot and adjuster quadrant bolts.
2   Push the pump in towards the engine.
3   Slip the belt off the pump pulley. Remove it by passing it under the fan blades.
4   Refit the belt in the reverse fashion and adjust the tension.
5   Deflection on the belt at a point mid way between the pulleys should be between 0.25 and 0.375 in (6 to 9 mm). Adjust by levering the pump on its pivot bolt. Then tighten the pivot and adjuster bolts.

18 Power steering system – filling and bleeding

1   Turn the steering wheel so that the roadwheels are pointing in the straight-ahead position.
2   Before filling the fluid reservoir, check the system completely to ensure that all the pipes, hoses and unions are satisfactory.
3   Fill the hydraulic reservoir with the recommended type of fluid (see Specifications) to a point 1 in (25 mm) below the base of the filler neck.
4   Loosen the pump adjuster/pivot bolts and nuts and relieve the drivebelt tension.
5   Rotate the hydraulic pump pulley, by hand, several times in a clockwise direction to prime the system.
6   Re-tension the drivebelt as described in Section 17, recheck the fluid level and top-up as necessary.
7   Start the engine and whilst allowing it to idle, turn the steering wheel so that the roadwheels are deflected, from the straight-ahead position to the full left-hand lock position. Return the roadwheels to the straight-ahead position and recheck the fluid level.
8   Repeat paragraph 7 but this time turn the steering to the right-hand lock position and then return it to the straight-ahead position. Recheck the fluid level and top-up as necessary.
9   Repeat paragraphs 7 and 8 until all air is expelled. Finally recheck and top-up the fluid level.

19 Steering wheel – removal and refitting

1   Turn the steering wheel until the roadwheels are pointing in the straight-ahead position.
2   Pull out the steering wheel trim pad and whilst grasping the rim of the steering wheel with one hand, undo the central retaining nut and remove the plain washers (photo).
3   Using Rover service tool 18G 1014 or a suitable puller, draw the steering wheel off the steering column taper. **Note**: *Do not, under any circumstances, attempt to drive or tap the steering wheel off the steering column as irreparable damage may result to the safety type column.*
4   Lift the steering wheel off the steering column shaft.
5   Before refitting the steering wheel, check that the arrow on the trafficator cancelling collar aligns with the centre of the trafficator stock.
6   Refit the steering wheel, locating the two lugs on the wheel with the two slots in the cancelling collar.
7   Tighten the steering wheel retaining nut to the recommended torque setting and then refit the trim pad.

20 Steering column assembly – removal and refitting

1   Open the bonnet and disconnect the battery earth lead.
2   Remove the driver's side glovebox.
3   Remove the nut and bolt that secure the upper universal coupling to the intermediate shaft.
4   Separate the four wiring multi-plug connectors (Fig. 11.13).
5   Undo the two bolts, washers and nyloc nuts that retain the steering column mounting bracket to the body.
6   Pull the steering column away from the car.
7   Before refitting the steering column, ensure that the roadwheels

Fig. 11.13 Steering column assembly (Sec 20)

Fig. 11.14 Steering column intermediate shaft (Sec 21)

2 *Nut and bolt securing intermediate shaft to steering column mast*
4 *Nut and bolt securing lower universal coupling to intermediate shaft*
5 *Nut and bolt securing lower universal coupling to steering rack pinion*

are in the straight-ahead position and the steering wheel centralised.
8   Engage the end of the steering column splines in the upper universal coupling.
9   Fit and tighten the steering column clamp bolt and nut.
10 Lift the steering column up and refit the steering column bracket to body bolts.
11 Reconnect the four multi-plugs and battery earth lead.

21 Steering intermediate shaft – removal and refitting

1   Raise the front of the car and support it.
2   Remove the securing nut and bolt where the intermediate shaft joins the steering column mast. In order to gain better access to this nut and bolt, it may be necessary to turn the steering wheel.
3   From within the car, lift the steering column inner shaft by approximately $\frac{1}{2}$ in (12.7 mm).
4   Remove the nut and bolt that secure the lower universal coupling to the steering rack pinion shaft.
5   Slide the coupling and intermediate shaft downwards to

Fig. 11.15 Steering column lock clamp plate and shear head bolt (Sec 22)

disengage the intermediate shaft from the steering column inner shaft.
6   Separate the intermediate shaft from the universal coupling and withdraw the shaft from the car.
7   Refitting is the reverse of the removal procedure, but before starting reassembly ensure that the roadwheels are in the straight-ahead position.

22 Steering lock/ignition switch – removal and refitting

Note: *It is necessary to purchase 2 new shear-head screws before starting this operation or it will not be possible to refit the steering lock/ignition switch.*
1   Withdraw the key from the switch and remove the nacelle halves (two screws).
2   Either remove the two shear-head screws that secure the steering lock/ignition switch using a hammer and a small chisel; or centre-punch and drill them, then use a screw extractor.
3   Remove the plug-in connector to the ignition switch and then remove the steering lock.
4   Refitting is the reverse of the removal procedure.

23 Roadwheels and tyres

1   Whenever the roadwheels are removed, it is a good idea to clean the insides to remove accumulations of mud and in the case of the front one, disc pad dust.
2   Check the condition of the wheel for rust and repaint if necessary.
3   Examine the wheel stud holes. If these are tending to become

elongated or the dished recesses in which the nuts seat have worn or become overcompressed, then the wheel will have to be renewed.

4   With a roadwheel removed, pick out any embedded flints from the tread and check for splits in the sidewalls or damage to the tyre carcass generally.

5   Where the depth of tread pattern is 1 mm or less, the tyre must be renewed.

6   Rotation of the roadwheels to even out wear is a worthwhile idea if the wheels have been balanced off the car. Include the spare wheel in the rotational pattern.

7   If the wheels have been balanced on the car, then they cannot be moved round the car as the balance of the wheel, tyre and hub will be upset. In fact their exact stud fitting positions must be marked before removing a roadwheel so that it can be returned to its original 'in-balance' state.

8   It is recommended that wheels are rebalanced halfway through the life of the tyres to compensate for the loss of tread rubber due to wear.

9   Finally, always keep the tyres (including the spare) inflated to the recommended pressures and always refit the dust caps on the tyre valves. Tyre pressures are best checked first thing in the morning when the tyres are cold.

---

24 Fault diagnosis – suspension and steering

Symptom	Reason/s
Steering feels vague, car wanders and 'floats' at speed	Tyre pressures uneven Shock absorbers worn Steering gear balljoints badly worn Steering mechanism free play excessive Front/rear suspension pick-up points out of alignment
Stiff and heavy steering	Tyre pressures too low No grease in steering gear Front wheel toe-in incorrect Steering gear incorrectly adjusted too tightly Steering column badly misaligned Power steering pump defective Power steering drivebelt slack or missing
Wheel wobble and vibration	Wheel nuts loose Front wheels and tyres out of balance Steering balljoints badly worn Hub bearings badly worn Steering gear free play excessive Front springs weak or broken

Chapter 12 Bodywork and fittings

For modifications, and information applicable to later models, see Supplement at end of manual

Contents

1 General description

The combined body and chassis underframe is made of steel fabrications welded together to form a 'monocoque' structure. Certain areas are reinforced to provide mounting points for the suspension, steering system, engine supports etc. Special pressure pads and beams are built into the doors and body structure to transmit any impact loads evenly; in fact, the doors will open normally after the car has undergone the standard 30 mph ECE 12 barrier-impact test.

All Rover 2300 and 2600 (SDI) models are manufactured with five doors, the fifth door taking the form of a one-piece rear tailgate. The rear tailgate is fitted with a Triplex heated window.

The front screen is of the Triplex Ten-Twenty laminated type and is bonded into position to carry a proportion of the body torsional stress. A great deal of development went into the design of this screen and a reduction of 99% in facial injuries is claimed owing to the thick interlayer laminate.

Not only is the body designed with safety in mind, but also fuel economy, performance and roominess were all prime considerations. The aerodynamically sound bodyshape was evolved from 'mock-up' models which underwent wind tunnel tests. Careful planning of the layout, and the positioning of the main mechanical components, helped to create the desired space to seat five passengers comfortably with an ample reserve for luggage, parcels etc. Where maximum load space is required, the rear seat backrest can be folded down flat and the rear parcel shelf removed.

2 Maintenance – bodywork and underframe

The general condition of the car's bodywork is the one thing that significantly affects it value. Maintenance is easy but needs to be regular and particular. Neglect, particularly after minor damage, can lead quickly to further deterioration and costly repair bills. It is important also to keep watch on those parts of the car not immediately visible, for instance the underside, inside all the wheel arches and the lower part of the engine compartment.

The basic maintenance routine for the bodywork is washing, preferably with a lot of water, from a hose. This will remove all the loose solids which may have stuck to the car. It is important to flush these off in such a way as to prevent grit from scratching the finish. The wheel arches and underbody need washing in the same way to remove any accumulated mud which will retain moisture and tend to encourage rust. Paradoxically enough, the best time to clean the underbody and wheel arches is in wet weather when the mud is thoroughly wet and soft. In very wet weather the underbody is usually cleaned of large accumulations automatically and this is a good time for inspection.

Periodically, it is a good idea to have the whole of the underside of the car steam cleaned, engine compartment included, so that a thorough inspection can be carried out to see what minor repairs and renovations are necessary. Steam cleaning is available at many garages and is necessary for the removal of the accumulation of oily grime which sometimes is allowed to cake thick in certain areas near the engine, gearbox and back axle. If steam facilities are not available, there are one or two excellent grease solvents available which can be brush applied. The dirt can then be simply hosed off.

After washing the paintwork, wipe off with a chamois leather to give an unspotted finish free from smears. A coat of clear protective wax polish will give added protection against chemical pollutants in the air. If the paintwork sheen has dulled or oxidised, use a cleaner/polisher combination to restore the brilliance of the shine. This requires a little effort, but is usually caused because regular washing has been neglected. Always check that the door and ventilator opening drain holes and pipes, are completely clear so that water can drain. Bright work should be treated in the same way as paintwork. Windscreens and windows can be kept clear of the smeary film which often appears, if a little ammonia is added to the water. If they are scratched, a good rub with a proprietary metal polish will often clear them. Never use any form of wax or other body or chromium polish on glass.

3 Maintenance – upholstery and carpets

Mats and carpets should be brushed or vacuum-cleaned regularly to keep them free of dirt. If they are badly stained, remove them from the car for scrubbing or sponging and make quite sure they are dry before refitting. Seat and interior trim panels can be kept clean by a wipe over with a damp cloth. If they do become stained (which can be more apparent on light coloured upholstery) use a little liquid detergent and a soft nail brush to scour the grime out of the grain of the material. Do not forget to keep the head lining clean in the same way as the upholstery. When using liquid cleaners inside the car do not over-wet the surfaces being cleaned. Excessive dampness could get into the seams and padded interior causing stains, offensive odour or even rot. If the inside of the car gets wet accidentally it is worthwhile taking some trouble to dry it out properly, particularly where carpets are involved. Do not leave oil or electric heaters inside the car for this purpose.

4 Minor bodywork damage repair

The photo sequence on pages 166 and 167 illustrate the operations detailed in the following sections.
Note: *For more detailed information about bodywork repair, the Haynes Publishing Group publish a book by Lindsay Porter called* The Car Bodywork Repair Manual. *This incorporates information on such aspects as rust treatment, painting and glass fibre repairs, as well as details on more ambitious repairs involving welding and panel beating.*

Repair of minor scratches in the car's bodywork

If the scratch is very superficial, and does not penetrate to the metal of the bodywork, repair is very simple. Lightly rub the area of the scratch with a paintwork renovator, or a very fine cutting paste, to remove loose paint from the scratch and to clear the surrounding bodywork of wax polish. Rinse the area with clean water.

Apply touch-up paint to the scratch using a thin paint brush; continue to apply thin layers of paint until the surface of the paint in the scratch is level with the surrounding paintwork. Allow the new paint at least two weeks to harden, then blend it into the surrounding paintwork by rubbing the scratch area, with a paintwork renovator or a very fine cutting paste. Finally, apply wax polish.

Where the scratch has penetrated right through to the metal of the bodywork, causing the metal to rust, a different repair technique is required. Remove any loose rust from the bottom of the scratch with a penknife, then apply rust inhibitor paint to prevent the formation of rust in the future. Using an applicator, fill the scratch with bodystopper paste. If required, this paste can be mixed with a cellulose thinner to provide a very thin paste which is ideal for filling narrow scratches. Before the stopper-paste in the scratch hardens wrap a piece of smooth cotton rag around the top of a finger. Dip the finger in cellulose thinners and then quickly sweep it across the surface of the stopper-paste in the scratch: this will ensure that the surface of the stopper-paste is slightly hollowed. The scratch can now be painted over as described earlier in this Section.

Repair of dents in the car's bodywork

When deep denting of the car's bodywork has taken place, the first task is to pull the dent out until the affected bodywork almost attains its original shape. There is little point in trying to restore the original shape completely as the metal in the damaged area will have stretched on impact and cannot be reshaped fully to its original contour. It is better to bring the level of the dent up to a point which is about $\frac{1}{8}$ in (3 mm) below the level of the surrounding bodywork. In cases where the dent is very shallow anyway, it is not worth trying to pull it out at all.

If the underside of the dent is accessible, it can be hammered out gently from behind, using a mallet with a wooden or plastic head. Whilst doing this, hold a suitable block of wood firmly against the impact from the hammer blows to prevent a large area of the bodywork from being 'belled-out'.

Should the dent be in a section of the bodywork which has double skin or some other factor making it inaccessible from behind, a different technique is called for. Drill several small holes through the metal inside the area particularly in the deeper section. Then screw long self-tapping screws into the holes just sufficiently for them to gain a good purchase in the metal. Now the dent can be pulled out by pulling on the protruding heads of the screws with a pair of pliers.

The next stage of the repair is the removal of the paint from the damaged area, and from an inch or so of the surrounding undamaged bodywork. This is accomplished most easily by using a wire brush or abrasive pad on a power drill, although it can be done just as effectively by hand using sheets of abrasive paper. To complete the preparation for filling, score the surface of the bare metal with a screwdriver or the tang of a file; alternatively, drill small holes in the affected area. This will provide a really good 'key' for the filler paste.

To complete the repair see the Section on filling and respraying.

Repair of rust holes or gashes in the car's bodywork

Remove all paint from the affected area and from an inch or so of the surrounding undamaged bodywork, using an abrasive pad or a wire brush on a power drill. If these are not available, a few sheets of abrasive paper will do the job just as effectively. With the paint removed you will be able to gauge the severity of the corrosion and therefore decide whether to renew the whole panel (if this is possible) or to repair the affected area. New body panels are not as expensive as most people think and it is often quicker and more satisfactory to fit a new panel than to attempt to repair large areas of corrosion.

Remove all fittings from the affected area except those which will act as a guide to the original shape of the damaged bodywork (eg headlamp shells etc). Then, using tin snips or a hacksaw blade, remove all loose metal and any other metal badly affected by corrosion. Hammer the edges of the hole inwards in order to create a slight depression for the filler paste.

Wire brush the affected area to remove the powdery rust from the surface of the remaining metal. Paint the affected area with rust inhibiting paint; if the back of the rusted area is accessible treat this also.

Before filling can take place it will be necessary to block the hole in some way. This can be achieved by the use of one of the following materials: Zinc gauze or aluminium tape.

Zinc gauze is probably the best material to use for a large hole. Cut a piece to the approximate size and shape of the hole to be filled, then position it in the hole so that its edges are below the level of the surrounding bodywork. It can be retained in position by several blobs of filler paste around its periphery.

Aluminium tape should be used for small or very narrow holes. Pull a piece off the roll and trim it to the approximate size and shape required, then pull off the backing paper (if used). Stick the tape over the hole, overlapping if the thickness of one piece is insufficient. Burnish down the edges of the tape with the handle of a screwdriver or similar, to ensure that the tape is securely attached to the metal underneath.

Bodywork repairs – filling and respraying

Before using this Section, see the Sections on dent, deep scratch, rust holes and gash repairs.

Many types of bodyfiller are available, but generally speaking those proprietary kits which contain a tin of filler paste and a tube of resin hardener are best for this type of repair. A wide, flexible plastic or nylon applicator will be found invaluable for imparting a smooth and well contoured finish to the surface of the filler.

Mix up a little filler on a clean piece of card or board. Use the hardener sparingly, following the maker's instructions on the packet, otherwise the filler will set very rapidly.

Using the applicator, apply the filler paste to the prepared area. Draw the applicator across the surface of the filler to achieve the correct contour and to level the filler surface. As soon as a contour that approximates the correct one is achieved, stop working the paste. If you carry on too long the paste will become sticky and begin to 'pick up' on the applicator. Continue to add thin layers of filler paste at twenty-minute intervals until the level of the filler is just proud of the surrounding bodywork.

Once the filler has hardened, excess can be removed using a plane or file. From then on, progressively finer grades of abrasive paper should be used, starting with a 40 grade production paper and finishing with 400 grade wet-and-dry paper. Always wrap the abrasive paper around a flat rubber, cork, or wooden block, otherwise the surface of the filler will not be completely flat. During the smoothing of the filler surface the wet-and-dry paper should be periodically rinsed in water. This will ensure that a very smooth finish is imparted to the filler at the final stage.

At this stage the dent should be surrounded by a ring of bare metal, which in turn should be encircled by the finely 'feathered' edge of the good paintwork. Rinse the repair area with clean water, until all of the dust produced by the rubbing-down operation has gone.

Spray the whole repair area with a light coat of primer to show up any imperfections in the surface of the filler. Repair these imperfections with fresh filler paste or bodystopper, and once more smooth the surface with abrasive paper. If bodystopper is used, it can be mixed with cellulose thinners to form a really thin paste which is ideal for filling small holes. Repeat this spray and repair procedure until you are satisfied that the surface of the filler and the feathered edge of the paintwork are perfect. Clean the repair area with clean water and allow to dry fully.

The repair area is now ready for final spraying. Paint spraying must be carried out in a warm, dry, windless and dust free atmosphere. This condition can be created artificially if you have access to a large indoor working area, but if you are forced to work in the open, you will have to pick your day very carefully. If you are working indoors, dousing the floor in the work area with water will help to settle the dust which would otherwise be in the atmosphere. If the repair area is confined to one body panel, mask off the surrounding panels; this will help to minimise the effects of a slight mis-match in paint colours. Bodywork fittings (eg chrome strips, door handles etc) will also need to be removed or masked off. Use genuine masking tape and several thicknesses of newspaper for the masking operations.

Before commencing to spray, agitate the aerosol can thoroughly, then spray a test area (an old tin, or similar) until the technique is mastered. Cover the repair area with a thick coat of primer; the thickness should be built up using several thin layers of paint rather than one thick layer. Using 400 grade wet-and-dry paper, rub down the surface of the primer until it is really smooth. While doing this, the work area should be thoroughly doused with water, and the wet-and-dry paper periodically rinsed in water. Allow to dry before spraying on more paint.

Spray on the top coat, again building up the thickness by using several thin layers of paint. Start spraying in the centre of the repair area and then using a circular motion, work outwards until the whole repair area and about 2 inches of the surrounding original paintwork is covered. Remove all masking material 10 to 15 minutes after spraying on the final coat of paint.

Allow the new paint at least two weeks to harden, then, using a paintwork renovator or a very fine cutting paste, blend the edges of the paint into the existing paintwork. Finally, apply wax polish.

5   Major body damage – repair

Where serious damage has occurred or large areas need renewal due to neglect, it means certainly that completely new sections or panels will need welding in and this is best left to professionals. If the damage is due to impact it will also be necessary to completely check the alignment of the body shell structure. Due to the principle of construction the strength and shape of the whole can be affected by damage to a part. In such instances the services of a Rover agent with specialist checking jigs are essential. If a body is left misaligned it is first of all dangerous as the car will not handle properly and secondly uneven stresses will be imposed on the steering, engine and transmission, causing abnormal wear or complete failure. Tyre wear may also be excessive.

6   Bumpers – removal and refitting

Front bumper

1   Refer to Fig. 12.1 and undo the four nuts, spring washers and plain washers that secure the rubber end caps to the brackets.
2   Lift away the rubber ends from the bumper and brackets.
3   Whilst supporting the bumper remove the two bolts, spring washers and plain washers that secure it to the brackets.
4   Lift the bumper bar away.

5   Refitting is the reverse of the removal procedure.

Rear bumper

6   The rear bumper components are retained to corner brackets in a similar manner to the front bumper (see Fig. 12.2).
7   Removal and refitting are identical procedures to that described in paragraphs 1 to 5 above.

7   Underbelly panel – removal and refitting

1   Open the bonnet and locate the fog lamp wiring harness next to the rear of the headlamp unit. Disconnect the leads at the snap connectors.
2   Refer to Fig. 12.3 and remove the self-tapping screws from the

Fig. 12.1 Front bumper fixing detail (Sec 6)

1   Nut and spring washer retaining rubber end cap
3   Bolt, spring washer and securing bumper to bracket

Fig. 12.2 Rear bumper fixing detail (Sec 6)

1   Nut, spring washer and plain washer retaining rubber end cap
2   Rubber end cap
3   Bolt, spring washer and plain washer securing bumper to bracket

Fig. 12.3 Underbelly panel (Sec 7)

2	*Side screw*	*4*	*Support straps*
3	*Forward edge facing screws*	*5*	*Centre fixing screw*
		6	*Rear edge fixing screw*

locations shown at either side and the centre.

3   Lift the panel away.

4   Refitting is the reverse of the removal procedure, but ensure that the fog lamp cables are connected up as follows: Black wire to black wire, blue/yellow wire to grey wire.

8   Bonnet – removal and refitting

1   Disconnect the battery earth lead.

2   Separate the two snap-connectors from the bonnet lamp leads, and the two wiring spade connectors at the bonnet lamp switch.

3   Pull the under-bonnet lamp wiring harness away from the retaining clips.

4   Separate the screenwasher hose at the T-piece.

5   With the help of an assistant, support the bonnet and mark around the bonnet hinge positions with a pencil.

Fig. 12.4 Bonnet hinge detail (left-hand) (Sec 8)

   5   *Screenwasher T-piece*
   8   *Hinge fixing screws and adjuster plate*

Fig. 12.5 Bonnet stay bar components (Sec 8)

   2   *Washers and split pins*

6   Remove the split-pin and washers that secure the stay bar to the bonnet.

7   Undo the four hinge retaining bolts and lift away the two adjuster plates that secure the hinges to the body.

8   Lift off the bonnet.

9   Refitting is the reverse of the removal procedure, but after completion close the bonnet and check that it is correctly aligned. If necessary, loosen the hinge retaining bolts and adjust the bonnet position.

9   Bonnet catches and controls

Catch removal, refitting and adjustment

1   Support the bonnet in the open position then remove the two screws, spring washers and flat washers to release the catch.

2   Refitting is the reverse of the removal procedure.

3   If necessary, adjust the catch to give a positive locking action and to eliminate free movement, as described in the following paragraphs.

4   Pull back the spring and loosen the locknut on the adjuster bolt.

5   Rotate the screw in, or out, as necessary, then tighten the locknut and check the operation of the catch. Adjust further as necessary.

Bonnet lock removal and refitting

6   Remove the cable trunnion, then slacken the pinch bolt and remove the cable from the lock (Fig. 12.7).

7   Remove the four bolts, single screw, spring washers and flat washers, then detach the lock.

8   Refitting is the reverse of the removal procedure.

Release cable removal and refitting

9   Initially proceed as described in paragraph 6. **Note:** *Do not close the bonnet with the release cable detached.*

10   Open the driver's side glovebox, unscrew the nut from the cable securing bracket beneath the facia, then withdraw the cable through the grommet in the bulkhead. Do not lose the nut and shakeproof washer.

11   Refitting is the reverse of the removal procedure, adjustment for satisfactory operation being made at the lock end of the cable.

10   Rear tailgate – removal and refitting

1   Disconnect the battery earth lead.

2   Open and support the tailgate.

3   Pull away the carpet from the body at the rear panel and disconnect the three wiring plug connectors (two on the left and one on the right) (Fig. 12.8).

4   Tie a length of string around the wiring plug connectors and pull each one through the door closing face aperture, together with its grommet. The length of string will facilitate guiding the looms through the aperture at a later stage.

5   With the tailgate open, release the retaining clips from the upper sockets on the support stays. Pull the support stays away from the ball pins.

Fig. 12.6 Adjusting the bonnet catch (Sec 9)

Fig. 12.7 Bonnet lock components (Sec 9)

2   *Inner cable trunnion and clamp bolt*
3   *Outer cable trunnion and clamp bolt*
4   *Lock retaining screw*
5   *Lock retaining bolts*

10.6 Rear tailgate (left-hand hinge)

6   Undo the four bolts that secure the tailgate to the hinges and lift the tailgate away (photo).
7   Refitting is the reverse of the removal procedure, but on completion, check that the tailgate is correctly aligned with the body. Adjustment can be achieved by loosening the hinge bolts and moving the tailgate to correct any misalignment.

11 Rear tailgate hinges – renewal

1   Remove the tailgate as described in Section 10.
2   Ease the rear edge of the headlining away from the 'Velcro' retaining strips.

3   Mark around the hinge with a pencil then remove the two retaining bolts, spring washers and plain washers.
4   Refitting is the reverse of the removal procedure. The door alignment can be adjusted by loosening the hinge retaining bolts, and moving the tailgate as necessary.

12 Rear tailgate lock and striker – removal, refitting and adjustment

Tailgate lock

1   Remove the four screws that retain the number plate lamps and the screws that retain the plastic moulding.
2   Pull the moulding away and detach the spade connectors at the rear of the number plate lamps.
3   From the recesses under the door, remove the two long screws, spring washers and shakeproof washers that retain the lock.
4   Withdraw the lock after detaching the three wiring connectors inside the door on the right-hand side.
5   Refitting is the reverse of the removal procedure.

Fig. 12.8 Tailgate components (Sec 10)

4   *Harness plugs*   5   *Support stay retaining clips*   6   *Tailgate to hinge bolts*

Fig. 12.9 Tailgate hinge (Sec 11)

2   'Velcro' retaining strip
3   Bolts

12.7 Lift the tailgate moulding away to gain access to the striker bolts

Tailgate lock striker

6   Remove the self-tapping screws that secure the luggage compartment right-hand sill moulding.
7   Lift the moulding away to gain access to the three bolts, plain and shakeproof washers that retain the striker unit (photo).

8   Refitting is the reverse of the removal procedure; but before fully tightening the striker retaining screws, check that the latching operations and body alignment are satisfactory. Where adjustment is necessary, loosen the striker retaining screws and move the striker within the limits of the vertical slots. Temporarily tighten the screws and check the adjustment.
9   On completion secure the striker retaining screws.

13   Door rattles – tracing and rectification

1   The most common cause of door rattles is a misaligned, loose or worn striker plate, but other causes may be:

   (a) *Loose door handles, window winder handles or door hinges*
   (b) *Loose, worn or misaligned door lock components*
   (c) *Loose or worn remote control mechanism*

2   If the striker catch is worn, renew and adjust, as described later in this Chapter.
3   Should the hinges be badly worn then it may become necessary for new ones to be fitted.

14   Doors – removal and refitting

Front doors
1   Disconnect the battery earth lead.
2   Release the window regulator handle plastic cover which is clipped into position. Pivot the cover to one side in order to gain access to the retaining screw.
3   Remove the retaining screw and withdraw the regulator handle (with plastic cover) and bezel (photo).
4   Remove a single self-tapping screw from the upper part of the door pull moulding. On the driver's door, this screw also retains the door lock switch protection ramp (photo).
5   Remove the ashtray as for normal emptying. Locate and remove the single screw that secures the ashtray housing to the inner door panel (photo) and withdraw the housing.
6   The door trim panel is retained to the door frame by conventional spring clips along its sides and bottom. To release the clips, insert a large flat blade screwdriver between the inner door panel and the trim pad. Position the blade over the spring clip retaining bridge as shown in Fig. 12.10 and prise out the clip. Repeat this operation for the remaining eight clips.
7   After releasing the nine spring clips, lift the trim panel up and off the window sill retaining channel.
8   Carefully peel off the adhesive tape and protective sheet from the door panel.
9   Separate the wiring connectors which are located at the lower edge of the door.
10 If the passenger's door is being removed then it will be necessary to remove the radio speaker and rubber shroud. Two snap-connectors are provided to enable the speaker wires to be easily disconnected.
11 Support the door then remove the six nuts, spring washers, plain washers and the clamping plates from inside the door frame.
12 Now the door can be lifted away.

14.3 The window regulator handle showing the retaining screw and plastic insert (trim panel already removed)

14.4 Removing the single screw from the upper part of the door pull moulding

14.5 Removing the door ashtray housing

This sequence of photographs deals with the repair of the dent and paintwork damage shown in this photo. The procedure will be similar for the repair of a hole. It should be noted that the procedures given here are simplified – more explicit instructions will be found in the text

In the case of a dent the first job – after removing surrounding trim – is to hammer out the dent where access is possible. This will minimise filling. Here, the large dent having been hammered out, the damaged area is being made slightly concave

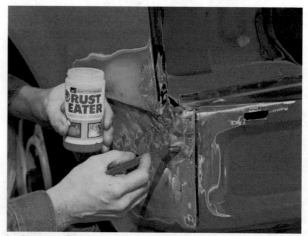

Now all paint must be removed from the damaged area, by rubbing with coarse abrasive paper. Alternatively, a wire brush or abrasive pad can be used in a power drill. Where the repair area meets good paintwork, the edge of the paintwork should be 'feathered', using a finer grade of abrasive paper

In the case of a hole caused by rusting, all damaged sheet-metal should be cut away before proceeding to this stage. Here, the damaged area is being treated with rust remover and inhibitor before being filled

Mix the body filler according to its manufacturer's instructions. In the case of corrosion damage, it will be necessary to block off any large holes before filling – this can be done with aluminium or plastic mesh, or aluminium tape. Make sure the area is absolutely clean before ...

... applying the filler. Filler should be applied with a flexible applicator, as shown, for best results; the wooden spatula being used for confined areas. Apply thin layers of filler at 20-minute intervals, until the surface of the filler is slightly proud of the surrounding bodywork

Initial shaping can be done with a Surform plane or Dreadnought file. Then, using progressively finer grades of wet-and-dry paper, wrapped around a sanding block, and copious amounts of clean water, rub down the filler until really smooth and flat. Again, feather the edges of adjoining paintwork

The whole repair area can now be sprayed or brush-painted with primer. If spraying, ensure adjoining areas are protected from over-spray. Note that at least one inch of the surrounding sound paintwork should be coated with primer. Primer has a 'thick' consistency, so will find small imperfections

Again, using plenty of water, rub down the primer with a fine grade wet-and-dry paper (400 grade is probably best) until it is really smooth and well blended into the surrounding paintwork. Any remaining imperfections can now be filled by carefully applied knifing stopper paste

When the stopper has hardened, rub down the repair area again before applying the final coat of primer. Before rubbing down this last coat of primer, ensure the repair area is blemish-free – use more stopper if necessary. To ensure that the surface of the primer is really smooth use some finishing compound

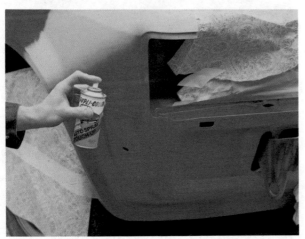

The top coat can now be applied. When working out of doors, pick a dry, warm and wind-free day. Ensure surrounding areas are protected from over-spray. Agitate the aerosol thoroughly, then spray the centre of the repair area, working outwards with a circular motion. Apply the paint as several thin coats

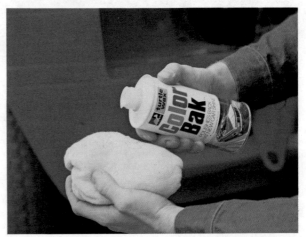

After a period of about two weeks, which the paint needs to harden fully, the surface of the repaired area can be 'cut' with a mild cutting compound prior to wax polishing. When carrying out bodywork repairs, remember that the quality of the finished job is proportional to the time and effort expended

Fig. 12.10 Removal procedure for door trim panel (Sec 14)

4   *Releasing the spring retainer clips with a screwdriver*
5   *Window sill channel retainer*

Fig. 12.11 Front door lock components (Sec 16)

2	*Steady bracket*	5	*Interior lock control*
3	*Latch*	6	*Operating rod*
4	*Latch release and lock relay rods*	7	*Operating rod*

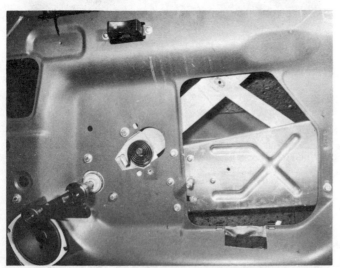

15.3 Window regulator and retaining bolts (one already removed)

16.2 A door lock steady bracket

13 Refitting is the reverse of the removal procedure, but after 'hanging' the door, check that it opens and closes satisfactorily and that it is also correctly aligned with the body shell. Adjustments can be made, if necessary, by loosening the hinge fixings and moving the door. Temporarily tighten the door fixings, after each adjustment, and make them secure when a satisfactory door fit is obtained.

Rear doors
14 The removal and refitting procedure for the rear doors is basically identical to that of the front doors (paragraphs 1 to 12). Points which refer specifically to either of the front doors should, however, be ignored.

---

15 Manual window regulator – removal and refitting

1 Wind the window glass fully upwards to the closed position then tape or wedge the glass in position.
2 Remove the door trim pad as described in Section 14, paragraphs

2 to 8.
3 Remove the four bolts that secure the regulator unit to the door frame (photo).
4 Disengage the scissor linkage and lifting studs from the horizontal glass support and the support plate channels by sliding it forwards or backwards as necessary.
5 Withdraw the window regulator assembly through the large aperture in the door frame.
6 Refitting is the reverse of the removal operation.

---

16 Door lock (front doors) – removal and refitting

1 Remove the window regulator assembly as described in Section 15.
2 Remove the two screws, plain and shakeproof washers and steady bracket that retain the lock to the inner door panel (photo).
3 Using a suitable Allen key, remove the four torque screws that retain the outer latch assembly to the door shut face. Lift the latch

assembly away.

4   Disconnect the latch release and lock relay rods from the outer handle by releasing the retaining clips.

5   Release the interior lock control from the inner door panel by removing the two retaining screws, plain and shakeproof washers. Note that the coloured dot on the assembly is facing towards the front.

6   Withdraw the interior locking control through the large aperture in the door frame after disconnecting the release operating rod retaining clip.

7   Disconnect the forward end of the operating rod at the remote control release unit.

8   At the lower edge of the door, separate the two wiring plug connectors.

9   Withdraw the lock unit, together with its four operating rods and solenoid wiring, through the large aperture in the inner door panel.

10   Refitting is the reverse of the removal procedure. When refitting the interior lock control, ensure that the coloured dot is facing towards the front.

Fig. 12.12 The rear door lock assembly (Sec 17)

3 Steady bracket	9 Interior lock control
4 Latch	10 Operating rod
5 Rubber mounting	11 Locking control rod
6 'Cheater' channel operating rod	12 Operating rod clip
8 Latch release operating rod	13 Childrens safety lock

Fig. 12.13 Side door lock striker (Sec 18)

1 Retaining screws	2 Striker components

17 Door lock (rear doors) – removal and refitting

1   Wind the window glass upwards to the fully closed position then tape or wedge the glass in position.

2   Remove the door trim pad as described in Section 14, paragraphs 2 to 8.

3   Remove the steady bracket that retains the lock to the inner door panel. The steady bracket is held in position by two screws, plain washers and shakeproof washers.

4   Using a suitable size Allen key, undo the four special torque screws that retain the latch assembly to the door shut face. Lift the latch assembly away (photo).

5   Carefully pull the rubber moulding out of the rear channel and hold it back out of the way using a strip of sticky tape.

6   Remove the door rear cheater channel, located at the rear edge of the door frame. This is retained from inside the car by a screw and a bolt, spring washer and plain washer, and a bracket.

7   Release the operating rod from the outside door handle by removing the retainer clip.

8   Release the interior lock control from the interior door panel by removing the two retaining screws, plain and shakeproof washers. Note that the coloured dot on the assembly is facing towards the front.

9   Withdraw the interior lock control after disconnecting the clip and operating rod.

10   Disconnect the clip that retains the locking control rod to the lock lever. The control rod can be withdrawn from the aperture next to the lock.

11   Disconnect the operating rod at the remote control release, after removing the spring retainer clip.

12   At the door shut face, remove the children's safety lock knob, which is simply a screwed on fixture.

13   Pull out the wiring block connector. Remove the lock unit, together with the operating rods and attached wiring loom.

14   Refitting is the reverse of the removal procedure. When refitting the interior lock control, ensure that the coloured dot is facing towards the front.

18 Door lock striker (side doors) – removal, refitting and adjustment

1   Remove the two special torque screws that secure the striker assembly to a tapped plate, located inside the door frame. An impact type screwdriver may be needed to undo these screws but if one of these tools is not available, an ordinary crosshead type screwdriver can sometimes be used, in conjunction with a hammer, to release the screws (photo).

2   Lift away the outer cover, rubber seal, striker plate, rubber gasket and backplate.

18.1 The door lock striker (driver's door)

3   Refitting is the reverse of the removal procedure. Before fully tightening the torque screws, check that the latching action and door alignment are correct. Where adjustments are necessary, loosen the torque screws and move the striker in the horizontal or vertical planes as necessary.
4   When correctly adjusted, it should be possible after closing the door, to press it in against its seals by a small amount. This measure ensures that the striker is not set in too far.
5   After correct adjustment has been made, it will be necessary to tighten the torque screws using a similar method as used for their removal.

19 Lock remote control – removal and refitting

1   Wind up the window to its fully closed position.
2   Remove the door trim pad as described in Section 14, paragraphs 2 to 8. Ignore any instructions referring to other doors.
3   Where work is being carried out on the driver's door, unplug the wiring plug connector at the locking control switch.
4   Remove the door pull which is retained by two bolts, plain and

Fig. 12.14 Lock remote control assembly (Sec 19)

   3   *Horseshoe retainer clip*
   4   *Operating rod retaining clip*
   5   *Remote control unit retaining screws*

19.5 Pull out the horse shoe shaped spring clip to remove the door catch lever

shakeproof washers.
5   Pull out the horse shoe shaped spring clip, that retains the remote control handle spindle, and withdraw the handle (photo).
6   Disconnect the operating rod from the remote control release by releasing the spring retainer clip.
7   Remove the three screws, and shakeproof washers that retain the remote control unit to the inner door panel. Withdraw the remote control unit through the large aperture in the door.
8   Refitting is the reverse of the removal process, but in order to prevent tension or compression being exerted on the lock release mechanism, it is advisable to tighten the remote control retaining screws after refitting the operating rod.

20 Front door lock barrel – removal and refitting

1   Remove the window regulator unit as described in Section 15.
2   Remove the two screws, plain and shakeproof washers and steady bracket that retain the lock to the inner door.
3   Remove the bolt, plain and shakeproof washers that locate the bottom of the rear glass guide channel.
4   Pull the rubber moulding strip to one side and restrain it using a piece of sticky tape.
5   Withdraw the guide channel from the door.
6   Prise off the circlip at the rear of the outside handle. Access to the circlip can be gained by using the rectangular shaped hole in the door panel.
7   Withdraw the indexing plate, lock operating lever and release lock indexing spring in that order.
8   The lock barrel can now be pressed out, together with its rubber O-ring.
9   Refitting is the reverse of the removal procedure, but ensure that the rubber O-ring is located under the head of the lock barrel before inserting it.

21 Outer door handle (front door) – removal and refitting

1   Remove the window regulator unit as described in Section 15.
2   Remove the two screws, plain and shakeproof washers and steady bracket that retain the lock to the inner door panel.
3   Remove the bolt, plain and shakeproof washers that locate the bottom of the rear glass guide channel.
4   Pull the rubber moulding strip to one side and restrain it with a piece of sticky tape.
5   Withdraw the guide channel from the door.
6   Disconnect the latch release and lock operating rods from the outside door handle, after releasing the retaining clips.
7   Remove the two handle retaining nuts, plain and shakeproof washers, in order to release the inner clamping plate.
8   Withdraw the handle from the door, noting the gasket between the two parts.
9   Refitting is the reverse of the removal procedure.

Fig. 12.15 Front door lock barrel and outer door handle (Sec 20)

6 *Circlip*	9 *Indexing spring*
7 *Indexing plate*	10 *Lock barrel*
8 *Lock operating lever*	11 *O-ring*

22 Outer door handle (rear door) – removal and refitting

1 Remove the window regulator unit as described in Section 15.
2 Remove the two screws, plain and shakeproof washers and steady bracket that retain the lock to the inner door panel.
3 Locate and remove a screw at the rear edge of the door frame which retains the upper cheater section of the rear glass guide channel.
4 Remove the bolt, plain and shakeproof washers that locate the bottom of the rear glass guide channel.
5 Withdraw the glass guide channel from the door.
6 Disconnect the latch release operating rod from the door handle.
7 Remove the two handle retaining nuts, plain and shakeproof washers, in order to release the inner clamping plate.
8 Withdraw the handle from the door, noting the gasket positioned between the two components.
9 Refitting is the reverse of the removal procedure. When relocating the bolt that secures the bottom of the rear guide channel, it will be found necessary to use a pair of long-nosed pliers.

23 Centre console (manual transmission models) – removal and refitting

1 Disconnect the battery earth lead.
2 Apply the handbrake and pull off the handbrake lever grip.
3 Using a flat blade screwdriver, prise out the rear cover panel which is retained by four spigots.
4 At the front end of the assembly, remove the two screws that secure it to the heater bracket.
5 Remove the further four screws that secure the console to the transmission tunnel. The exact location of these screws is shown in Fig. 12.16 at either end of the assembly.
6 Carefully prise out the cigar lighter and housing from the console. Disconnect the single snap connector and pull off the two spade connectors from the cigar lighter.
7 Unscrew and remove the gear lever knob.
8 Lift up the choke control lever. Remove the spring clip that retains the choke inner cable to the control lever.
9 Raise the rear of the console and guide the choke cable through the console.
10 Pull off the two spade connectors from the choke warning light switch.

11 On models with electrically operated windows, pull out the four harness plugs from the operating switches.
12 Lift the console up and withdraw it from the car.
13 Refitting is the reverse of the removal procedure.

24 Centre console (automatic transmission models) – removal and refitting

1 Disconnect the battery earth lead.
2 Using a small pin punch, drive out the roll pin that retains the plastic selector lever sleeve.
3 Apply the handbrake and pull off the handbrake lever grip.
4 Remove the two retaining screws and withdraw the selector lever shroud. The selector indicator panel can be lowered into the recess of the console.
5 Using a flat blade screwdriver, prise out the rear cover panel, which is retained by four spigots.
6 At the forward end of the console, remove the two screws that retain it to the heater bracket.
7 Refer to Fig. 12.17 and remove the four screws that retain the console to the transmission tunnel (two screws at either end).
8 Prise out the cigar lighter and housing. Disconnect the single snap connector and the two spade connectors. Lift the housing away from the console.
9 Raise the choke control lever and remove the clip that retains the choke inner cable.
10 Raise the rear of the console and guide the choke cable through the console.
11 Pull off the two spade connectors at the choke warning light switch.
12 On models fitted with electrically operated windows, pull out the four harness plugs at the operating switches.
13 Lift the console up and withdraw it from the car.
14 Refitting is the reverse of the removal procedure.

25 Glovebox – removal and refitting

1 Open the glovebox and disconnect the support straps from it (photo).
2 Remove the two screws at the rear of the glovebox that secure it to the pivot brackets.
3 Lift the glovebox away after detaching it from the spigots on the

Fig. 12.16 Centre console (manual transmission models) (Sec 23)

   3   *Rear cover panel*
   4   *Console to heater bracket screw*
   5   *Console to transmission tunnel screw*
   6   *Cigar lighter*
   7   *Wiring connectors – cigar lighter*
   8   *Fixing clip – choke cable*
 12   *Harness plugs (four shown are for electric windows)*

Fig. 12.17 Centre console (automatic transmission models) (Sec 24)

2   Roll pin
4   Gear shift lever shroud
5   Rear cover panel
6   Console to heater bracket screw
7   Console to transmission tunnel screw
8   Cigar lighter
9   Wiring connectors – cigar lighter
10 Fixing clip – choke cable
12 Choke cable
14 Harness plugs (four shown are for electric windows)

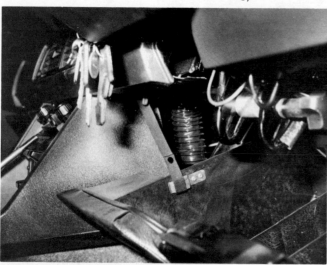

25.1 Driver's side glovebox open showing supporting straps

pivot brackets.
4   Refitting is the reverse of the removal procedure.

26 Facia – removal and refitting

1   Disconnect the battery earth lead.
2   Remove both the gloveboxes as described in Section 25.
3   Unscrew the nut that secures the bonnet release cable to the bracket and detach the cable from the bracket.
4   Remove the instrument housing and the time clock as described in Chapter 10.
5   Remove the steering wheel as described in Chapter 11.
6   Remove the steering column upper nacelle. This is retained by a single screw.
7   Remove the six bolts and washers that secure the facia to the outer body brackets (three bolts at either side of the car).
8   Remove the two bolts and washers that secure both the facia and the relay bracket to the bulkhead.

9   Pull the two demister vents away from the heater unit.
10 Disconnect the right-hand side vent hose from the demister vent and move it away from the steering column.
11 Disconnect the wiring connectors to each of the glovebox lamps, and the map light.
12 Lift the facia away, and at the same time, guide the wiring harness and the speedometer cable through the apertures in the top part of the facia.
13 Refitting is the reverse of the removal procedure.

27 Front seats and runners – removal and refitting

1   Release the seat belt brackets from their fixing studs at the seat runners.
2   Using a suitable size Allen key or Rover service tool 18G 1256A, remove the screws, clamping plate and rectangular washers that secure the seat pivot tube to the floor panel (Fig. 12.19).
3   Using either of the tools mentioned in paragraph 2, remove the two screws that retain the cushion frame to the bracket fitted to the seat runners.
4   Separate the wiring harness plug located between the seat and the console.
5   Lift out the seat sufficiently to disconnect the harness plug from its underside.
6   Remove the two plastic straps that retain the harness to the seat frame.
7   The seat can now be lifted from the car.
8   To remove the seat runners, simply remove the six screws and rectangular washers that secure the assembly to the floor (Fig. 12.20).
9   Refitting is the reverse of the removal procedure.

28 Rear seat cushion, squab wings and squab – removal and refitting

1   The reat seat cushion is secured to the floor panel by two clips beneath the forward edge. Release the cushion from these clips and lift it out.
2   Tilt the seat squab forward and remove the bolts and washers (one either side) that retain the squab wing brackets to the body frame.
3   Raise the squab wings sufficiently to disengage the retainers from the body bracket.
4   Having removed the left and right-hand squab wings remove the four bolts and washers (two either side), that secure the seat squab

Fig. 12.18 Removing the facia (left-hand drive model shown) (Sec 26)

2   Bonnet release control
5   Steering column and column
    rake angle adjuster
6   Nacelle half and retaining
    screw

7   Bolts securing facia to outer
    body brackets
8   Bolts securing facia and
    relay bracket to bulkhead
9   Glovebox

10   Demister valve
12   Glovebox lamp
13   Map light
14   Wiring harness and
     speedometer cable assembly

Fig. 12.19 Front seat fixings (Sec 27)

2   Screw and clamping plate
3   Screw cushion frame to
    seat runner bracket
4   Harness plug

5   Harness plug
6   Harness retaining
    clip
8   Bearing block

Fig. 12.21 Rear seat squab wing fixing (Sec 28)

2   Squab wing bracket, bolt and washer
3   Retainer

brackets to the body.
5   The seat squab can now be lifted away from the car.
6   Refitting is the reverse of the removal procedure.

29 Seat belt (front) – removal and refitting

1   Disconnect the swivel bracket from the bracket which is attached to the seat runner by removing the retaining bolt. Note the positions of the spacer, wave washers and plastic washer.
2   Pull the carpet away to expose the reel cover plate and remove the two cover plate retaining screws.
3   Lift the cover plate away. Remove the single screw and washer that secure the reel assembly to the base of the 'B' post.
4   Remove the 'B' post lower trim panel (two screws) after prising off the five front and three rear carpet retainer clips.
5   Remove the two screws that secure the 'B' post seat belt guide piece.

Fig. 12.20 Front seat runner assembly (Sec 27)

1   Seat belt bracket, washer and nut
3   Screw seat runner to floor

Fig. 12.22 Front seat belt assembly (Sec 29)

1   Swivel bracket, wavey washers, spacer, seat runner bracket and
    bolt
2   Reel cover plate screws
3   Reel retaining screw
5   Seat belt guide piece screws
6   Upper swivel bracket cover
7   Swivel bracket, bolt, wavey washer and spacer

6   Carefully prise off the plastic swivel bracket cover. Remove the bolt, wave washer and spacer that secure the swivel bracket to the 'B' post.
7   Where necessary the seat belt switch can be removed as described in Chapter 10, Section 35.

30 Seat belt (rear) – removal and refitting

1   Remove the rear seat cushion as described in Section 28.
2   Remove the bolt, shakeproof washer, bracket, and plastic washer that anchor the seat belt to the floor panel.
3   Carefully prise off the plastic swivel bracket cover. Remove the bolt, swivel bracket, wave washer, spacer and plastic washer that anchor the seat belt to the 'D' post.
4   Guide the belt, and its attached brackets, through the cut out in the rear parcel tray extension panel.
5   Pull the carpet away to expose the reel assembly. Remove the screw and spring washer that secure it to the body.
6   The remaining section of the seat belt is anchored to the floor panel by a bolt, swivel bracket, spacer and plastic washer.
7   Refitting is the reverse of the removal procedure.

31 Door glass (front) – removal and refitting

1   Remove the window regulator assembly as described in Section 15.
2   Release the interior sealing strip which is retained by five clips to the window sill.
3   Release the interior waist rail moulding which is retained by four clips.
4   Remove the sticky tape or wedge, that secures the glass to the door frame.
5   Withdraw the glass, by raising it and tilting it upwards, from the outside of the door. Take care when removing the glass as it is easily scratched if it comes into direct contact with the door frame.
6   Refitting is the reverse of the removal procedure.

32 Door glass (rear) – removal and refitting

1   Remove the window regulator unit as described in Section 15.
2   Release the interior sealing strip. This is retained to the window sill by five clips.
3   Release the interior waist rail moulding. This is retained by four clips.
4   At the rear edge of the door frame, remove the screw which retains the upper cheater section of the rear glass guide channel.
5   Remove the locating bolt, plain and shakeproof washer from the bottom part of the rearmost glass guide channel.
6   Withdraw the guide channel, after pulling out and taping the rubber moulding to one side.
7   Remove the tape or wedge, that secures the glass to the top door frame.
8   Withdraw the glass from the outside of the door by tilting the glass upwards at the front. Take care when carrying out this operation, because the glass can easily be scratched if allowed to come into contact with the door frame.
9   Refitting is the reverse of the removal procedure.

33 Windscreen – removal and refitting

The windscreen is retained in the aperture by a neoprene based material, which is supplied in round strip form. It contains a resistance wire core which is heated by electric current to cure the sealing strip after it is fitted. Fitting of the windscreen requires special techniques and equipment. This should never be attempted by the do-it-yourself owner. This is definitely a job for the Rover dealer or a windscreen specialist.

34 Heated rear window – removal and refitting

1   Using a blunt tool, break the existing seal.
2   Disconnect the two wiring harness plugs at the rear window connection.
3   With help from an assistant, push out the glass taking care that it is not scratched.
4   Remove the weatherstrip and finishers from the glass.
5   When refitting, ensure that the edges of the glass and body

Fig. 12.23 Rear seat belt assembly (Sec 30)

2   Seat belt anchorage to floor
3   Swivel bracket components
4   Cut-out in rear parcel tray extension panel
5   Reel assembly
6   Floor mounted swivel bracket components

aperture are clean and dry. Apply a mastic sealing compound to the glass channel, then fit the weatherstrip and finishers around the windscreen (Fig. 12.24).
6   Insert a strong draw-cord into the weatherstrip inner channel, allowing the ends to protrude from the lower edge.
7   With an assistant holding the glass centrally in the aperture, apply steady pressure and pull the cord ends so that the lip of the weatherstrip is pulled over the body flange.
8   Seal the outer channel to the body flange using the mastic sealer.
9   Reconnect the two wiring harness plugs.

35 Quarter light glass – removal and refitting

1   Remove the appropriate seat squab wing as described in Section 28.
2   On cars fitted with rear seat belts, prise off the plastic swivel bracket cover. Remove the bolt, spring washer and spacer that secure the swivel bracket to the 'D' post.
3   Pull the 'D' post upper trim panel away from the body and disengage the upper fixing clip. Slide the trim panel downwards to disengage the lower fixing clip and to remove the trim panel.
4   Remove the screw that secures the forward end of the 'E' post trim panel to the body. Slide the trim panel forwards to release its lower fixing clip.
5   Lift out the parcel tray and loosen the parcel tray stops.
6   Carefully prise off the single retaining clip located at the rear end of the extension panel. Where rear seat belts are fitted, it will be necessary to remove the appropriate seat belt (Section 30) before the rear parcel tray extension panel can be lifted away.
7   Using a drill with a $\frac{1}{8}$ in (3 mm) diameter bit, drill out the four 'pop' rivets that retain the front edge of the 'D' post capping.
8   Withdraw the 'D' post capping, after disengaging the two tongues on the rear edge from the channel in the rear quarter light weatherstrip.
9   Using a blunt tool, break the seal between the body and the weatherstrip.
10   Withdraw the end cap from the front end of the waist moulding and prise each end of the moulding off the retaining clips.
11   With the help of an assistant, push out the glass together with the weatherstrip and waist moulding, taking care not to scratch the glass.
12   Note the positions of the waist moulding and weatherstrip, then remove them from the glass.

Fig. 12.24 Fitting a heated rear window (Sec 34)

2   *Wiring connector for heater element*   4   *Weatherstrip finisher*   6   *Draw-cord*

Fig. 12.25 Quarter light components (Sec 35)

5   *'D' post capping*
6   *Weatherstrip*
7   *End cap and waist moulding*

13 When refitting, ensure that the edges of the glass and the body aperture are clean and dry. Apply a mastic sealing compound to the glass channel, and fit the weatherstrip to the glass. The waist moulding can now be slid into position in the weatherstrip outer channel.

14 Insert a strong draw-cord into the weatherstrip inner channel, allowing the ends to protrude from the lower edge.

15 With an assistant holding the glass centrally in the aperture, apply steady pressure. Pull the cord ends so that the lip of the weatherstrip is pulled over the body flange.

16 Press the waist moulding down onto the retaining clips and refit the end cap to the forward edge of the moulding.

17 Refit the 'D' post capping by engaging the two tongues in the channel. Use a 'pop' rivet gun to relocate the front edge.

18 The remainder of the reassembly procedure is the reverse of the removal.

36 Heater and ventilation unit – removal and refitting

1   Disconnect the battery earth lead.

2   Drain the cooling system as described in Chapter 2.

3   Loosen the heater hose clips and pull the hoses off the bulkhead connections. Note their exact locations for refitting.

4   Remove the radio and facia assembly (Section 26, and Chapter 10, Section 43).

5   Remove the two heater rear fixing nuts, plain and spring washers as shown in Fig. 12.26.

6   From within the car, remove the screws that retain the triangular shaped air duct covers located either side of the transmission tunnel. Note that these duct covers are fitted with their open side upwards,

facing the front of the car.

7   Release the rectangular shaped air duct covers from each side of the transmission tunnel by pressing out the centres of the special Rokut plastic rivets. Note that the vanes of these covers are inclined rearwards to deflect the air in the required direction.

8   Remove the centre console (Section 23 manual transmission models or Section 24 automatic transmission models).

9   Remove the two large bolts, plain and spring washers from the heater support bracket which secures the lower side of the heater. When removed, these console front mounting brackets will also be released.

10 Loosen the two bolts, plain and shakeproof washers that secure the slotted heater bracket to the floor. This will enable the bracket to be released and lifted, with the heater, to clear the angle piece on the floor.

11 Remove the four bolts, plain and shakeproof washers that secure the glovebox mounting brackets and fibre optic master bulb unit. These are located at either side of the heater base plate.

12 Lift the heater in a rearwards direction, allowing the fixing studs at its rear, to clear the front bulkhead.

13 Disconnect the radio aerial from the radio.

14 Pull off the five wiring spade connectors from the heater control illumination panel.

15 Remove the heater motor end cover. Disconnect the red feed cable spade connector beneath the motor and the earth wire connection under the heater.

16 Plug the inlet and outlet water pipes to prevent the coolant from spilling, then lift the complete heater assembly away.

17 Refitting is the reverse of the removal procedure. After completion refill the cooling system as described in Chapter 2.

37 Fan (blower) motor – removal and refitting

1   Remove the heater as described in the previous Section.

2   Loosen the trunnion and disconnect the air intake control rod.

3   Remove the retaining screws and lift off the air inlet box.

4   Drill out the three 'pop' rivets which secure the upper casing to the lower casing.

5   Drill out a further 'pop' rivet that secures the pipe bracket to the upper casing.

6   Pull off the spade connector from the top of the motor and release the three remaining wires from the clip on the heater base.

7   Detach the clips that secure the two halves of the casing and separate the two parts.

8   Lift away the motor assembly and pull the rotor unit from the motor shaft.

9   Remove the rubber mounting strips carefully from the motor housing and locating tab.

10 When refitting the motor, apply adhesive to the rubber mounting strips, and stick them to the motor housing.

Fig. 12.26 Heater fixing detail (Sec 36)

6 Triangular air duct fixing screw
7 'Rokut' plastic rivet for retaining rectangular air duct
12 Screw retaining top heater bracket
15 Heater support bracket to floor bolt
16 Fibre optic lamp and glovebox mounting bracket retaining bolts
17 Rear fixing studs
18 Radio aerial lead
20 Heater motor cover
21 Earth wire
22 Heater coolant pipes

12.27 Fan (blower) motor components and fitting diagram (Sec 37)

10 Rotor unit
11 Rubber mounting strips
13 Protrusion ($\frac{3}{16}$ in/5mm) of shaft through rotor hub

11 Press the rotor onto the motor shaft, exerting even pressure to prevent possible distortion. The rotor should be pressed on until $\frac{3}{16}$ in (5 mm) of the shaft protrudes through the rotor hub.

12 Fit the motor assembly so that its locating tang is correctly positioned in the lower half of the heater casing.

13 Reposition the foam sealing strips. Lower the upper casing onto the lower casing, whilst ensuring that the flap pivot shafts are correctly relocated.

14 Secure the upper and lower casings together using the retaining clips. The locking sprags of the retaining clips locate under the thicker parts of the lower casing.

15 Secure the pipe bracket to the upper casing using a 'pop' rivet.

16 Fit three further 'pop' rivets to secure the upper casing to the lower casing.

17 Refit the air inlet box and reconnect the air inlet control rod. Ensure that the trunnion is positioned to permit full movement of the air intake control lever and flap.

18 Refit the heater unit as described in the previous Section.

38 Fan (blower) motor resistor unit – removal and refitting

1 Disconnect the battery earth lead.
2 Remove the facia panel as described in Section 26.
3 Disconnect the wiring connection at the fan (blower) motor.
4 Use a soldering iron to unsolder, from the back of the resistor unit, the wire which runs from the blower switch to the resistor.
5 Remove the seal from around the resistor unit.

Fig. 12.28 Fan (blower) motor resistor unit (Sec 38)

3   Wiring connector
6   Press spring clip at point arrowed to release the resistor unit
7   Spring retainer clip

6   Push the edge of the spring clip that secures the resistor into the heater casing and withdraw the resistor and spring clip.
7   Remove the spring clip from the resistor unit.

8   Refitting is the reverse of the removal procedure.

39 Heater matrix – removal and refitting

1   Remove the heater unit as described in Section 36.
2   Separate the upper and lower casings as described in Section 37, paragraphs 2 to 7.
3   Lift off the face level flap.
4   Lift the air blend flap upwards and disconnect the operating link from the lever.
5   Extract the thick packing seal from the matrix casing and withdraw the matrix by holding the pipe bracket and pipes. Push the pipes up through the heater casing.
6   Hold the pipes and pull the matrix off.
7   Where a matrix is leaking, repair is best entrusted to a radiator repair specialist. Seldom does a do-it-yourself repair prove satisfactory.
8   Refitting is the reverse of the removal procedure. When fitting the matrix pipes always fit new pipe seals. Lubricate both the seals and pipes with a smear of rubber grease or soapy water to facilitate fitment.

Rover 'new' 2000 model

Chapter 13 Supplement:
Revisions and information on later models

Contents

1 Introduction

This Supplement contains information which is additional to, or a revision of, material in the preceding Chapters. Although much of the material relates to the 'O' Series 2000 engine, some items apply to all models.

The Sections in the Supplement follow the same order as the Chapters to which they relate. The Specifications are all grouped together for convenience, but they too follow Chapter order.

It is recommended that before any particular operation is undertaken, reference be made to the appropriate Section(s) of the Supplement. In this way any changes to procedure or components can be noted before referring to the main Chapters.

2 Specifications

The Specifications below are revisions of, or additional to, those given at the beginning of the preceding Chapters.

Engine – 2000
General
Engine type	4-stroke, 4-cylinder, in-line, belt driven overhead cam
Maker's designation	O Series
Bore	3.324 in (84.45 mm)
Stroke	3.503 in (89.00 mm)
Cubic capacity	121.68 cu in (1994 cc)
Compression ratio	9.0:1
Compression pressure	150 to 170 lbf/in² (10.5 to 11.9 kgf/cm²)
Firing order	1-3-4-2
Location of No 1 cylinder	Nearest radiator

Valve clearances
Standard clearance (inlet and exhaust, cold)	0.012 ± 0.001 in (0.30 ± 0.03 mm)
Adjust only if less than	0.008 in (0.20 mm)

Crankshaft
Main bearing journal diameter	2.1262 to 2.1270 in (54.005 to 54.026 mm)
Crankpin diameter	1.8754 to 1.8759 in (47.635 to 47.647 mm)
Endfloat	0.001 to 0.005 in (0.03 to 0.13 mm)

Main bearings
Number	5
Running clearance	0.001 to 0.003 in (0.025 to 0.076 mm)
Undersizes available	0.01, 0.02, 0.03 and 0.04 in (0.254, 0.508, 0.762 and 1.016 mm)

Big-end bearings
Running clearance	0.0015 to 0.0032 in (0.038 to 0.081 mm)
Undersizes available	As for main bearings

Pistons and rings
Piston clearance in bore:	
Below oil control ring	0.0008 to 0.0024 in (0.02 to 0.06 mm)
At bottom of skirt	0.0004 to 0.0015 in (0.01 to 0.04 mm)
Oversize available	0.02 in (0.508 mm)
Number of piston rings	2 compression, 1 oil control
Ring-to-groove clearance (compression rings)	0.0015 to 0.0027 in (0.04 to 0.07 mm)
Piston ring end gap:	
Compression rings	0.012 to 0.020 in (0.3 to 0.5 mm)
Oil control rails	0.015 to 0.055 in (0.4 to 1.4 mm)
Oil control expander	Zero (ends butt)

Gudgeon pins
Diameter	0.8125 to 0.8127 in (20.638 to 20.643 mm)
Fit in connecting rod	Press fit
Fit in piston	Hand push fit at 60°F (16°C)

Camshaft

Endfloat .... 0.003 to 0.007 in (0.07 to 0.18 mm)
Journal diameter .... 1.888 to 1.889 in (47.96 to 47.97 mm)
Bearing clearance .... 0.0017 to 0.0037 in (0.043 to 0.094 mm)

Valves

Face angle .... 45° 30′
Seat angle .... 45° 00′
Head diameter:
  Inlet .... 1.575 in (40 mm)
  Exhaust .... 1.339 in (34 mm)
Stem diameter:
  Inlet .... 0.2917 to 0.2923 in (7.41 to 7.42 mm)
  Exhaust .... 0.2909 to 0.2917 in (7.39 to 7.41 mm)
Stem-to-guide clearance:
  Inlet .... 0.001 to 0.002 in (0.03 to 0.05 mm)
  Exhaust .... 0.0015 to 0.0027 in (0.04 to 0.07 mm)

Valve guides

Outside diameter .... 0.474 to 0.475 in (12.04 to 12.06 mm)
Bore .... 0.2933 to 0.2937 in (7.45 to 7.46 mm)
Height above cylinder head when fitted .... 0.394 in (10 mm)

Valve springs

Free length .... 1.646 in (41.81 mm)
Fitted length .... 1.375 in (34.92 mm)

Valve timing

Clearance for checking purposes .... 0.012 in (0.30 mm)
Inlet opens .... 12° BTDC
Inlet closes .... 48° ABDC
Exhaust opens .... 54° BBDC
Exhaust closes .... 22° ATDC

Camshaft drivebelt tension

Force needed to bring outer face of belt into line with reference
mark on water pump inlet:
  New belt .... 13 lbf (6 kgf)
  Used belt .... 11 lbf (5 kgf)

Lubrication system

Filter type .... Full flow, disposable cartridge, with built-in bypass valve
Oil pressure (hot):
  Running .... 60 to 90 lbf/in² (4.2 to 6.3 kgf/cm²)
  Idling .... 40 to 60 lbf/in² (2.8 to 4.2 kgf/cm²)
Warning light switch operating pressure .... 6 to 10 lbf/in² (0.42 to 0.70 kgf/cm²)
Pressure relief valve spring free length .... 1.525 in (38.7 mm)
Oil pump clearances:
  Housing to outer rotor .... 0.005 to 0.009 in (0.126 to 0.229 mm)
  Inner rotor lobe to outer rotor .... 0.001 to 0.011 in (0.025 to 0.279 mm)
  Outer rotor endfloat .... 0.001 to 0.003 in (0.025 to 0.076 mm)
Oil type/specification* .... Multigrade engine oil, viscosity range SAE 10W/30 to 15W/50, to API
                                                                                      SE or SF (Duckhams QXR, Hypergrade, or 10W/40 Motor Oil)
Oil capacity (drain and refill) .... 7 pints (4 litres) including filter

*Austin Rover specify a 10W/40 oil to meet warranty requirements for models produced after August 1983. Duckhams QXR and 10W/40 Motor Oil
are available to meet these requirements

Torque wrench settings (2000 engine)

	lbf ft	Nm
Camshaft top cover bolts	13	18
Camshaft sprocket bolt	48	65
Camshaft end cover bolts	9	12
Big-end bearing cap nuts*	33	45
Crankshaft pulley bolt*†	68	92
Cylinder head bolts*:		
Stage 1	30	41
Stage 2	60	81
Stage 3	Tighten by a further 60° or to 80 lbf ft (108 Nm), whichever comes first	
Driveplate-to-crankshaft bolts (GM180 transmission)	81	110
Engine backplate screws (8 mm)	22	30
Engine backplate screws (10 mm)	37	50
Flywheel bolts*†	42	57
Main bearing cap bolts	77	105
Manifolds to cylinder head	18	24
Oil pressure warning switch	9	12
Oil pump to cylinder block	8	11
Oil separator to cylinder block	22	30
Sump drain plug	27	37

	lbf ft	Nm
Block drain plug (when fitted)	27	37
Screws not specified, into aluminium:		
M6	8	11
M8	18	24
Screws not specified, into cast iron:		
M6	8	11
M8	22	30
M10	37	50

* Lightly oil threads
† Further tightening is permissible if necessary to align lockwasher tabs

Engine – 2300 and 2600 (1982 on)

Pistons
Clearance in bore:
  Top of skirt:
    2300 .... 0.0015 to 0.0031 in (0.038 to 0.079 mm)
    2600 .... 0.0057 to 0.0073 in (0.145 to 0.186 mm)
  Bottom of skirt:
    2300 .... 0.0006 to 0.0016 in (0.015 to 0.041 mm)
    2600 .... 0.0006 to 0.0020 in (0.015 to 0.051 mm)

Gudgeon pins
Diameter:
  Red .... 0.9375 to 0.9376 in (23.812 to 23.815 mm)
  Green .... 0.9374 to 0.9375 in (23.810 to 23.812 mm)
Clearance in connecting rod:
  Red .... 0.0001 to 0.0006 in (0.003 to 0.015 mm)
  Green .... 0.0002 to 0.0006 in (0.006 to 0.015 mm)

Camshaft
Endfloat .... 0.002 to 0.009 in (0.05 to 0.22 mm)

Valves
Stem-to-guide clearance:
  Inlet .... 0.0007 to 0.0023 in (0.0178 to 0.0582 mm)
  Exhaust .... 0.001 to 0.003 in (0.0254 to 0.0762 mm)

Valve timing
Inlet opens .... 16° BTDC
Inlet closes .... 56° ABDC
Exhaust opens .... 56° BBDC
Exhaust closes .... 16° ATDC

Lubrication system
Oil pressure (hot):
  Running .... 55 to 70 lbf/in² (3.9 to 4.9 kgf/cm²)
  Idling .... 36 to 54 lbf/in² (2.5 to 3.8 kgf/cm²)
Warning light switch operating pressure .... 6 to 10 lbf/in² (0.4 to 0.7 kgf/cm²)
Oil pump clearances:
  Housing to outer rotor .... 0.0059 to 0.0060 in (0.150 to 0.156 mm)
  Inner rotor lobe to outer rotor .... 0.0010 to 0.0011 in (0.0254 to 0.0279 mm)
  Outer rotor endfloat .... 0.0010 to 0.0025 in (0.0254 to 0.0635 mm)

Cooling system
Thermostat
Opening temperature (2000 and later 2300/2600 models) .... 190°F (88°C)

Cooling fan (2000 models)
Type .... Electrically driven, thermostatically controlled
Thermoswitch operating temperature .... 190°F (88°C)

Coolant capacity (2000 models) .... 13.0 pints (7.4 litres)

Torque wrench settings (2000 model)

	lbf ft	Nm
Water pump bolts	8	11
Water pump pulley to hub	9	12

Fuel and exhaust systems
Carburettors (2000 model)
Make and type .... Twin SU HIF 44 with Zenith FASD or electronic fuel management
Specification number:
  With FASD .... FZX 1383
  With electronic fuel management .... FZX 1450
Piston spring .... Red

Jet size:
    With FASD .... 0.10 in
    With electronic fuel management .... 0.07 in
Needle:
    With FASD .... BFG
    With electronic fuel management .... BFX

Carburettors (2300 model, 1982 on)
Make and type .... Twin SU HIF 44 with Zenith FASD or electronic fuel management
Specification number:
    With FASD .... FZX 1384
    With electronic fuel management .... FZX 1452
Piston spring .... Yellow
Jet size .... 0.10 in
Needle:
    With FASD .... BHF
    With electronic fuel management .... BFH

Carburettors (2600 models, 1982 on)
As for 2300 model (above), except
Specification number:
    With FASD .... FZX 1390
    With electronic fuel management .... FZX 1454
Needle .... BFJ

Idle speed
2000 model:
    With FASD .... 750 to 800 rpm
    With electronic fuel management:
        Manual transmission .... 700 to 800 rpm
        Automatic transmission .... 750 to 850 rpm
2300 and 2600 models:
    With FASD .... 750 to 850 rpm
    With electronic fuel management .... 700 to 800 rpm

CO emission at idle:
With FASD .... 2 to 3%
With electronic fuel management:
    2000 model .... 1.5 to 3.5%
    2300 and 2600 models .... 1 to 3%

Torque wrench settings

	lbf ft	Nm
Carburettor to manifold	19	26
Manifold to cylinder head	18	24

Ignition system
Distributor with contact breaker points (2000 model)
Make and type .... Lucas 48D4
Direction of rotation .... Anti-clockwise (viewed from above)
Contact breaker gap .... 0.014 to 0.016 in (0.35 to 0.40 mm)
Dwell angle .... 47 to 59°

Distributor (breakerless)
2000 model:
    Make and type .... Lucas 65DM4
    Direction of rotation .... Anti-clockwise (viewed from above)
2300 and 2600 models:
    Make and type .... Lucas 54DLM6
    Direction of rotation .... Anti-clockwise (viewed from above)
Air gap .... Not less than 0.006 in (0.15 mm)

Spark plugs

	Unipart	Champion
2000 model	GSP 4563	S9YC
2300 and 2600 models	GSP 4573	S12YC
Electrode gap:		
Models up to 1984:		
2000 model	0.035 in (0.90 mm)	0.035 in (0.90 mm)
2300 and 2600 models	0.024 to 0.026 in (0.60 to 0.66 mm)	0.024 in (0.60 mm)
Models 1985 on:		
2000 model	0.039 in (1.0 mm)	0.035 in (0.90 mm)
2300 and 2600 models	0.039 in (1.0 mm)	0.024 in (0.60 mm)

Firing order (2000 model) .... 1 - 3 - 4 - 2 (No 1 nearest radiator)

Ignition timing (2000 model)
Static (approximate setting only) .... 10° BTDC
At 2500 rpm (vacuum pipe disconnected and plugged) .... 25° BTDC

Ignition coil
With contact breaker distributor:
  All models 1982 on:
    Make and type .... Unipart GCL 130 with ballast resistor
    Primary resistance .... 1.2 to 1.5 ohms
With breakerless distributor:
  Make and type:
    2000 model .... Ducellier 520 067A or Bosch ADU 8779
    2300 and 2600 models .... Ducellier 520 074A, Bosch ADU 9288 or Bosch ADU 8228
Primary resistance:
  2000 model .... 0.78 to 0.86 ohms
  2300 and 2600 models .... 0.71 to 0.81 ohms

Ignition module (breakerless distributor)
Make and type:
  2000 model .... Lucas 14AB
  2300 and 2600 models .... Lucas 9EM

Torque wrench settings

	lbf ft	Nm
Distributor flange nuts	19	26
Spark plugs	7	10

Clutch (2000 model)
General
Clutch type .... Single dry plate, diaphragm spring pressure plate, hydraulic actuation
Driven plate diameter .... 8.5 in (215 mm) nominal

Torque wrench settings

	lbf ft	Nm
Clutch to flywheel	17	23

Manual gearbox
Ratios (1982 on)
Fifth 0.792:1
Fourth 1.000:1
Third 1.396:1
Second 2.087:1
First 3.321:1
Reverse 3.428:1

Automatic transmission (1982 on)
General
Make and type .... Borg-Warner 66 or GM 180
Fluid type/specification:
  Borg-Warner .... ATF to specification M2C 33G (Duckhams Q-Matic)
  GM 180 .... Dexron IID type ATF (Duckhams D-Matic)
Fluid capacity (from dry):
  Borg-Warner .... 9.3 pints (5.3 litres)
  GM 180 .... 12.3 pints (7.0 litres)

Ratios
Borg-Warner 66:
  Top 1.00:1
  Second 1.45:1
  First 2.39:1
  Reverse 2.09:1
GM 180:
  Top 1.00:1
  Second 1.48:1
  First 2.40:1
  Reverse 1.92:1

Torque wrench settings (GM 180)

	lbf ft	Nm
Driveplate to crankshaft:		
2000 model	74 to 88	100 to 119
2300 and 2600 models	52	71
Transmission-to-engine dowel bolt	18	24
Converter to driveplate	55	75
Servo cover	7	9
Oil pan (sump)	7	9

Rear axle
Ratios (2000 model)
Manual transmission 3.90:1
Automatic transmission 3.45:1

Electrical system
Alternator (1982 on)
Make and type .... Lucas A133
Maximum output:
    2000 model .... 65 amps at 6000 rpm
    2300 and 2600 models .... 55 amps at 6000 rpm
Rotor winding resistance at 68°F (20°C) .... 3.2 ohms
Control voltage .... 13.6 to 14.4 volts
Brush length (protrusion):
    New .... 0.8 in (20 mm)
    Wear limit .... 0.4 in (10 mm)
Brush spring tension (brush face flush with brush box) .... 4.7 to 9.8 ozf (1.3 to 2.7 N)

Fuses (1982 on, typical)   **Circuits protected**
Main fuse box:
    A1 (5 amp*) .... Instrument illumination, side and tail lights, number plate lights
    A2 (10 amp) .... Front fog lamps, or spare
    A3 (3 amp) .... Radio
    A4 (7.5 or 15 amp) .... Electric aerial and (on 2000 model only) engine cooling fan. Use 15 amp fuse with fan
    A5 (7.5 amp) .... Rear fog lights
    B1 (25 amp) .... Heater or air conditioning blower
    B2 (7.5 amp) .... Heater or air conditioning relay
    B3 (10 amp) .... Gauges and warning lamps, electric mirror switch, automatic transmission selector light, reversing lamps, trip computer display
    B4 (15 amp) .... Windscreen wash/wipe
    B5 (7.5 amp)* .... Direction indicators, stop-lamps
    C1 (7.5 amp) .... Air conditioning clutch
    C2 (10 amp) .... Horns
    C3 (20 amp) .... Cigarette lighter(s), clock, interior lamps, under-bonnet lamp, trip computer input
    C4 (10 amp) .... Hazard warning flasher
    C5 .... Spare
Luggage area fuse box:
    No 1 (25 amp) .... Heated rear window
    No 2 (5 amp) .... Luggage area lamp, reading lamps
    No 3 (10 amp) .... Rear wash/wipe
    No 4 (25 amp) .... Sliding roof
    No 5 (25 amp) or in-line (30 amp) .... Central door locking
Increase rating to 10 amp (A1) and 15 amp (B5) when a towing socket is fitted

Torque wrench settings (2000 engine)	lbf ft	Nm
Alternator adjusting link:		
To alternator	9	12
To cylinder block	38	51
Starter motor mounting bolts	27	37

Suspension and steering

Torque wrench settings (power steering components)	lbf ft	Nm
Pulley to pump	18	24
Pump bracket bolts (to block or timing cover)	18	24
Pump bracket to pump	30	41
Pump pivot bolt	25	34

Air conditioning system
General
Refrigerant type R12
Compressor drivebelt tension .... 0.25 to 0.40 in (6 to 10 mm) deflection under firm thumb pressure at mid-point of longest run

Torque wrench settings	lbf ft	Nm
Compressor bracket to block	37	50
Compressor bracket to compressor	37	50
Compressor drive pulley to crankshaft pulley	21	28
Tensioner bracket to mounting bracket	37	50

Under-bonnet view of a Rover 2000

1 Brake fluid reservoir
2 Clutch fluid reservoir
3 Oil filler cap
4 Distributor
5 Crankcase ventilation
  pipe

6 Rear carburettor
7 FASD
8 Front carburettor
9 Fuel filter
10 Expansion tank cap

11 Coolant hose (FASD to
   radiator)
12 Coolant hose (expansion
   tank to radiator)
13 Expansion tank cap

14 Expansion tank overflow
   hose
15 Air cleaner
16 Oil filter
17 Coolant hose (manifold

   to thermostat)
18 Thermostat
19 Alternator
20 Battery
21 Ignition coil

Underside view of a Rover 2000 – front end

1	Anti-roll bar	4	Brake pad warning	6	Brake hydraulic union	9	Gearbox drain plug	12	Clutch hydraulic damper
2	Steering rack gaiter		light connector	7	Exhaust manifold	10	Clutch slave cylinder	13	Steering column
3	Crossmember	5	Brake caliper	8	Exhaust joint	11	Starter motor		

Underside view of a Rover 2000 — rear end

1 Brake flexible hose
2 Exhaust pipe
3 Propeller shaft flange
4 Handbrake cable
5 Fuel tank

6 Semi-trailing arm
   (radius rod)
7 Handbrake operating
   lever
8 Watts linkage

9 Differential housing
10 Handbrake compensator
11 Exhaust hanger
12 Rear crossmember
   mounting

3 Engine (2000 model)

General description

1 The 'O' Series engine fitted to 2000 models is a four-cylinder ohc water-cooled unit. The engine is widely used in the vehicles in the BL range.

2 The combined crankcase and cylinder block is of cast iron construction and houses the pistons, connecting rods and crankshaft. The solid skirt aluminium alloy pistons are retained on the connecting rods by gudgeon pins which are an interference fit in the connecting rod small-end bore. The connecting rods are attached to the crankshaft by renewable shell type big-end bearings.

3 The forged steel crankshaft is carried in five main bearings also of the renewable shell type. Crankshaft endfloat is controlled by thrust washers which are located on either side of the centre main bearing.

4 The camshaft is located in the cylinder head and is retained in position by an aluminium cover which is bolted to the upper face of the cylinder head. The camshaft is supported by three bearing journals machined directly in the head and camshaft cover. Drive to the camshaft is via a toothed composite rubber belt from a sprocket on the front end of the crankshaft. A spring-loaded tensioner is fitted to eliminate backlash and prevent slackness of the belt.

5 Two valves per cylinder are mounted vertically in the aluminium cylinder head. The valves are operated by bucket type tappets acted upon directly by the lobes of the camshaft. Valve/tappet clearance adjustment is by selective shims.

6 The cylinder head is of the non-crossflow type, all eight inlet and exhaust ports being on the left-hand side.

7 Engine lubrication is by the conventional forced feed system.

Fig. 13.1 Internal components of 2000 engine (Sec 3)

1 Camshaft drivebelt tensioner	14 Oil seal	25 Piston	36 Connecting rod bolt
2 Camshaft drivebelt	15 Piston and connecting rod	26 Bolt	37 Connecting rod
3 Camshaft gear	16 Gudgeon pin	27 Lock washer	38 Crankshaft gear
4 Oil seal	17 Piston rings (compression)	28 Pulley	39 LED bracket
5 Roll pin	18 Piston ring – oil control	29 Timing disc	40 LED plug
6 Camshaft	19 Valve seat (exhaust)	30 Timing pointer	41 Thrust washers
7 Plug	20 Valve seat (inlet)	31 Flange	42 Connecting rod nut
8 Tappet (cam follower)	21 Valve guide	32 Woodruff key (pulley and gear)	43 Connecting rod cap
9 Shim	22 Exhaust valve	33 Woodruff key (oil pump)	44 Big-end bearing shells
10 Collets	23 Inlet valve	34 Crankshaft	45 Flywheel dowel
11 Top cup	24 Thrust washers	35 Main bearing shells	46 Spigot bearing (manual gearbox)
12 Valve spring			47 Bush (torque converter)
13 Bottom cup			

Engine – removal (alone)

8 Because of the small size of the 2000 engine relative to the engine bay, it is easily removed by itself. Suitable lifting tackle will be required, as will a jack or other suitable support for the gearbox.

9 Disconnect the battery earth lead.

10 Remove the bonnet and store it in a safe place.

11 Drain the cooling system by disconnecting the radiator bottom hose. Take precautions against scalding if the engine is hot.

12 Drain the oil from the engine.

13 On models with power steering, remove the pump mounting bolts. Remove the drivebelt and place the pump to one side.

14 Although not essential, access will be improved if the radiator and fan are now removed. The same applies to the air cleaner unit and its associated hoses.

15 Disconnect the throttle cable from the carburettor linkage (photo). On automatic transmission models, also disconnect the downshift cable.

16 Disconnect and plug the carburettor fuel feed pipe. Be prepared for some fuel spillage.

17 Disconnect the coolant hoses and the brake servo hose from the inlet manifold.

18 Remove the air cleaner adaptor and its support struts (photo).

3.15 Throttle cable connection to carburettor linkage

19 Disconnect the coolant hoses from the Fully Automatic Starting Device (FASD) (if fitted).

20 Free the carburettor breather (overflow) pipes from their clips.

21 If not already done, disconnect the coolant top hose at the thermostat and the bottom hose at the engine.

22 Raise and securely support the front of the car.

23 On manual gearbox models, remove the clutch slave cylinder mounting bolts, withdraw the cylinder and tie it up out of the way. Recover the shim (when fitted) and keep it with the cylinder. The pushrod will remain attached to the release lever.

24 On automatic transmission models, unclip the oil cooler pipes.

25 Unbolt the stiffener plate bolt from the bellhousing. (The other end of this plate is attached to the engine sump).

26 Unbolt the exhaust bracket from the bellhousing, noting which way round it fits, and disconnect the exhaust pipe from the manifold flange.

27 Unbolt and remove the starter motor. The bracket at the brush end of the starter motor is a tight fit, but if the dipstick is removed, the starter motor and bracket can be extracted with the aid of a little manipulation.

28 Remove those engine-to-bellhousing bolts which are accessible from below.

29 Support the front of the gearbox with a jack. Use a block of wood between the jack head and the gearbox.

30 Disconnect all electrical leads from the engine (photo), labelling them if there is any possibility of confusion. Similarly disconnect any remaining hoses. Do not forget to disconnect the earth strap from the right-hand side of the cylinder block.

31 Fit lifting brackets to the engine, or pass stout rope or chain around it. Engage the lifting tackle and take the weight of the engine.

32 Remove the remaining engine-to-bellhousing nuts and bolts. Some of these bolts are rather awkward to get at.

33 Remove the engine mounting bolts on each side (raise or lower the lifting tackle slightly if necessary to allow the bolts to be extracted).

34 Slacken, but do not remove, the engine mounting brace bolts. Move the braces out of the way of the engine mountings.

35 Draw the engine forwards (or move the vehicle backwards, if the hoist is fixed) until it is clear of the gearbox input shaft. Initial reluctance of the engine to move away from the gearbox may be overcome by judicious levering between the mating flanges. **Do not** allow the weight of the engine to hang upon the gearbox input shaft, nor attempt to lift the engine until it is clear of the shaft.

36 Lift the engine clear of the car (photo) and take it to the bench.

Engine – refitting (alone)

37 Clean the mating surfaces of the engine and the bellhousing.

38 Apply a smear of grease or anti-seize compound to the nose of the input shaft and the input shaft splines.

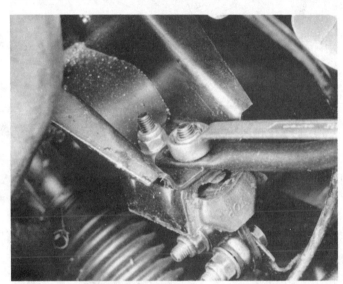

3.18 Disconnecting an air cleaner adaptor support strut from the engine mounting bracket

3.30 Disconnecting the oil pressure gauge sender. Warning light switch is just behind

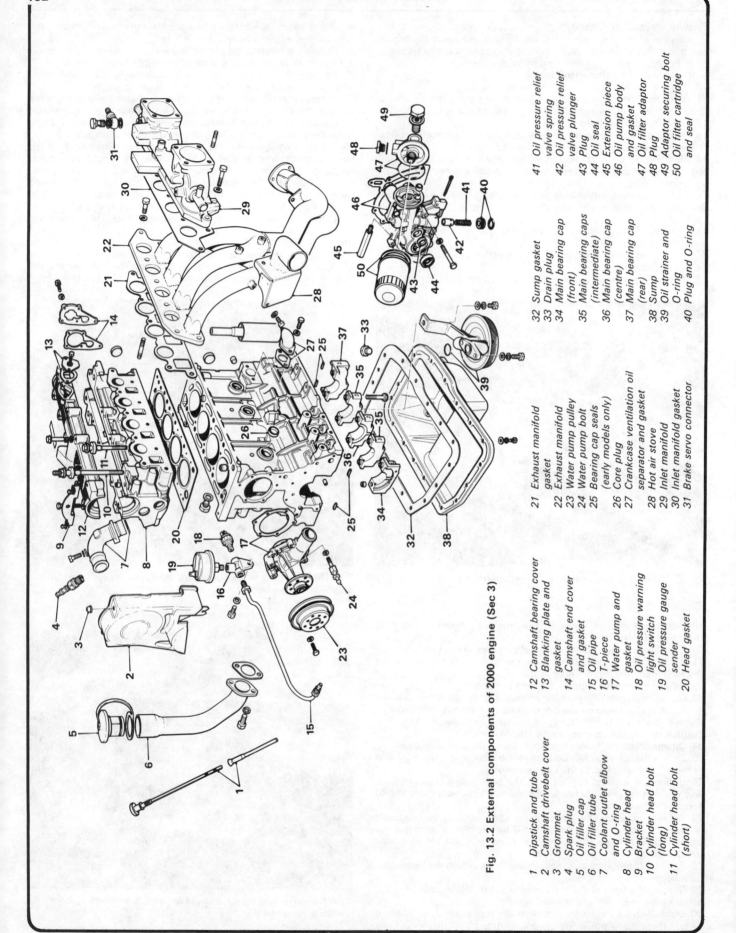

Fig. 13.2 External components of 2000 engine (Sec 3)

1 Dipstick and tube
2 Camshaft drivebelt cover
3 Grommet
4 Spark plug
5 Oil filler cap
6 Oil filler tube
7 Coolant outlet elbow
  and O-ring
8 Cylinder head
9 Bracket
10 Cylinder head bolt
  (long)
11 Cylinder head bolt
  (short)
12 Camshaft bearing cover
13 Blanking plate and
  gasket
14 Camshaft end cover
  and gasket
15 Oil pipe
16 T-piece
17 Water pump and
  gasket
18 Oil pressure warning
  light switch
19 Oil pressure gauge
  sender
20 Head gasket
21 Exhaust manifold
  gasket
22 Exhaust manifold
23 Water pump pulley
24 Water pump bolt
25 Bearing cap seals
  (early models only)
26 Core plug
27 Crankcase ventilation oil
  separator and gasket
28 Hot air stove
29 Inlet manifold
30 Inlet manifold gasket
31 Brake servo connector
32 Sump gasket
33 Drain plug
34 Main bearing cap
  (front)
35 Main bearing caps
  (intermediate)
36 Main bearing cap
  (centre)
37 Main bearing cap
  (rear)
38 Sump
39 Oil strainer and
  O-ring
40 Plug and O-ring
41 Oil pressure relief
  valve spring
42 Oil pressure relief
  valve plunger
43 Plug
44 Oil seal
45 Extension piece
46 Oil pump body
  and gasket
47 Oil filter adaptor
48 Plug
49 Adaptor securing bolt
50 Oil filter cartridge
  and seal

3.36 Removing the engine

Fig. 13.4 Engine mounting (2000 engine) – RH shown (Sec 3)

1	Mounting bolts	4	Brace bolts
2	Mounting	5	Crossmember
3	Brace		

39 Make sure that the clutch disc is properly centralised.

40 Sling the engine so that it hangs at a similar angle to that which it has when fitted.

41 Two people should be present when the engine is lowered into the car, one to operate the hoist and one to guide the engine and guard against trapped hoses, wires etc.

42 If difficulty is experienced in mating the input shaft to the clutch, engage a gear to stop the input shaft turning and rock the engine gently from side to side whilst applying pressure rearwards. If the input shaft splines still will not enter the clutch disc, either the angle of the engine is wrong or the clutch disc is not centralised.

43 Make sure that the dowels are properly engaged before fitting the engine-to-bellhousing nuts and bolts.

44 The remainder of refitting is essentially a reversal of the removal procedure. Make sure that all fluids and lubricants have been replenished before attempting to start the engine.

Valve clearances – checking and adjusting

To retain the camshaft in position during the checking operation, BL special tools 18G 1301 and 18G 1302 will be required. If these tools are not available it is possible to make up suitable alternatives as described below and shown in the photos. Read through the entire section first to familiarize yourself with the procedure, and then obtain or make up the special tools before proceeding.

45 Unscrew the distributor cap securing screws, lift off the cap and place it to one side.

46 Mark the relative position of the distributor mounting flange to the camshaft cover as a guide to refitting. Disconnect the vacuum pipe from the vacuum advance unit and LT lead at the wiring connector.

47 Undo and remove the two distributor securing nuts and washers and withdraw the distributor.

48 Turn the crankshaft to the 90° BTDC position. This is achieved when the dimple on the rear face of the camshaft sprocket is opposite the pointer on the upper surface of the camshaft cover. At the same time the single notch in the crankshaft timing disc is opposite the timing pointer (photos). The crankshaft can be turned using a socket on the crankshaft pulley bolt or, on cars with manual transmission only, by engaging top gear and moving the car forward. Removal of the spark plugs will enable the crankshaft to be turned with greater ease.

49 Free the coolant hose from its strap and lift away the camshaft drivebelt cover.

Fig. 13.3 Sectional view of front of 2000 engine (Sec 3)

3.48A Timing pointer aligned with single notch ...

3.48B ... and dimple on camshaft gear (arrowed) aligned with pointer on cover

50 If BL special tools 18G 1301 and 18G 1302 are not available, make up the three camshaft retaining brackets and a rear support plate to the dimensions shown in Figs. 13.5 and 13.6 (photos) using suitable scrap metal and angle iron.

51 Undo and remove the five bolts securing the camshaft rear end cover and lift off the cover and gasket. Fit the homemade rear support plate or tool 18G 1302 in position and secure with two of the rear end cover retaining bolts. Make sure that the rounded bolt head of the homemade tool, or the tapered projection of the BL tool, fits squarely into the recess at the rear of the camshaft (photo).

52 Slacken evenly, and in a side-to-side sequence, each of the nine bolts securing the camshaft cover to the cylinder head. Remove the bolts and then lift off the camshaft cover.

Fig. 13.5 Camshaft rear support plate dimensions (Sec 3)

A = 0.31 in (7.93 mm)
B = 1.00 in (25.4 mm)
C = 0.25 in (6.35 mm) diameter clearance for
    ^{1}/4 UNF nut and bolt
D = 1.25 in (31.75 mm)
E = 2.00 in (50.80 mm)

F = 1.50 in (38.10 mm)
G = 0.62 in (15.87 mm)
H = 0.31 in (7.93 mm)
J = 1.87 in (47.62 mm)
K = 0.12 in (3.17 mm)
L = 2.50 in (63.50 mm)

H.10927

3.50A The camshaft rear support plate ...

3.50B ... and three retaining brackets

3.51 Rear support plate in position

H.10926

Fig. 13.6 Camshaft retaining bracket dimensions (Sec 3)

1   Front bracket
2   Centre bracket
3   Rear bracket
A   Front and rear bracket – 4.00 in (101.6 mm)
    Centre bracket – 5.75 in (146.05 mm)
B   Plywood or other soft material positioned centrally on base of
    bracket
C   = 0.125 in (3.175 mm)
D   = 1.187 in (30.162 mm)
E   = 1.187 in (30.162 mm)
F   = 0.312 in (7.937 mm)

G   Front and centre brackets – 0.5 in (12.7 mm)
    Rear bracket – 0.75 in (19.05 mm)
H   Front bracket – 0.437 in (11.112 mm)
    Centre bracket – 0.75 in (19.05 mm)
    Rear bracket – 0.375 in (9.525 mm)
J   Front and rear bracket – 3.125 in (79.37 mm)
    Centre bracket – 4.25 in (107.95 mm)
K   Front bracket – 0.437 in (11.112 mm)
    Centre bracket – 0.75 in (19.05 mm)
    Rear bracket – 0.5 in (12.70 mm)
L   = 0.437 in (11.112 in)

53 Place the three clamps of BL special tool 18G 1301 or the three homemade brackets in position over the camshaft bearings and secure with the camshaft cover retaining bolts (photo). When in position the clamps or brackets should be exerting a light pressure only on the camshaft bearing journals; sufficient to hold the camshaft firmly in place while still allowing it to be rotated.
54 Release the camshaft drivebelt tensioner and slip the belt off the camshaft gear.
55 Rotate the camshaft in the normal direction of rotation to bring each pair of cam lobes to the vertical position, ie 1 and 4, 2 and 5, 6 and 7, 3 and 8. As each pair of cam lobes reaches the vertical position measure and record the clearance between the heel of the cam lobe and the tappet using feeler gauges (photo).
56 The standard valve clearance is given in the Specifications. Provided that the measured clearances do not exceed this figure or are not less than 0.008 in (0.20 mm), adjustment is not necessary and the camshaft cover and components can be refitted. If, however, adjustment is required proceed as follows.
57 Undo and remove the bolt securing the camshaft gear to the camshaft and withdraw the gear.
58 Remove the camshaft rear support plate and then progressively slacken the camshaft retaining bracket bolts. When the spring tension is released, remove the bolts and lift away the brackets.
59 Lift the camshaft out of its location in the cylinder head and carefully remove the front oil seal.
60 Remove each tappet requiring adjustment in turn and extract the shim from the valve spring cup (or from inside the tappet). Measure and record the thickness of the shim with a micrometer.

3.53 One of the camshaft retaining brackets in position

3.55 Measuring a valve clearance

Fig. 13.7 Checking No 3 valve clearance using BL special tools (Sec 3)

1 Tool 18G 1301 (part)	4 Camshaft
2 Pressure pad bolts	5 Feeler gauge
3 Pressure pad	

61 If the measured clearance was too small, then a smaller shim is required. If the clearance was too large, then a larger shim is required, ie:

A   B – C =   Shim thickness required
Where: A =   Measured clearance
      B =   Thickness of existing shim
      C =   Standard tappet clearance

62 Shims are available in thicknesses between 0.091 and 0.117 in (2.32 and 2.98 mm), increasing in thickness by increments of 0.002 in (0.05 or 0.06 mm).
63 Having selected each required new shim, place it in the spring cup on top of the valve and refit the tappet in its original bore.
64 Liberally lubricate the camshaft bearing journals with engine oil and place the camshaft in position. Lubricate the outer circumference and sealing lip of the oil seal and position it over the camshaft until it is in contact with the register in the cylinder head.
65 Remove all traces of old sealant from the camshaft cover and cylinder head and ensure that the mating faces are clean and dry.
66 Apply a very thin bead, 1/16 in (1.5 mm) diameter, of RTV silicone sealant to the mating face of the camshaft cover. Refit the cover and

timing belt cover bracket and then tighten the retaining bolts evenly and progressively to the specified torque.
67 Refit the camshaft rear end cover using a new gasket if necessary.
68 Refit the camshaft gear and fully tighten the retaining bolt.
69 Ensure that the crankshaft is still at the 90° BTDC position and then turn the camshaft until the dimple on the gear is aligned with the pointer on the cover.
70 Refit and tension the camshaft drivebelt (timing belt) as described later in this Section.
71 Refit the remaining components in the reverse order to removal. Check the ignition timing on completion as described in Section 7.

Camshaft drivebelt – checking, tensioning and renewal
72 The condition and tension of the camshaft drivebelt must be checked every 24 000 miles (40 000 km) or two years and adjusted if necessary. If defective, it must be renewed. A new belt **must** be fitted after 48 000 miles (80 000 km) or four years. A broken belt will result in

piston/valve contact, possibly with expensive results.

73 Free the coolant hose and remove the camshaft drivebelt cover.

74 Examine the camshaft drivebelt. If the teeth are worn or show signs of uneven wear, cracking or oil contamination, the belt must be renewed. The source of oil contamination must also be dealt with.

75 Check the tension of the camshaft drivebelt by attaching a spring balance to the belt at the point in line with the water pump inlet pipe. Measure the pull required to align the outside face of the belt with the moulded line on the inlet pipe (Fig. 13.8).

Fig. 13.8 Checking camshaft drivebelt tension (Sec 3)

1 Camshaft gear	5 Crankshaft gear
2 Drivebelt	6 Hook
3 Tensioner	7 Spring balance
4 Moulded line on water pump inlet	

76 The force needed to align a correctly tensioned drivebelt as described is as given in the Specifications. If the belt is in good condition but slack, it must be adjusted as follows:

(a) Slacken the belt tensioner securing nuts
(b) Push the tensioner against the belt and tighten the securing nuts
(c) Recheck the tension and readjust if necessary

77 To remove the camshaft drivebelt, first remove the alternator/water pump drivebelt and (if fitted) the power steering pump drivebelt.

78 Turn the crankshaft to 90° BTDC, No 1 piston rising on compression. In this position the 'V' notch in the timing disc will be opposite the pointer, and the dimple on the rear face of the camshaft gear will be opposite the pointer on the camshaft cover.

Note: *It is essential that the crankshaft is set at this position before the camshaft drivebelt is removed. The crankshaft must not be turned while the camshaft is disconnected, as this will result in damage to the valves and pistons.*

79 Slacken the belt tensioner nuts and release the belt tension.

80 Ease the belt off the camshaft gear.

81 Extract the belt from the crankshaft gear. It will probably be necessary to withdraw the plug from the LED sensor bracket and to bend the timing pointer upwards slightly in order to provide sufficient clearance around the timing disc.

82 Fitting a new belt is carried out in the reverse order to removal, noting the following points:

(a) Do not twist the new belt or bend it sharply
(b) Make sure that the crankshaft is still at 90° BTDC and that the camshaft timing marks are still aligned
(c) Adjust the camshaft drivebelt tension as previously described
(d) Adjust the tension of the alternator/water pump drivebelt and (if applicable) the power steering pump drivebelt on completion

Cylinder head – removal (engine in car)

83 Disconnect the battery earth lead.

84 Drain the cooling system as described in Section 5.

85 Remove the distributor as described in Section 7.

86 Number the spark plug leads and then detach them from the spark plugs. Disconnect the HT lead from the coil tower and remove the distributor cap complete with leads.

87 Disconnect the temperature gauge lead from the right-hand side of the cylinder head.

88 Remove the carburettors and the inlet manifold as described in Section 6. On automatic models, disconnect the downshift cable from the throttle linkage.

89 Remove the exhaust manifold by detaching it from the exhaust pipe flange and from the cylinder head.

90 Remove the crankcase breather.

91 Remove the camshaft drivebelt as previously described. *Do not rotate the crankshaft from now on.* If the same belt is to be re-used there is no need to take it off the crankshaft gear, but take care not to damage or contaminate it.

92 Slacken the cylinder head bolts in the reverse of the sequence shown in Fig. 13.15. Remove the bolts.

93 The cylinder head can now be removed by lifting upwards. If it is reluctant to move, lever between the two lugs provided for this purpose on the right-hand side. *Do not attempt to prise the head from the block by inserting a screwdriver between their mating faces, or serious damage may result.*

94 With the cylinder head removed, retrieve the gasket from the block.

Cylinder head – removal (engine on bench)

95 Proceed as described above, disregarding the instructions to disconnect the controls and services which have already been dealt with when removing the engine.

Flywheel, crankshaft rear oil seal and engine backplate – removal

96 If the engine is in the car, remove the gearbox or automatic transmission and the clutch or torque converter.

97 Lock the flywheel using a suitable wedge in mesh with the starter ring gear. Undo the bolts that secure the flywheel or torque converter driveplate to the crankshaft in a diagonal and progressive manner. Remove the bolts and the locking plate.

98 Mark the relative positions of the flywheel or driveplate to the crankshaft to ensure correct refitment. Lift away the flywheel or driveplate.

99 Undo and remove the bolts that secure the crankshaft rear oil seal retainer and lift away the retainer.

100 The engine backplate retaining bolts can now be removed and the backplate complete with oil seal and gasket lifted off. With the backplate removed tap out the old oil seal using a suitable drift.

Sump – removal

101 If the engine is in the car, perform the following preliminary operations:

(a) Raise and securely support the front of the vehicle
(b) Drain the engine oil
(c) Bring the crankshaft to 90° BTDC ('V' mark aligned)
(d) Unbolt the clutch slave cylinder and tie it up out of the way
(c) Remove the sump stiffener plate bolts

102 Undo and remove the bolts which secure the sump. Note that the bolt fitted at the right-hand rear of the sump is longer that the others.

103 Remove the sump and its gasket.

Crankshaft pulley, gear and oil pump – removal

104 Remove the camshaft drivebelt as previously described.

105 Relieve the lockwasher tabs from around the crankshaft pulley bolt. Jam the crankshaft and unscrew the bolt. The bolt is large (30

mm across flats) and probably tight. Make sure that the crankshaft does not move from its 90° BTDC position if the cylinder head is still fitted.

106 Ease the pulley off the crankshaft. Use a couple of screwdrivers to lever carefully behind the pulley if necessary.

107 With the pulley removed, the timing disc, gear and flange can be removed. Recover the Woodruff key from the nose of the crankshaft after removing these components.

108 Disconnect the oil pressure switch feed pipe from the right-hand

side of the oil pump.

109 Slacken evenly the bolts which secure the oil pump to the crankcase. Remove the bolts and lift away the oil pump, then recover the gasket.

110 If the object of the exercise is to renew the crankshaft front oil seal, this is most easily done with the oil pump removed as described. Special equipment is needed to extract the old seal from the oil pump *in situ*.

Fig. 13.9 Crankshaft pulley, oil pump and associated components (Sec 3)

1 Pulley bolt and lock washer
2 Pulley
3 Timing disc
4 Crankshaft gear
5 Flange
6 Oil pump
7 Bolt
8 Plug

Fig. 13.10 Crankshaft and bottom end components (Sec 3)

1 Main bearing cap seals (early models only)	3 Main bearing cap (centre)	5 Connecting rod cap
2 Cylinder block	4 Thrust washers	6 Main bearing cap identifying marks

Pistons, connecting rods and big-end bearings – removal

111 If the engine is in the car, first remove the cylinder head and the sump as previously described.

112 Turn the crankshaft so that all the pistons are halfway down their bores. Stuff the bores with rags, then carefully scrape the carbon ring from round the top of each bore. If there is a pronounced wear ridge, this too should be scraped away with a tool known as a ridge reamer. (Failure to observe these points may lead to damage to the pistons as they are removed; if they are to be renewed in any case, this may not matter). Remove the rags and clean the bores on completion.

113 Remove the oil pick-up pipe and strainer. Recover the gasket from the pipe flange.

114 Inspect the big-end caps and connecting rods for identification marks which will enable each cap to be refitted to its own rod and the right way round. Make suitable marks if none are present.

115 Remove the big-end cap securing nuts.

116 Remove the big-end caps, keeping them in order. Also keep the bearing shells with their respective caps if the shells are to be re-used. If the caps are difficult to remove, tap them gently with a soft-faced hammer.

117 Push the piston/connecting rod assemblies upwards and out through the top of the block. Note that each piston crown carries a 'FRONT' marking and/or an arrow or groove to ensure correct orientation when refitting.

118 To remove the bearing shells from cap and connecting rod, press the shell at the end remote from the tab and it will pop out.

Crankshaft and main bearings – removal

119 The engine must be removed from the car for this task.

120 Remove the cylinder head, the sump, the pistons and connecting rods, the engine backplate and the oil pump, all as previously described.

121 Check that there are identifying marks on the main bearing caps. Each cap should carry a number (No 1 at the front of the engine); caps 2, 3 and 4 also carry arrows which point to the front of the engine.

122 Unscrew and remove the main bearing cap bolts. Remove the caps and the bottom half of each bearing shell, keeping the shells with their respective caps if they are to be re-used.

123 Note the joint seals fitted to the front and rear main bearing caps (early models only) and the thrust washers fitted on each side of the centre cap. Keep the thrust washer halves with the centre cap and bearing.

124 Lift the crankshaft out of the crankcase, then retrieve the top half main bearing shells and the thrust washer halves from their crankcase location. Keep the shells in order if they are to be re-used.

Cylinder head and camshaft assembly – dismantling

125 If not already done, remove the distributor, the manifolds and the coolant outlet elbow from the cylinder head.

126 Unscrew and remove the coolant temperature sender.

127 Unscrew and remove the bolt which secures the camshaft gear. Pull the gear off the camshaft.

128 Unbolt and remove the camshaft and cover. Recover the gasket.

129 Slacken the nine bolts that secure the camshaft bearing cover in a progressive and even sequence until the valve spring tension is released, then remove the bolts, release the oil filler cap and lift away the cover bracket.

130 Lift off the camshaft bearing cover.

131 Remove the camshaft complete with the front oil seal from the cylinder head. Pull the oil seal off the front of the camshaft.

132 Lift out each tappet and shim and lay them out in the correct order, 1 to 8, to ensure that they can be refitted in their original positions.

133 To remove the valves, compress each spring in turn with a universal valve spring compressor until the two halves of the collet can be removed. Release the compressor and lift away the spring top cup, valve spring, oil seal (inlet valves only), valve spring seat (bottom cup) and the valve.

134 If, when the valve spring compressor is screwed down, the valve spring top cup refuses to free and expose the split collet, do not continue to screw down on the compressor, but gently tap the top of the tool directly over the cup with a light hammer. This should free the cup. To avoid the compressor jumping off the valve retaining cup when it is tapped, hold the compressor firmly in position.

135 It is essential that the valves are kept in their correct order unless they are so badly worn or burnt that they are to be renewed. If they are going to be refitted, place them in their correct sequences along with the tappets and shims previously removed. Also keep the valve springs, cups and collets in the same order.

Gudgeon pins – removal

136 The gudgeon pins are a press fit in the connecting rod and it is important that no damage is caused during removal and refitting. Because of this, should it be necessary to fit new pistons or connecting rods, take the parts along to the local BL garage who will have the special equipment required to carry out this work.

Piston rings – removal

137 To remove the piston rings, slide them carefully over the top of the piston, taking care not to scratch the aluminium alloy of the piston. Never slide them off the bottom of the piston skirt. It is very easy to break the piston rings if they are pulled off roughly so this operation should be done with extreme caution. It is helpful to use an old 0.020 in (0.5 mm) feeler gauge to facilitate their removal as follows:

138 Lift one end of the piston ring to be removed out of its groove and insert the end of the feeler gauge under it.

139 Turn the feeler gauge slowly round the piston; as the ring comes out of its groove it rests on the land above. It can then be eased off the piston with the feeler gauge stopping it from slipping into any empty grooves.

Fig. 13.11 Piston rings – 2000 engine (Sec 3)

1 Top compression ring
2 Second compression ring
3 Oil control (scraper) ring rails
4 Oil control (scraper) ring expander
5 Piston

Oil filter – renewal

140 The oil filter is a throw-away cartridge type screwed into the left-hand side of the oil housing.

141 Simply unscrew the old unit; if it is very tight use a strap wrench to slacken it.

142 Fit a new sealing ring in position and smear it with engine oil, then screw the new filter on, *hand-tight only*.

143 Run the engine and check for oil leaks.

Oil pump – dismantling, inspection and reassembly

144 Scribe an alignment mark on the pump housing and pump backplate to ensure that the backplate is refitted in its original position at reassembly.

145 Using a 3 mm Allen key, remove the backplate securing screws and lift off the backplate (photos).
146 Remove the outer and inner rotors.
147 Remove the split pin that retains the pressure relief valve, then remove the plug from the housing by pushing down on the relief valve spring with a screwdriver through the oil return hole. Collect the spring and valve plunger. Discard the plug O-ring seal.
148 Remove the crankshaft front oil seal from the oil pump housing.
149 Thoroughly clean all component parts then check the rotor endfloat and lobe clearance.
150 Fit the outer rotor in the housing and, using a feeler gauge, check the clearance between the outer rotor and the pump body A in Fig. 13.13.

151 Fit the inner rotor and measure the lobe clearance B and C in Fig. 13.13 (photo).
152 Measure the outer rotor to housing face clearance D in Fig. 13.13.
153 If any of these clearances exceed the limits shown in the Specifications, the pump must be renewed.
154 Check the free length of the pressure relief valve spring. If its length differs from the dimension shown in the Specifications, renew the spring.
155 Reassembly is the reverse of the dismantling procedure. Liberally lubricate the oil pump components with engine oil, fit a new O-ring on the pressure relief valve plug and a new crankshaft front oil seal in the pump housing (photo).

3.145A Remove the oil pump backplate securing screws ...

3.145B ... and lift off the backplate

Fig. 13.12 Oil pump pressure relief valve (Sec 3)

1	Pump body	4	Spring
2	Split pin	5	Plug
3	Plunger	6	O-ring

Fig. 13.13 Oil pump measurement points. For A, B, C and D see text (Sec 3)

1	Pump body	4	Outer rotor
2	Backplate	5	Inner rotor
3	Straight-edge		

3.151 Measure the lobe clearance with a feeler gauge

3.155 Fitting a new seal in the oil pump housing

Examination and renovation (general)
156 The principles behind examination and renovation of engine components apply equally, regardless of the number of cylinders. Refer to the appropriate Sections of Chapter 1, as listed below; where necessary, refer also to the Specifications at the beginning of this Chapter.

Cylinder head decarbonisation – Section 20
Valves and valve springs – Section 22
Valve grinding – Section 23
Valve guides – Section 24
Cylinder bores – Section 40
Crankshaft and bearings – Section 45

Pistons and piston rings – examination and renovation
157 If the old pistons are to be refitted, carefully remove the piston rings and then thoroughly clean them. Take particular care to clean out the piston ring grooves. Do not scratch the aluminium in any way. If new rings are to be fitted to the old pistons, then the top ring should be of the stepped type so as to clear the ridge left above the previous top ring. If a normal but oversize new ring is fitted, it will hit the ridge and break, because the new ring will not have worn in the same way as the old.
158 Before fitting the rings on the pistons, each should be inserted approximately 3 in (76 mm) down the cylinder bore and the ring end gap measured with a feeler gauge. This should be between the limits given in the Specifications at the beginning of this Chapter. It is essential that the gap is measured at the bottom of the ring travel, for if it is measured at the top of a worn bore and gives a perfect fit, it could easily seize at the bottom. If the ring gap is too small, rub down the ends of the ring with a very fine file until the gap is correct when fitted. To keep the rings square in the bore for measurement, line each one up in turn with an old piston inserted in the bore upside down.
159 The groove clearance of the new rings in old pistons should be within the tolerance given in the Specifications. If it is not enough, the rings could stick in the piston grooves causing loss of compression. The ring grooves in the piston in this case will need machining out to accept the new rings.
160 Before fitting new rings onto an old piston, clean out the grooves with a piece of broken ring. Protect your fingers when doing this – piston rings are sharp!
161 If new pistons are obtained, the rings will be included, so it must be emphasised that the top ring be stepped if fitted to a cylinder bore that has not been rebored or has not had the top ridge removed.

Tappets – examination
162 The faces of the tappets in contact with the lobes on the camshaft should show no signs of pitting, scoring or other forms of wear. They should not be a loose fit in the cylinder head.
163 Tappets with any of these defects must be renewed.

Camshaft and camshaft bearings – examination and renovation
164 Check the camshaft journals and cams for scoring and wear. If there are very slight scoring marks, these can be removed with emery cloth or a fine oil stone. The greatest care must be taken to keep the cam profiles smooth.
165 Examine the ignition distributor drivegear for wear or chipping of the gear teeth.
166 Examine the camshaft bearing surfaces in the cylinder head and camshaft bearing cover, if they are scored and worn it means a new cylinder head and camshaft cover will be required.

Flywheel starter ring gear – examination and renovation
167 If the teeth on the flywheel starter ring gear are badly worn, or if some are missing, then it will be necessary to remove the ring. This is achieved by splitting the old ring using a cold chisel. Care must be taken not to damage the flywheel during this process. Take suitable precautions to avoid injury caused by flying fragments.
168 To fit a new ring gear, it will be necessary to heat it gently and evenly with an oxy-acetylene flame until a temperature of approximately 350°C (660°F) is reached. This is indicated by a grey/brown surface colour. With the ring gear at this temperature, fit it to the flywheel with the bevelled edge of the teeth facing the engine facing end of the flywheel. The ring gear should be either pressed or lightly tapped onto its register and left to cool naturally, when the contraction of the metal on cooling will ensure that it is a secure and permanent fit. Great care must be taken not to overheat the ring gear, for if this happens the temper of the ring gear will be lost.
169 An alternative method is to use a high temperature oven to heat the ring.
170 Because of the need of oxy-acetylene equipment or a special oven it is not normally practical for refitment to take place at home. Take the flywheel and new starting ring to an engineering works willing to do the job.

Engine reassembly – general
171 Before reassembly begins, all components of the engine must be cleaned of oil, sludge and old gaskets, and the working area should also be cleared and clean. In addition to the normal range of good quality socket spanners and general tools which are essential, the following must also be available:

Complete set of gaskets
Supply of clean rags
Clean oil can full of clean engine oil
Torque wrench
Suitable jointing compound
All new parts as necessary

Crankshaft – refitting

172 Ensure that the crankcase is thoroughly clean and that all the oilways are clear. If possible, blow them out with compressed air. Treat the crankshaft in the same fashion and then inject engine oil into the crankshaft oilways.

173 Fit the five upper halves of the main bearing shells to their location in the crankcase after wiping the location clean.

174 Note that on the back of each bearing is a tab which engages in locating grooves in either the crankcase or the main bearing cap housings (photo).

175 If new bearings are being fitted, carefully clean away all traces of the protective grease with which they are coated.

176 With the five upper bearing shells securely in place, wipe the lower bearing cap housings and fit the five lower shell bearings to their caps, ensuring that the right shell goes into the right cap if the old bearings are being refitted.

177 Wipe the recesses either side of the centre main bearing which locate the upper halves of the thrust washers.

178 Introduce the upper halves of the thrust washers (the halves without tabs) into their grooves either side of the centre main bearing with their oil grooves facing outwards (photo).

179 Generously lubricate the crankshaft journals and the upper and lower main bearing shells and carefully lower the crankshaft into position. Make sure that it is the right way round (photo).

180 Fit the main bearing caps into position, ensuring that they locate properly. The mating surfaces must be spotlessly clean or the caps will not seat correctly.

181 When refitting the centre main bearing cap, ensure that the thrust washers, generously lubricated, are fitted with their oil grooves facing outwards and the locating tab of each washer is in the slot in the bearing cap (photo).

182 Refit the main bearing cap bolts and screw them up finger-tight.

183 Test the crankshaft for freedom of rotation. Should it be very stiff to turn or possess high spots, a most careful inspection must be made, preferably by a skilled mechanic with a micrometer to trace the cause of the trouble. It is very seldom that any trouble of this nature will be experienced when fitting the crankshaft.

184 Tighten the main bearing cap bolts to the specified torque and recheck the crankshaft for freedom of rotation.

185 Using a screwdriver between one crankshaft web and main bearing cap, lever the crankshaft forwards and check the endfloat using feeler gauges. This should be as shown in the Specifications. If excessive, new thrust washers must be fitted.

Pistons and connecting rods – reassembly

186 As the gudgeon pin is a press fit in the connecting rod this operation must be carried out by a BL dealer or motor engineering specialist.

3.174 The tab on the bearing shell locates in the groove

3.178 The thrust washers are fitted with the oil grooves facing outwards

3.179 Lower the crankshaft into position

3.181 Fitting the centre main bearing cap and thrust washers

Piston rings – refitting

187 Check that the piston ring grooves and oilways are thoroughly clean and unblocked. Piston rings must always be fitted over the head of the piston and *never* from the bottom.

188 The easiest method to use when fitting rings is to position two 0.015 in (0.38 mm) feeler blades on either side of the piston and slide the rings down over the blades. This will stop the rings from dropping into a vacant ring groove. When the ring is adjacent to its correct groove, slide out the feeler blades and the ring will drop.

189 The procedure for fitting the rings is as follows. Start by sliding the bottom rail of the oil control ring down the piston and position it below the bottom piston ring groove. Fit the oil control expander into the bottom ring groove and then move the bottom oil control ring rail into the bottom groove. Now fit the top oil control ring rail into the bottom groove. Make sure that the ends of the expander are butting together and not overlapping. Position the gaps of the two rails and the expander at 90° to each other.

190 Fit the second compression ring to its groove with the step towards the gudgeon pin and the word TOP or the letter T facing the top of the piston.

191 Fit the chrome plated top compression ring to its groove with the word TOP or the letter T facing the top of the piston.

192 When all the piston rings are in place, set the ring gaps of the compression rings at 90° to each other and away from the thrust (left-hand) side of the piston.

Pistons – refitting

193 Wipe the cylinder bores clean with a clean rag.

194 The pistons, complete with connecting rods, must be fitted to their bores from the top of the block.

195 Check that the two upper piston ring gaps are spaced at 90° to each other.

196 Check that the piston is the correct one for the cylinder bore and that the small-end offset of the connecting rod is correct for the bore; see Fig. 13.14.

197 Lubricate the cylinder bore and piston with clean engine oil.

198 Fit a universal piston ring compressor over the rings. A large diameter worm-drive hose clip will serve as a ring compressor if the proper tool is not available.

199 Insert the first piston into its bore making sure that the front of the piston (marked on top with the word FRONT or an arrow) is towards the front of the engine (photo).

200 Slide the piston connecting rod assembly down the bore until the bottom of the piston ring compressor rests on the cylinder block face. Now gently but firmly tap the piston through the compressor using a block of wood or the handle of a mallet (photo).

Connecting rods to crankshaft – reassembly

201 Wipe the connecting rod half of the big-end bearing location and the underside of the shell bearing clean (as for the main bearing shells)

and fit the shell in position with its locating tab engaged with the corresponding groove in the connecting rod. Always fit new shells (photo).

Fig. 13.14 Correct relationship of connecting rod offsets and oil squirt holes (arrowed) (Sec 3)

3.199 Piston FRONT marking or arrow shows correct fitted position

3.200 Carefully tap the piston into the cylinder bore

3.201 Connecting rod big-end assembly

202 Generously lubricate the crankpin journals with engine oil and turn the crankshaft so that the crankpin is in the most advantageous position for the connecting rod to be drawn onto it.
203 Fit the bearing shell to the connecting rod cap in the same way as with the connecting rod itself.
204 Generously lubricate the shell bearing and offer up the connecting rod bearing cap to the connecting rod. Note that the bearing shell grooves in the connecting rod and cap must both be on the same side (photo).
205 Refit the connecting rod cap retaining nuts and tighten them to the specified torque.

Oil strainer and sump – refitting
206 Refit the oil strainer. Always use a new flange gasket or O-ring. Fit the two bolts that secure the oil strainer flange to the crankcase and the bolt that secures the support stay (photo).
207 Ensure that all traces of the old gasket have been removed from the mating faces of the sump and crankcase.
208 Apply a jointing compound to the joint faces of the front and rear main bearing caps and fit new cork seals to the caps (photo). Later models do not have cork seals: RTV jointing compound should be used instead.
209 Place a new sump gasket on the crankcase. Use a little grease to keep the gasket in position and then fit the oil sump (photo).
210 Refit the sump securing bolts and spring washers; the longer bolt is fitted at the rear right-hand location. Tighten the bolts to the specified torque.

Oil pump – refitting
211 Ensure that the joint faces of the crankcase and oil pump housing are clean. Position a new gasket on the oil pump.
212 Fit the oil pump drive key in the crankshaft (photo).
213 Fit a protective sleeve over the end of the crankshaft (photo). Line up the keyway in the pump with the drive key on the crankshaft and fit the oil pump. Take care not to damage the oil seal.
214 Fit the securing bolts, timing pointer and LED sensor bracket. The long bolt is fitted adjacent to the core plug. Tighten the bolts to the specified torque.

215 Prime the oil pump by removing the bottom plug and injecting oil into the pump. Refit the oil pressure switch feed pipe.

Engine backplate – refitting
216 Lubricate a new seal with SAE 90EP oil and fit the seal in the backplate with the top of the seal facing to the front of the engine.
217 Ensure that the seal is pressed in square, with the front of the seal flush with the front face of the backplate (photo).
218 Locate the rear oil seal retainer, then fit the retainer and backplate securing bolts.
219 Tighten the oil seal retainer securing bolts and the backplate securing bolts to the specified torque.

Crankshaft gear, timing disc and pulley – refitting
220 Fit the drive key on the crankshaft (photo).
221 Fit the gear flange followed by the gear, then the timing disc and the crankshaft pulley (photos).
222 Using a new lockwasher, fit the crankshaft pulley securing bolt.
223 Fit two bolts temporarily in the rear flange of the crankshaft, and use a lever between them to prevent the crankshaft from turning whilst tightening the crankshaft pulley bolt to the specified torque.
224 Lock the bolt by bending over two tabs of the lockwasher.

Valves – refitting
225 With the valves and valve seats suitably prepared and in their correct order, start with No 1 cylinder.
226 Lubricate the valve stem with oil and insert the valve into its guide (photo).
227 On inlet valves, fit a new oil seal well-lubricated with engine oil.
228 Fit the valve spring seat (bottom cup), valve spring and valve spring cup over the valve stem (photos).
229 Using a valve spring compressor tool, compress the valve spring until the split collets can be slid into positon, then carefully release the valve spring compressor in order not to displace the collets (photo).
230 Refit the other valves in the same way. When they are all fitted, tap the end of each valve stem using a plastic-faced hammer or a block of hardwood interposed. This will settle the valve components ready for checking the valve clearances.

3.204 Fitting a connecting rod cap

3.206 Fit the oil pick-up strainer

3.208 Cork seals (arrowed) will not be found on later models

3.209 Fitting the sump

3.212 Oil pump drive key correctly located in crankshaft

3.213 Wrap some tape around the end of the crankshaft to prevent damage to the oil seal

3.217 Fit a new oil seal to the engine backplate

3.220 Crankshaft gear Woodruff key

3.221A Slide on the flange and the gear ...

3.221B ... followed by the timing disc and the pulley

3.226 Insert the valve in the guide

3.228A Fit the valve spring seat (bottom cup) ...

3.228B ... then fit the valve spring and top cup

3.229 Compress the valve spring and fit the collets

3.232 Position a new head gasket on the block

Cylinder head, camshaft and camshaft cover – refitting
231 Ensure that the mating faces of the cylinder block and cylinder head are perfectly clean and dry.
232 Position a new cylinder head gasket on the cylinder block, locating it over the dowels in the block (photo). The gasket is pre-coated and must be fitted dry. Do not use grease or jointing compound on the gasket.
233 Check that the crankshaft is positioned at 90° BTDC.
234 Lower the cylinder head into position, locating it over the dowels. Ensure that the retaining bolt threads are clean, and then lightly oil the threads and the undersides of the bolt heads. Screw the bolts in finger tight. Progressively tighten the bolts in the order shown in Fig. 13.15 in the stages given in the Specifications.
235 Place the valve clearance adjusting shims into their original valve spring cap recesses. Lubricate the valve tappets and place them over

Fig. 13.15 Cylinder head bolt tightening sequence (Sec 3)

the top of each valve spring cap in their original positions (photo).
236 Liberally lubricate the camshaft journals and place the camshaft in position on the cylinder head.
237 Using BL special tool 18G 1301 or the alternative brackets described earlier, secure the camshaft in position in the cylinder head. When in position the clamps or brackets should be exerting a light pressure only on the camshaft bearing journals; sufficient to hold the camshaft firmly in place while still allowing it to be rotated.
238 Refer to paragraphs 55 to 70 and check/adjust the valve tappet clearances.
239 If the engine is in the car, reverse the operations described in paragraphs 83 to 90.
240 After refitting the cylinder head, run the engine at a fast idle for 15 minutes, then switch off and allow it to cool. Now slacken each cylinder head bolt individually in the correct sequence, half a turn, and then retighten to the specified torque.

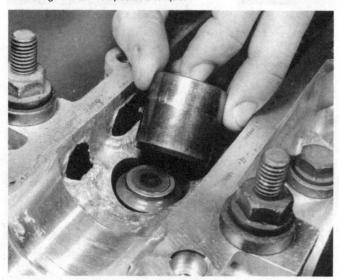

3.235 Fit the valve shims and tappets

Flywheel and clutch – refitting
241 If the flywheel bolts were retained with a locking compound, thoroughly clean the crankshaft threads. Clean the mating faces of the crankshaft and flywheel. Fit the flywheel, locating it on the dowel in the end of the crankshaft flange, and with the alignment marks made at removal correctly matched.
242 Refit the locking plate and use six **new** securing bolts (of encapsulated type, or with a locking compound). Using a suitable wedge, lock the flywheel and tighten the securing bolts in a diagonal and progressive manner to the specified torque.
243 Lock the bolts by bending over the locking plate.
244 Refit the clutch assembly as described in Chapter 5.
245 If a GM 180 automatic transmission is fitted, refer to Section 9.

Final assembly
246 Refit the exhaust and inlet manifolds, using new gaskets.
247 Refit the coolant temperature sender.
248 Refit the coolant outlet elbow.
249 Refit the distributor as described in Section 7.
250 Refit the alternator as described in Chapter 10.
251 Fit new spark plugs and a new oil filter cartridge.

Initial start-up after overhaul or major repair
252 The following check list should ensure the engine starts safely and with the minimum of delay:

(a) Fuel lines connected and tightened
(b) Water hoses connected and all clips tightened
(c) Coolant drain plug fitted and tightened (when applicable)
(d) Cooling system replenished
(e) Sump drain plug fitted and tight
(f) Oil in engine
(g) LT wiring connected to distributor and coil
(h) Temperature gauge and oil pressure warning light wires connected
(i) Camshaft drivebelt correctly fitted and ignition timing set statically
(j) Distributor rotor arm, cap and HT leads fitted

(k) Throttle cable connected
(l) Earth strap connected
(m) Alternator and starter motor leads connected
(n) Battery fully charged and leads connected
(o) Oil or fluid in gearbox or automatic transmission
(p) Clutch hydraulic system bled (where applicable)

253 Remember that the fuel pump will only operate when the starter motor is cranking (until engine oil pressure has been established), so if the fuel system has been dismantled a couple of attempts to start may be necessary to prime the fuel system.
254 As soon as the engine fires and runs, keep it going at a fast idle only and bring it up to normal working temperature.
255 As the engine warms up there will be odd smells and some smoke from parts getting hot and burning off oil deposits. Look for leaks of petrol, water or oil, which will be obvious if serious. Check also the exhaust joints, as these do not always find their exact gas-tight positions until the heat and vibration have acted upon them, and it is almost certain that they will require further tightening. This should be done, of course, with the engine stopped.
256 When normal running temperature has been reached, adjust the carburettor settings as described in Section 6.
257 Stop the engine and wait a few minutes to see if any lubricant or coolant is dripping out when the engine is stationary.
258 After the engine has run for fifteen minutes, switch it off and retorque the cylinder head as described in paragraph 240. Also check the tightness of the manifold and sump bolts.
259 Road test the car to check that the ignition and carburettor settings are correct and that the engine is delivering the necessary smoothness and power. Do not race the engine – if new bearings and/or pistons have been fitted, it should be treated as a new engine and run in at reduced speed for the first 1000 miles (1610 km).

4 Engine – general

Low oil level warning system – description
1 Certain later models are equipped with a low oil level warning system. One of the central cluster of warning lights carries a symbol depicting a dripping dipstick. When the oil level is satisfactory, the warning light will flash up to three times when the ignition is switched on, and then extinguish. If the oil level is low, the light will flash for 10 to 20 seconds and then extinguish.
2 A false low warning may be given if the car is parked on a slope. Note that the oil level of a running engine is not monitored.
3 The prudent owner will continue to check the engine oil level at regular intervals in the traditional fashion. The dipstick should be used in any case to verify a low level warning before topping up.
4 An open-circuit in the wiring between the oil level sensor (which is screwed into the side of the sump) and the warning module (behind the tachometer) will cause false low warnings. Testing of sensor and module is by substitution of a known good unit.

Valve clearance adjustment (2300/2600 models)
5 If the range of shims specified in Chapter 1 is not adequate, shims originally intended for the 'slant 4' engine (as fitted to the 'old' 2000/2200 models) may be used. These are available in thicknesses from 0.074 to 0.352 in (1.88 to 8.94 mm).

Camshaft cover refitting (2300/2600 models)
6 Later models are fitted with an improved gasket beneath the camshaft cover. The gasket may be recognised by its foil insert. The cover fitting procedure when using this gasket is as follows.
7 Clean the camshaft cover and apply RTV jointing compound to the mating surfaces of the camshaft cover and the gasket.
8 Immediately (or as directed by the maker of the jointing compound) place the gasket on the cam cover, invert the cover and gasket and press down firmly onto a flat surface so that the gasket is firmly bonded to the cam cover.
9 Place the cam cover and gasket in position on the camshaft carrier. Do not use any jointing compound on the face of the gasket which faces the camshaft carrier.
10 Apply threaded locking compound to the threads of the camshaft cover retaining screws, then tighten them evenly to 7 lbf ft (10 Nm). Run the engine for a few minutes and then retighten the screws to the same torque (obviously this must be done before the thread locking compound has set). Do not overtighten the screws as this may distort the gasket and cause leaks.

Engine overhaul (2300/2600 models)
11 The oil pressure reducing restrictor (located in the cylinder block-to-cylinder head oilway) should be inspected and cleaned before refitting the cylinder head. This will reduce the possibility of camshaft failure through lack of lubrication.
12 If any jointing compound is used, be sure that none blocks the oilways.

Cylinder head gasket (with GM 180 transmission)
13 The identification tag on a new gasket may foul the transmission. This tag should be bent out of the way; do not cut if off.

---

5 Cooling system

Description (2000 model)
1 The cooling system on the 2000 model is similar to that described in Chapter 2. The most significant difference is the use of a thermostatically controlled electric cooling fan instead of the viscous coupled fan used on the larger engines.
2 Except as detailed below, the procedures in Chapter 2 may be followed for the 2000 model.

Draining (2000 model)
3 With the vehicle on level ground and the system cold, remove the expansion tank cap.

4 Move the heater controls to the 'HOT' position.
5 Place a drain pan under the radiator. Remove the bottom hose from the radiator and allow the coolant to drain.
6 On early models, the cylinder block drain plug may be removed and the block drained. The plug is located on the right-hand side of the cylinder block. Use a piece of cardboard to divert the flow of coolant away from the starter motor. Later models do not have a cylinder block drain plug.

Filling (2000 model)
7 Refit the radiator bottom hose and (if removed) the cylinder block drain plug. Make sure that all hoses are in good condition and that their clips are tight.
8 Fill the system via the expansion tank filler until the level is up to the plate in the expansion tank. Refit the expension tank cap.
9 Run the engine for five minutes, then allow it to cool. Check the level in the expansion tank and top up as necessary.

Radiator – removal and refitting (2000 and later 2300/2600 models)
10 Proceed as described in Chapter 2, Section 5, but note that the thermoswitch or coolant level sensor lead must be disconnected before the radiator is removed, and reconnected on completion. The sensor or thermoswitch is located just below the radiator top hose.

Fig. 13.16 Cooling system components – 2000 model (Sec 5)

1 Radiator	5 Thermostat
2 Cooling fan motor	6 Cylinder block drain plug (early
3 Fan thermoswitch	models only)
4 Water pump	7 Expansion tank

Cooling fan – removal and refitting (2000 model)

11 Disconnect the battery earth lead.
12 Unbolt the radiator top rail and fan support mountings (photo). Release the radiator from its mountings and move it out of the way, being careful not to strain the hoses.
13 Unplug the electrical connector from the fan motor and remove the fan complete with mountings.
14 If it is wished to renew the fan motor, first remove the fan blades after releasing the C-clip which holds them to the spindle. Unbolt and remove the motor, noting the location of the bushes and spacers. A defective motor must be renewed.
15 Refitting is a reversal of the removal procedure.

Thermoswitch – testing, removal and refitting (2000 model)

16 If the electric cooling fan fails to operate even though the coolant temperature is high, the thermoswitch may be at fault. The switch may be tested as follows.
17 Unplug the electrical connector from the thermoswitch. Bridge the connector terminals with a short length of wire (eg fuse wire) (photo). Switch on the ignition and the cooling fan should operate. Do not allow the bridge wire to touch earthed metal.

5.12 Unbolt the radiator top rail

18 If the cooling fan does not operate when the above test is performed, there is a fault in the fan motor or in the wiring which feeds it. (Do not forget to check the appropriate fuse).
19 If the cooling fan operates when the test is performed, but does not operate normally when the coolant temperature is known to exceed 190°F (88°C), then the thermoswitch is faulty and must be renewed as follows.
20 Remove the expansion tank filler cap. *Take care to avoid scalding if the coolant is hot.*
21 If not already done, unplug the electrical connector from the thermoswitch. Have ready a container to catch escaping coolant, and the new thermoswitch (complete with seal).
22 Remove the switch retaining plate and extract the switch with its seal. Insert the new switch and seal promptly, and little coolant will be lost.
23 Secure the switch with the retaining plate and reconnect the electrical connector.
24 Top up the cooling system and refit the expansion tank cap, then run the engine at a fast tickover and check that the cooling fan cuts in before the coolant boils.
25 Allow the engine to cool, then top up the cooling system if necessary. Check that the switch seal is not leaking.

Water pump – removal and refitting (2000 model)

26 Disconnect the battery earth lead.
27 Drain the cooling system as previously described.
28 Slacken the alternator pivot and link bolts. Move the alternator towards the engine and remove the water pump/alternator drivebelt. Unbolt and remove the water pump pulley.

29 Disconnect the hoses from the water pump.
30 Remove the camshaft drivebelt by pulling it off its mounting spigots.
31 Undo and remove the two nuts which secure the camshaft drivebelt tensioner. Lift away the tensioner. **Do not** turn the engine while the tensioner is removed.
32 Undo and remove the five bolts and one stud which secure the water pump. Lift the pump away, passing it between the runs of the camshaft drivebelt. Take care not to displace the belt.
33 Remove the water pump gasket.
34 Collect the two bolts on which the drivebelt tensioner is located from the rear of the water pump body.
35 A defective pump should be renewed; repair is not a practical proposition for the home mechanic.
36 Fit the new pump, using a new gasket. Make sure that the pump and block mating surfaces are clean.
37 Make sure that the two bolts for the camshaft drivebelt tensioner are in place, then fit the water pump securing bolts and tighten them evenly to the specified torque.
38 Refit the camshaft drivebelt tensioner. Tension the belt as described in Section 3 and refit the cover.
39 Connect the hoses to the water pump and secure them.

5.17 Testing the fan thermoswitch. The connector terminals are bridged with a paper clip

40 Fit the pulley to the water pump, then refit and tension the drivebelt. The belt deflection is 0.3 to 0.7 in (7.0 to 19.0 mm).
41 Refill the cooling system and reconnect the battery.
42 Run the engine until it is warm, then allow it to cool and top up the expansion tank if necessary.

Thermostat – removal and refitting (2000 model)

43 Partially drain the cooling system. Roughly a gallon (four or five litres) should be sufficient. Recover the coolant if it is fit for re-use.
44 Disconnect the hoses from the thermostat. Remove the thermostat, noting that its fitted position is stamped on it (photo).
45 The thermostat may be tested if wished as described in Chapter 2, Section 11, although it is difficult to see the moving parts.
46 Refit in the reverse order to removal. Refill the cooling system, run the engine for a few minutes, allow it to cool and top up the expansion tank as necessary.

Viscous fan coupling – removal and refitting (later 2300/2600 models)

47 On later models the viscous fan coupling is secured to the water pump shaft by a bolt. This bolt has a *left-hand thread*, ie it is undone by turning its head clockwise (viewed from above).
48 To prevent the pump shaft turning when attempting to undo the bolt, grip the pulley by passing an old drivebelt round it and clamping the drivebelt with a self-gripping wrench.
49 With the bolt removed, the coupling may be removed from the water pump shaft.
50 Refitting is a reversal of removal.

5.44 Disconnect the hoses from the thermostat. Arrow on housing points to radiator

5.58 Withdrawing the expansion tank level sensor from its grommet

Low coolant level warning system – description and testing

51 Most later models are equipped with a low coolant level warning system. On 2000 models the system uses a sensor in the expansion tank only; on the larger engined models there is also a sensor in the radiator. On all models the sensors are wired to a low coolant warning module, situated inside the instrument housing. This module causes the low coolant warning light to illuminate for up to eight seconds when the ignition is switched on. This serves to show the driver that the bulb is intact. Should the light remain on indefinitely, or come on whilst driving, the coolant level should be checked and topped up if necessary. *Take adequate precautions against scalding* if you wish to add coolant to a hot engine. Do not add cold water to a seriously overheated engine, or damage may result.

52 If the low coolant level warning system is suspected of giving false alarms, make sure first that the correct filling procedure has been adopted. Refer to Chapter 2, Section 4 for 2300/2600 models, and note that on those models *a full expansion tank does not guarantee a full cooling system.*

53 If the cooling system is known to be full, but the low level warning light remains on, the system may be tested as follows.

54 With the ignition off, disconnect the wires from the expansion tank sensor. Join the two wiring connectors together and earth them (connect them to the battery negative terminal or to engine metal) by means of a suitable test lead. (On 2000 models there is only one connector, which should simply be earthed).

55 Switch on the ignition, obsrving the low coolant level warning light. The light should illuminate for a few seconds and then go out. If it remains on, either the low coolant warning or the lead from the module to the expansion tank is defective. Access to the module is gained by removing the instrument housing top cover (Chapter 10, Section 35).

56 If the test just described is satisfactory, leave the ignition on and disconnect and separate the expansion tank sensor connectors. This action (producing an open-circuit at the sensor connection point) mimics a 'low level' signal and should cause the warning light to illuminate within eight seconds.

57 If the above test is satisfactory, proceed to the radiator level sensor (not 2000 models). With the expansion tank sensor reconnected, repeat the earthing and open-circuit tests described in paragraphs 54 to 56. (There is only a single lead to the radiator sensor). Similar results should be obtained, ie short-circuiting the lead to earth should give an 'OK' result, and producing an open-circuit should give a low level warning. Failure to obtain an 'OK' result means either that the lead from the expansion tank to the radiator sensor is defective, or that the expansion tank sensor is defective.

58 Assuming that all the above tests have had satisfactory results, if a false low level warning is obtained when the radiator sensor is reconnected, then that sensor is defective and must be renewed

(photo).

59 Always renew the grommet or seal at the same time when renewing a sensor.

6 Fuel and exhaust systems

Air cleaner (1982 on) – description

1 Later models have an air cleaner which is mounted remotely from the carburettors, to which it is connected by a large hose and an adaptor. The air temperature control valve, of the same type as that described in Chapter 3, is secured to the bottom of the air cleaner housing by a large worm drive clip (photo).

6.1 Later type air cleaner, inverted to show fitting of air temperature control valve

Air cleaner (1982 on) – element renewal

2 Undo the clips which secure the housing lid, lift off the lid and extract the element (photo). Wipe clean inside the housing, then fit the new element and secure the lid.

Air cleaner (1982 on) – removal and refitting

3 Release the hose which joins the air cleaner to the carburettor adaptor.

4 Remove the nuts and bolts which secure the air cleaner bracket, then remove the air cleaner complete with bracket and air temperature

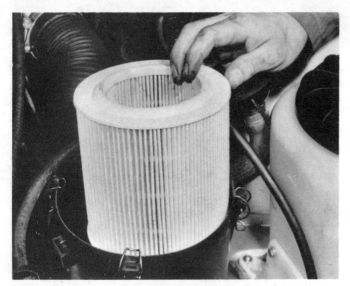

6.2 Removing the air cleaner element

6.13 Removing the air cleaner adaptor

control valve. Disengage the hot and cold air pick-up hoses as the unit is withdrawn.
5   Refitting is a reversal of removal.

HIF carburettor – description

6   Later models are fitted with twin SU HIF series carburettors. The principles of operation of this type of carburettor are identical to the earlier type SU carburettors described in Chapter 3; the main difference in the HIF is that the float chamber is below the main jet instead of beside it.
7   On the vehicles considered in this book, a separate cold start device (choke) is used. The operation of this item is automatic, being dependent on coolant temperature and throttle position; it is therefore known as the FASD (fully automatic starting device). Models from 1985 (VIN 322702) are fitted with an electronically controlled fuel management system in place of the FASD.

Tamperproofing of carburettor adjustment screws

8   Owners of later models may find that tamperproof plugs or seals have been fitted to one or more carburettor adjusting screws. The object of such tamperproofing is to discourage, and to detect, adjustment by unqualified operators.
9   Before removing a tamperproof device, satisfy yourself that you are not breaking any local, national or international anti-pollution regulations. At the time of writing it is not an offence in the UK to remove tamperproof plugs, but in some EEC countries it is an offence to use a vehicle on the road with the tamperproof plugs missing.
10 When carburettor adjustment is complete, have new tamperproof plugs fitted where this is required by law. Such plugs are normally held by authorised dealers.

HIF carburettor – adjustment

11 As with the earlier type carburettor, adjustment is confined to setting the idle speed and mixture. Because of the design of the SU carburettor, correct idle mixture adjustment ensures correct mixture throughout the range of operation.
12 Refer to the preliminary remarks in Chapter 3, Section 7, which apply equally to the HIF carburettor. A cheap substitute for an exhaust gas analyser is a device such as Gunson's Colortune'. In the absence of an independent tachometer it is permissible to adjust the idle speed 'by ear', but the inexperienced mechanic should not attempt the same for mixture adjustment or carburettor balance.

Carburettors without electronic fuel management

13 Commence operations by removing the air cleaner adaptor from the carburettor mouths (photo).
14 Remove the suction chamber from each carburettor (taking care not to inadvertently exchange parts between carburettors). With the suction chamber removed, lift out the piston and check that the needle guide is secure and that it is not protruding from the piston face.
15 Still with the suction chamber and piston removed, turn the mixture adjuster screw anti-clockwise to bring the jet flush with the

bridge, then turn the screw two full turns clockwise to provide a roughly correct starting position. Repeat the procedure on the other carburettor.
16 Check that the throttle disc operates correctly and without restriction, then remove the piston dampers from the suction chambers. Refit the pistons and the suction chambers, taking care not to wind up the piston springs.
17 Lift each piston in turn and check that it falls freely back onto the bridge. If not, overhaul is required.
18 Top up the damper tubes with clean engine oil to the level of the top of the hollow piston rod. Refit the dampers.
19 Slacken the throttle interconnection clamp (Fig. 13.17 or 13.18). Connect a tachometer to the engine, then run it at a fast idle until it has reached normal running temperature. (Turn both idle speed adjusting screws equally to achieve the required engine speed).
20 Allow the engine to run at a fast idle for five minutes after normal temperature has been reached, then check (by feeling for suction) that the FASD inlet port is not admitting any air. If it is, the FASD is faulty.
21 Increase the engine speed to 2500 rpm and hold it at this speed for 30 seconds. Repeat the operation every three minutes while adjustment is taking place.
22 Act on both idle speed adjusting screws by equal amounts to reduce the engine speed to 800 rpm.
23 Fit the airflow meter or balancing device to the carburettors as instructed by the makers of the meter. Act on the idle speed adjusting screws of both carburettors, not necessarily equally, until the carburettors are drawing in equal amounts of air (and the engine is still running). Remove the airflow meter.
24 If necessary, turn each idle speed adjusting screw equally to bring the idle speed within the correct range (see Specifications).
25 Turn each mixture adjusting screw equally to obtain the highest possible idle speed. From this position, turn each screw equally in an anti-clockwise direction until the idle speed just starts to fall, then clockwise again until maximum speed is just regained.
26 If necessary, turn each idle speed adjusting screw equally to bring the idle speed back within the specified limits.
27 If an exhaust gas analyser (CO meter) or other mixture checking device is available, connect it as instructed by its maker. If necessary, turn each mixture adjusting screw equally by the minimum amount necessary to give the desired CO level. Turning the screws clockwise richens the mixture (increased CO) and *vice versa*. Disconnect the CO meter when adjustment is correct.
28 Hold the throttle interconnecting lever against its fork while tightening the throttle interconnection clamp. Refit the airflow meter or balancing device and check that the carburettors are still balanced when the throttle is opened to give an engine speed of 1500 rpm; if not, adjust the interconnection clamp. Make sure that there is a small amount of endfloat (0.03 in/0.8 mm approx) on the throttle interconnection rod.
29 Disconnect all measuring instruments and refit the air cleaner adaptor.

Fig. 13.17 SU HIF carburettors – 2000 model (Sec 6)

1	Throttle cable and adjuster	3	Idle mixture adjusting screws	5	Fuel feed hose	8	Distributor vacuum advance hose	10	FASD delay switch
2	Idle speed adjusting screws	4	Throttle interconnection clamp	6	Fuel overflow hoses	9	Coolant hoses for FASD	11	FASD outlet pipe
				7	Crankcase ventilation hose				

Not all models have FASD

Fig. 13.18 SU HIF carburettors – 2300 and 2600 models (Sec 6)

1	Throttle cable and adjuster	3	Idle speed adjusting screws	5	Throttle interconnection clamp	8	Distributor vacuum advance hose	10	FASD delay switch connector
2	Throttle lever stop screw	4	Idle mixture adjusting screws	6	Fuel overflow hoses	9	Coolant hoses for FASD	11	FASD outlet pipe
				7	Crankcase ventilation hoses				

Not all models have FASD

Fig. 13.19 Throttle linkage – 2000 model (Sec 6)

1	Cable adjuster	3	Bracket
2	Downshift cable (when fitted)	4	Link rod

Carburettors with electronic fuel management

30 Ensure all electrical equipment is switched off. Remove the air cleaner assembly.

31 Disconnect the coolant thermistor multi-plug and bridge the terminals. Switch on the ignition; this will ensure that the mixture control device is fully off. Switch off the ignition.

32 Check that the throttle operates correctly, and that the cable has 0.04 in (1.0 mm) free play when the pedal is released.

33 Slacken the clamp on the throttle interconnection rod (Figs. 13.17 and 13.18).

34 Adjust both idle speed adjusting screws until they are just touching the lever, then screw them clockwise a further 1 1/2 turns.

35 Remove the suction chamber from the carburettors (taking care not to interchange parts) and withdraw the damper. Check that the needle guide is secure and flush with the piston face.

36 With the suction chamber and damper still removed, turn the mixture adjusting screw to bring the jet flush with the bridge, then turn the screw 2 turns clockwise for an initial setting. Repeat the procedure on the other carburettor.

37 Refit the suction chambers (without the dampers); taking care not to wind up the piston spring. Lift the piston and check that it falls freely onto the bridge. If not, complete overhaul is required.

38 Top up the damper oil level and refit the damper.

39 Remove the bridging wire from the coolant thermistor multi-plug. Reconnect the plug.

40 Connect a tachometer and start the engine. Turn the idle speed screws equally until the engine runs at 1500 rpm; allow it to warm-up at this speed for a few minutes. When the engine is at its normal operating temperature let it idle at 1500 rpm for another 5 minutes.

Note: During the following procedure a clearance must be maintained between the fast idle screw and the stepper motor pin (B in Fig. 13.20), and also at the lost motion link (A). Maintain clearance by adjusting the relevant screws.

41 Increase the engine speed to 2500 rpm and hold it at this speed for 30 seconds. Repeat this clearing operation every 3 minutes while adjustments are being made.

42 Turn the idle speed screws by equal amounts until the engine is running at its specified idle. The recommended idle should be achieved by speed reduction, not increase. If the idle is allowed to fall 100 rpm below that specified the electronic control unit (ECU) anti-stall

mechanism will come into action. If this occurs, wait 2 minutes for the conditions to stabilise.

43 Fit an airflow meter or balancing device to the carburettors, as instructed by the makers of the meter. Act on the idle speed adjusting screws of both carburettors, not necessarily equally, until the carburettors are drawing in equal amounts of air.

44 Treat each carburettor separately and adjust the mixture adjusting screws until the fastest engine speed is obtained. Turn the screw anti-clockwise until the speed just commences to fall, then clockwise just enough to reattain the fastest idle.

45 Readjust the engine idle speed (paragraph 42).

46 Fit an exhaust gas analyser, in accordance with the manufacturer's instructions, and check the CO reading. Adjust the mixture screw on both carburettors to obtain the correct reading (see Specifications). Turn clockwise to richen the mixture, and vice versa. Disconnect the gas analyser on completion.

47 Hold the throttle interconnection lever against its fork and tighten the clamp. Ensure that the interconnection rod has about 0.03 in (0.8 mm) endfloat.

48 Increase the engine idle to 1500 rpm and check the carburettor balance with the airflow meter. Reset the clamp, if necessary.

49 Switch off the ignition and check the lost motion link clearance (A in Fig. 13.20). Turn the screw to obtain a clearance of 0.06 to 0.08 in (1.5 to 2.0 mm).

50 Disconnect the coolant thermistor multi-plug and start the engine, compare the fast idle speed with that given in the Specifications. Turn the fast idle adjusting screws to obtain the correct speed. Ensure that the carburettors remain balanced by using the airflow meter.

51 Switch off the engine and detach the airflow meter. Reconnect the coolant thermistor multi-plug and refit the air cleaner assembly.

52 Start the engine and make a final check that the CO reading and idle speed are correct.

HIF carburettor – removal and refitting.
Carburettors without electronic fuel management

53 Disconnect the battery earth lead.

54 Unbolt and remove the air cleaner adaptor from the carburettors.

55 Disconnect the fuel hose from the T-piece or carburettor (photo). Be prepared for some fuel spillage. Plug the open ends of the hose.

56 Disconnect the vacuum line from the carburettor to which it is attached. Unhook the overflow hoses from their brackets.

57 Disconnect the crankcase ventilation hose from each carburettor.

58 Relieve any residual pressure in the cooling system by removing the expansion tank cap. Take precautions against scalding if the engine is hot.

59 Place a drip tray under the FASD, then disconnect the coolant hoses from it (photo). Plug the hoses.

60 Disconnect the delay switch wiring from the FASD.

61 On 2000 models, disconnect the throttle link rod. On 2300/2600 models, disconnect the return spring from the bracket and the operating rod from the interconnection lever.

62 Remove the carburettor retaining nuts.

63 Release the FASD outlet pipe and remove the carburettors and FASD together.

64 If it is only wished to remove one carburettor, follow whichever of the above paragraphs are applicable. Additionally, loosen the retaining nuts on the carburettor which is not being removed, and release the throttle interconnecting shaft.

Refitting is a reversal of removal, noting the following points:

(a) *Use new gaskets between the carburettors and the manifold*
(b) *Tighten the carburettor securing nuts to the specified torque*
(c) *Top up the carburettor dampers if necessary*
(d) *Adjust the carburettor balance and the idle speed and mixture as previously described*
(e) *Check the coolant level and top up if necessary*

Carburettors with electronic fuel management

65 Removal and refitting is basically as given for carburettors without electronic fuel management, but some connections do not apply.

HIF carburettor – overhaul
Carburettors without electronic fuel management

66 With the carburettor removed from the vehicle, unbolt and remove the FASD (when applicable).

67 Remove the piston damper, pour the oil out of the damper tube and remove the suction chamber.

Fig. 13.20 SU HIF carburettor with electronic fuel management (Sec 6)

1 Damper oil level	3 Throttle cable	5 Fast idle adjustment screw	A Lost motion link clearance
2 Idle speed screw	4 Throttle lever adjustment screw	6 Fast idle pushrod	B Fast idle screw-to-stepper
		7 Mixture screw	motor clearance

6.55 Disconnecting a fuel hose from a carburettor

6.59 Disconnect the fuel hoses from the FASD

68 Remove the piston and the piston spring.

69 Undo the grub screw in the side of the piston and remove the needle, needle guide and bias spring.

70 Scribe or paint alignment marks between the carburettor body and the float chamber cover (and the FASD adaptor, where applicable). Remove the float chamber cover and the adaptor elbow.

71 Remove the idle mixture adjusting screw. Extract its seal.

72 Remove the jet retaining screw and spring.

73 Extract the jet together with the bi-metal lever. Disengage the lever from the jet.

74 Unscrew the float pivot and remove the float. Remove the needle valve and its seat.

75 Remove the jet bearing by unscrewing its retaining nut.

76 Observe how the throttle return spring is fitted, then remove the nut

from the spindle and take off the washers, levers and spring.
77 When fitted, remove the idle stop lever from the other end of the spindle.
78 Undo the throttle disc retaining screws (they may be tight) and remove the throttle disc.

79 Remove the throttle spindle, noting which way round it is fitted. Remove the throttle spindle seals from the carburettor body.
80 Clean all components in fuel or in a suitable solvent, taking precautions appropriate to the cleaning agent used. Do not use abrasive cleaning methods, particularly on the inside of the suction chamber or on the piston, except as a last resort.
81 Blow through the jet and all other orifices with clean compressed air. If an air line is not available, a blast from a foot pump is better than nothing.
82 Renew all gaskets and seals as a matter of course. The needle valve and seat should also be renewed if the carburettor has seen much use. The jet and jet needle should be renewed as a pair if either component shows evidence of wear (ridges or grooves). Repair and overhaul kits are available from main dealers or carburettor specialists.
83 Insert the piston into the suction chamber and hold them horizontally. Spin the piston and check that it does not stick anywhere. A sticking piston is best renewed; the thrifty owner may wish to experiment with steel wool or the finest abrasive paper to relieve high spots and so prevent sticking, but this cannot be considered good practice.
84 Commence reassembly by inserting the throttle spindle (without the seals) and fitting the throttle disc to the spindle. The disc fits so that the top opens towards the piston, with the overrun valve (when fitted) at the bottom.
85 Insert the screws which secure the throttle disc to the spindle, but do not tighten them. Operate the throttle lever a few times, then tighten the screws and lock the ends. Ideally new screws should be used, and their ends locked by splaying or peening. It is clearly undesirable for one of these screws to fall out in service!
86 Fit new throttle spindle seals and press them home with a suitable diameter tube or small socket. The correct fitted position of the seals is just below the flange face.
87 Refit the throttle return spring, levers, washers and nuts. Refit the idle stop lever (when applicable) to the other end of the spindle. Tighten and lock the spindle nut.
88 Refit the jet bearing and secure it with its nut.
89 Refit the fuel inlet strainer and the needle valve seat. Hold the needle valve itself in position and offer up the float. Insert the float pivot and make sure that the wire clip on the needle valve is engaged with the float.
90 Check the float level by inverting the carburettor and measuring the dimension shown in Fig. 13.22. Adjust if necessary by carefully bending the float arm.

Fig. 13.21 Exploded view of the SU HIF carburettor used with the FASD system (Sec 6)

1 Piston damper	18 Locknut and tab washer
2 Suction chamber	19 Jet bearing
3 Piston spring	20 Jet bearing nut
4 Piston	21 Jet
5 Needle retaining screw	22 Bi-metal lever
6 Needle bias spring	23 Spring
7 Needle	24 Jet retaining screw
8 Needle guide	25 Float
9 Piston lifting pin	26 Float pivot
10 Spring and circlip	27 Seal
11 Throttle spindle seals	28 Needle
12 Throttle spindle	29 Needle seat
13 Throttle disc	30 Fuel strainer
14 Throttle disc screws	31 Float chamber cover
15 Throttle spring	32 Seal
16 Throttle lever	33 Identification tag
17 Throttle lever	

Fig. 13.22 Checking the HIF carburettor float level (Sec 6)

With electronic fuel management: A = 0.051 ± 0.011 in (1.25 ± 0.25 mm)

With FASD: A = 0.22 ± 0.02 in (5.6 ± 0.5 mm)

91 Assemble the jet and the bi-metal lever, if they were separated, and fit the jet to its bearing. Make sure that the slot in the adjusting lever engages with the end of the mixture adjusting screw, then tighten the jet retaining screw. Set the jet flush with the carburettor bridge.

92 Refit the FASD elbow, if applicable, so that it points towards the jet. Fit a new sealing ring in the groove and refit and secure the float chamber cover.

93 Fit the needle to the piston and secure it with a new grub screw. Make sure it is the correct needle (see Specifications). The needle and its guide should be aligned as shown (Fig. 13.23).

Fig. 13.23 Correct fitting of HIF carburettor needle, spring and guide. Etch mark is arrowed (Sec 6)

94 Fit the piston to the carburettor and temporarily cover it with the suction chamber without the spring. Mark the correct relative positions of the carburettor body and the suction chamber, remove the suction chamber and refit it with the spring in place on the piston. By keeping the marks aligned, spring wind-up can be avoided.

95 When applicable, fit the FASD to the carburettor and secure it. Do not overtighten the through-bolts.

Carburettors with electronic fuel management

96 Remove the carburettor.

97 Clean off the exterior of the carburettor using paraffin, or a suitable solvent and wipe dry.

98 Unscrew the three retaining screws and lift off the suction chamber and piston assembly (photo).

99 Unscrew the damper from the suction chamber (photo), and drain the oil from the piston rod.

100 Push the piston up to expose the retaining circlip (photo). Extract the circlip and withdraw the piston and spring assembly (photo).

101 Unscrew the needle guide locking screw and withdraw the needle, guide and spring (photo).

102 Mark the relationship of the float chamber cover to the carburettor body. Unscrew the four retaining screws and lift off the cover and O-ring seal (photo).

103 Unscrew the jet adjusting lever retaining screw and withdraw the jet and adjusting lever assembly (photo). Disengage the jet from the lever.

104 Unscrew the float pivot screw (photo) and lift out the float and fuel needle valve (photo). Unscrew the needle valve seat from the base of the float chamber (photo).

105 Unscrew the jet bearing locking nut (photo) and remove the jet bearing (photo).

106 Undo the three retaining screws and remove the fuel shut-off valve and solenoid assembly (photo). Recover the gasket.

107 Dismantling the remaining components is not recommended, as these parts are not available separately. If the throttle levers, linkage or spindle appear worn, or in any way damaged, it will be necessary to renew the complete carburettor. Do not remove the mixture control

6.98 Removing the carburettor suction chamber and piston

6.99 Unscrew the damper and drain the oil

6.100A Extract the retaining circlip ...

6.100B ... to allow removal of the piston and spring

6.101 Slacken the needle guide locking screw and withdraw the needle, guide and spring

6.102 Lift off the float chamber cover after removing the four screws

6.103 Removing the jet and adjusting lever assembly

6.104A Unscrew the float pivot screw and remove the float ...

6.104B ... followed by the needle valve ...

6.104C ... and needle valve seat

6.105A Unscrew the jet bearing locknut ...

6.105B ... and lift out the jet bearing

6.106 Remove the fuel shut-off valve and solenoid

6.108 Ensure that the filter in the fuel needle valve seat is clean

stepper motor or vacuum switch. These components are set to each individual carburettor during manufacture and may not operate correctly if disturbed.

108 Check the condition of the float needle valve and seat and renew these components if there is any sign of pitting or wear ridges, particularly on the needle. Ensure that the filter in the seat assembly is clean (photo).

109 Examine the carburettor body for cracks and damage, and ensure that the brass fittings and piston guide are secure.

110 Clean the inside of the suction chamber and the outer circumference of the piston with a petrol-moistened rag and allow to air dry. Insert the piston into the suction chamber without the spring. Hold the assembly in a horizontal position and spin the piston. If there is any tendency for the piston to bind, renew the piston and dashpot assembly.

111 Connect a 12 volt supply to the terminals of the fuel shut-off valve solenoid and ensure that the valve closes. If not, renew the solenoid.

112 Check the piston needle and jet bearing for any signs of ovality, or wear ridges.

113 Shake the float and listen for any trapped fuel which may have entered through a tiny crack or fracture.

114 Check the condition of all gaskets, seals and connecting hoses and renew any that show signs of deterioration.

115 Begin reassembly by refitting the jet bearing and retaining nut to the carburettor body.

116 Refit the fuel needle valve and seat, followed by the float and float pivot screw.

117 Allow the float to close the needle valve under its own weight and measure the distance from the centre of the float to the face of the carburettor body, as shown in Fig. 13.21. If the measured dimension is outside the float height setting specified, carefully bend the brass contact pad on the float to achieve the required setting.

118 Engage the jet with the cut-out in the adjusting lever, ensuring that the jet head moves freely. Position the jet in the jet bearing and, at the same time, engage the slot in the adjusting lever with the protruding tip of the mixture adjustment screw. Secure the assembly with the retaining screw.

119 Turn the mixture adjustment screw as necessary to bring the top of

the jet flush with the jet bearing upper face when viewed from above. Now turn the adjustment screw two complete turns clockwise to obtain an initial mixture setting.

120 Fit a new O-ring seal to the float chamber cover. Fit the cover with the previously made marks aligned and secure with the four retaining screws.

121 Refit the piston needle, spring and needle guide to the piston (photo), ensuring that the needle guide is flush with the underside of the piston and the triangular etch mark on the guide is between the two transfer holes in the piston (photo). Refit and tighten the locking screw.

122 Temporarily refit the piston and dashpot to the carburettor body without the spring. Engage the piston in its guide, and, with the suction chamber in its correct position relative to the retaining screws, mark the piston-to-suction chamber relationship. Remove the suction chamber and piston.

123 Fit the spring to the piston, align the previously made marks and slide the suction chamber over the piston and spring. Avoid turning the piston in the suction chamber, otherwise the spring will be wound up.

124 Push the piston up and refit the circlip to the piston rod.

125 Refit the piston and suction chamber, and secure with the three retaining screws tightened evenly. Fill the piston damper with engine oil up to the top of the piston rod and refit the damper.

126 Refit the fuel shut-off valve using a new gasket, if necessary, and secure the unit with the three screws.

Fig. 13.24 Exploded view of the SU HIF carburettor used with the electronic fuel management system (Sec 6)

1   Piston damper
2   Retaining circlip
3   Suction chamber
4   Piston
5   Piston spring
6   Needle guide locking screw
7   Needle bias spring
8   Jet needle
9   Needle guide
10   Idle speed adjustment screw
11   Adjustment screw seal
12   Mixture adjustment screw
13   Fuel shut-off valve and housing
14   Fuel shut-off solenoid
15   Throttle return spring
16   Throttle spindle seal
17   Throttle plate
18   Throttle spindle
19   Carburettor body
20   Vacuum switch
21   Mixture control stepper motor
22   Fast idle pushrod
23   Jet bearing
24   Jet bearing nut
25   Jet assembly
26   Float needle seat
27   Float needle
28   Bi-metal jet lever
29   Float
30   Jet lever retaining screw
31   Float chamber cover seal
32   Float chamber cover
33   Throttle lever and return spring
34   Fast idle adjustment screw
35   Lost motion link and return spring
36   Throttle lever adjustment screw

6.121A Refit the needle, spring and guide to the piston ...

6.121B ... with the guide flush with the piston base, and the etch mark (arrowed) positioned as shown

FASD – description

127 The FASD is attached to the side of the front or rear carburettor. It provides additional fuel/air mixture when the engine is cold, according to temperature and load.

128 When the starter motor is cranking a cold engine, and for the first few seconds of cold running, a delay valve causes the FASD to provide a particularly rich mixture. The valve is electrically operated.

129 As the engine warms up, coolant circulated to the FASD acts on a temperature-sensitive capsule, so causing the quantity of additional mixture supplied to reduce. At a given coolant temperature the FASD closes completely.

130 During warm-up the FASD also provides additional fuel for acceleration by means of an accelerator pump.

FASD – removal and refitting

131 On 2000 models, remove the rear carburettor as previously described, complete with FASD (photo). Remove the through-bolts and separate the FASD from the carburettor (photos). Be prepared for fuel spillage.

132 On 2300/2600 models, disconnect the battery earth lead, then proceed as follows.

133 Remove the air cleaner adaptor from the carburettor throats.

134 Remove the expansion tank filler cap, taking precautions against scalding if the engine is hot.

135 Place a drip tray under the FASD, then disconnect the coolant hoses from it. Plug the hoses.

136 Remove the FASD outlet pipe and the seal retainer. Disconnect the electrical cables from the delay valve.

137 Remove the through-bolts and separate the FASD from the front carburettor. Be prepared for fuel-spillage.

138 On all models, refitting is a reversal of removal. Do not overtighten the through-bolts which secure the FASD to the carburettor. Make sure that the delay valve is fitted the right way round (photo).

139 Remember to check the coolant level after the engine has been run again.

FASD – fault finding and adjustment

140 Before looking for a fault in the FASD, make sure that all other engine systems are in good order and that the correct starting procedure is being followed.

141 It is possible for a fault in the FASD module (located behind the minor instruments) to stop the delay valve opening. In such a case the engine will start well from cold and will run well when hot, but in the intervening period will show symptoms of excessive richness (eg lumpiness and black smoke). This condition is confirmed if battery voltage is not present across the cables supplying the delay valve when the engine is running.

142 If starting and initial running are satisfactory, but the FASD seems to stay on too long, check that with the engine hot, coolant is circulating past the FASD capsule. On 2000 models there is a restrictor

6.131A Removing the rear carburettor and FASD (2000 model)

6.131B Remove the through-bolts (arrowed) ...

6.131C ... and separate the FASD from the carburettor

6.138 Fit the delay valve as shown

in the hose between the FASD and the radiator, which may become blocked by foreign matter; on 2300/2600 models it is possible for the coolant feed to be blocked by the fitting of an incorrect (early pattern) inlet manifold gasket.

143 Reluctance to start and run when cold may be due to fuel starvation. Remove the FASD adaptor (accessible after removing the float chamber cover) and check particularly that the non-return valve ball is not dislodged.

144 If the above points are all in order, but it is still felt that the FASD is not functioning correctly, adjustment may be attempted. To carry out adjustment it will be necessary to possess a means of determining when airflow through the FASD has ceased – a paper or cardboard disc with a hole in the centre may suffice – and a means of accurately measuring the temperature of the FASD water jacket. Temperature-sensitive labels are available from Rover dealers (a Unipart spare). If the reader can judge correctly a temperature of 65°C (150°F) with the hand, there will be no need for temperature-sensitive labels. One further item is required for adjusting, namely a 1.5 mm Allen key.

145 Remove the air cleaner adaptor from the carburettor throats.

146 With the engine cold, remove the rubber plug from the end of the adjustment tube. Insert the Allen key into the tube, long end first, until it engages with the adjuster (photos).

147 If a temperature-sensitive label is being used, degrease the water jacket and attach the label so that it can be seen. Do not put it on the jacket flange, or incorrect readings may result.

148 Start the engine and allow it to idle. (If the engine will not start, turn the Allen key two full turns clockwise and try again.)

149 With the engine idling and cold, place the airflow detector over the FASD air intake so that the passage of air holds it in place.

150 As soon as the water jacket temperature reaches 65°C (150°F), turn the Allen key clockwise until the FASD stops taking in air (indicated by the airflow detector falling off). This must be done within 30 seconds of the desired temperature being reached; otherwise, allow the engine to cool for not less than an hour and start again.

151 When adjustment is complete, remove the Allen key and refit the rubber plug. Refit the air cleaner adaptor.

152 If the above procedure fails to give satisfactory operation of the FASD, renewal would appear to be the only solution. No provision is made for overhaul. Note that the delay valve and the FASD itself can be renewed separately.

Inlet manifold (2000 model) – removal and refitting

153 If it is only wished to renew the gasket, there is no need to drain the cooling system, disconnect the coolant hoses or separate the carburettor from the manifold. Otherwise, follow the instructions

6.146A Remove the rubber ring ...

6.146B ... and insert the Allen key (FASD removed for clarity)

below.

154 Disconnect the battery earth lead.

155 Drain the cooling system.

156 Remove the air cleaner adaptor from the carburettor throats.

157 Remove the carburettors and FASD from the manifold as previously described.

158 Disconnect or remove from the manifold the coolant hoses, the heater rail, the brake servo pipe and the throttle bracket.

159 Remove the crankcase ventilation hose and its seal.

160 Undo and remove the manifold securing nuts and bolts.

161 Withdraw the manifold, carefully passing the heater rail over it.

162 Refitting is a reversal of removal. Make sure the manifold and cylinder head mating faces are clean. Use a new gasket and tighten the retaining nuts and bolts, in criss-cross sequence, to the specified torque.

Electronic fuel management system – description

163 Fuel enrichment for cold starting is by an internal valve which admits more fuel into the airstream passing through the carburettor. This valve is operated by a stepper motor which also controls the engine idling speed. An electronic control unit (ECU) which is a small microprocessor receives inputs from the coolant thermister, ambient air temperature sensor, accelerator pedal switch and ignition coil, and adjusts the engine idle speed and mixture accordingly. The ECU also controls the operation of a fuel shut-off valve which comes into operation when decelerating or descending a hill. If, during these conditions, the engine speed is in excess of 1300 rpm, the ambient air

Fig. 13.25 FASD adjustment diagram (Sec 6)

A   Hole
B   Water jacket
C   Position for
    temperature-sensitive label
D   Airflow detector
E   Allen key

temperature and engine temperature are above a predetermined value, and the accelerator pedal switch is closed (pedal released), the valve will be opened and closed at half second intervals. This introduces a partial vacuum to the top of the float chamber thus weakening the mixture. The fuel shut-off circuit is de-activated if the engine speed suddenly drops, ie when declutching. When accelerating, a vacuum operated switch acts upon the mixture control, allowing more fuel to be drawn through, resulting in the necessary richer mixture.

164 The overall effect of this type of carburettor is that it will remain in tune during the lengthy service intervals and also under varying operating conditions and temperature changes. The design of the unit and its related systems ensures a fine degree of mixture control over the complete throttle range, coupled with enhanced engine fuel economy.

Fuel shut-off solenoids

165 The fuel shut-off solenoids on Vanden Plas models with electronic fuel management and cruise control do not operate, even though they are fitted.

166 The wiring for these solenoids must not be connected.

7 Ignition system

Distributor – general

1 All 2000 models produced before 1985, and late 2300/2600 models (also produced before 1985) have distributors equipped with 'self-cleaning' contact breaker points. These points have a fork which engages in a peg on the distributor baseplate; movement of the baseplate by the vacuum advance mechanism produces a wiping action at the point faces. The normal 'pip and crater' build-up is thereby much reduced.

2 For removal and refitting of self-cleaning points, refer to Chapter 4, Section 4. Make sure on reassembly that the fork on the points engages with the peg on the baseplate.

3 Set the gap on new points as described in Chapter 4, Section 3; then if possible check the dwell angle as described below.

4 All models produced from 1985 are fitted with modular breakerless distributors. These are discussed below.

Dwell angle – definition and adjustment

5 Dwell angle is defined as the angle through which the distributor cam rotates between the instants of closure and opening of the points during one ignition cycle. The correct dwell angle is given in the Specifications, either at the beginning of Chapter 4 or at the beginning of this Chapter. The dwell angle for four-cylinder models is obviously greater than that for six-cylinder, since there are only four ignition cycles in 360° rotation instead of six.

6 Dwell angle is measured using a special electrical meter. Many such meters incorporate other test functions useful on motor vehicles, and are a useful addition to the electrically competent mechanic's tool kit.

7 Connect the dwell meter in accordance with its maker's instructions – usually to the distributor LT terminal and to earth. Measure the dwell angle as instructed by the meter maker, with the engine either idling or cranking. Make sure that the correct scale (4-cylinder or 6-cylinder) is selected.

8 If the dwell angle is outside the specified limits, alter the points gap to correct it. Reducing the points gap increases the dwell angle and *vice versa*.

9 If the correct dwell angle cannot be achieved without using a points gap grossly different from that specified, of if the dwell angle fluctuates substantially with the engine idling or cranking, this suggests that the distributor cam, or the distributor itself, is worn. Expert advice should be sought in this case.

10 When the dwell angle is correct, check the ignition timing and adjust if necessary.

Distributor (2000 models) – contact breaker type
Removal and refitting

11 Disconnect the battery earth lead.

12 Disconnect the LT lead (photo) and the vacuum pipe from the distributor. Remove the distributor cap and move it out of the way.

13 Turn the crankshaft, using a spanner on the pulley nut, in a clockwise direction, until the rotor arm is approaching the 2 o'clock position. Continue turning until the crankshaft pulley timing marks are

Fig. 13.26 Distributor components (contact breaker type) – 2000 model (Sec 7)

1 Distributor cap	10 Roll pin
2 Rotor arm	11 Vacuum unit
3 Condenser	12 Vacuum unit arm
4 Baseplate	13 Spacer
5 Felt pad	14 Centrifugal advance
6 Washer	mechanism
7 LT lead	15 Contact breaker points
8 Washer	16 Carbon brush
9 Drivegear	

7.12 Distributor LT lead connector in wiring harness

7.13 Timing marks aligned at 10° BTDC

aligned at 10° BTDC (photo). The rotor arm should now be at roughly the 3 o'clock position.
14 Undo and remove the two nuts which secure the distributor to the camshaft cover. Withdraw the distributor.
15 Always fit a new O-ring seal before refitting the distributor.
16 Make sure that the engine is still set at 10° BTDC on the compression stroke for No 1 cylinder. If this position has been accidentally lost, turn the crankshaft anti-clockwise until the 'V' on the timing disc aligns with the pointer, and the dimple on the camshaft sprocket aligns with the pointer on the camshaft cover. In this position the engine is at 90° BTDC, No 1 on compression; turn the crankshaft clockwise until the 10° BTDC mark is aligned, then proceed as follows.
17 Hold the distributor so that the vacuum unit is about 45° below the horizontal and pointing to the rear of the engine. Turn the rotor arm to the 1 o'clock position. Offer the distributor to the camshaft cover: the distributor flange should pass over the studs, and as the drivegear engages with the camshaft gear, the rotor arm will move to the 3 o'clock position.
18 Refit the retaining nuts, but before tightening them, turn the distributor body one way or the other so that the contact breaker points are just opening. (They should, of course, be correctly gapped). Refer to Chapter 4, Section 8, for details of how to determine accurately when the points are opening.
19 Refit the distributor cap and connect the LT lead. Reconnect the battery earth lead.
20 The engine will now run, but for the best results the dwell angle and then the dynamic timing should be checked and adjusted if necessary.
21 On completion, tighten the distributor flange nuts to the specified torque.

Overhaul
22 Refer to Chapter 4, Section 6, for an idea of the procedure to be followed, and to Fig. 13.26 for details of the distributor components.
23 Before spending much time dismantling the distributor, make sure that spares will be available if needed.

Ignition timing
24 Procedures for static and dynamic timing are given in Chapter 4, Section 8. Static timing must be regarded only as a preliminary to dynamic timing, which is essential for best results.
25 The 2000 engine is timed to No 1 cylinder, to which the stroboscopic timing light should be connected. The timing marks are shown in Fig. 13.27.

Distributor (2000 model) – breakerless type
Removal and refitting
26 Disconnect the battery earth lead.
27 Turn the crankshaft, using a spanner on the pulley nut, in a

clockwise direction until piston No 1 is at TDC on its compression stroke.
28 Remove the distributor cap and check that the rotor arm is aligned with the No 1 segment in the cap.
29 Disconnect the vacuum pipe and the amplifier multi-plug.
30 Undo and remove the nuts/bolts which secure the distributor. Withdraw the distributor.
31 Ensure that the engine has No 1 piston at TDC on its compression stroke. Hold the distributor adjacent to its mounted location with the vacuum unit pointing towards No 1 spark plug.
32 Insert the distributor into its location and note which way and how much the rotor arm rotates.
33 Withdraw the distributor and position the rotor arm so that, when the distributor is fitted, the rotor arm will be aligned with the No 1 segment in the distributor cap.
34 Connect the amplifier multi-plug and refit the distributor cap. Reconnect the battery.
35 Set the ignition timing (see below), tighten the securing nuts/bolts and reconnect the vacuum pipe.

H.15690

Fig. 13.27 Ignition timing marks – 2000 model (Sec 7)

Overhaul
36 Before dismantling this distributor, check the availability of new components.
37 Pull the rotor arm off the mainshaft.
38 Unscrew the amplifier retaining screws and remove the amplifier, gasket and connector block. **Note:** *the amplifier contains beryllia and must not be opened or crushed.*
39 Remove the securing screws and separate the upper housing from the lower housing.
40 Lift the clamp ring and pick-up winding from the upper housing.
41 Unscrew the vacuum unit retaining screw. Release the circlip from the mainshaft and remove the thrust washer. Withdraw the stator pack from the vacuum link and remove the vacuum unit.

42 Take off the drivegear by tapping out the securing pin with a suitable punch. Pull the mainshaft from the housing. Do not attempt to remove the reluctor from the shaft.

43 Examine all components and renew any which are worn or damaged.

44 Reassembly is a reversal of dismantling, but note the following:

(a) *Lightly lubricate bush and bearing surfaces, pivots, and the advance mechanism with engine oil*

(b) *Lubricate the vacuum link with a general purpose grease*

(c) *Smear heat conducting silicone grease on the amplifier mounting face*

(d) *Renew the O-ring seal*

Ignition timing

45 Engines with this distributor must be timed dynamically, as described in Chapter 4, Section 8. Use the setting given in the Specifications, and note that the engine is timed on No 1 cylinder. Timing marks are shown in Fig. 13.27.

Distributor (2300/2600 models) – breakerless type
Removal and refitting

46 This is basically as given in Chapter 4, Section 5, but note that there is also an amplifier module lead to disconnect.

Overhaul

47 Check the availability of new parts before dismantling this distributor.

48 Remove the rotor arm and flash guard. Release the circlip and remove the washer, O-ring, reluctor and coupling ring.

49 Remove the screws securing the vacuum unit and, with a downward movement, detach the operating link from the peg on the underside of the baseplate.

50 Remove the amplifier module and plate. **Note:** *the amplifier contains beryllia and must not be opened or crushed.*

51 Remove the harness guide and release the harness grommet.

52 Remove the screws securing the baseplate and pick-up assembly, and lift the pick-up assembly from the distributor body.

53 Renew any components which are worn or damaged.

54 Reassembly is a reversal of dismantling, but note the following:

(a) *Lightly lubricate the bush and bearing surfaces, pivots, advance mechanism and vacuum link with a molybdenum disulphide based oil*

(b) *Adjust the reluctor air gap before fitting the flash guard and rotor arm*

Ignition timing

55 This distributor must be timed dynamically, as described in Chapter 4, Section 8. Use the setting given in the Specifications.

Reluctor air gap – setting

56 Disconnect the distributor harness multi-plug, and remove the distributor cap, rotor arm and flash guard.

57 Rotate the crankshaft until one of the reluctor teeth is aligned with the pick-up limb. Check the air gap with a feeler gauge.

58 If necessary, adjust the nuts securing the pick-up assembly and move it to achieve the specified gap.

59 Refit the flash guard, rotor arm, distributor cap and harness multi-plug.

Fig. 13.28 Distributor components (breakerless type) – 2000 model (Sec 7)

1	Distributor cap, brush and spring	8	Reluctor, centrifugal advance and shaft assembly
2	Rotor arm	9	Internal thrust washer
3	Upper housing	10	Lower housing
4	Vacuum unit	11	O-ring seal
5	Stator pack, thrust washers and circlip	12	Washer and drivegear
6	Pick-up assembly	13	Connector block and gasket
7	Clamp ring	14	Amplifier module

Fig. 13.29 Distributor components (breakerless type) – 2300 and 2600 models (Sec 7)

1	Distributor cap, brush and spring	6	Pick-up and baseplate assembly
2	Rotor arm	7	Reluctor shaft
3	Flash guard	8	Distributor body
4	Circlip, washer and O-ring seal	9	Amplifier module
5	Reluctor and coupling ring	10	Vacuum unit
		11	O-ring seal

8 Manual gearbox

Gearbox – removal and refitting (2000 model)
1 Disconnect the battery earth lead.
2 Remove the gear lever as described in Chapter 6, Section 2, paragraphs 2 to 7.
3 Raise and securely support the vehicle.
4 Scribe an alignment mark on the flange, then disconnect the propeller shaft from the gearbox. Tie the shaft up to one side of the gearbox.
5 Disconnect the wires from the reversing light switch.
6 Disconnect the speedometer cable or the speedometer transducer multi-plug (as applicable). Move the wires out of the way.
7 Disconnect the exhaust pipe at the manifold and remove the exhaust bracket from the rear of the gearbox. Move the exhaust pipe out of the way, being careful not to strain the remaining mountings.
8 Remove the two bolts which secure the clutch slave cylinder. Carefully withdraw the slave cylinder, retrieving the shim, and tie it up so that the hydraulic hose is not strained.
9 Unbolt the starter motor. There is no need to actually remove the motor.
10 Remove the bolts which secure the sump stiffener plate to the gearbox.
11 Support the gearbox on a jack with a piece of wood between the jack head and the gearbox. A trolley jack is best as it will be easier to withdraw the gearbox.
12 Unbolt and remove the rear crossmember and retaining plates.
13 Insert a piece of wood, as tightly fitting as possible, between the back of the cylinder head and bulkhead. This will stop the engine tipping backwards when the gearbox is removed.
14 Remove the nuts and bolts which secure the gearbox bellhousing to the engine.
15 With the aid of an assistant, withdraw the gearbox from the engine and lower it to the ground. The gearbox is too heavy for one person of average strength to lower safely. Do not allow the gearbox to hang by its input shaft when withdrawing it; damage to the shaft and/or to the clutch may result.
16 Refitting is basically the reversal of the removal procedure. Refer to Chapter 6, Section 2, paragraph 28, for guidance when refitting the gear lever.
17 Make sure that there is adequate clearance between the gearbox mounting spacer and the crossmember. The gap should be 0.12 in (3 mm). If adjustment is necessary, slacken the locknut, adjust the centre bolt to achieve the specified gap, then tighten the locknut (photo).

Gearbox 'chatter' (2000 model)
18 If the transmission 'chatters' at idle, this noise can be reduced by increasing the engine idle speed to between 800 and 850 rpm.

8.17 Gap (arrowed) between spacer and crossmember must be as stated in text

9 Automatic transmission (GM 180)

Description
1 During 1982, the Borg-Warner 66 automatic transmission was superseded by the GM 180.
2 The most important feature of this transmission from the owner's point of view is the fact that it requires a different type of ATF from that used in the previous transmission and in the power steering reservoir. Refer to *Recommended lubricants and fluids* (at the beginning of the book) for details.

Maintenance
3 Every 6000 miles (10 000 km), or at the first sign of any malfunction, check the automatic fluid levels as follows.
4 Drive the car for at least 15 miles (25 km) to bring the transmission fliud to operating temperature. Park on level ground, and with the engine running and the footbrake applied, move the selector lever through all positions three times, finishing in position 'P'.
5 With the engine still running, 'P' selected and the handbrake applied, open the bonnet and locate the automatic transmission dipstick (on the left-hand side of the engine bay, towards the rear). Withdraw the dipstick, wipe it with a clean non-fluffy rag, reinsert it and withdraw it again. If the level is at or below the minimum mark, top up with fresh fluid of the specified type. *Take great care not to introduce foreign matter into the filler/dipstick tube.*
6 Every 24 000 miles (40 000 km) the transmission should be drained by removing the sump. The filter and gasket should be renewed, the sump refitted with a new gasket and the transmission refilled with fresh fluid. If the car is operated under arduous conditions this work should be undertaken every 12 000 miles (20 000 km). If the ATF is contaminated, also flush the fluid cooler (which is part of the radiator).
7 Only about 4 pints (2.3 litres) of ATF will be needed to refill the transmission after draining as described – the remainder of the fluid is retained in the torque converter. Refill a cold transmission to the level of the triangle on the dipstick (below the minimum mark). Recheck the level when the transmission has reached operating temperature.
8 Also every 24 000 miles (40 000 km) or earlier, if operating under arduous conditions, adjust the low brake band, or have the work done by a Rover dealer or automatic transmission specialist.

Removal and refitting
9 Position the car on ramps, or jack it up and support on axle stands. Select N and disconnect the battery.
10 Disconnect the downshift cable at the carburettor.
11 Disconnect and unclip the vacuum pipe from the transmission modulator valve.
12 Unbolt and remove the dipstick tube and remove the seal. Plug the vacant hole.
13 Unclip the selector rod.
14 Disconnect the wiring from the speed transducer and inhibitor switch.
15 Remove the front and intermediate exhaust pipes.
16 Remove the propeller shaft (Chapter 7).
17 Remove the engine sump stiffening plate bolts.
18 Remove the bottom starter motor securing bolt and disconnect the strap. On 2000 models, remove the starter motor.
19 On 2300 and 2600 models, remove the driveplate cover fitted at the bottom of the converter housing.
20 Unscrew the driveplate bolts; turning the engine as necessary.
21 Support the rear of the engine and take the weight of the transmission on a trolley jack.
22 Unbolt the mounting bracket from the underbody and detach the oil cooler pipe bracket.
23 Lower the transmission far enough to disconnect the oil cooler pipes. Tie the pipes to one side.
24 Unscrew the remaining transmission-to-engine bolts, and recover the dipstick tube support bracket.
25 Withdraw the transmission until the torque converter clears the crankshaft spigot then lower it to the ground.
26 Refitting is a reversal of removal, with reference to Chapter 6, Section 11 where applicable. Finally adjust the downshift cable (this Section).

Transmission – mating to 2000 engine
27 Certain items must be checked before refitting a 2000 engine and/or a GM 180 transmission, particularly if the crankshaft or the

engine itself has been renewed. Refer to Fig. 13.30.

28 Make sure that the crankshaft dowels are correctly positioned, and that the dowel shanks are correctly located in the driveplate.

29 Note that the driveplate adaptor is fitted with the chamfer on its outer edge facing the driveplate, and that the radiused edge of the driveplate backing plate is fitted against the driveplate. Tighten the driveplate-to-crankshaft bolts to the specified torque.

30 Check the condition of the torque converter bush. Renew the torque converter if necessary.

31 When mating the engine and gearbox, make sure that the dowel on the engine backplate enters its proper location in the transmission casing. Fit, but do not tighten, the dowel bolt followed by the other retaining bolts. Tighten the dowel bolt to its specified torque, then tighten the other bolts.

32 Tighten the converter-to-driveplate bolts to the specified torque.

H.15684

Fig. 13.30 Points to check on 2000 engine with GM 180 automatic transmission (Sec 9)

A Dowel	D Torque converter bush
B Driveplate adaptor	E Dowel bolt
C Driveplate backing plate	F Dowel

Downshift cable – checking and adjustment

33 Press the accelerator pedal to the floor and wedge it in that position.

34 Check that the carburettors are fully open against the throttle stops, and that the downshift cable is fully withdrawn from the transmission.

35 To adjust, slacken the two outer downshift cable locknuts at the support bracket.

36 *2000 models:* With the throttle fully open, adjust the tension of the

downshift outer cable until the downshift lever at the carburettor just contacts the stop. Tighten the locknuts.

37 *2300 and 2600 models:* With the accelerator pedal released, turn the cable adjuster nut until the downshift lever is just touching the lever stop. Tighten the locknuts.

38 Check that, when the accelerator pedal is fully depressed, the downshift cable is fully withdrawn and does not act as a throttle stop.

Low brake band – adjustment

39 Position the car on ramps, or support it on axle stands.

40 Position a suitable container beneath the sump then undo the sump pan and drain the fluid.

41 Remove the brake band servo cover and gasket. Be prepared for some fluid spillage.

42 Loosen the adjusting screw locknut, then tighten the screw to 3.3 lbf ft (4.5 Nm) using an Allen key.

43 Hold the piston sleeve stationary with a spanner and unscrew the adjusting screw five turns. Tighten the locknut.

44 Refit the servo cover and gasket, followed by the sump pan and gasket. Tighten all bolts to the specified torque.

45 Refill the transmission with fluid. Warm up the engine and check the level, as described earlier.

Fig. 13.31 Downshift cable adjustment – 2300 and 2600 models with GM 180 transmission (Sec 9)

1 Outer cable and locknuts	4 Lever stop
2 Cable bracket	5 Throttle lever and stop
3 Downshift lever	screw

Fig. 13.32 Low brake band adjustment (Sec 9)

1 Servo cover and gasket	3 Piston sleeve
2 Adjustment screw and locknut	

Selector rod – adjustment

46 Position the car on ramps, or support it on axle stands.
47 Set the gear lever in N.
48 Unclip the selector rod from the selector lever (at the transmission).
49 Set the transmission in N by turning the selector lever fully anti-clockwise, then rotating it 2 detents clockwise.
50 Release the locknuts and turn the adjuster until the selector rod aligns with the hole in the selector lever. Clip the rod to the lever and tighten the locknuts.
51 Check that the engine will only start in P and N. If necessary, adjust the starter inhibitor switch.

Starter inhibitor switch – adjustment

52 Position the car on ramps, or support it on axle stands.
53 Set the gear lever to N and slacken the nut which secures the switch.
54 Rotate the switch fully anti-clockwise, then turn it clockwise until a distinct click is heard. The switch-to-shaft alignment marks should now correspond.
55 Rotate the switch clockwise a further 0.06 in (1.5 mm), measured at the switch locknut, then tighten the locknut.

Speed transducer – removal and refitting

56 Chock the rear wheels, and support the rear of the car on axle stands.
57 Disconnect the wiring from the speed transducer.
58 Unscrew the securing bolt and remove the transducer from the extension housing. Be prepared for a little oil spillage.
59 Fit a new O-ring seal and lubricate the housing.
60 Push the transducer into position, making sure that the driven gear meshes correctly.
61 Insert and tighten the securing bolt, then reconnect the wiring. Route the wiring over the top of the extension housing; away from the exhaust.

Fig. 13.33 Selector rod adjustment and starter inhibitor switch setting (Sec 9)

1	Gear lever	5	Selector lever
2	Operating lever	6	Switch adjustment bolt
3	Adjuster	7	Switch cursor
4	Selector rod	8	Alignment marks

10 Rear axle

Halfshaft bearing and oil seals – addition of circlip (later models)

1   From 1981 a circlip has been fitted to the halfshaft between the bearing retainer and the inner oil seal. The purpose of the circlip is to stop the halfshaft parting company with the axle in the event of bearing failure.

2   Since the modification is to the halfshaft itself and not to the axle casing, later pattern halfshafts may be fitted to early pattern axles.

3   If a bearing and/or oil seal kit is purchased, the circlip which it contains may be discarded if the components are to be fitted to an early pattern halfshaft.

Low brake fluid warning system

11   If the warning lamp does not light when the starter is engaged the bulb should be renewed. If the lamp lights at any other time, top up the master cylinder reservoir immediately. If the lamp lights repeatedly the entire hydraulic system must be checked for leaks.

12   To check the brake fluid level switch, remove the reservoir cap (ignition on) annd check that the warning lamp illuminates.

Pad wear warning system

13   If the warning lamp does not light when the starter is engaged the bulb should be renewed. If it illuminates when the brakes are applied, the brake pads must be renewed without delay.

14   Operation of the warning light is controlled by wires embedded in the brake pad friction lining. When the lining has worn so far that the

Fig. 13.34 Sectional views of old pattern (A) and new pattern (B) halfshaft bearing and oil seals (Sec 10)

11 Braking system

Brake servo knock (all models)

1   If a knocking noise is heard from the brake servo, proceed as follows.

2   With the engine not running, press the brake pedal several times to dissipate any residual vacuum.

3   Extract the non-return valve and its seal, leaving the valve attached to the vacuum hose.

4   Have an assistant depress the brake pedal as far as it will go. With the pedal depressed, stick a finger in through the non-return valve hole and rotate the metal plate inside through approximately 10°. The assistant may then release the pedal.

5   Refit the non-return valve and its seal.

6   Road test the car. If servo knock is still present, repeat the above procedure until it is cured. If no cure is forthcoming, renewal of the servo may be the only solution.

Brake servo hose routing (later 2300/2600 models)

7   To reduce the possibility of fuel entering the servo, the routing of the hose from the inlet manifold to the servo has been changed (Fig. 13.35).

8   Earlier models can be modified by fitting a new hose. Depending on available stocks, it may be necessary to cut the new hose to length; 34 in (864 mm) is the correct length for RHD vehicles.

Warning circuits

9   Later models have warning systems to indicate low brake fluid and pad wear.

10   The warning lights illuminate as a check for operation when the starter motor is engaged.

wires touch the disc, an electrical circuit is completed and the warning light is activated.

15   It is necessary to disconnect the wires at the caliper when removing the pads, and to reconnect them on completion.

16   The conscientious owner will wish to inspect the brake pads at regular intervals, even when not prompted by the warning light.

Fig. 13.35 Correct routing of brake servo hose (A) – 2300 and 2600 models (Sec 11)

12 Electrical system

Alternator type A133 – description and brush renewal

1   The type A133 alternator may be found on later models. It is a more compact version of the ACR series alternator fitted previously.

2   To renew the brushes, first remove the alternator from the vehicle (Chapter 10, Section 8).

3   Disconnect and remove the interference suppression capacitor from the end cover.

4   Undo the screws or nuts which secure the end cover. Remove the cover.

5   Unscrew the surge protection diode securing screw. Either move the diode carefully out of the way, or disconnect it from the rectifier board and remove it.

6   Make a careful note of the regulator lead colours and fitting arrangements, then disconnect the regulator leads from the rectifier board and the brushbox.

7   Remove the regulator screw and withdraw the regulator. Note that the regulator securing screw also holds one of the brush mounting plates in position.

8   Remove the two securing screws and withdraw the brushbox. Extract the free brush, then undo the securing screw to release the other brush. Remove the sealing pad.

9   Renew the brushes if they are at or approaching the minimum specified length. Check the brush spring pressure with the brush ends flush with the end of the brushbox; renew the springs if they have become weak.

10 Reassemble the alternator in the reverse sequence to dismantling. Refit the alternator as described in Chapter 10 and tension the drivebelt; the belt deflection for this alternator is 0.3 to 0.7 in (7 to 19 mm).

Fig. 13.36 Exploded view of type A133 alternator (Sec 12)

1   Drive end bracket
2   Bearing pack
3   Rotor
4   Slip rings and bearing
5   Stator
6   Slip ring end bracket
7   Brushbox
8   Rectifier (diode) pack
9   Surge protection diode
10 Cover
11 Through-bolt
12 Brushes
13 Regulator
14 Interference suppression capacitor

Relays and electronic control units (1982 on) – general

11 Cars built in 1982 and later model years have more relays than those described in Chapter 10. In addition a good many electronic control units (ECU) have made their appearance. The paragraphs which follow will enable the owner to locate a particular relay or ECU. A relay or an ECU may appear identical to one used elsewhere in the vehicle, but this does not mean that they are interchangeable. Malfunction and/or damage may result from haphazard interchanging of units.

12 The **FASD (auto choke) ECU**, if fitted, is located behind the instrument housing which holds the fuel, temperature and oil pressure gauges. It has two white/black cables running to it, one white/blue cable and one brown/purple.

13 The fuel management system ECU, if fitted, is located behind the passenger's glovebox.

14 The **low oil level indicator module** is located behind the speedometer multi-plug. Its cable colours are black, white, yellow, white/orange and yellow/orange.

15 The **brake warning and dip beam relay diode unit** is located on the relay bank behind the left-hand glovebox. The function of the unit is twofold: it provides an automatic testing facility for the brake fluid level and brake pad wear warning lights, and it also activates headlamp dipped beam (via the appropriate relay) in the event of main beam failure. The colours of the cables supplying the diode unit are black/purple, black/white, blue/white, black/orange and blue/orange; the cables are connected by a multi-plug.

16 The **wiper programme unit** is located behind the right-hand instrument cluster. Its cables are coloured yellow, blue, orange, black, brown and red.

17 The **low coolant level indicator module** is located inside the main instrument housing. It has four black cables; fortunately these are connected to a multi-plug which can only be fitted one way round.

18 The **courtesy light delay unit** is located on the relay bank behind the left-hand glovebox. Its cable colours are white, purple, black, purple/white and purple/black.

19 The **headlamp dipped beam relay** is located on the relay bank behind the left-hand glovebox. Its cable colours are brown, blue, blue/orange and blue/black.

20 The **headlamp main beam relay** is located next to the dipped beam relay. Its cable colours are brown, black, blue/slate and blue/white.

21 The **fog guard relay** is also located on the relay bank behind the left-hand glovebox. Its function is to control the operation of the rear fog lamps so that they will illuminate with dipped beam or front fog lamps lit, but not with main beam lit (unless the front fog lamps are also lit). The cable colours of the fog guard relay are brown, black, blue/black, blue/yellow and red/purple.

22 The **central door locking control unit** is located on the right-hand side of the luggage area, behind the auxiliary fuse box. Its cable colours are red, black, grey, brown and two each of green/grey and blue/orange. When this unit is protected by a line fuse, the fuse is in the red lead. Earlier models are protected by a fuse in the auxiliary fuse box.

23 The **heated rear window relay** is now located on the right-hand side of the luggage area, behind the auxiliary fuse box. Its cable colours are brown/red, white/green, green and brown/red.

24 The **starter solenoid relay** is now located inside the right-hand wing valance, under the bonnet. Its cable colours are white, red, brown, white/brown and black.

25 The **rear wiper programme unit** is located on the right-hand side of the luggage area, behind the auxiliary fuse box. Its cable colours are yellow, blue, red, brown and orange.

26 The **air conditioning condenser fan relay** (when fitted) is located inside the right-hand wing valance, under the bonnet. Its cable colours are green/orange, brown, black/green and black.

27 The **headlamp power wash programme unit** is mounted on the left-hand wing valance, next to the headlamp washer reservoir. Its cable colours are red/blue, brown, light green/black, black and light green/purple.

Fuse box locations and fuse ratings (1982 on)

28 On later models, the main fuse box is located beneath the mat in the passenger's front tray. An auxiliary fuse box is fitted at the rear of the car, behind the carpet at the rear of the right-hand wheel arch (photos).

29 The manufacturer's recommended fuse ratings are given in the Specifications. Note that the ratings of the fuses serving the rear lights and the direction indicators (A1 and B5 respectively) must be increased when a towing socket is fitted.

Towing socket wiring (all models) – precautions

30 To avoid damage to the bulb failure indicator unit (when fitted), note that if a towing socket is fitted, the wiring for the trailer lights must be taken from the input side of the BFIU and **not** from the rear lamp unit itself.

31 The cables providing the inputs to the BFIU are coloured red/orange (for tail lights) and green/purple (for stop-lights). The other cables of interest are coloured green/white (RH indicator), green/red (LH indicator), and red (rear fog lamp).

32 On models already fitted with a dashboard warning light to show when the trailer direction indicators are operational, a green/light green cable will be found next to the flasher unit. This lead should be connected to the trailer warning light terminal of the heavy duty flasher unit or relay which will have to be fitted in conjunction with the towing socket. The warning light will then be operational.

Instrument panel lamps (1982 on) – renewal

33 To renew an instrument illumination or warning lamp on later models, first disconnect the battery earth lead.

34 Remove the screw which secures the instrument panel top cover

12.28A Main fuse box is located beneath passenger's front tray

12.28B Auxiliary fuse box is in luggage area

12.34 Instrument panel cover securing screw may be covered by a cap

12.35 Removing a warning light bulb

(photo). Remove the cover by sliding it to the passenger's side to release its studs.
35 Extract the appropriate bulb holder by twisting it anti-clockwise and pulling it (photo). Remove the capless bulb from its holder and push in a new one.
36 Refit in the reverse order to removal.

Instrument panel switches (1982 on) – removal and refitting

37 Disconnect the battery earth lead.
38 Remove the instrument panel top cover as described above.
39 Disconnect the wiring multi-plug from the appropriate switch.
40 Ease the switch and its wiring out from the front of the instrument panel.
41 Refit in the reverse order to removal.

Minor instruments (1982 on) – removal and refitting

42 Disconnect the battery earth lead.
43 Remove the instrument panel top cover as described in paragraph 34.
44 Disconnect the multi-plug from the digital clock (if fitted).
45 If a trip computer is fitted, remove the instrument panel front cover, then disconnect the multi-plug and the blade connector from the computer.
46 If fitted, release the FASD ECU from its bracket behind the instruments, then remove the bracket.
47 Disconnect the instrument wiring multi-plug.
48 Remove the retaining screws, then extract the instruments through the rear of the instrument panel.
49 Refit in the reverse order to removal. Reset the clock or computer on completion, when applicable, and check the instruments for correct operation.

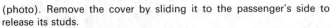

Fig. 13.37 Rear view of minor instrument pack (Sec 12)

1 Panel illumination lamps
2 Thermal delay unit
3 Blade connectors
4 Printed circuit
5 Plastic retainer
6 Voltage stabilizer
7 Fuel gauge retaining nuts
8 Warning lamps
9 Temperature gauge retaining nuts
10 Leads for digital clock (when fitted)
11 Oil pressure gauge retaining nuts

Speedometer/tachometer (1982 on) – removal and refitting

50 Disconnect the battery earth lead.
51 Remove the instrument panel top cover as described in paragraph 34.
52 Disconnect the multi-plug from the speedometer and tachometer and remove their securing screws.
53 Slacken the screws which secure the plate carrying the low oil level warning unit and the wash/wipe programme unit. (This plate is immediately behind the speedometer and tachometer).
54 Move the plate aside, then extract the speedometer/tachometer assembly through the rear of the instrument panel.
55 Refit in the reverse order to removal. Reset the clock or computer on completion, when applicable, and check the speedometer and tachometer for correct operation.

Minor instruments

66 Remove the lens from the instrument pack.
67 Remove the shroud and faceplate, taking care not to strain the connections to the digital clock (when applicable).
68 Remove the retaining screws or nuts from the appropriate gauge and extract the gauge from its housing. Note that when a digital clock is fitted, two of the leads are normally secured by the oil pressure gauge retaining nuts.
69 Reassemble in the reverse order to dismantling, making sure to relocate the clock leads correctly (when applicable).

Speedometer or tachometer

70 From the front of the instrument pack remove the lens, the shroud and the warning lamp symbol plate.
71 Remove the retaining screws or nuts and extract the tachometer or speedometer.

Fig. 13.38 Rear view of speedometer/tachometer instrument pack (Sec 12)

1 *Panel illumination lamps*	3 *Warning lamps*	5 *Printed circuit*
2 *Speedometer retaining nuts*	4 *Plastic retainer*	6 *Tachometer retaining screws*

Instrument panel (1982 on) – removal and refitting (complete)

56 Disconnect the battery earth lead.
57 Remove the glovebox on the driver's side.
58 Remove the instrument panel top cover as described in paragraph 34.
59 Remove the instrument panel front cover.
60 Remove the instrument panel mounting nuts and bolts.
61 Ease the instrument panel away from the facia so that the wiring connectors are accessible.
62 Label or sketch the various connectors if there is any possibility of confusion on reassembly, then disconnect all multi-plugs, blade connectors etc from the instruments, switches, clock or computer (as applicable).
63 Remove the instrument panel.
64 Refit in the reverse order to removal. Reset the clock or computer on completion and check the instruments for correct operation.

Instrument panel (1982 on) – dismantling

65 With the instrument panel or the appropriate instrument pack removed, as described above, individual instruments or components may be removed and refitted as follows.

Fig. 13.39 Speedometer trip meter control engagement (Sec 12)

1 *Instrument housing*	3 *Reset control*
2 *Speedometer*	

72 Reassemble in the reverse order to dismantling, making sure in the case of the speedometer that the trip meter reset control is located correctly.

Printed circuit

73 Remove the instruments from the printed circuit board as already described.

74 Remove all bulb holders from the printed circuit board. Also remove all nuts, bolts, screws, leads, and hardware such as the instrument voltage stabilizer, the thermal delay unit and any blade connectors.

75 Release the plastic retainers and remove the printed circuit.

76 Transfer all the hardware, bulbs and gauges to the new printed circuit when it is fitted.

Digital clock

77 With the minor instrument pack removed, disconnect the clock leads from the printed circuit. Note their locations for use when reassembling. Release the leads from their securing tape.

78 Undo and remove the clock securing screws, then remove the clock.

79 Fit a new clock in the reverse order to removal.

Electronic speedometer (1982 on) – description and fault diagnosis

80 All later models are fitted with an electronic speedometer. This instrument operates in the same way as the familiar electronic tachometer. The input to the speedometer consists of electrical impulses by a transducer which is fitted to the gearbox in the same place as the old mechanical cable take-off. Inside the speedometer a stepper motor drives the mileage recorders.

81 In the event of malfunction, the first check must be of the wiring between the transducer and the instrument panel, not forgetting the printed circuit.

82 If the wiring is in order, subsequent checking consists of substituting a known good transducer or speedometer head. The following points may exist in determining which unit is defective:

(a) When a trip computer is fitted, if its distance-related functions are satisfactory, the speedometer transducer is almost certainly OK.

(b) If the speedometer needle returns to zero with the ignition off, but stays above zero with the ignition on, the transducer is probably defective.

(c) If the speedometer needle stays above zero with the ignition off the instrument itself is defective.

(d) An absence of speed or mileage readings when cold, followed by inaccurate readings after a few miles, denotes a faulty transducer.

83 On vehicles not equipped with a trip computer, the spare plug and socket in the instrument wiring harness which would feed distance information to the trip computer **must not** be connected together; this can lead to transducer failure.

84 Note that the number of gear teeth on the speedometer transducer varies according to final drive ratio, so a transducer taken from another car will not necessarily give satisfactory results. The transducers are colour coded black (20 teeth, 3.08:1 final drive), orange (23 teeth, 3.45:1 final drive) or red (22 teeth, 3.90:1 final drive).

Central door locking system (all models) – precaution

85 When the battery has been disconnected on models with a central door locking system, make sure before reconnecting it that both front door interior locking buttons are in the unlocked (raised) position.

86 Failure to observe the above point can cause damage to the central door locking control unit as a result of a current surge when the battery is reconnected.

Heated rear window (all models) – inhibition of operation

87 On all 2000 models, wiring of the heated rear window relay is such that the relay is de-energised whenever the engine cooling fan is operating.

88 On all models with air conditioning, similar wiring disables the heated rear window whenever the condenser cooling fans are operating.

89 Both the above arrangements are designed to prevent overloading of the car's electrical system. No attempt should be made to bypass them.

Radio aerial (original equipment) – removal and refitting

90 Remove the radio as described in Chapter 10, Section 43.

91 Remove the passenger side glovebox as described in Chapter 12, Section 25.

92 Lift up the carpet in the passenger footwell and carefully free the large grommet from the left-hand panel. Feed the aerial lead through the grommet from the inside of the car.

93 Slacken, but do not remove, the aerial mounting nut so that the aerial is free to move. Swivel the aerial so that its base can be grasped through the grommet hole.

94 Have an assistant remove the aerial mounting nut and retrieve the dome, spacer and seal. Pull the aerial into the car through the grommet hole.

95 Refit in the reverse order to removal. Extend the aerial to make sure it is properly positioned before tightening the mounting nut.

Fig. 13.40 Radio aerial fitting details (Sec 12)

3   Large grommet
7   Mounting components

Key to Fig. 13.41

No	Description	Grid Reference	No	Description	Grid Reference
1	Starter motor and solenoid	A1	53	Fuel tank and pump unit	B3
2	Alternator	A1	54	Temperature transmitter	B3
3	Battery	A1	55	Oil pressure transmitter	B3
4	Terminal stud	A1	56	Oil pressure switch	B3
5	Starter relay	A1	57	Rear screen heater switch	B4
6	Engine sensing socket	A2	58	Rear screen heater relay	B4
7	Transducer	A1	59	Rear screen heater	B4
8	Coil	A2	60	Rear screen heater warning light	B4
9	Distributor	A2	61	Main beam warning light	B1
10	Ignition switch	A2	62	Headlamp main beam	B1
11	Starter inhibitor switch – automatic	A2	63	Headlamp dip beam	B1
12	Ballast resistor	A2	64	Front foglamp warning light	B1
13	Speed transducer	A2	65	Front foglamp	B1
14	Screen washer pump	A3	66	Rear foglamp warning light	B1
15	Screen washer switch	A3	67	Rear foglamp	C1
16	Front wash/wipe switch	A3	68	Front foglamp switch	B2
17	Front wiper program unit	A3	69	Rear foglamp switch	B2
18	Wiper motor	A3	70	Rear foglamp relay	B2
19	Rear wash/wipe switch	A4	71	Diode unit	B2
20	Screen washer pump	A4	72	Hazard flasher unit	B3
21	Rear wiper program unit	A4	73	Low coolant level warning light	B3
22	Rear wiper motor	A4	74	Expansion tank probes	B3
23	RH front door switch/motor	A1	75	Radiator probe	B3
24	LH front door switch/motor	B1	76	Low coolant level indicator	B3
25	RH rear door motor	A1	77	Low oil level unit	B3
26	LH rear door motor	B2	78	Low oil level switch	B3
27	Tail door motor	A1	79	Brake pad wear switch	B3
28	Central door locking control unit	B2	80	Brake fluid level indicator	B3
29	FASD – Fully Automatic Starting Device	A2	81	Speedometer	B4
30	FASD control unit	A2	82	Tachometer	B4
31	Automatic gearbox selector lever illumination	A3	83	Ignition warning light	B4
32	Reversing lamp switch	A3	84	Low oil level warning light	B4
33	Reversing lamps	A4	85	Brake pad wear warning light	B4
34	Seat belt warning light	A4	86	Handbrake warning light	B4
35	Seat belt sensor switch	A4	87	Handbrake switch	B4
36	Driver's seat belt buckle switch	A4	88	Brake failure warning light	B4
37	Passenger's seat belt buckle switch	A4	89	Bulb failure warning light	B4
38	Boot lamp	A4	90	Front foglamp switch illumination	C1
39	Boot lamp switch	A4	91	Rear foglamp switch illumination	C1
40	RH reading lamp and switch	A4	92	Rear screen heater switch illumination	C1
41	LH reading lamp and switch	B4	93	Hazard switch illumination	C1
42	Lighting switch	B2	94	Interior lamp switch illumination	C1
43	Headlamp dip and flash switch	B2	95	Sunroof switch illumination	C1
44	Main beam relay	B2	96	Rear wash/wipe switch illumination	C1
45	Dip beam relay	B2	97	Window lift isolation switch illumination	C1
46	Voltage stabilizer	B3	98	Fibre optic light source	C1
47	Low fuel warning light	A3	99	Clock illumination	C1
48	Fuel gauge	B3	100	Trip computer illumination	C1
49	Temperature gauge	B3	101	Cigar lighter illumination	C2
50	Oil pressure warning light	B3	102	Glovebox illumination	C2
51	Oil pressure warning light	B3	103	Glovebox switch	C2
52	Thermal delay switch	A3	104	Number plate illumination	C2
			105	Illumination rheostat	C3

Key to Fig. 13.41 (continued)

No	Description	Grid Reference	No	Description	Grid Reference
106	Ballast resistor	C3	123	Stop-lamp	C1
107	Horn push	C3	124	Sidelamp	C1
108	RH horn	C3	125	Bulb failure monitor unit	C2
109	LH Horn	C3	126	Stop-lamp switch	C2
110	RH interior light	C4	127	Panel illumination	C3
111	RH door open lamp	C4	128	LH rear flasher lamp	C1
112	RH front door switch	C4	129	LH side repeater lamp facility	C1
113	RH rear door switch	C4	130	LH front flasher lamp	C1
114	LH door open lamp	C4	131	LH flasher warning lamp	C1
115	LH front door switch	C4	132	RH rear flasher lamp	C1
116	LH interior light	C4	133	RH side repeater lamp facility	C1
117	Map light and switch	C4	134	RH front flasher lamp	C1
118	LH rear door switch	C4	135	RH flasher warning light	C1
119	Clock	C4	136	Direction indicator switch	C2
120	Interior light switch	C4	137	Flasher unit	C2
121	Cigar lighter	C4	138	Hazard switch	C3
122	Tail lamp	C1			

Colour code

B	Black	N	Brown	S	Slate
G	Green	O	Orange	U	Blue
K	Pink	P	Purple	W	White
LG	Light green	R	Red	Y	Yellow

Supplementary circuits

Points are identified on each main diagram by a letter-number code. Use the following list to identify the appropriate supplementary diagram.

E	Electric windows	J	Trip computer
F	Electric mirrors	K	Electric sunroof
G	Radio, cassette	M	Heater, air conditioning

Symbols used in the wiring diagrams

1. Component earthed
2. Component earthed by its fixing
3. If fitted
4. Line connector
5. Sealed joint
6. Printed circuit connector
7. Printed circuit

Fig. 13.41 Wiring diagram for all models – 1981 to 1983

Fig. 13.41 Wiring diagram for all models – 1981 to 1983 (continued)

Fig. 13.42 Main wiring diagram for all models – 1984

Fig. 13.42 Main wiring diagram for all models – 1984 (continued)

Key to Fig. 13.42

No.	Description	Grid reference	No.	Description	Grid reference
1	Alternator	A1	46	Water temperature indicator	B3
3	Battery	A1	47	Water temperature transducer	B3
4	Starter motor solenoid	A1	49	Reverse lamp switch	A3
5	Starter motor	A1	50	Reverse lamp(s)	A4
6	Lighting switch	B2	53	Fog lamp switch	B2
7	Headlamp dip switch	B2	54	Fog lamp(s)	C1
8	Headlamp dip beam	B1	56	Clock	C4
9	Headlamp main beam	B1	57	Cigar lighter	C4
10	Main beam warning lamp	B1	64	Voltage stabiliser	B3
11	RH side lamp	C1	65	Boot lamp switch	B4
12	LH side lamp	C1	66	Boot lamp	B4
14	Panel illumination lamp(s)	C1,C3	67	Line fuse	A4,B4
15	Number plate illumination lamp(s)	C2	75	Automatic gearbox ignition inhibitor switch	A2
16	Stop lamp(s)	C1	76	Automatic gearbox selector indicator lamp	B3
17	RH tail lamp	C1	77	Windscreen washer motor	A3
18	Stop lamp switch	C3	78	Windscreen washer switch	A3
19	Fuse box	Various	82	Switch illumination lamp(s)	C1
20	Interior lamp(s)	C4	95	Tachometer	B4
21	Interior lamp door switch	C4	101	Map light switch	C4
22	LH tail lamp	C1	102	Map light	C4
23	Horn(s)	C3	110	Direction indicator repeater lamps	C1
24	Horn push	C3	115	Heated rear screen switch	B4
26	Direction indicator switch	C2	116	Heated rear screen	B4
27	Direction indicator warning lamp(s)	C1	118	Windscreen washer/wiper switch	A3
28	RH front direction indicator lamp	C1	134	Oil level indicator	B4
29	LH front direction indicator lamp	C1	135	Oil level indicator switch	B3
30	RH rear direction indicator lamp	C1	136	Oil level sump unit	B3
31	LH rear direction indicator lamp	C1	147	Oil pressure transducer	B3
34	Fuel level indicator	B3	150	Heated rear screen warning lamp	B4
37	Windscreen wiper motor	A3	153	Hazard warning switch	C2
38	Ignition/starter switch	A2	164	Ballast resistor or resistive cable	C3
39	Ignition coil	A2	165	Handbrake warning lamp switch	B4
40	Distributor	A2	166	Handbrake warning lamp	B4
41	Fuel pump/tank unit	B3	174	Starter solenoid relay	A2
42	Oil pressure switch	B3	176	Fuel level warning lamp	B3
43	Oil pressure warning lamp or indicator	B3	182	Brake fluid level switch	C4
44	Ignition or no charge warning lamp	B4	208	Cigar lighter illumination lamp	C2
45	Headlamp flash switch	B2	210	Panel illumination lamp rheostat/resistor	C3

Key to Fig. 13.42 (continued)

No.	Description	Grid reference	No.	Description	Grid reference
231	Headlamp relay	B2	308	Direction indicator/hazard flasher unit	B3
240	Heated rear screen relay	B4	314	Clock illumination lamp (console)	C1
242	Two way interior lamp switch	C4	316	Coolant level sensor/switch	B3
246	Glove box illumination lamp	C2	324	Parcel shelf/map lamp	B4
247	Glove box illumination switch	C2	325	Brake pad wear warning lamp	B4
248	Bonnet lamp	C4	326	Brake pad wear sensor	B3
249	Bonnet lamp switch	C4	333	Bulb failure warning lamp	C4
255	Fibre optics illumination bulb	C1	337	Bulb fail units(s)	C2
256	Brake warning blocking diode	B2	338	Low fuel warning light delay unit	B3
270	Rear screen wiper motor	A4	344	Door lock motor	B1
271	Rear screen washer motor	A4	345	Door lock motor control unit	B1
272	Rear screen wipe wash switch	A4	356	Speed transducer	A2
273	Front fog lamp(s) relay	C2	367	Trailer towing warning light	B3
274	LH door lamp	C4	394	Radiator switch	B3
275	RH door lamp	C4	400	Fuseable link	A1
286	Fog rearguard lamp switch	C2	401	Interior lamp delay unit	C4
287	Fog rearguard warning lamp	C1	448	Speedometer	B4
288	Fog rearguard lamp(s)	C1	449	Oil pressure gauge	B3
293	Foglamp warning lamp	B1	450	Low coolant level indicator	B3
296	Fuel pump protection relay	B3	451	Low coolant warning lamp	B3
297	Brake failure warning lamp	C4	480	FASD	A2
298	Windscreen wiper delay unit	A3,A4	481	FASD control unit	B2

Connection codes

A1	Digital clock pick-up point	B3,C4
A2	Auxiliary ignition feed to fuse A4 pick-up point	A2,C4
A3	Linklead – used in place of relay when front fog option is not required	B2
A4	Eureka wire	A2

Not all items are fitted to all models

See key to Fig. 13.41 for symbols used and colour code.

Key to Fig. 13.43

No.	Description	Grid reference	No.	Description	Grid reference
1	Alternator	A1	46	Water temperature indicator	B3
3	Battery	A1	49	Reverse lamp switch	A3
4	Starter motor solenoid	A1	50	Reverse lamp(s)	A4
5	Starter motor	A1	53	Fog lamp switch	C2
6	Lighting switch	B2	54	Fog lamp(s)	B1
7	Headlamp dip switch	B2	56	Clock	C4
8	Headlamp dip beam	B1	57	Cigar lighter	C4
9	Headlamp main beam	B1	64	Voltage stabiliser	B3
10	Main beam warning lamp	B1	65	Boot lamp switch	B4
11	RH side lamp	C1	66	Boot lamp	B4
12	LH side lamp	C1	67	Line fuse	A4,B4
14	Panel illumination lamp(s)	C1,C3	75	Automatic gearbox ignition inhibitor switch	A2
15	Number plate illumination lamp(s)	C2	76	Automatic gearbox selector indicator lamp	B3
16	Stop lamp(s)	C1	77	Windscreen washer motor	A3
17	RH tail lamp	C1	78	Windscreen washer switch	A3
18	Stop lamp switch	C2	82	Switch illumination lamp(s)	C1
19	Fuse box	Various	95	Tachometer	B4
20	Interior lamp(s)	C4	101	Map light switch	C4
21	Interior lamp door switch	C4	102	Map light	C4
22	LH tail lamp	C1	110	Direction indicator repeater lamps	C1
23	Horn(s)	C3	115	Heated rear screen switch	B4
24	Horn push	C3	116	Heater rear screen	B4
26	Direction indicator switch	C2	118	Windscreen washer/wiper switch	A3
27	Direction indicator warning lamp(s)	C1	134	Oil level indicator	B4
28	RH front direction indicator lamp	C1	135	Oil level indicator switch	B3
29	LH front direction indicator lamp	C1	136	Oil level sump unit	B3
30	RH rear direction indicator lamp	C1	147	Oil pressure transducer	B3
31	LH rear direction indicator lamp	C1	150	Heated rear screen warning lamp	B4
34	Fuel level indicator	B3	153	Hazard warning switch	C2
37	Windscreen wiper motor	A3	164	Ballast resistor or resistive cable	C3
38	Ignition/starter switch	A2	165	Handbrake warning lamp switch	B4
39	Ignition coil	A2	166	Handbrake warning lamp	B4
40	Distributor	A2	174	Starter solenoid relay	A1
41	Fuel pump/tank unit	B3	176	Fuel level warning lamp	B3
42	Oil pressure switch	B3	182	Brake fluid level switch	C3
43	Oil pressure warning lamp or indicator	B3	208	Cigar lighter illumination lamp	C2
44	Ignition or no charge warning lamp	B4	210	Panel illumination lamp rheostat/resistor	C3
45	Headlamp flash switch	B2	231	Headlamp relay	B1,B2

Key to Fig. 13.43 (continued)

No.	Description	Grid reference	No.	Description	Grid reference
240	Heated rear screen relay	B4	308	Direction indicator/hazard flasher unit	B2
242	Two way interior lamp switch	C4	314	Clock illumination lamp (console)	C1
246	Glove box illumination lamp	C2	316	Coolant level sensor/switch	B3
247	Glove box illumination switch	C2	324	Parcel shelf/map lamp	B4
248	Bonnet lamp	C4	325	Brake pad wear warning lamp	B4
249	Bonnet lamp switch	C4	326	Brake pad wear sensor	B3
255	Fibre optics illumination bulb	C1	333	Bulb failure warning lamp	C4
256	Brake warning blocking diode	B2	337	Bulb fail unit(s)	C2
270	Rear screen wiper motor	B4	338	Low fuel warning light delay unit	B3
271	Rear screen washer motor	A4	344	Door lock motor	B1
272	Rear screen wipe wash switch	A4	345	Door lock motor control unit	A1
273	Front fog lamp(s) relay	B2	356	Speed transducer	A2
274	LH door lamp	C4	367	Trailer towing warning light	B3
275	RH door lamp	C4	394	Radiator switch	B3
286	Fog rearguard lamp switch	C2	400	Fuseable link	A1
287	Fog rearguard warning lamp	C1	401	Interior lamp delay unit	C4
288	Fog rearguard lamp(s)	C1	448	Speedometer	B4
293	Foglamp warning lamp	B1	449	Oil pressure gauge	B3
296	Fuel pump protection relay	B3	450	Low coolant level indicator	B3
297	Brake failure warning lamp	C4	451	Low coolant warning lamp	B3
298	Windscreen wiper delay unit	A4			

Connection codes

A1	Digital clock pick-up point	B3,C4
A2	Auxiliary ignition feed to fuse A4 pick-up point	A2,C4
A3	Linklead – used in place of relay when front fog option is not required	B2

Not all items are fitted to all models

See key to Fig. 13.41 for symbols used and colour code.

Fig. 13.43 Main wiring diagram for all models – 1985

Fig. 13.43 Main wiring diagram for all models – 1985 (continued)

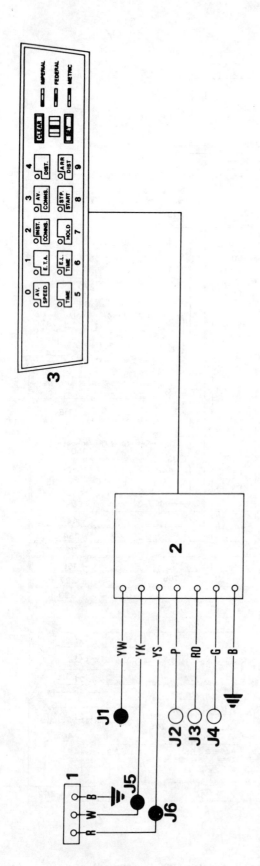

Fig. 13.44 Supplementary wiring diagram – trip computer (typical)

1   Fuel transducer
2   Trip computer
3   Keyboard

Connection codes

No	Description	No	Description
J1	Speed transducer pick-up point	J3	Trip computer illumination
J2	Trip computer pick-up point	J4	Trip computer pick-up point

Fig. 13.45 Supplementary wiring diagram – electric windows (typical)

1	Thermal cut-out	12	LH rear window close relay
2	LH front window open relay	13	LH rear window lift switch
3	RH front window open relay	14	RH rear window lift motor
4	LH front window lift motor	15	RH rear window close relay
5	LH front window close relay	16	RH rear window lift switch
6	LH front window lift switch	17	Driver's master switch (LH rear window)
7	RH front window lift motor	18	Driver's master switch (LH front window)
8	RH front window close relay	19	Driver's master switch (RH rear window)
9	LH rear window open relay	20	Driver's master switch (RH front window)
10	RH rear window open relay	21	Isolation switch
11	LH rear window lift motor		

Connection codes

No	Description	No	Description
E1	Thermal cut-out pick-up point	F1	Passenger's electric door mirror pick-up point (see electric door mirror diagram)
E2	Passenger front window lift switch pick-up point		
E3	Driver's front window master switch pick-up point	F2	Driver's electric door mirror pick-up point (see electric door mirror diagram)
E4	Window isolation switch pick-up point		

Fig. 13.46 Supplementary wiring diagram – ignition system (typical)

No	Description	No	Description
1	Radiator probe	7	From ignition switch
2	Cooling fan motor	8	Coil
3	Heated rear screen switch	9	Distributor
4	Ignition switch	10	To tachometer
5	To starter motor	11	FASD
6	Ballast resistor	12	FASD control unit

Connection codes

No	Description	No	Description
A3	Fuse 3 amp	G1	Radio pick-up point
A4	Fuse 7.5 amp	K2	Sunroof switch pick-up point. Radiator cooling fan (2000 only)

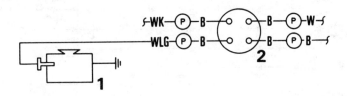

Fig. 13.47 Supplementary wiring diagram – low coolant warning circuit (typical)

1 Expansion tank sensor 2 Low coolant level indicator module

Fig. 13.48 Supplementary wiring diagram – heater blower (typical)

1	Blower motor switch	4	Heater relay
2	Overheat switch	5	Fuses
3	Heater motor		

Connection codes

No	Description	No	Description
M1	Heater pick-up point	M2	Blower motor pick-up point

Fig. 13.49 Supplementary wiring diagram – air conditioning (typical)

No	Description	No	Description
1	Blower motor	7	Fast idle solenoid
2	Air conditioning relay	8	Mode microswitch
3	Resistor assembly	9	Ambient temperature switch
4	Vacuum solenoid	10	Magnetic clutch relay
5	Blower speed switch	11	Cooling fan relay
6	Compressor	12	Cooling fan

Connection codes

No	Description	No	Description
M1	Cooling fan relay pick-up point	M4	Magnetic clutch pick-up point
M2	Blower motor pick-up point	M5	Magnetic clutch pick-up point
M3	Cooling fan pick-up point	M6	Heated rear screen connection

Fig. 13.50 Supplementary wiring diagram – radio/cassette (typical). Dotted lines show circuit for mono radio

1	LH front speaker	7	In-line fuse – 3 amp
2	RH front speaker	8	Choke – radio/cassette only
3	LH rear speaker	9	Electric aerial circuit
4	RH rear speaker	10	Electric aerial relay
5	Speaker balance control	11	Electric aerial motor
6	Radio or radio/cassette		

Connection codes

No	Description	No	Description
G1	Radio pick-up point	G3	AC810 and AC820 radio battery feed
G2	Electric aerial pick-up point (3500 only)		

Fig. 13.51 Supplementary wiring diagram – electric door mirrors (typical)

1	LH door mirror and demist element	3	Door mirror changeover switch
2	RH door mirror and demist element	4	Door mirror control switch

Connection codes

No	Description	No	Description
F1	Passenger's door mirror demist element pick-up point (see electric window circuit)	F2	Driver's door mirror demist element pick-up point
		F3	Door mirror control switch pick-up point

Trip computer – description

96 A trip computer is available as an optional extra on certain models. The computer displays time and date information; it can also process and display information relating to fuel consumption (both instantaneous and average) and speed. If the driver enters the length of the journey proposed, the computer will count down the distance to destination and will display an estimated time of arrival. A stopwatch function is also available.

97 Full operating instructions for the trip computer are provided in the operator's handbook supplied with the car. The information given below is intended to assist the owner in tracing possible faults.

Trip computer – checking procedure

98 Disconnect the battery for at least two minutes, then reconnect it. (See paragraph 85 for vehicles with central door locking).

99 Switch on the ignition and watch the computer display. The 'AV SPEED' LED should light and the alpha-numeric display should show a sequence of five figure eights, from left to right, finishing with a colon in the centre position. The other LEDs should then illuminate in sequence from left to right. After the 'ARR DIST' LED has been illuminated, the 'EL TIME' LED will illuminate once more and the display will start to record elapsed time.

100 Any deviation from the above sequence indicates a fault, either in the keyboard or in the cable and connectors which link the keyboard to the display unit.

101 If the test is satisfactory so far, press the 'CLEAR' button until the display disappears, then release it. Elapsed time will again be displayed, starting from the time when the 'CLEAR' button was pressed.

102 Set the clock as follows. Press the 'TIME' button once, then press the 'SET' button; the word 'SET' will be displayed. Press the correct buttons to enter the time in 24-hour format, then press the 'SET' button again. The clock should now start.

103 To set the date, press the 'TIME' button once (if time is already being displayed) or twice (if any other information is being displayed), then press the 'SET' button. Press the correct buttons to enter the date in numerical form, day first, prefixing single digits with a zero. Thus the 1st of May will be entered as 01 05, the 14th of July as 14 07, and so on. Press the 'SET' button again; the calender is now operational. The computer display will revert to showing clock time, but the date can be recalled by pressing the 'TIME' button once or twice (as above).

104 To set the stop watch to zero, press the 'STP START' button once: the figures displayed should be the same as for elapsed time. Press the 'STP START' button again and the colon should stop flashing. Press 'CLEAR' to zero the display; the stop watch will start counting when the 'STP START' button is pressed for a third time. The stopwatch will continue to count, first in minutes and seconds, then in hours and minutes, while other computer functions are in use.

105 Any road test of the computer must be over a distance of at least 1.5 miles (or 1/5 kilometres, if metric units are preferred). To set an arrival distance of 1.5 miles, press 'ARR DIST), 'SET', '1', '5' and 'SET'. (Note that the last digit entered is always preceded by the decimal point when displayed).

106 Drive the car on the chosen test route, trying (so far as road safety and speed limits allow) to drive at a steady 50 mph (80 kph). After one mile press the 'AV CONS' button: the fuel consumption displayed should be roughly 15 to 25 mpg (11 to 19 litres/100 km). Press the 'INST CONS' button and note the reading; if a steady speed is maintained, the 'AV CONS' reading should approach the 'INST CONS' reading.

107 Press the 'ARR DIST' button and check that the display is counting downwards in tenths of a mile (or kilometre); similarly, pressing the 'DIST' button should show the display counting upwards in tenths.

108 Press the 'ETA' button and check that the display shows a sensible time of arrival, given the distance left to cover and the speed of the vehicle.

109 This completes the road test of the computer. Faults may be due to the computer itself, its wiring, or a faulty transducer. The following points may be of interest when tracing a fault:

(a) If speed- and distance-related information is unsatisfactory, and the speedometer is also malfunctioning, the speedometer transducer is faulty or disconnected

(b) If the fuel consumption (instantaneous or average) is claimed to be 0.0 mph (or 0.01/100 km), the fuel flow sensor is faulty or disconnected. Similar conclusions may be drawn from an 'INST CONS' reading of 6553.5

110 When tracing computer wiring, note that many wire colours change across multi-plugs. This does not necessarily mean that the wiring is incorrect.

111 If the computer 'locks up', ie it will neither accept commands nor display information, disconnect the battery for at least two minutes, then set the computer up as previously described. 'Lock-up' can be caused by incorrect operation, voltage irregularities or strong electromagnetic fields.

Trip computer – removal and refitting

112 Disconnect the battery earth lead.

113 Remove the minor instrument pack.

114 Remove the screws which secure the trip computer to the instrument shroud and lens, then remove the computer.

115 Refit in the reverse order to removal. Reset the computer on completion.

Electric door mirrors – general

116 Electrically adjustable door mirrors, with built-in heating elements for defrosting purposes, are fitted to some models.

117 Where damage to the heating element or mirror glass occurs it is not necessary to renew the whole mirror assembly; a glass with the element attached is available separately. Unfortunately, no renewal information was available at the time of writing.

Horns

118 The horns are located in front of the radiator.

119 To remove a horn, first disconnect the battery earth lead.

120 Remove the securing nut and washer, and feed the horn downwards through the air slot.

121 Disconnect the Lucar connectors.

122 Refitting is the reversal of removal; the connectors may be fitted either way round.

Tailgate wiper motor

Removal

123 Disconnect the battery earth lead.

124 Remove the wiper arm (Chapter 10, Section 39)

125 Open the tailgate and remove the wiper motor cover.

126 Disconnect the motor fixings, unplug the multi-plug, and remove the wiper motor.

Refitting

127 Fit the grommet and spindle spacer to the motor. The remaining refitting procedure is the reversal of removal.

128 Before refitting the wiper arm, reconnect the battery and turn the motor on and off, to ensure the spindle is in the 'park' position.

Headlamp washer components – removal and refitting

Jets

129 Remove the front bumper overrider, and disconnect the washer tube and clip from the jet.

130 Remove the jet from the overrider.

131 Refitting is a reversal of removal.

Reservoir and pump

132 Raise the bonnet and release the bolts securing the reservoir filler neck. Remove the filler neck from the filler tube.

133 Remove the underbelly panel. Release the bolts securing the reservoir to the valance, and lower the reservoir.

134 Remove the pump from the reservoir, drain the washer fluid and remove the reservoir.

135 Refitting is a reversal of removal, but do not refill the reservoir until it is fitted.

Fig. 13.52 Supplementary wiring diagram – electric sunroof (typical)

1	Sunroof relay	3	Sunroof motor
2	Sunroof relay	4	Sunroof switch

Connection codes

No	Description	No	Description
K1	Sunroof pick-up point	K2	FASD module unit pick-up point

Fig. 13.53 Supplementary wiring diagram – headlamp washers (typical). Dotted lines show non-UK circuit

1	In-line fuse – 25 amp	4	Level indicator module
2	Powerwash relay	5	Powerwash bottle probes
3	Powerwash pump	6	Underbonnet lamp switch

Connection codes

No	Description	No	Description
L1	Powerwash pick-up point	L2	Powerwash pump

13 Suspension and steering

Anti-roll bar mountings – models with 175 section tyres
1   Anti-roll bar end mountings differ according to the tyre profile fitted and the date of production (Fig. 13.54).
2   Earlier models with 175 section tyres can be modified to the latest standard by discarding the two washers fitted underneath each nut and fitting a new single washer, of the correct pattern, instead. Obtain the correct washers from a Rover dealer.

Anti-roll bar bushes
3   From VIN 299418 improved bushes were fitted between the anti-roll bar and suspension lower link arms (Fig. 13.55). The new bushes can be fitted as replacements on earlier models, and are supplied as a mounting kit of washers, bushes and nuts.
4   Disconnect the anti-roll bar from the suspension arms and discard the washers, bushes and nuts.
5   Fit the new black steel washers to both ends of the anti-roll bar, followed by the tubular spacer and bush.
6   Pass the ends of the anti-roll bar through the suspension arms.
7   To both ends of the anti-roll bar now fit the white bush and shouldered plastic washer, followed by the plated steel washer and nut. Tighten the nut to the specified torque (Chapter 11).
8   Fit the plastic nut locking caps so that the slots align with holes in the anti-roll bar and fit split pins. Where a spring clip locked the original nut, this must be retained and the locking cap and split pin discarded.

Fig. 13.54 Old pattern (A) and later pattern (B) anti-roll bar mountings used with 175 section tyres (Sec 13)

Fig. 13.55 Anti-roll bar improved fitting kit components (Sec 13)

1	Washer (black)	5	Plastic washer
2	Bush	6	Washer
3	Spacer	7	Nut
4	Bush (white)	8	Locking cap

Fig. 13.56 Suspension height (H) measuring points (Sec 13)

Self-levelling rear suspension – checking procedure

9 On models equipped with self-levelling rear suspension, it may be found that the rear of the car settles somewhat when the luggage area is laden and the vehicle is parked for some time (eg overnight). This is not in itself a fault, provided that normal suspension height is restored when the vehicle is driven.

10 If some other malfunction of the self-levelling units is suspected, proceed as follows.

11 Inspect the self-levelling units for oil leakage. Traces of seepage are permissible; dripping, gushing or other major leaks are not. A unit which is leaking significantly must be renewed.

12 With the luggage area unladen and the underside of the vehicle free of heavy mud deposits, measure and record the distance from the centre of each rear wheel to the point on the wing vertically above the wheel centre (Fig. 13.56). The distances should be between 15.75 and 17.75 in (400 and 450 mm); if not, renew the self-levelling unit(s) on the side(s) concerned.

13 Load the rear seat and luggage area with 440 to 550 lb (200 to 250 kg). Human ballast of known weight is probably most convenient for the DIY operator, particularly as it should not need to be lifted into the car.

14 Have an assistant (of roughly the driver's weight) sit in the driving seat, then measure and record the distances described in paragraph 12 again.

15 Drive the car over at least 3 miles (5 km) of undulating road. Bring the car to rest by light brake applications, and do not allow the ballast to move. With the driver's seat still occupied, measure and record the distances described in paragraph 12 again. The ballast may now be unloaded.

16 Subtract the initial loaded height (paragraph 14) from the final loaded height (paragraph 15). If the difference is at least one inch (25 mm) the self-levelling unit is operating correctly. A difference of less than one inch (25 mm) indicates that the self-levelling unit on that side should be renewed.

Rear suspension trailing link mounting – later models

17 To reduce noise coming from the trailing link and the rear axle bracket, additional washers are fitted to each mounting on later models.

18 Earlier models can be fitted with such washers if so wished. Suitable washers should be available from a Rover dealer.

19 At VIN 297222 a different trailing link was introduced and washer A (Fig. 13.57) was no longer needed. Washer B should still be fitted.

Fig. 13.57 Additional washers (arrowed) fitted to trailing link mounting (Sec 13)

A and B see text

Rear suspension crossmember-to-body mounting (all models)

20 If a problem is experienced with the rear suspension crossmember hitting the body, this can be rectified by fitting additional washers to the mounting as shown (Fig. 13.58).

Fig. 13.58 Additional washers (A) and existing washers (B) on rear crossmember mounting (Sec 13)

14 Bodywork and fittings

Front spoiler – removal and refitting

1 Remove the blanking plugs, then undo the nuts and bolts which secure the spoiler to the under-panel and the wing flange.

2 Remove the spoiler.

3 Refitting is a reversal of removal.

Front bumper overrider – removal and refitting

4 When fitted, disconnect the headlight washer by prising out the elbow connector.

5 Undo the nut which secures the overrider and remove the overrider.

6 Refitting is a reversal of removal.

Rear parcel shelf extension panel – removal and refitting

7 Lift out the parcel shelf.

8 Slacken the parcel shelf stops and free the rear end of the extension panel from the body by pulling it towards the centre of the car.

9 Lift the extension panel from the stops and free it from under the seat squab.

10 If a rear seat belt is fitted, remove the floor bracket and the swivel bracket as described in Chapter 12, Section 30. Feed the belt through the extension panel.

11 The extension panel may now be removed.

12 Refitting is a reversal of removal.

Headlining – removal and refitting

13 Disconnect the battery earth lead.

14 Remove the trim pads from the 'A' posts (to the front of the front doors). These pads are each secured by two screws.

15 Remove the upper trim pads from the 'D' posts as described in Chapter 12, Section 35, paragraphs 2 and 3.

16 Remove the grab handles. Their securing screws are accessible after sliding off the end caps.

17 Remove the sun visors and the sun visor hinge clips.

18 Support the headlining, then remove the interior mirror and its bracket.

19 Free the rear edge of the headlining from the Velcro strips which hold it to the car. **Note:** Some models use clips instead of Velcro. No further information was available at the time of writing.

20 The headlining can now be removed from the car.

21 Refitting is a reversal of removal.

Sliding roof assembly (manual) – removal and refitting

22 Remove the headlining as described above.

23 Disconnect the four drain hoses (one at each corner).

24 Remove the six nuts and washers which secure the sliding roof frame.

25 Remove the sliding roof assembly from the car.

26 Refitting is a reversal of removal. Check for correct operation and adjust if necessary as described above.

Sliding roof (manual) – panel removal and refitting

27 Open the sliding roof as far as it will go.

28 Apply a layer of masking tape to the rear edge of the hole in the roof so that the paintwork of the sliding panel is not damaged during removal.

29 Remove the four screws from the front of the sliding panel.

30 Slide the panel forwards until it is about one inch (25 mm) short of the closed position. Lift the front of the panel, being careful not to damage the rubber seal.

31 Move the panel forwards to disengage it from the retaining springs at the rear, then lift it away from the car.

32 Refitting is a reversal of removal.

Sliding roof (manual) – adjustment

33 Remove the sliding panel as described above.

34 Operate the catch and study the action of the locking teeth.

35 Slacken the nuts which secure the linkage and extend or retract the teeth as required.

36 Tighten the nuts and check for correct operation.

37 Refit the sliding panel.

Sliding roof assembly (electric) – removal and refitting

38 Remove the headlining, the rear parcel shelf and the parcel shelf extension panels, as described earlier in this Section.

39 Remove the right-hand section of the luggage compartment floor.

40 Remove the cover from the sliding roof mirror and disconnect the wires at the multi-plug.

41 Undo the screws which secure the motor and remove the motor from behind its bracket.

42 Undo the cable clamp nuts and remove the motor.

43 Remove the spare wheel, lift back the carpets and unclip the operating cable straps.

44 Disconnect the drain hoses from the sliding roof.

45 Remove the six nuts and washers which secure the sliding roof frame. Lower the frame.

46 Secure the two halves of each outer operating cable by taping them together. Pull the cables through the 'D' posts.

47 Extract the sliding roof assembly through the rear of the car.

48 Refitting is a reversal of removal.

Heater fan switch – removal and refitting

49 Remove the radio as described in Chapter 10, Section 43.
50 Remove the console as described in Chapter 12, Section 23 or 24.
51 Pull off the control knobs from the heater levers.
52 Remove the radio mounting plate and extract the screws which secure the heater control front plate. Carefully withdraw the heater control front plate from the control levers, being careful not to strain the fibre optic lines.

53 Extract the screws which secure the heater control plate. Lift out the plate.
54 The heater fan switch is now accessible. Remove its securing screws and withdraw it. Make a note of the wiring connections before disconnecting the switch.
55 Refitting is a reversal of removal. Check for correct operation on completion.

Fig. 13.59 Heater unit attachments on later models (Sec 14)

1 Locknut	7 Console bracket	13 Glovebox rail bolts
2 Large washer	8 Lower mounting bolt	14 Retaining plate
3 Mounting stud and nut	9 Air vent control	15 Footwell duct
4 Upper mounting bolt	10 Temperature control	16 Duct retaining screws
5 Coolant hoses	11 Fan (blower) control	17 Bracket retaining bolts
6 Glovebox rail bracket	12 Air distribution control	18 Slotted bracket

Fig. 13.60 Major components of VIR air conditioning system (Sec 14)

1 Compressor	4 Evaporator	c Water valve
2 Condenser	a Vacuum reservoir	d Air inlet/blower unit
3 VIR (valves in receiver) unit	b High pressure switch	e Heater/cooler unit

Heater (later type) – removal and refitting

56 Disconnect the battery negative lead.

57 Drain the cooling system (Chapter 2 or Section 5 of this Supplement).

58 Remove the centre console, radio and facia (Chapters 10, 12 and 13).

59 Disconnect the heater hoses in the engine compartment.

60 Remove the nut and washer holding the bulkhead insulation, then remove the heater mounting nuts from the bulkhead.

61 Working inside the car, remove the console bracket then pull off the heater control knobs, unbolt the control panel and unclip the fibre optic leads. Disconnect the leads and remove the control panel.

62 Remove the triangular and rectangular air duct covers then remove the air duct screws from under the carpets.

63 Unbolt the glovebox brackets and move them to one side. Note that the fibre optic bulb is mounted on the right-hand bracket. Recover the plates from the brackets.

64 Unbolt the heater and console brackets from the slotted mounting bracket, and remove the upper mounting bolt from the bulkhead.

65 Disconnect the heater motor and relay wiring.

66 Loosen the slotted mounting bracket bolts then lift the heater and withdraw the bracket.

67 Remove the footwell ducts then position the instrument wiring loom to one side and withdraw the heater from the car.

68 Refitting is a reversal of removal. Refill the cooling system as described in Chapter 2 or Section 5 of this Supplement.

Air conditioning system – description and precautions

69 Available as an optional extra on certain models, the air conditioning systems works on the same principle as a domestic refrigerator or freezer. A compressor, belt-driven from the crankshaft pulley, pumps refrigerant into a condenser unit. After cooling and drying, the refrigerant evaporates under controlled conditions in an evaporator inside the heater/air conditioning unit, so cooling the incoming air.

70 Certain precautions must be observed when dealing with the air conditioning system, both for personal safety and to avoid damaging the system. These are as follows:

   (a) **Do not** undertake any work which would require the disconnection of a refrigerant hose, unless the system has first been discharged by a refrigeration engineer or other specialist.

   (b) **Do not** leave any part of the refrigeration circuit open to the air after it has been discharged

   (c) **Do not** apply heat (eg welding or steam cleaning) near any air conditioning components

71 The refrigerant gas is not of itself poisonous, but it forms poisonous gases when exposed to flame or other combustion (eg a lighted cigarette). If spilled onto skin in its liquid form it can cause damage through rapid cooling. It follows that refrigerant leaks should not be approached closely and should be repaired without delay.

72 Do not attempt to operate the air conditioning system if it is known to be short of refrigerant.

Air conditioning system – maintenance

73 Operate the air conditioning system for a few minutes at monthly intervals when it is not otherwise being used (eg in winter). This will ensure the continued distribution of lubricant and refrigerant round the system.

74 Check the tension and condition of the compressor drivebelt at regular intervals. The drivebelt is adjusted in the same fashion as the water pump/alternator and power steering pump drivebelts. Where drive is via the idler pulley, this may have its own separate adjuster.

75 A sight glass on the VIR (valves in receiver) unit (Fig. 13.61) can be inspected to provide evidence of the state of the refrigerant charge. With the air conditioning system operating, the sight glass should display a clear stream of refrigerant, perhaps with occasional bubbles. Many bubbles, or even foam, are indications that the refrigerant level is low; oil streaks on the glass show that the refrigerant charge is zero. A clouded sight glass means that dessicant has escaped from the drier, or possibly that the compressor is defective.

76 Any abnormal sight glass reading should be investigated without delay. It is in any case wise to have the air conditioning system inspected professionally every year.

Air conditioning system – later type

77 During 1983 the VIR (valves in receiver) air conditioning system was superseded by a system known as CCOT (clutch cylinder orifice tube).

78 The CCOT system has an accumulator in place of the VIR unit, and there is a clutch cycling pressure switch which controls system operation.

79 Maintenance is as described above, but there is no sight glass.

Fig. 13.61 Location of sight glass on VIR unit (Sec 14)

Facia (later type) – removal and refitting

80 Disconnect the battery earth lead.

81 Remove the steering wheel (Chapter 11, Section 19), and the glovebox (Chapter 12, Section 25).

82 Remove the fuse box cover to gain access to the securing screws. Remove the fuse box.

83 Remove the instrument cover, and disconnect the multi-plugs and other connectors.

84 Slacken the steering column adjusting nut, lower the column, and remove the cowls (upper and lower).

85 Unplug the direction indicator and lighting switch multi-plugs. Remove the direction indicator switch assembly.

86 Unbolt the bonnet cable release lever/bracket.

87 Disconnect the demister and face level vent tubes from the heater.

88 Remove the facia retaining bolts, and manoeuvre the facia out of the car.

89 Refitting is the reversal of removal.

Fault diagnosis

Introduction

The vehicle owner who does his or her own maintenance according to the recommended schedules should not have to use this section of the manual very often. Modern component reliability is such that, provided those items subject to wear or deterioration are inspected or renewed at the specified intervals, sudden failure is comparatively rare. Faults do not usually just happen as a result of sudden failure, but develop over a period of time. Major mechanical failures in particular are usually preceded by characteristic symptoms over hundreds or even thousands of miles. Those components which do occasionally fail without warning are often small and easily carried in the vehicle.

With any fault finding, the first step is to decide where to begin investigations. Sometimes this is obvious, but on other occasions a little detective work will be necessary. The owner who makes half a dozen haphazard adjustments or replacements may be successful in curing a fault (or its symptoms), but he will be none the wiser if the fault recurs and he may well have spent more time and money than was necessary. A calm and logical approach will be found to be more satisfactory in the long run. Always take into account any warning signs or abnormalities that may have been noticed in the period preceding the fault – power loss, high or low gauge readings, unusual noises or smells, etc – and remember that failure of components such as fuses or spark plugs may only be pointers to some underlying fault.

The pages which follow here are intended to help in cases of failure to start or breakdown on the road. There is also a Fault Diagnosis Section at the end of each Chapter which should be consulted if the preliminary checks prove unfruitful. Whatever the fault, certain basic principles apply. These are as follows:

Verify the fault. This is simply a matter of being sure that you know what the symptoms are before starting work. This is particularly important if you are investigating a fault for someone else who may not have described it very accurately.

Don't overlook the obvious. For example, if the vehicle won't start, is there petrol in the tank? (Don't take anyone else's word on this particular point, and don't trust the fuel gauge either!) If an electrical fault is indicated, look for loose or broken wires before digging out the test gear.

Cure the disease, not the symptom. Substituting a flat battery with a fully charged one will get you off the hard shoulder, but if the underlying cause is not attended to, the new battery will go the same way. Similarly, changing oil-fouled spark plugs for a new set will get you moving again, but remember that the reason for the fouling (if it wasn't simply an incorrect grade of plug) will have to be established and corrected.

Don't take anything for granted. Particularly, don't forget that a 'new' component may itself be defective (especially if it's been rattling round in the boot for months), and don't leave components out of a fault diagnosis sequence just because they are new or recently fitted. When you do finally diagnose a difficult fault, you'll probably realise that all the evidence was there from the start.

Electrical faults

Electrical faults can be more puzzling than straightforward mechanical failures, but they are no less susceptible to logical analysis if the basic principles of operation are understood. Vehicle electrical wiring exists in extremely unfavourable conditions – heat, vibration and chemical attack – and the first things to look for are loose or corroded connections and broken or chafed wires, especially where the wires pass through holes in the bodywork or are subject to vibration.

All metal-bodied vehicles in current production have one pole of the battery 'earthed', ie connected to the vehicle bodywork, and in nearly all modern vehicles it is the negative (–) terminal. The various electrical components – motors, bulb holders etc – are also connected to earth, either by means of a lead or directly by their mountings. Electric current flows through the component and then back to the battery via the bodywork. If the component mounting is loose or corroded, or if a good path back to the battery is not available, the circuit will be incomplete and malfunction will result. The engine and/or gearbox are also earthed by means of flexible metal straps to the body or subframe; if these straps are loose or missing, starter motor, generator and ignition trouble may result.

Assuming the earth return to be satisfactory, electrical faults will be due either to component malfunction or to defects in the current supply. Individual components are dealt with in Chapter 10. If supply wires are broken or cracked internally this results in an open-circuit, and the easiest way to check for this is to bypass the suspect wire temporarily with a length of wire having a crocodile clip or suitable connector at each end. Alternatively, a 12V test lamp can be used to verify the presence of supply voltage at various points along the wire and the break can be thus isolated.

If a bare portion of a live wire touches the bodywork or other earthed metal part, the electricity will take the low-resistance path thus formed back to the battery: this is known as a short-circuit. Hopefully a short-circuit will blow a fuse, but otherwise it may cause burning of the insulation (and possibly further short-circuits) or even a fire. This is why it is inadvisable to bypass persistently blowing fuses with silver foil or wire.

A simple test lamp is useful for tracing electrical faults

Carrying a few spares can save you a long walk!

Spares and tool kit

Most vehicles are supplied only with sufficient tools for wheel changing; the *Maintenance and minor repair* tool kit detailed in *Tools and working facilities,* with the addition of a hammer, is probably sufficient for those repairs that most motorists would consider attempting at the roadside. In addition a few items which can be fitted without too much trouble in the event of a breakdown should be carried. Experience and available space will modify the list below, but the following may save having to call on professional assistance:

Spark plugs, clean and correctly gapped
HT lead and plug cap – long enough to reach the plug furthest from the distributor
Distributor rotor, condenser and contact breaker points
Drivebelt(s) – emergency type may suffice
Spare fuses
Set of principal light bulbs
Tin of radiator sealer and hose bandage
Exhaust bandage
Roll of insulating tape
Length of soft iron wire
Length of electrical flex
Torch or inspection lamp (can double as test lamp)
Battery jump leads
Tow-rope
Ignition waterproofing aerosol
Litre of engine oil
Sealed can of hydraulic fluid
Emergency windscreen
'Jubilee' clips
Tube of filler paste

If spare fuel is carried, a can designed for the purpose should be used to minimise risks of leakage and collision damage. A first aid kit and a warning triangle, whilst not at present compulsory in the UK, are obviously sensible items to carry in addition to the above.

When touring abroad it may be advisable to carry additional spares which, even if you cannot fit them yourself, could save having to wait while parts are obtained. The items below may be worth considering:

Throttle cable
Cylinder head gasket
Alternator brushes

One of the motoring organisations will be able to advise on availability of fuel etc in foreign countries.

Engine will not start

Engine fails to turn when starter operated

Flat battery (recharge, use jump leads, or push start)
Battery terminals loose or corroded
Battery earth to body defective
Engine earth strap loose or broken
Starter motor (or solenoid) wiring loose or broken
Automatic transmission selector in wrong position, or inhibitor switch faulty
Ignition/starter switch faulty
Major mechanical failure (seizure)
Starter or solenoid internal fault (see Chapter 10)

Jump start lead connections for negative earth vehicles – connect leads in order shown

Starter motor turns engine slowly

Partially discharged battery (recharge, use jump leads, or push start)
Battery terminals loose or corroded
Battery earth to body defective
Engine earth strap loose
Starter motor (or solenoid) wiring loose
Starter motor internal fault (see Chapter 10)

Starter motor spins without turning engine

Flat battery
Starter motor pinion sticking on sleeve
Flywheel gear teeth damaged or worn
Starter motor mounting bolts loose

Engine turns normally but fails to start

Damp or dirty HT leads and distributor cap (crank engine and check for spark) (photo)
Dirty or incorrectly gapped distributor points (if applicable)
No fuel in tank (check for delivery at carburettor) (photo)
Excessive choke (hot engine) or insufficient choke (cold engine)
Fouled or incorrectly gapped spark plugs (remove, clean and regap)
Other ignition system fault (see Chapter 4)
Other fuel system fault (see Chapter 3)
Poor compression (see Chapter 1)
Major mechanical failure (eg camshaft drive)

Engine fires but will not run

Insufficient choke (cold engine)
Air leaks at carburettor or inlet manifold
Fuel starvation (see Chapter 3)
Ballast resistor defective, or other ignition fault (see Chapter 4)

Engine cuts out and will not restart

Engine cuts out suddenly – ignition fault

Loose or disconnected LT wires
Wet HT leads or distributor cap (after traversing water splash)
Coil or condenser failure (check for spark)
Other ignition fault (see Chapter 4)

Engine misfires before cutting out – fuel fault

Fuel tank empty
Fuel pump defective or filter blocked (check for delivery)
Fuel tank filler vent blocked (suction will be evident on releasing cap)
Carburettor needle valve sticking
Carburettor jets blocked (fuel contaminated)
Other fuel system fault (see Chapter 3)

Engine cuts out – other causes

Serious overheating
Major mechanical failure (eg camshaft drive)

Engine overheats

Ignition (no-charge) warning light illuminated

Slack or broken drivebelt (photo) – retension or renew (Chapter 2)

Ignition warning light not illuminated

Coolant loss due to internal or external leakage (see Chapter 2)
Thermostat defective
Low oil level
Brakes binding
Radiator clogged externally or internally
Electric cooling fan not operating correctly (2000 only)
Engine waterways clogged
Ignition timing incorrect or automatic advance malfunctioning
Mixture too weak

Note: *Do not add cold water to an overheated engine or damage may result*

Low engine oil pressure

Gauge reads low or warning light illuminated with engine running

Oil level low or incorrect grade
Defective gauge or sender unit
Wire to sender unit earthed
Engine overheating
Oil filter clogged or bypass valve defective
Oil pressure relief valve defective
Oil pick-up strainer clogged
Oil pump worn or mountings loose
Worn main or big-end bearings

Note: *Low oil pressure in a high-mileage engine at tickover is not necessarily a cause for concern. Sudden pressure loss at speed is far more significant. In any event, check the gauge or warning light sender before condemning the engine.*

Engine noises

Pre-ignition (pinking) on acceleration

Incorrect grade of fuel
Ignition timing incorrect
Distributor faulty or worn
Worn or maladjusted carburettor
Excessive carbon build-up in engine

Whistling or wheezing noises

Leaking vacuum hose
Leaking carburettor or manifold gasket
Blowing head gasket

Crank engine and check for a spark. Note use of insulated tool

Check for fuel delivery with engine cranking. Take precautions against fire

A slack drivebelt can cause overheating and battery charging problems

Tapping or rattling
    Incorrect valve clearances
    Worn valve gear
    Worn timing chain or belt
    Broken piston ring (ticking noise)

Knocking or thumping
    Unintentional mechanical contact (eg fan blades)

Worn drivebelt
Peripheral component fault (generator, water pump etc)
Worn big-end bearings (regular heavy knocking, perhaps less under load)
Worn main bearings (rumbling and knocking, perhaps worsening under load)
Piston slap (most noticeable when cold)

General repair procedures

Whenever servicing, repair or overhaul work is carried out on the car or its components, it is necessary to observe the following procedures and instructions. This will assist in carrying out the operation efficiently and to a professional standard of workmanship.

Joint mating faces and gaskets

Where a gasket is used between the mating faces of two components, ensure that it is renewed oh reassembly, and fit it dry unless otherwise stated in the repair procedure. Make sure that the mating faces are clean and dry with all traces of old gasket removed. When cleaning a joint face, use a tool which is not likely to score or damage the face, and remove any burrs or nicks with an oilstone or fine file.

Make sure that tapped holes are cleaned with a pipe cleaner, and keep them free of jointing compound if this is being used unless specifically instructed otherwise.

Ensure that all orifices, channels or pipes are clear and blow through them, preferably using compressed air.

Oil seals

Whenever an oil seal is removed from its working location, either individually or as part of an assembly, it should be renewed.

The very fine sealing lip of the seal is easily damaged and will not seal if the surface it contacts is not completely clean and free from scratches, nicks or grooves. If the original sealing surface of the component cannot be restored, the component should be renewed.

Protect the lips of the seal from any surface which may damage them in the course of fitting. Use tape or a conical sleeve where possible. Lubricate the seal lips with oil before fitting and, on dual lipped seals, fill the space between the lips with grease.

Unless otherwise stated, oil seals must be fitted with their sealing lips toward the lubricant to be sealed.

Use a tubular drift or block of wood of the appropriate size to install the seal and, if the seal housing is shouldered, drive the seal down to the shoulder. If the seal housing is unshouldered, the seal should be fitted with its face flush with the housing top face.

Screw threads and fastenings

Always ensure that a blind tapped hole is completely free from oil, grease, water or other fluid before installing the bolt or stud. Failure to do this could cause the housing to crack due to the hydraulic action of the bolt or stud as it is screwed in.

When tightening a castellated nut to accept a split pin, tighten the nut to the specified torque, where applicable, and then tighten further to the next split pin hole. Never slacken the nut to align a split pin hole unless stated in the repair procedure.

When checking or retightening a nut or bolt to a specified torque setting, slacken the nut or bolt by a quarter of a turn, and then retighten to the specified setting.

Locknuts, locktabs and washers

Any fastening which will rotate against a component or housing in the course of tightening should always have a washer between it and the relevant component or housing.

Spring or split washers should always be renewed when they are used to lock a critical component such as a big-end bearing retaining nut or bolt.

Locktabs which are folded over to retain a nut or bolt should always be renewed.

Self-locking nuts can be reused in non-critical areas, providing resistance can be felt when the locking portion passes over the bolt or stud thread.

Split pins must always be replaced with new ones of the correct size for the hole.

Special tools

Some repair procedures in this manual entail the use of special tools such as a press, two or three-legged pullers, spring compressors etc. Wherever possible, suitable readily available alternatives to the manufacturer's special tools are described, and are shown in use. In some instances, where no alternative is possible, it has been necessary to resort to the use of a manufacturer's tool and this has been done for reasons of safety as well as the efficient completion of the repair operation. Unless you are highly skilled and have a thorough understanding of the procedure described, never attempt to bypass the use of any special tool when the procedure described specifies its use. Not only is there a very great risk of personal injury, but expensive damage could be caused to the components involved.

Conversion factors

Length (distance)

Inches (in)	X	25.4	= Millimetres (mm)	X	0.0394 = Inches (in)
Feet (ft)	X	0.305	= Metres (m)	X	3.281 = Feet (ft)
Miles	X	1.609	= Kilometres (km)	X	0.621 = Miles

Volume (capacity)

Cubic inches (cu in; in^3)	X	16.387	= Cubic centimetres (cc; cm^3)	X	0.061 = Cubic inches (cu in; in^3)
Imperial pints (Imp pt)	X	0.568	= Litres (l)	X	1.76 = Imperial pints (Imp pt)
Imperial quarts (Imp qt)	X	1.137	= Litres (l)	X	0.88 = Imperial quarts (Imp qt)
Imperial quarts (Imp qt)	X	1.201	= US quarts (US qt)	X	0.833 = Imperial quarts (Imp qt)
US quarts (US qt)	X	0.946	= Litres (l)	X	1.057 = US quarts (US qt)
Imperial gallons (Imp gal)	X	4.546	= Litres (l)	X	0.22 = Imperial gallons (Imp gal)
Imperial gallons (Imp gal)	X	1.201	= US gallons (US gal)	X	0.833 = Imperial gallons (Imp gal)
US gallons (US gal)	X	3.785	= Litres (l)	X	0.264 = US gallons (US gal)

Mass (weight)

Ounces (oz)	X	28.35	= Grams (g)	X	0.035 = Ounces (oz)
Pounds (lb)	X	0.454	= Kilograms (kg)	X	2.205 = Pounds (lb)

Force

Ounces-force (ozf; oz)	X	0.278	= Newtons (N)	X	3.6 = Ounces-force (ozf; oz)
Pounds-force (lbf; lb)	X	4.448	= Newtons (N)	X	0.225 = Pounds-force (lbf; lb)
Newtons (N)	X	0.1	= Kilograms-force (kgf; kg)	X	9.81 = Newtons (N)

Pressure

Pounds-force per square inch (psi; lbf/in^2; lb/in^2)	X	0.070	= Kilograms-force per square centimetre (kgf/cm^2; kg/cm^2)	X	14.223 = Pounds-force per square inch (psi; lbf/in^2; lb/in^2)
Pounds-force per square inch (psi; lbf/in^2; lb/in^2)	X	0.068	= Atmospheres (atm)	X	14.696 = Pounds-force per square inch (psi; lbf/in^2; lb/in^2)
Pounds-force per square inch (psi; lbf/in^2; lb/in^2)	X	0.069	= Bars	X	14.5 = Pounds-force per square inch (psi; lbf/in^2; lb/in^2)
Pounds-force per square inch (psi; lbf/in^2; lb/in^2)	X	6.895	= Kilopascals (kPa)	X	0.145 = Pounds-force per square inch (psi; lbf/in^2; lb/in^2)
Kilopascals (kPa)	X	0.01	= Kilograms-force per square centimetre (kgf/cm^2; kg/cm^2)	X	98.1 = Kilopascals (kPa)

Torque (moment of force)

Pounds-force inches (lbf in; lb in)	X	1.152	= Kilograms-force centimetre (kgf cm; kg cm)	X	0.868 = Pounds-force inches (lbf in; lb in)
Pounds-force inches (lbf in; lb in)	X	0.113	= Newton metres (Nm)	X	8.85 = Pounds-force inches (lbf in; lb in)
Pounds-force inches (lbf in; lb in)	X	0.083	= Pounds-force feet (lbf ft; lb ft)	X	12 = Pounds-force inches (lbf in; lb in)
Pounds-force feet (lbf ft; lb ft)	X	0.138	= Kilograms-force metres (kgf m; kg m)	X	7.233 = Pounds-force feet (lbf ft; lb ft)
Pounds-force feet (lbf ft; lb ft)	X	1.356	= Newton metres (Nm)	X	0.738 = Pounds-force feet (lbf ft; lb ft)
Newton metres (Nm)	X	0.102	= Kilograms-force metres (kgf m; kg m)	X	9.804 = Newton metres (Nm)

Power

Horsepower (hp)	X	745.7	= Watts (W)	X	0.0013 = Horsepower (hp)

Velocity (speed)

Miles per hour (miles/hr; mph)	X	1.609	= Kilometres per hour (km/hr; kph)	X	0.621 = Miles per hour (miles/hr; mph)

Fuel consumption*

Miles per gallon, Imperial (mpg)	X	0.354	= Kilometres per litre (km/l)	X	2.825 = Miles per gallon, Imperial (mpg)
Miles per gallon, US (mpg)	X	0.425	= Kilometres per litre (km/l)	X	2.352 = Miles per gallon, US (mpg)

Temperature

Degrees Fahrenheit = (°C x 1.8) + 32

Degrees Celsius (Degrees Centigrade; °C) = (°F - 32) x 0.56

*It is common practice to convert from miles per gallon (mpg) to litres/100 kilometres (l/100km), where mpg (Imperial) x l/100 km = 282 and mpg (US) x l/100 km = 235

Index

Printed by
J H Haynes & Co Ltd
Sparkford Nr Yeovil
Somerset BA22 7JJ England